TEXTB

Revenue Law

CONSULTANT EDITOR: LORD TEMPLEMAN
EDITOR: HUGH MCCROSSAN
LLM, ATII

OLD BAILEY PRESS

OLD BAILEY PRESS
200 Greyhound Road, London W14 9RY

1st edition 1997

© Old Bailey Press Ltd 1997

Previous editions published under The HLT Group Ltd.

All Old Bailey Press publications enjoy copyright protection and the copyright belongs to the Old Bailey Press Ltd.

All rights reserved. No part of this publication may be reproduced or transmitted in any form or by any means, electronic, mechanical, photocopying, recording or otherwise, or stored in any retrieval system of any nature without either the written permission of the copyright holder, application for which should be made to the Old Bailey Press Ltd, or a licence permitting restricted copying in the United Kingdom issued by the Copyright Licensing Agency.

Any person who infringes the above in relation to this publication may be liable to criminal prosecution and civil claims for damages.

ISBN 1 85836 227 X

British Library Cataloguing-in-Publication.
A CIP Catalogue record for this book is available from the British Library.

Acknowledgement
The publishers and author would like to thank the Incorporated Council of Law Reporting for England and Wales for kind permission to reproduce extracts from the Weekly Law Reports, and Butterworths for their kind permission to reproduce extracts from the All England Law Reports.

Printed and bound in Great Britain

Contents

Preface *vii*

Table of Cases *ix*

Table of Statutes *xv*

1 **Introduction** *1*

2 **The Taxation of Income of Non-corporate Bodies** *2*

The legislation – The annual review – The tax years – The schedular system of taxation – The unified system of taxation – Exemptions from income tax – Persons exempt from income tax

3 **Total Income** *9*

Method of charging tax – Investment and savings income – Computation of total income – Relief for interest paid: ss353–379 ICTA 1988 – Charges on income – Personal reliefs – The taxation of married couples

4 **Schedule A** *22*

The new Schedule A (post 6 April 1995) – Section 15 ICTA 1988 (old Schedule A rules) – Business and trading considerations – The 'Schedule A business' – Basis of assessment: s22 – Allowable expenditure and capital allowances (new Schedule A) – Expenditure incurred in void period (old Schedule A rules) – Premiums: ss34–49 ICTA 1988 and capital gains tax – Charge on assignment of a lease at an undervalue – Allowances for losses – Income from furnished lettings – Foreign element – Anti-avoidance provisions of s33A ICTA 1988

5 **The Taxation of Woodlands** *36*

Introduction – The old system: Schedule B – The new system: FA 1988

6 **Schedule D Cases I and II: Profits of a Trade, Profession or Vocation** *38*

The scope of the charge: s18 ICTA 1988 – What constitutes 'trading' – The badges of trade – Special cases – The computation of profits – Trading receipts – Trading stock – Trading expenses: revenue and capital – 1996–97: Fundamental changes to the Schedule D basis of assessment (also applicable to new businesses 1994–95 onwards) – The basis of assessment (pre-FA 1994 changes) – Losses – Losses under the new Schedule D current year basis of assessment – Post-cessation receipts

7 **Capital Allowances** *72*

Introduction – Allowances on plant and machinery: CAA 1990 – Allowances on security assets – Allowances on expenditure on stands at sports grounds – Industrial buildings allowances

8 Schedule E *84*

Scope of the charge – Basis of the charge – The meaning of 'emoluments therefrom' – Basis of assessment – Statutory treatment of benefits in kind – Terminal payments – Payments in respect of restrictive covenants – Expenses taxable and allowable under Schedule E – Removal expenses – Redundancy payments

9 The Foreign Element of Schedules D And E *111*

Domicile, residence and ordinary residence – Foreign element of Schedule D Cases I and II – Schedule D Cases IV and V – The foreign basis of computation under Schedule D – The foreign element of Schedule E

10 Partnership Taxation *124*

Introduction – Existence of a partnership – Mode of assessment and liability for tax – Change of partners – Partnership losses – Partnership retirement annuities – Partnerships controlled abroad or trading abroad

11 Schedule D Case VI *133*

Scope of the charge – 'Annual' profits – Furnished lettings – Computation of income

12 Schedule D Case III *136*

Introduction – Definitions – Collection of the tax – Section 349(2) and (3) ICTA 1988 and interest payments – Sections 348-9, 347A–B ICTA 1988: annuities and other annual payments – Tax-free payments – Purchased life annuities

13 Trust Income *151*

Introduction – The taxation of the trustee – The scope of the charge on the trustees – The taxation of the beneficiary – Sections 686 and 687 ICTA 1988 – Payments out of capital treated as income – Income tax and the administration of an estate

14 Settlements – Anti-avoidance *166*

Introduction – Chapters 1A and 1B ICTA 1988, ss660A et seq – Preliminary concepts – Children's settlements: s660B ICTA 1988 – Section 660A(4)–(9) ICTA 1988 – Other anti-avoidance provisions: ss677 and 678 ICTA 1988

15 Matrimonial Taxation *176*

Introduction – Income taxation of married couples living together – Income tax position of separated couples and maintenance payments – Mortgage interest relief on separation – Capital gains tax treatment of married couples – Capital gains tax on separation – The disposal of the matrimonial home by one spouse to the other – Inheritance tax and married couples

16 Corporation Tax *182*

Introduction – The charge to corporation tax – The rate of corporation tax – Charges on income – Interest payments by companies (loan relationships) – Losses – Reform: the pay and file system and self-assessment

17 Dividends and Distributions of Companies *199*

Introduction – 'Distribution' – 'Qualifying distribution' – Set-off of ACT against mainstream corporation tax: s239 ICTA 1988 – Treatment of surplus ACT – Franked payments made to individuals – Franked payments made to other companies – The uses of surplus franked investment income – Special rules for groups and consortia – The purchase by a company of its own shares and 'special dividends'

18 Close Companies *213*

Introduction – 'Close company' – 'Participator' – 'Associate' – 'Loan creditor' – 'Control' – Extended meaning of 'distribution' – Loans to participators – Apportionment of income and chargeable gains – Small companies' rates are not available to CICs – Profit distributions by CICs – Transfer of assets at an undervalue: s125 TCGA 1992

19 Capital Gains Tax: General *221*

Introduction – The charge – Persons chargeable – Non-resident with UK branch or agency – Chargeable assets – 'Disposal' – Timing of a disposal – Computation – Calculation of gains and losses – Valuation of disposal consideration – Exemptions and reliefs – Partnership – Company transactions

20 Death and Settled Property in CGT *261*

Death – Variations of dispositions made on death – Losses unused at the date of death – Settled property: introduction – 'Settled property' – 'Trustees' – Gifts in settlement – Sales of trust assets – Persons becoming absolutely entitled to settled property and the settlement comes to an end – Termination of a life interest where the settlement continues – Disposal by a beneficiary of his interest – The foreign element of trusts in CGT

21 Inheritance Tax: General *275*

Introduction – The basic charging provisions – Transfer of value – The value transferred – The rate of tax – Liability for IHT and 'grossing up' and calculation of IHT – Death – Gifts with reservation of benefit: Schedule 20 and s102 FA 1986 – Associated operations – Excluded property

22 IHT Reliefs and Related Provisions *297*

Introduction – Potentially exempt transfers – Exemptions and reliefs applying to lifetime transfers only – Exemptions and reliefs available both during the transferor's lifetime and on death – Reliefs available only on death

23 IHT and Settled Property *312*

Introduction – 'Settlement' – 'Interest in possession' – Consequence of the existence of an interest in possession – The charging provisions – 'Excluded property' – Liability for tax and the beneficiary's cumulative total – The discretionary trust regime – The principal charge to tax – The charge at other times – Charitable purpose trusts – Accumulation and maintenance trusts: s71 – Property becoming held for charitable purposes or by exempt bodies

24 Administration, Assessments and Back Duty *329*

Administration – Returns and assessments – Self-assessment – Appeals – Judicial review – Back duty – Interest – *Pepper* v *Hart*: statutory interpretation

25 Value Added Tax 342
Introduction – Taxable supplies – Importation – Exempt supplies – Zero-rated supplies – The computation of the charge – Special cases

26 Anti-avoidance 360
Introduction – *The Duke of Westminster's Case* and beyond – *Ramsay* and the 'new approach' – Pre-ordination – The tax avoidance motive – Summary

27 Recent Cases 373
Schedule D Cases I and II – Capital allowances – Schedule E – Settlements: anti-avoidance – Corporation tax – Close companies – Value added tax – Anti-avoidance

Preface

This book has been written specifically for students. No matter which course is being followed, Old Bailey Press books are clear and concise, and provide comprehensive and up-to-date coverage.

The *Revenue Law* textbook is designed for use by all undergraduates who have Revenue Law within their syllabuses. It will also be an invaluable aid to those studying for the Law Society Legal Practice Course Examination, the Bar Examination and the Bar Vocational Course.

This edition of the *Revenue Law* textbook incorporates the changes introduced by the Finance Act 1997, in particular the changes to the taxation of 'special dividends' introduced in Schedule 7 of the Act, being dividends paid on the occasion of the purchase by a company of its own shares and on other occasions when share capital is repaid: see Chapter 17.

The developments in this edition represent the law as at 1 May 1997, by which date the Finance Act 1996 had received the Royal Assent.

Table of Cases

Aberdeen Construction Group Ltd *v* IRC [1978] STC 127   *247*
Alexander von Glehn *v* IRC (1920) 12 TC 232   *56*
Allan *v* IRC, Cullen *v* IRC [1994] STC 943   *110*
Allied Domecq plc *v* Customs and Excise Commissioners [1996] STC 898   *357, 384*
Anders Utkilens Rederi A/S *v* O/Y Lovisa Stevedoring Co A/B [1985] STC 301   *268*
Aspden *v* Hildesley [1982] STC 206   *180, 243*
Associated Restaurants Ltd *v* Warland *see* Wimpey International Ltd *v* Warland
Attorney-General *v* Seccombe [1911] 2 KB 688   *292*
Attorney-General *v* Worrall [1895] 1 QB 99   *291*
Attwood *v* Anduff Car Wash Ltd [1996] STC 110   *74, 376*

BLP Group *v* Customs and Excise Commissioners [1995] STC 424   *351*
BSC Footwear Ltd *v* Ridgway (1971) 47 TC 495   *48*
Baker *v* Archer-Shee [1927] AC 844   *154, 155, 158*
Ball *v* National and Grindlay's Bank (1971) 47 TC 287   *189*
Batey *v* Wakefield 55 TC 550   *248, 249*
Baylis *v* Roberts [1989] STC 693   *63*
Beak *v* Robson [1943] AC 352   *105*
Beauchamp *v* FW Woolworth plc [1989] STC 570; [1987] STC 279   *53*
Bennett *v* IRC [1995] STC 54   *300*
Bennett *v* Ogston (1930) 15 TC 374   *137*
Blakiston *v* Cooper (1908) 5 TC 347   *90*
Bolton *v* International Drilling Ltd [1983] STC 70   *53*
Bond *v* Pickford [1983] STC 517   *266*
Booth *v* Ellard [1980] STC 555   *267*
Bott (E) *v* Price [1987] STC 100   *189*
Bourne *v* Norwich Crematorium (1967) 44 TC 165   *81*
Bowden *v* Russell and Russell (1965) 42 TC 301   *54, 55*

Bradley *v* London Electricity plc [1996] STC 1054   *74, 376*
Bray *v* Best [1989] 1 All ER 969   *92*
British Airways plc *v* Customs and Excise Commissioners [1990] STC 643   *348*
British Airways *v* Customs and Excise Commissioners [1996] STC 1127   *348*
British Insulated and Helsby Cables Ltd *v* Atherton [1926] AC 205; (1925) 10 TC 155   *52, 189*
Brodie's Will Trustees *v* IRC (1933) 17 TC 432   *161*
Brown *v* Bullock (1961) 40 TC 1   *108*
Burmah Steamship Co Ltd *v* IRC (1930) 16 TC 67   *46, 366*
Butler (Inspector of Taxes) *v* Wildin [1989] STC 22   *171*
Butt *v* Haxby [1983] STC 239   *66*
Bye *v* Coren [1986] STC 393   *4*

Cairns *v* MacDiarmid [1983] STC 178   *138*
Campbell *v* IRC [1970] AC 77   *140*
Campbell Connelly & Co Ltd *v* Barnett [1994] STC 50   *253*
Cape Brandy Syndicate *v* IRC [1920] 1 KB 71   *360*
Carlisle and Silloth Golf Club *v* Smith (1913) 6 TC 198   *42*
Carr *v* Sayer [1992] STC 396   *74*
Carver *v* Duncan [1984] STC 556   *159*
Cenlon Finance *v* Ellwood [1961] Ch 634   *332, 336*
Chancery Lane Safe Deposit and Offices Ltd *v* IRC (1965) 43 TC 83   *146, 188*
Chevron Petroleum (UK) Ltd *v* BP Petroleum Development Ltd [1981] STC 689   *137*
Chick *v* Commissioner of Stamp Duties [1958] AC 435   *291*
Chinese Channel (Hong Kong) Limited, The *v* Customs and Excise Commissioners [1996] Decision No 14003   *347*
Chinn *v* Collins [1981] AC 583   *168, 363*
Clarke *v* Mayo [1994] STC 570   *255*
Colquhoun *v* Brooks (1889) 2 TC 490   *115, 118*

Table of Cases

Commissioner of Stamp Duties (Queensland) v Livingston [1965] AC 694   *164*
Commissioner of Stamp Duties v Perpetual Trustee Co Ltd [1943] AC 435   *289*
Commissioners v Glassborrow [1975] QB 465   *359*
Conservative and Unionist Central Office v Burrell [1980] 3 All ER 42   *182*
Cooke v Beach Station Caravans Ltd (1974) 49 TC 514   *73*
Cooke v Blacklaws [1985] STC 1   *86*
Cooper v Cadwalader (1904) 5 TC 107   *112*
Coperman v Coleman, for Coleman Minors (1939) 22 TC 594   *380*
Craven v White [1988] STC 477   *363, 365, 366, 367, 368, 369, 370, 371*
Crowe v Appleby 51 TC 374   *268*
Cunard's Trustees v IRC [1946] 1 All ER 159   *161, 162, 163*
Customs and Excise Commissioners v Faith Construction Ltd [1988] STC 35   *370*
Customs and Excise Commissioners v Leightons Ltd; Customs and Excise Commissioners v Eye-Tech Opticians [1995] STC 458   *348*
Customs and Excise Commissioners v Morrison's Academy Boarding House Association [1978] STC 1   *344*
Customs and Excise Commissioners v Robert Gordon's College [1995] STC 1093   *351*

Dale v De Soissons (1950) 32 TC 108; [1950] 2 All ER 460   *104, 110*
Davenport v Chilver [1983] STC 426   *224, 226*
Davies v Braithwaite (1931) 18 TC 198   *85, 116*
Davis v Powell [1977] STC 32; [1977] STC 426   *224*
Dawson v IRC [1989] 2 All ER 289   *152*
De Beers Consolidated Mines Ltd v Howe [1906] AC 455; 5 TC 198   *114*
De Rothschild v Lawrenson [1995] STC 623   *273*
Deeny and Others v Gooda Walker Ltd (In Voluntary Liquidation) and Others (Inland Revenue Commissioners as Third Party) and Related Appeals [1996] STC 299   *45, 373*
Dewar v IRC [1935] 2 KB 351   *165*
Ditchfield v Sharp [1983] STC 590   *141*
Donald Fisher (Ealing) Ltd v Spencer [1989] STC 256   *46, 225*
Drummond v Austin-Brown [1984] STC 321   *224*
Drummond v Collins [1915] AC 1011   *118*
Duke of Westminster's Case, The see IRC v Duke of Westminster

Duple Motor Bodies Ltd v Ostime (1961) 39 TC 537   *49*

EC Commission v UK [1988] STC 456   *354*
Earl Fitzwilliam's Agreement, Re [1950] Ch 448   *289*
Earl Howe v IRC [1919] 2 KB 415   *139*
Earlspring Properties Ltd v Guest [1995] STC 479   *218*
Eastham v Leigh London and Provincial Properties Ltd [1971] Ch 871   *231*
Edwards v Bairstow and Harrison [1956] AC 14   *40, 335, 365*
Edwards v Clinch [1982] AC 845; [1981] Ch 1   *85*
Eilbeck v Rawling [1982] AC 300; [1981] STC 174; 54 TC 101   *361, 362*
Empire Stores Ltd v Customs and Excise Commissioners [1994] STC 623   *355*
Ensign Tankers (Leasing) Ltd v Stokes [1992] STC 226   *42, 370*
Erichsen v Last (1881) 4 TC 422   *116*
Euro Hotel (Belgravia) Ltd, Re [1975] 3 All ER 1075   *137*

Fall v Hitchen [1973] 1 All ER 368   *85*
Fetherstonaugh v IRC [1984] STC 261   *305*
Ferguson v IRC [1970] AC 412   *149*
Fine Art Developments plc v Customs and Excise Commissioners (No 2) [1996] STC 246   *355*
Firestone Tyre and Rubber Co Ltd v Lewellin [1957] 1 All ER 561; (1957) 37 TC 111   *116*
Fitzpatrick v IRC (No 2) [1994] 1 WLR 306; [1994] STC 237   *108*
Fitzwilliam (Countess) and Others v IRC [1993] 1 WLR 1189; [1993] STC 502   *370*
Fletcher v IRC [1972] AC 414   *42*
Floor v Davis [1979] STC 379; [1978] STC 436   *229, 258, 361*
Foley v Fletcher (1858) 28 LJ Ex 100   *139*
Foster v Williams; Horan v Williams [1997] STC (SCD) 112   *225*
Frankland v IRC [1996] STC 735   *287, 302*
Frost v Feltham [1981] STC 115   *14*
Fry v Salisbury House Estate Ltd [1930] AC 432   *4, 7, 27*
Furniss v Dawson [1984] STC 153; [1984] AC 474   *168, 294, 317, 364, 365, 366, 371*

Gallagher v Jones, Threlfall v Jones [1993] STC 537   *50, 58, 59*

Gilbert v Hemsley [1981] STC 703   *101*
Gittos v Barclay (1985) 55 TC 633   *25*
Glaxo Group Ltd v IRC [1996] STC 191   *50*
Glenboig Union Fireclay Co Ltd v IRC (1921) 12 TC 427   *46*
Glynn v Commissioner of Inland Revenue [1990] STC 227   *88*
Golding v Kaufman [1985] STC 152   *230*
Goodbrand v Loffland Brothers North Sea Inc [1997] STC 102   *242*
Goodwin v Curtis [1996] STC 1146   *250*
Gray v Matheson [1993] STC 178   *332, 336*
Gray v Seymours Garden Centre [1995] STC 706   *73, 74, 376*
Great Western Railway Co Ltd v Bater [1920] 3 KB 266   *84*
Griffin v Craig-Harvey [1994] STC 54   *250*
Griffiths v Jackson and Pearman [1983] STC 184   *25*

Hafton Properties Ltd v McHugh [1987] STC 16   *117*
Hall v Lorimer [1994] 1 WLR 209; [1994] STC 23   *85*
Hamblett v Godfrey [1987] STC 60   *87, 90, 105*
Hamilton-Russell's Executors v IRC [1943] 1 All ER 474   *154, 157*
Hampton v Fortes Autogrill Ltd [1980] STC 80   *73*
Harrison v Nairn Williamson Ltd [1976] STC 67   *258*
Harrison (TC) Group Ltd v Customs and Excise Commissioners [1996] STC 898   *357, 384*
Hart v Briscoe [1979] Ch 110   *266*
Harvey v Sivyer [1985] STC 434   *169, 172*
Heather v PE Consulting Ltd [1973] Ch 189   *189*
Heaton v Bell [1970] AC 728; (1969) 46 TC 211   *94, 101*
Higgs v Olivier [1952] Ch 311   *45, 46*
Hoare Trustees v Gardner [1979] Ch 110   *266*
Hobbs v Hussey [1942] 1 KB 491   *134*
Hochstrasser v Mayes (1959) 38 TC 673   *87, 89, 110*
Honour v Norris [1992] STC 304   *249*
Horton v Young (1971) 47 TC 60   *55, 108*
Hoye v Forsdyke [1981] STC 711   *121*
Hunter v Dewhurst (1932) 16 TC 605   *90*

Imperial Chemical Industries plc v Colmer (Inspector of Taxes) [1996] STC 352   *196, 380*

Inglewood v IRC [1983] STC 133   *326*
Ingram's (Lady) Executors v IRC [1995] STC 564   *290, 291*
IRC v Aken [1988] STC 69   *43*
IRC v Barclay, Curle and Co Ltd (1969) 45 TC 221   *73*
IRC v Berrill [1981] STC 784   *158*
IRC v Biggar [1982] STC 677   *46*
IRC v Church Commissioners [1977] AC 329   *140*
IRC v Cleveley's Investment Trust Co (1971) 47 TC 300   *247*
IRC v Cochrane's Executors [1974] STC 335   *266*
IRC v Cock, Russell and Co Ltd (1949) 29 TC 387   *48*
IRC v Countess of Longford [1928] AC 252   *153*
IRC v Crawley [1987] STC 147   *147*
IRC v Duke of Westminster [1936] AC 1; 19 TC 490   *360, 361, 363*
IRC v Levy [1982] STC 442   *168, 169*
IRC v Livingston (1927) 11 TC 538   *41*
IRC v Lysaght [1928] AC 234   *113*
IRC v Maxse [1919] 1 KB 647   *39*
IRC v National Federation of Self-Employed and Small Businesses Ltd [1981] STC 260   *337*
IRC v Nelson and Sons (1939) 22 TC 716   *49*
IRC v Plummer [1980] AC 896   *146, 168, 169, 188, 363*
IRC v Reinhold (1953) 34 TC 389   *40, 42*
IRC v Scottish & Newcastle Breweries [1982] STC 296   *74*
IRC v Ufitec Group Ltd [1977] STC 363   *231*
IRC v Universities Superannuation Scheme Ltd [1997] STC 1   *371, 386*
IRC v Wesleyan and General Assurance Society [1946] 2 All ER 749   *363*
IRC v Whitworth Park Coal Co Ltd [1961] AC 31; (1959) 38 TC 531; [1958] Ch 792   *139, 142, 146*
IRC v Wilkinson [1992] STC 454   *4*
IRC v Willoughby [1995] STC 143   *370*
Irving v Tesco Stores (1987) TC 1   *394*

JP Harrison (Watford) Ltd v Griffiths (1962) 40 TC 281   *335*
Jacgilden (Weston Hall) Ltd v Castle (1969) 45 TC 685   *51*
Jarrold v Boustead [1964] 3 All ER 76   *89*
Jefferson v Jefferson [1956] P 136   *150*
Jeffs v Ringtons Ltd [1986] STC 144   *189*
John Hood and Co Ltd v Magee (1918) 7 TC 327   *114*

Table of Cases

Johnston v Britannia Airways Ltd [1994] STC 763   *58, 59*
Joint v Bracken Developments Ltd [1994] STC 300   *218*
Jones v Leeming [1930] AC 415; (1930) 15 TC 333   *43, 134*

Kidson v MacDonald [1974] Ch 339   *267, 268*
Kildrummy (Jersey) Ltd v IRC [1990] STC 657   *291*
Kirby v Thorn EMI [1987] STC 621   *228, 258*

Laidler v Perry [1966] AC 16; (1965) 42 TC 351   *90*
Lang v Rice [1984] STC 172   *46*
Law Shipping Co Ltd v IRC (1924) 12 TC 621   *24, 56*
Lawson v Johnson Matthey plc [1992] STC 466   *52*
Levene v IRC [1928] AC 217   *113*
Lewis v IRC [1933] 2 KB 557   *126*
Lewis v Rook [1992] STC 171   *249*
Loewenstein v De Salis (1926) 10 TC 424   *112*
Lomax v Newton (1953) 34 TC 558   *108*
Lomax v Peter Dixon Ltd (1943) 25 TC 353   *141*
London and Thames Haven Oil Wharves Ltd v Attwooll (1996) 43 TC 491   *374*
Lubbock Fine v Customs and Excise Commissioners [1994] STC 101   *351*
Lupton v Potts [1969] 1 WLR 1749   *108*

McClure v Petre [1988] STC 749   *23*
McGregor v Adcock [1977] STC 206   *255*
McGregor v Randall [1984] STC 223   *90, 104*
MacKinlay v Arthur Young McClelland Moores [1990] 1 All ER 45; [1989] STC 898   *55*
McMenamin v Diggles [1991] STC 419   *85*
McMillan v Guest [1942] AC 561   *85*
MacPherson v IRC [1988] STC 362; [1987] STC 73   *318*
Mairs v Haughey [1993] 3 WLR 393   *110*
Mallalieu v Drummond [1983] STC 665   *54*
Mangin v IRC [1971] 1 All ER 179   *363*
Mann v Nash (1932) 16 TC 532   *43*
Markey v Sanders [1987] STC 256   *248*
Marren v Ingles [1980] STC 500   *228*
Marshall v Kerr [1994] 3 WLR 299   *171, 263*
Martin v Lowry [1927] AC 312   *40*
Mason v Innes [1967] Ch 1079   *51*
Melluish v BMI (No 3) Ltd v IRC [1995] STC 964   *75, 76*
Merseyside Cablevision v Customs and Excise Commissioners [1987] VATTR 134   *345*

Methuen-Cambell v Walters [1979] QB 525   *249*
Miller v IRC [1987] STC 108   *315*
Mills v IRC [1975] AC 38   *171*
Miners v Atkinson [1997] STC 58   *108*
Mitchell v BW Noble Ltd (1927) 11 TC 372   *57*
Mitchell and Edon v Ross [1962] AC 814   *85*
Moodie v IRC, Sotnick v IRC [1993] STC 188   *168, 363*
Moore & Osborn v IRC [1984] STC 236   *316*
Moorhouse v Dooland (1954) 36 TC 1   *90*
Moss Empires Ltd v IRC [1937] AC 785   *139*
Muir v Muir [1943] AC 468   *266*
Munby v Furlong (1977) 50 TC 491   *73*
Munro v Commissioner for Stamp Duties [1934] AC 61   *290*

Neville Russell v Customs and Excise Commissioners [1987] VATTR 194   *346*
Newson v Robertson (1952) 33 TC 452   *55*
Nicholls v IRC [1975] STC 278   *290, 291*
Nichols v Gibson [1996] STC 1008   *7, 88, 104, 114*
Nicoll v Austin (1935) 19 TC 531   *87, 95, 96, 100*

Oakes v Commissioner of Stamp Duties [1954] AC 57   *289, 290*
O'Brien v Benson's Hosiery (Holdings) Ltd [1979] STC 735   *224, 225*
Ockenden v Mackley [1982] STC 513; [1982] 1 WLR 787   *35*
Odeon Associated Cinemas v Jones (1971) 48 TC 257   *56, 58*
Ogilvie v Kitton (1908) 5 TC 338   *115*
O'Keefe v Southport Printers Ltd [1984] STC 443   *57*
Overseas Containers (Finance) Ltd v Stoker [1989] STC 364   *42*

Padmore v IRC [1989] STC 493; [1987] STC 36   *116, 132*
Park, deceased (No 2), Re [1972] Ch 385   *301*
Parkside Leasing v Smith [1985] STC 63   *142*
Partridge v Mallandaine (1886) 2 TC 179   *39*
Parway Estates Limited v IRC 45 TC 135   *231*
Pearson v IRC [1980] 2 WLR 872   *289, 313, 314, 315*
Pennine Raceway Ltd v Kirklees Metropolitan Council (No 2) [1989] STC 122   *225*
Pepper v Hart [1992] 3 WLR 1032; [1992] STC 898   *97, 98, 340*

Peracha v Miley (Inspector of Taxes) [1990] STC 512   *139*
Perrons v Spackman [1981] STC 739   *108*
Petrotim Securities Ltd v Ayres (1963) 41 TC 389   *51*
Pettitt, Re [1922] 2 Ch 765   *150*
Pickford v Quirke (1927) 13 TC 251   *41*
Piggott v Staines Investments [1995] STC 114   *371*
Pilkington v IRC [1964] AC 612   *327*
Plumbly v Spencer [1996] STC (SCD) 295   *255*
Pook v Owen [1970] AC 244; [1969] TR 113   *107, 108*
Primback Ltd v Customs and Excise Commissioners [1996] STC 757   *352*
Pritchard v Arundale [1971] 3 All ER 1011   *88, 89, 103*

R v Barnet LBC, ex parte Shah [1983] 2 AC 309   *113*
R v Commissioner, ex parte Stipplechoice Ltd [1988] STC 556   *337*
R v HM Inspector of Taxes, ex parte Kissane [1986] STC 152   *337*
R v International Stock Exchange of the United Kingdom and the Republic of Ireland, ex parte Else (1982) Ltd [1993] QB 534   *386*
R v IRC, ex parte Fulford-Dobson [1987] STC 344   *222*
R v IRC, ex parte Matrix Securities Ltd [1994] 1 WLR 334   *332*
R v IRC, ex parte MFK [1990] 1 WLR 1545; [1989] STC 873   *337*
R v IRC, ex parte Preston [1985] AC 836; [1985] STC 282   *337*
R v O'Kane and Clarke, ex parte Northern Bank Ltd [1996] STC 1249   *331*
Ramsay (WT) Ltd v IRC [1982] AC 300; [1981] STC 174; 54 TC 101   *168, 247, 361, 362, 364, 365, 366, 370, 371*
Ransom v Higgs (1974) 50 TC 1   *39, 42*
Reckitt, Re [1932] 2 Ch 144   *149*
Reed v Clark [1985] STC 323   *114, 116*
Reed v Young [1986] STC 285; [1984] STC 38   *67, 124, 126, 131*
Reid's Trustees v IRC (1929) 14 TC 512   *152*
Rice, BJ & Associates v Customs and Excise Commissioners [1996] STI 273   *346*
Richardson v Worrall [1985] STC 693   *95, 102*
Ricketts v Colquhoun [1926] AC 1   *106*
Riley v Coglan (1968) 44 TC 481   *89*
Robson v Dixon [1972] 3 All ER 671   *113*

Rolfe v Nagel [1982] STC 53   *47*
Rolls Royce Motors Ltd v Bamford [1976] STC 162; [1951] TC 319   *67, 193*
Roome v Edwards [1981] STC 96   *266*
Royscot Leasing Ltd and Royscot Industrial Leasing Ltd v Customs and Excise Commissioners [1996] STC 898   *357, 384*
Russell v IRC [1988] STC 195   *287*
Rutledge v IRC (1929) 14 TC 490   *40*

St Aubyn v Attorney-General [1952] AC 15   *289*
Sainsbury (J) plc v O'Connor [1991] STC 318   *210*
Sansom v Peay [1976] STC 494   *251*
Sargent v Barnes [1978] STC 322   *56*
Schofield v R and H Hall Ltd (1974) 49 TC 538   *73*
Scorer v Olin Energy [1985] STC 218; [1984] STC 141   *192, 332, 336*
Sharkey v Wernher [1956] AC 58; (1955) 36 TC 271   *50, 51, 245*
Shepherd v Lyntress Ltd [1989] STC 517   *369*
Sheppard and Another (Trustees of the Woodlands Trust) v IRC (No 2) [1993] STC 240   *388*
Sherdley v Sherdley [1988] AC 213; [1987] STC 217   *169*
Shilton v Wilmhurst [1991] STC 88   *88, 89, 105*
Sidey v Phillips [1987] STC 87   *85*
Simmons v IRC [1980] STC 350   *41, 43*
Smith v Abbott [1994] 1 WLR 306; [1994] STC 237   *108, 109*
Smith v Schofield [1993] STC 268   *240*
Sotnick v IRC *see* Moodie v IRC
Southern v Aldwych Properties Ltd [1940] 2 KB 266   *24*
Southern Railway of Peru v Owen [1957] AC 334   *59*
Stanley v IRC [1944] 1 KB 255   *157*
Stanton v Drayton Investment Ltd [1982] STC 585   *242*
Starke & Another (Brown's Executors) v IRC [1995] 1 WLR 1439; [1995] STC 689   *307*
Steele v EVC International NV [1996] STC 785   *216, 382*
Stekel v Ellice [1973] 1 WLR 191   *126*
Stephenson v Barclays Bank [1975] 1 All ER 625   *268*
Stevenson v Wishart [1987] STC 266   *161, 162*
Stokes v Costain Property Investments Ltd [1984] STC 204   *75*

Stone & Temple Ltd v Waters [1995] STC 1   59
Strong & Co of Romsey Ltd v Woodfield (1906) 5 TC 215   56

Taylor v Provan [1975] AC 194   *107, 108*
Templeton v Jacobs [1996] 2 WLR 1433; [1996] STC 991   *96, 377*
Tenbry Investments Ltd v Peugeot Talbot Motor Co Ltd [1992] STC 791   *148*
Tennant v Smith [1892] AC 150   *86, 93*
Thomas v Marshall [1953] AC 543   *172*
Thomas v Reynolds [1987] STC 135   *73, 74*
Threlfall v Jones see Gallagher v Jones
Todd v Mudd [1987] STC 141   *251, 254*
Tomlinson v Glynn's Executor and Trustee Co Ltd [1970] Ch 112   *267, 268*
Tucker v Granada Motorway Services Ltd [1979] STC 393   *52*

UDT v Kirkwood [1966] 2 QB 431   *143*
Unit Construction v Bullock (1959) 38 TC 712   *114–115*

Vallambrosa Rubber Co Ltd v Farmer (1910) 5 TC 529   *52, 58, 59*
Van den Berghs v Clark [1935] AC 431; (1935) 19 TC 390   *47, 58*
Vertigan v Brady [1988] STC 91   *93*
Vestey v IRC [1962] Ch 861   *140*
Vibroplant Ltd v Holland [1982] STC 164   *81*
Virgin Atlantic Airways Ltd v Customs and Excise Commissioners [1995] STC 341   *348*
Vodafone Cellular Ltd v Shaw [1997] STC 734   *58*

Wain v Cameron [1995] STC 555   *45*
Walding v IRC [1996] STC 13   *305*
Wales v Tilley [1943] AC 386   *90, 104*

Walker v Joint Credit Card Co Ltd [1982] STC 427   *52*
Walls v Sinnett [1987] STC 236   *85*
Watkis v Ashford, Sparkes and Harward [1985] STC 451   *55*
Watton v Tippett [1996] STC 101   *254*
Weight v Salmon (1935) 19 TC 174   *103*
Wellcome Trust Ltd v Customs and Excise Commissioners [1996] STC 945   *344*
Wharf Properties Ltd v CIR [1996] 2 WLR 334; [1997] STC 351   *53, 374*
Whitehead v Tubbs Elastic Ltd [1984] STC 1   *53, 57*
Whittles v Uniholdings Ltd [1996] STC 914   *371*
Wicks v Firth [1983] AC 214; [1983] STC 25   *88, 93, 99, 100, 101*
Wilcock v Eve [1995] STC 18   *109*
Wilcock v Frigate Investments Ltd [1982] STC 198   *188*
Wilkins v Rogerson [1961] Ch 133   *87, 94, 95*
Williams v Bullivant [1983] STC 107   *230*
Williams v Evans [1982] STC 498   *253*
Williams v Merrylees [1987] STC 445   *248*
Williams v Simmonds (1981) 55 TC 17   *104*
Williams v Singer [1921] 1 AC 41   *118, 152*
Willingale v International Commercial Bank [1978] STC 75   *44*
Wimpey International Ltd v Warland; Associated Restaurants Ltd v Warland [1989] STC 273; [1988] STC 149; [1988] CLY 753   *74, 376*
Wisdom v Chamberlain (1969) 45 TC 92   *40*

Yarmouth v France (1887) 19 QBD 647   *73, 377*
Yates v Starkey [1951] Ch 465   *169*
Young v Pearce; Young v Scrutton [1996] STC 743   *170, 378*

Zim Properties v Proctor [1985] STC 90   *225, 226, 227*

Table of Statutes

Administration of Estates Act 1925
    s47A   *288*
    s51(3)   *157*
Agricultural Holdings Act 1948
    s34(2)   *224*
Agricultural Holdings Act 1986   *279*
Agriculture Tenancies Act 1995   *307*

Bill of Rights 1688
    Article 9   *341*
Banking Act 1987   *143*

Capital Allowances Act 1968   *72*
    s3(4A)   *82*
    s3(4B)   *82*
Capital Allowances Act 1990   *72, 73, 74, 78, 79, 80, 81, 216*
    s4(1)   *82*
    s9(1)   *83*
    s9(5)   *83*
    s18   *80, 82*
    s18(1)   *80*
    s18(3)   *81*
    s18(7)   *81*
    s20   *82*
    ss22–83   *80*
    s24   *75, 77, 376*
    a24(1)   *75*
    s25   *77*
    s27   *75*
    s29   *75*
    ss30–33   *79*
    ss34–36   *79*
    s37   *78*
    s38   *78*
    s38A–38H   *78*
    s38A(2)   *78*
    s38B   *78*
    s38D   *78*
    s38F   *78*
    ss39–50   *79*
    ss51–59   *75, 76*
    s53   *76*
    s61   *29*
    s67A   *74*

Capital Allowances Act 1990 (*contd.*)
    s70   *80*
    s71   *79*
    s71(2)   *80*
    s72   *79*
    s79   *78*
    s140   *76*
    s140(2)   *76*
    s144   *83*
    s145   *83*
    s160   *74*
    s161   *75*
    s161(2)   *216*
    s161(7)   *81*
    Schedule AA1   *73, 74*
Capital Gains Tax Act 1979   *221, 365*
    s62(3)   *369*
    s77   *362*
    s115   *25*
    s152   *251*
    s258(3)   *244*
Capital Transfer Tax Act 1984   *276*
Companies Act 1985
    ss159–181   *210*

Finance Act 1960   *387*
Finance Act 1965   *221*
Finance Act 1971   *72, 80*
    s32(3)   *10*
    s44   *376*
    s72   *70*
Finance Act 1972   *72, 342*
    s3(6)   *385*
Finance Act 1980
    s79   *244, 269, 270*
Finance Act 1981   *174*
    s80   *274*
    s80(2)   *274*
Finance Act 1982   *174, 233, 235, 259*
    s60   *201*
    s80   *232*
    s82   *244, 269*
Finance Act 1984   *8, 72, 81, 99, 336*
    s36   *141*
    s50   *25*

Finance Act 1984 (*contd.*)
    Schedule 9   *141*
    Schedule 11   *25*
Finance Act 1985   *72, 233, 235, 260*
Finance Act 1986   *289, 297*
    s102   *275, 288, 291, 292*
    s102(1)   *290*
    s102(3)   *293*
    s102(4)   *293*
    Schedule 20   *275, 288, 292*
Finance Act (No 2) 1987
    ss82–90   *197*
    s95   *197*
    s96   *298, 316*
    Schedule 6   *197*
Finance Act 1988   *4, 13, 31, 36, 114, 144, 167, 233, 236*
    s31   *19*
    ss31–35   *18*
    s36   *15*
    s36(3)   *155*
    s38   *178*
    s38(5)   *178*
    s44   *179*
    s65   *5, 36*
    s66(1)   *114*
    s73   *105*
    ss77–89   *103*
    s104   *180*
    Schedule 3   *18*
    Schedule 6   *5, 36*
    Schedule 10   *274*
Finance Act 1989   *214, 219*
    s36   *92*
    s37   *92*
    s53   *96*
    s103   *214, 219*
    s110   *152, 153*
    s124   *243*
    Schedule 12   *220*
Finance Act 1990
    s21   *103*
    s28   *144*
    s30   *11, 144*
    s71   *13*
    s83   *248*
    s84   *247*
    s102   *75*
    Schedule 5   *144*
    Schedule 13   *75*
Finance Act 1991
    s30   *103*
    s31   *109*

Finance Act 1991 (*contd.*)
    s64   *66*
    s72   *68, 257*
    s73   *192*
Finance Act 1992   *35, 102*
Finance Act (No 2) 1992   *74, 304*
    s75   *335*
    Schedule 5   *19*
    Schedule 10   *33*
    Schedule 16   *335, 336*
Finance Act 1993   *59, 112, 192*
    s171   *45, 373, 374*
    s184   *45, 374*
    s184(1)   *374*
    Schedule 3   *101*
    Schedule 6   *255*
    Schedule 7   *253, 255, 256*
Finance Act 1994   *7, 38, 60, 142, 143, 205, 333, 351*
    s81   *13*
    s85   *178*
    s88   *102*
    s89   *95*
    s117   *73, 74*
    ss125–130   *91*
    ss178–199   *3, 333*
    ss181–183   *198*
    ss184–189   *124*
    s199   *3*
    s199(3)   *3*
    ss200–205   *60*
    ss200–208   *7*
    s206   *142*
    s207   *119*
    s211   *76*
    s221   *29*
    Schedule 19   *3, 333*
Finance Act 1995   *25, 111, 117, 125, 126, 151, 333, 351, 380*
    s39   *6*
    s39(2)   *6, 12, 23, 26*
    ss39–42   *25*
    s40   *34*
    s41   *34*
    s42   *6*
    s42(1)   *13*
    s43   *101*
    ss103–116   *333*
    s117   *124, 125, 126*
    s125   *117*
    ss126–129   *117*
    s127   *117*
    s128   *113*

Finance Act 1995 (*contd.*)
    Schedule 6   *6, 25, 26, 28, 29, 30, 32, 34*
    Schedule 16   *35*
    Schedule 17   *167*
    Schedule 18   *164*
    Schedule 21   *333*
    Schedule 23   *117*
Finance Act 1996   *2, 4, 5, 10, 12, 59, 102, 136, 141, 143, 187, 188, 189, 190, 191, 219, 248, 257, 304, 307, 358*
    ss80–105   *191*
    s81   *191*
    s106   *93, 94*
    s107   *102*
    s141   *254*
    s145   *18*
    s147(1)   *58*
    s173   *218*
    s184   *304*
    Schedules 8–15   *191*
    Schedule 13   *141*
    Schedule 41   *304*
Finance Act 1997   *75, 351, 358*
    s37   *350*
    s39   *357, 358*
    s40   *359*
    s41   *359*
    s59   *185*
    s62   *108*
    s68   *384*
    s73   *372, 388*
    s81   *370*
    s82   *51, 59*
    s86   *76*
    Schedule 7   *211, 212*
    Schedule 12   *51, 59*
    Schedule 14   *78*
    Schedule 16   *76*
    Schedule 17   *358*

Fire Safety and Safety of Places of Sport Act 1987   *80*

Income and Corporation Taxes Act 1925
    s31   *327*
    s31(1)   *158, 327, 328*
    s32   *327*
    s69(2)   *156*
Income and Corporation Taxes Act 1970
    s258   *380*
    s258(2)   *381*
    s258(5)   *381*
    s258(7)   *381*
    s258(8)   *381*

Income and Corporation Taxes Act 1988   *2, 6, 126, 214, 336*
    s1   *153*
    s1(2)   *153*
    s1A   *10, 11, 153, 200*
    s1A(1)   *12, 153*
    s1A(2)   *12, 142, 153*
    s3   *145, 146*
    s4   *145, 147*
    s4(1A)   *10, 142*
    s6   *182*
    s6(2)   *183*
    s8(3)   *183*
    s9   *183*
    s11   *182*
    s11(2)   *182*
    s12(1)   *183*
    s13   *185, 186, 187, 219*
    s13(1)   *219*
    s13A   *15, 216, 219*
    s13A(3)   *219, 220*
    s13(2)   *185*
    s14   *200*
    s14(2)   *202*
    s15   *6, 22, 23, 24, 27, 37, 151*
    s15(1)   *6, 24*
    s15(2)   *6*
    s18   *6, 38, 43, 115, 118, 133, 134, 151*
    s18(3)   *6, 7, 136*
    s18(3A)   *6*
    s19   *7, 84, 86, 88, 89, 90, 94, 101, 104, 105, 110*
    s19(1)   *86, 88*
    s19(4A)   *89, 92*
    s20   *7, 206*
    s20(1)   *7, 11, 200, 206, 388*
    s21   *6, 22*
    s22   *6, 22, 27*
    s24   *30*
    ss25–28   *6*
    s25   *24*
    s25(2)   *24*
    s32   *75*
    s33   *28*
    s33A   *22, 28, 35*
    s33B   *35*
    ss34–39   *22, 30*
    s34   *30, 31, 32*
    s34(1)   *31*
    s34(8)   *30*
    s35   *32*
    s38   *31*
    s41   *27*

xviii *Table of Statutes*

Income and Corporation Taxes Act 1988 (*contd.*)
- s41(2)   34
- s42A   34
- s46   8
- s53   43
- s53(1)   43
- s53(2)   43
- s53(3)   43
- s59   155
- ss60–64   6
- s60   60, 61, 64, 65
- s60(1)   62, 63
- s61   60, 65, 130
- s61(1)   61, 62, 63
- s61(3)   61, 62
- s61(4)   130
- s62   60, 61, 62, 63, 130
- s62(1)   62
- s63   60, 65, 129–130
- s63(1)   63, 64, 130
- ss64–67   142
- s64   6, 142
- ss65–67   119
- s65   6, 34, 118, 120, 223
- s65A   34
- s65(1)   6, 118
- s65(2)   6, 118
- s65(2A)   24, 35
- s65(2B)   24
- s66   142
- s66(1)   6
- s67   142
- s69   7
- s69(2)   156
- s74   6, 12, 23, 28, 35, 52, 53, 58, 59
- s74(a)   6, 54, 55
- s74(b)   55
- s74(c)   56
- s74(d)   56
- s74(e)   56
- s74(j)   57
- s74(n)   57
- s75   195, 208
- s76   208
- s80   66
- s82   34, 57
- s87   56
- s90   57
- s98   28
- ss100–102   65
- s100   49
- s100(1)   49
- s101   49

Income and Corporation Taxes Act 1988 (*contd.*)
- s102(2)   49
- s103   70
- s104   70
- s108   153
- s111   125, 126
- s112   131, 132
- s112(4)   116, 132
- s112(5)   116, 132
- s113   65, 129, 130
- s113(1)   65, 130
- s113(2)   129, 130
- s117   66, 131
- s119   10
- s120   10
- s125   137, 168
- ss131–207   7
- s131   7, 86, 88
- s131(1)   88
- s131(2)   120
- s132   7
- s135   103
- s141   94, 95
- s142   94, 95
- s143   47, 94, 95
- s144   47, 95
- s145   14, 93, 94, 217
- s145(4)   93
- s146   93, 94
- s146A   94
- s146(11)   94
- s148   7, 88, 89, 104, 105, 247
- ss153–168   96
- s153   107
- s153(1)   106
- s154   96, 97, 100, 103, 217, 377, 378
- s154(1)   93, 96, 378
- s154(2)   377
- s154(b)   101
- s155   99
- s155(1)   101
- s155(2)   96, 378
- s155(7)   91
- s155A   103
- s156   217
- s156(1)   97
- s156(2)   97
- s156(3)   98
- s156(4)   98
- s156(5)   98, 99
- s156(8)   98
- s157   100, 101, 102
- s158   100, 102

Income and Corporation Taxes Act 1988 (*contd.*)
- s159 *100*
- s159A *103*
- s160 *102, 103, 217*
- s160(1B) *102*
- s161 *102*
- s162 *103*
- s165 *99, 100*
- s167 *96*
- s168(5) *101*
- s177(1) *192*
- s187 *104*
- s188 *104, 247*
- s188(4) *89, 105*
- s191 *107*
- s192 *7*
- s193 *121*
- s193(1) *121, 123*
- s198 *7, 96, 106, 107, 108*
- s202A *3, 7, 89, 92*
- s202A(2) *92*
- s202B *92*
- s203 *91*
- ss203B–K *91*
- s207 *112*
- s207A *11*
- s208 *183, 186*
- ss209–211 *201*
- s209 *217, 260*
- s209(2) *57, 210, 220*
- s210 *201*
- s211 *202*
- s218 *216*
- s219 *210, 211*
- s219(1) *211*
- s220(5) *210*
- s229(1) *216*
- s231 *185, 206*
- s231(2) *207*
- s231(3) *11, 207, 382*
- s231(3A–D) *207, 220*
- s233(1) *206*
- s235 *202*
- s238 *207*
- s238(1) *185*
- s239 *199, 203, 204*
- s239(3) *204, 205*
- s239(4) *204*
- s240 *204*
- s240(11) *216*
- s241 *207*
- s241(3) *208*
- s242 *208*

Income and Corporation Taxes Act 1988 (*contd.*)
- s242(5) *209*
- s242(6) *209*
- s244(2) *208*
- s245 *204*
- s245B *204*
- s246A *205, 212*
- s246C *205*
- s246D *205*
- s246E *205, 212*
- ss246J–M *205*
- ss246S–Y *206*
- s247 *209*
- s247(4) *210*
- s247(5A) *209*
- s248 *189, 209*
- s249 *188*
- s256(2) *177*
- s257(1) *16, 19, 177, 178*
- s257(2) *18*
- s257(3) *18*
- s257A *177*
- s257A(1) *17, 18, 19, 178, 179*
- s257A(2) *18*
- s257A(3) *18*
- s257BA *177*
- s257B *17, 19, 21*
- s257D *19*
- s257E *19*
- s257F *19, 178*
- s257F(1) *17*
- s259 *17, 18*
- s259(4A) *17*
- s262 *17*
- s265 *18*
- s266 *150*
- s276 *145, 146*
- s278 *18*
- s278(2) *18*
- s279 *19*
- s282A *19, 177*
- s282A(1) *19*
- s282A(4) *19*
- s282B *19, 177*
- s286(3A) *243*
- s312 *216*
- s313 *88, 104, 105*
- s325 *8*
- s326 *8*
- s326A *8, 144*
- s329A *8*
- s331 *8, 99, 100*
- s334 *116*

Income and Corporation Taxes Act 1988 (*contd.*)
- s335 *113*
- s335(1) *112*
- s335(2) *112*
- s336 *112*
- s336(1) *112*
- s337 *189*
- s337(2) *189*
- s337(3) *189*
- s337A *188*
- ss338–340 *188*
- s338 *188, 190*
- s338(1) *188, 190*
- s338(2) *188*
- s338(3) *188*
- s338(4) *190*
- s338(5) *189*
- s339(8) *189*
- s343 *194*
- s343(6) *195*
- s344 *194*
- s347A *16, 136, 137, 143, 144, 148, 167, 283, 300*
- s347A(2) *137, 144, 145, 148, 167*
- s347B *136, 137, 144, 169, 178, 179*
- s347B(1) *179*
- s347B(2) *179*
- s347B(3) *179*
- s347B(8)–(12) *179*
- s348 *136, 137, 143, 144, 145, 146, 147, 148, 150, 155, 168, 210*
- s348(1) *145, 148*
- s348(2) *188*
- s349 *57, 67, 136, 137, 138, 143, 144, 146, 147, 148, 149, 150, 165, 190, 210*
- s349(1) *143, 146, 148*
- s349(2) *136, 143, 146*
- s349(3) *136, 138, 143, 146*
- s350 *144, 190, 210*
- s350(1) *148*
- ss353–358 *28*
- ss353–379 *9, 12*
- s353 *12, 14, 102, 143*
- s353(3) *12*
- ss354–368 *12*
- s354 *13, 14, 28, 179*
- s354(1) *13*
- s355 *13*
- s355(1) *6, 12*
- s355(1A) *14*
- s355(2) *14*
- s356 *14*
- s356A *13*

Income and Corporation Taxes Act 1988 (*contd.*)
- s356B *13, 14, 177*
- s356C *13*
- s357 *13*
- s359 *15*
- s360 *14*
- s360(3A) *15*
- s361 *15*
- s362 *15*
- s364 *15*
- s365 *15*
- ss369–379 *13*
- s369 *28*
- s369(1A) *13*
- s371 *14*
- s375A *28*
- s379A *35*
- s379(2) *33*
- s379(9) *33*
- s380 *26, 66, 67, 68, 69, 70, 131, 135, 257*
- s380(1) *66, 69*
- s381 *66, 68, 69, 131*
- s384 *66*
- s385 *66, 67, 68, 69, 131*
- s386 *66, 67, 68, 70*
- s387 *67, 70*
- s388 *66, 67, 69*
- s392 *135*
- ss393–396 *192*
- s393 *192*
- s393(1) *193*
- s393(2) *192, 193, 194*
- s393(8) *193*
- s393A *193, 195*
- s393A(1) *192, 193*
- s393A(3) *192*
- s394 *195*
- s396 *194*
- s397 *66, 69, 194*
- s401 *28, 58, 67*
- s401(1A) *190*
- s401(1B) *28*
- s402 *195*
- s402(3) *381*
- s402(4) *381*
- s402(6) *195*
- s408 *196*
- s410 *216, 384*
- s413(3) *381*
- s413(5) *196, 381*
- s414 *214*
- s414(1) *219*

Table of Statutes xxi

Income and Corporation Taxes Act 1988 (*contd.*)
  s416 *215, 216, 383, 384*
  s416(2) *383*
  s416(6) *214, 216*
  s417 *214*
  s417(3) *215*
  s417(5) *216*
  s417(7) *215*
  s418 *217*
  s418(2) *217*
  s418(4) *217*
  s419 *217, 218*
  s419(2) *217*
  s419(4) *218*
  s420(2) *217*
  s421 *218*
  ss423–430 *214, 219*
  s460 *337*
  s477A *11, 144*
  s480A *11, 144*
  s503 *25, 26, 28, 34, 135*
  s504 *25, 34*
  s505 *8*
  s505(1) *146*
  s573(2) *208*
  s577 *52, 57*
  s577A *57*
  s579 *57, 109, 110*
  s588 *57*
  s589A *57*
  s589B *57*
  s617(5) *58*
  s619 *150*
  s630 *131*
  s640 *131*
  s656 *150*
  ss660–676 *167*
  ss660–685 *166*
  s660 *167, 168*
  ss660A–G *133, 167, 380*
  s660A–682 *168*
  s660A *159, 166, 167, 170, 171, 162, 173, 263, 380*
  s660A(4) *166, 173*
  s660A(5) *166, 173*
  s660A(6) *166, 170, 173*
  s660A(7) *166, 170, 173*
  s660A(8) *166, 173*
  s660A(9) *166, 173*
  s660B *166, 167, 172*
  s660B(1) *172*
  s660B(2) *172, 173*
  s660B(3) *172, 173*

Income and Corporation Taxes Act 1988 (*contd.*)
  s660C *133, 167*
  s660D *167, 172*
  s660E *167*
  s660F *167*
  s660G *167, 168, 170, 171, 172, 273*
  s661 *167*
  s663 *168, 169, 170, 171, 286*
  s664 *286*
  s670 *169*
  s672 *379*
  s672(1) *379*
  s674A(1) *379, 380*
  s677 *166, 167, 169, 174, 175*
  s677(9) *174*
  s677(10) *174*
  s678 *166, 167, 174, 175*
  s681(4) *379, 380*
  s682 *131*
  ss683–685 *167*
  s683 *174, 177*
  s685 *170, 177*
  s685(4A) *379, 380*
  s686 *10, 12, 151, 153, 157, 158, 160, 163, 264*
  s686(1) *157*
  s686(1A) *157*
  s686(2) *157, 159*
  s686(2A) *158*
  s687 *10, 151, 157, 159, 162*
  s687(2) *12, 159, 160, 161*
  ss695–702 *163*
  s695 *164*
  s696 *164*
  s698(3) *165*
  s701(3A) *164*
  ss703–708 *388*
  s703 *372, 386*
  s703(3) *133, 387*
  s704 *372, 386, 388*
  s709 *372, 386, 388*
  s709(1) *372, 387, 388*
  s709(2) *212*
  s709(4) *388*
  s739 *370*
  s739(1A) *370*
  s740(4) *133*
  s767(5) *216*
  s770 *50*
  s770(d) *50*
  s770(1) *50*
  s773 *216*
  s774 *216*

Table of Statutes

Income and Corporation Taxes Act 1988 (*contd.*)
    s776(3)   *133*
    s832   *157*
    s832(1)   *26, 38, 182*
    s833   *10*
    s834(1)   *183*
    s835   *11, 137, 143, 147*
    s835(6)   *11, 16, 145, 146*
    s837   *93*
    s838   *195*
    s839   *35, 216, 384*
    s839(7)   *382, 383*
    s840   *195, 216*
    Schedule 4   *141*
    Schedule 6   *101*
    Schedule 7   *102, 273*
    Schedule 9   *103*
    Schedule 11A   *109*
    Schedule 12   *121, 122*
    Schedule 13   *203*
    Schedule 17A   *209, 210*
    Schedule 18   *209, 210*
    Part XV   *145, 151, 178*
    Part XVII   *360*
    Chapter 1A   *151, 166*
    Chapter 1B   *166*
Income Tax Act 1945   *72*
Inheritance (Provision for Family and Dependants) Act 1975   *288*
Inheritance Tax Act 1984   *276, 286, 293, 297, 312*
    s1   *276*
    s2(1)   *276, 297, 312*
    s3(1)   *276, 277, 280*
    s3(2)   *295*
    s3(3)   *276*
    s3A   *297, 298, 316, 317, 320*
    s4   *285*
    s4(1)   *284, 285, 311, 316, 317, 319*
    s5   *282, 293*
    s5(1)   *280*
    s5(3)   *282*
    s5(4)   *282*
    s6   *295*
    s6(1)   *319*
    s6(2)   *324*
    s6(3)   *295*
    s6(4)   *295*
    s7   *281*
    s7(2)   *281, 322, 324*
    s7(4)   *281, 293*
    s7(5)   *281*
    s10   *181, 277, 279, 302, 318*

Inheritance Tax Act 1984 (*contd.*)
    s10(1)   *277, 294, 318, 323, 326, 328*
    s11   *181, 278, 279, 300, 302*
    s11(3)   *279*
    s11(6)   *181, 278*
    s12   *279*
    s13   *279*
    s14   *279*
    s15   *279*
    s16   *279*
    s17   *263*
    s17(a)   *286*
    s18   *181, 292, 293, 302*
    s18(1)   *287*
    s19   *292, 293, 298, 299, 300, 301, 317*
    s19(2)   *299*
    s20   *292, 299, 300, 317*
    s21   *292, 300, 317*
    s22   *292, 301, 317*
    s22(4)   *301*
    s23   *292, 302, 303*
    s24   *244, 292, 303*
    s24A   *303*
    s25   *292, 302, 328*
    s26   *244, 292, 303, 309, 328*
    s26(1)   *252*
    s26(2)   *252, 303*
    s27   *244, 292*
    s28   *292*
    s30   *244, 309*
    s30(3B)   *310*
    s31   *309*
    s31(1)   *309*
    s32   *310*
    s33   *310*
    s43   *313*
    s43(3)   *296*
    ss44–93   *282*
    s48   *295*
    s48(1)   *319*
    s48(3)   *318, 324*
    s48(4)–(7)   *295*
    ss49–54   *313*
    s49(1)   *285, 287, 296, 316, 318*
    s50   *316*
    s51(1)   *301, 317, 318*
    s52   *318*
    s52(1)   *316, 317, 318, 319*
    s52(3)   *318*
    s53(1)   *318*
    s53(2)   *318*
    s54A   *298, 317*
    s54B   *298, 317*

Table of Statutes xxiii

Inheritance Tax Act 1984 (*contd.*)
  s57 *301*
  s57(1) *317*
  ss58–85 *313, 320*
  s58 *321, 325*
  s59 *320*
  s62 *321*
  s64 *321, 322, 325, 326*
  s65 *287, 322, 323, 324, 326*
  s65(1) *323, 324*
  s65(4) *288*
  s66 *321, 322, 324, 325*
  s66(1) *322*
  s66(2) *322*
  s66(3) *322*
  s66(4) *322*
  s67 *321, 323*
  s68 *324, 325*
  s69 *324, 325*
  s70 *325, 328*
  s71 *298, 312, 321, 326, 327, 328*
  s71(1) *326, 327*
  s71(3) *327*
  s71(4) *328*
  s76 *328*
  s89 *298*
  ss103–114 *304*
  s104(1) *304*
  s105(1) *26, 305*
  s105(3) *26, 304, 305*
  s106 *304, 305*
  s113 *305*
  s113A *304, 306*
  s113B *304, 306*
  ss115–124 *306, 310*
  s115(2) *306, 307*
  s116 *307*
  s116(2) *308*
  s116(3) *307*
  s116(5A) *307*
  s116(5B) *307*
  s117 *307, 308, 309*
  s118 *307*
  s122 *308*
  s124 *309*
  s124A *306, 309*
  s124B *306, 309*
  ss125–130 *310*
  s125 *310*
  s126 *310, 311*
  s129 *311*
  s141 *311*
  s142 *263, 286, 287*

Inheritance Tax Act 1984 (*contd.*)
  s142(1) *286, 287*
  s142(5) *287*
  s143 *287*
  s144 *287, 302*
  s144(2) *287*
  s145 *287, 288*
  s146 *287, 288*
  s153 *295*
  s154 *311*
  s155 *295*
  s158 *295*
  s171 *284*
  ss199–201 *281*
  s199 *281, 282*
  s199(2) *286*
  s200 *282*
  s200(1) *286*
  s201 *282*
  s201(1) *319*
  s204(6) *282, 286*
  s204(7) *282, 286*
  s204(8) *282*
  s263 *301*
  s267 *295*
  s267(2) *295*
  s268 *293, 294, 301*
  s268(1) *293*
  s268(2) *294*
  s269 *305*
  s270 *277*
  Schedule 1 *280, 281, 324*
  Part II *297*
  Part VIII *329*

Landlord and Tenant Act 1954
  s25 *224*
Law of Property Act 1925 *291*

Married Women's Property Act 1882 *298*

Partnership Act 1890
  s1 *125*
Perjury Act 1911
  s5 *338*
Provisional Collection of Taxes Act 1968 *3*

Statutory Instruments
  SI 1969/735 *224*
  SI 1990/2231 *11*
  SI 1990/2232 *11*
  SI 1992/3121 *347*
  SI 1992/3222 *357*

Table of Statutes

Statutory Instruments (*contd.*)
  SI 1995/282   *351*
  SI 1995/2518   *343, 359*
  SI 1995/2902   *34*

Taxation of Chargeable Gains Act 1992   *221, 222, 226, 231, 235, 265, 272*
  s1(1)   *221, 223*
  s3   *232*
  s4   *231, 232*
  s4(1A)   *222*
  s5   *264*
  s7   *231*
  s9   *112*
  s9(2)   *112*
  s10   *182, 222*
  s10(2)   *223*
  s10(5)   *223*
  s12   *223*
  s13   *219, 223*
  s13(7)   *223*
  s16   *239*
  s16(1)   *262*
  s17   *1, 180, 242, 243, 258, 269*
  s17(1)   *242, 258, 269*
  s17(2)   *258*
  s18   *180, 242, 243*
  s19(1)   *246*
  s21   *224, 225*
  s21(1)   *223*
  s21(2)   *227, 228*
  s22   *227, 228*
  s22(1)   *224, 231*
  s22(2)   *231*
  s23(1)   *230*
  s24   *230*
  s24(1)   *230*
  s24(2)   *230*
  s25   *1*
  s25(1)   *223*
  s25(3)   *223*
  s26   *228*
  s27   *231*
  s28   *231*
  s28(1)   *231*
  s28(2)   *231*
  s29   *229*
  s29(2)   *258*
  s30   *229*
  s32   *253*
  s35   *240, 241, 243*
  s35(2)   *236*
  s35(3)   *236, 237, 238, 240*

Taxation of Chargeable Gains Act 1992 (*contd.*)
  s35(4)   *236*
  s35(5)   *236, 237*
  s37(1)   *246*
  s38   *233*
  s38(1)   *235*
  s42   *234, 236*
  s44   *243*
  s46   *239, 268*
  s46(1)   *270*
  s48   *239, 242*
  s51   *246*
  s52(2)   *246*
  s53(1)   *235*
  s55   *236, 271*
  s55(1)   *235*
  s58   *180, 231, 238, 243*
  s60   *257, 265*
  s60(1)   *265, 266, 267, 268*
  s60(2)   *265, 266*
  s62   *262, 263, 270, 286*
  s62(2)   *264*
  s62(3)   *262*
  s62(4)   *262, 263*
  s62(5)   *262*
  s62(6)   *263, 286, 287*
  s62(7)   *262*
  s62(10)   *262*
  s67   *238, 243*
  ss68–79   *264*
  s68   *265*
  s69   *269*
  s70   *269*
  ss71–73   *1*
  s71   *270*
  s71(1)   *270*
  s72   *270*
  s72(1)   *270*
  s73   *238*
  s73(1)   *263, 270*
  s74   *270*
  s76   *271, 272*
  s76(1)   *272*
  s77   *264*
  s77(2)   *274*
  s77(3)   *264*
  ss80–85   *272*
  s80   *272, 273*
  s80(4)   *272*
  s81   *272*
  s85(1)   *272, 273*
  s85(3)   *272*
  ss87–90   *273*

Taxation of Chargeable Gains Act 1992 (*contd.*)
   s87   *272, 273, 274*
   s87(2)   *274*
   s88(3)   *273*
   s89   *274*
   s89(1)   *274*
   s89(2)   *274*
   s90   *274*
   s97   *273*
   s97(1)   *273*
   s97(4)   *273*
   s115   *257*
   s117   *248*
   s122   *220*
   s122(1)   *259*
   s122(2)   *259*
   s122(5)   *259*
   s125   *213, 220*
   ss126–138   *226*
   s126   *362*
   s127   *226, 259*
   s132   *247*
   ss135–138   *364*
   s135   *259*
   s140(2)   *227*
   ss152–158   *252*
   s152   *25, 26, 253, 256*
   s153   *253*
   s153A   *254*
   s157   *253*
   s161   *245*
   s163   *25, 26, 254, 255*
   s163(1)   *254*
   s163(2)   *254, 255*
   s163(3)   *255*
   s163(4)   *255*
   s163(5)   *255*
   s164   *25, 254*
   s164(6)   *255*
   s164(7)   *255*
   ss164A–M   *256*
   s165   *26, 238, 244, 269, 270*
   s166   *245*
   s167   *245*
   s168   *245*
   s170   *195*
   s172   *223*
   s222   *251*
   s222(2)   *249*
   s223   *180, 248*
   s223(2)   *180*
   s224(1)   *250*
   s225   *251*

Taxation of Chargeable Gains Act 1992 (*contd.*)
   s247   *238*
   s251   *247*
   s252   *254*
   s253   *247*
   s253(4)   *247*
   s253(6)   *248*
   s253(7)   *248*
   s253(8)   *248*
   s254   *247, 248*
   s256   *252*
   s257   *252*
   s258   *252*
   s260   *244, 269, 270*
   s260(2)   *244*
   s262   *251*
   s263   *246*
   s268   *246*
   s269   *246*
   s286   *180, 242, 277*
   s286(4)   *257*
   Schedule 1   *233*
   Schedule 2   *240, 260*
   Schedule 3   *238*
   Schedule 4   *238*
   Schedule 5   *172*
   Schedule 6   *25, 26, 254*
   Schedule 7   *244*
   Schedule 8   *31, 239*
   Schedule 9   *238*
Taxes Act 1970   *72*
   s181   *88*
Taxes Management Act 1970   *2, 151, 197, 329, 333*
   s7   *330*
   s8   *330*
   s8(1A)   *330*
   s8(3)   *330*
   s8A   *330*
   s9   *330, 331*
   s9(2)   *330, 333*
   s9A   *330, 331*
   ss10–11   *331*
   s10   *218*
   s11AA   *331*
   s11AB   *331*
   s12AA   *330*
   s12AB   *330*
   a12AC   *330*
   s15   *330*
   s19   *331*
   s19A   *331*
   s20   *331*

Taxes Management Act 1970 (*contd.*)
    s20(3)   *331*
    s20A   *331*
    s20B   *331*
    s20C   *331*
    ss28A–28F   *331*
    s29(1)   *331*
    s30A   *331*
    s30B   *330*
    s31(5A–E)   *335*
    s32   *4*
    s33   *332*
    s34   *332, 338*
    s36   *338*
    s44(3A)   *335*
    s54   *332, 336*
    s55   *336*
    s56   *40, 335*
    s59A   *334, 340*
    s59B   *222, 231, 340*
    s59C   *340*
    s72   *152*
    s73   *152*
    s76   *152*
    ss78–85   *111, 117*
    s83   *117*
    s86   *337*
    s86(4)   *337*
    ss88–91   *218*
    s88   *218*
    s91   *218*
    s93   *339*
    s95(2)   *339*
    s99   *331*
    s106   *149*
    s106(2)   *149, 150*
    s109   *218*
Trustee Act 1925
    s31   *155, 157, 267, 315*
    s31(1)   *155, 156, 157, 315*
    s31(2)   *155, 156, 157*
    s31(3)   *156*

Value Added Tax 1983
    s14(10)   *384, 385*
Value Added Tax Act 1994   *342, 343, 344, 348, 358*

Value Added Tax Act 1994 (*contd.*)
    s1   *26, 343*
    s1(2)   *356*
    s1(4)   *349*
    s3   *346*
    s4   *344*
    s4(2)   *344, 245*
    s5(2)   *345*
    s6   *344*
    s7   *346*
    s8   *343*
    s9   *347*
    s16   *347*
    s19   *355*
    s21   *349*
    s24   *343, 355*
    s24(1)   *356, 357*
    s24(3)   *357*
    s25(1)   *356*
    s25(2)   *356*
    s25(3)   *357*
    s25(5)   *357*
    s25(7)   *385*
    s26   *343, 355, 356*
    s26(2)   *350, 356*
    s30   *352, 353*
    s31   *350*
    s36(4A)   *358*
    s36(5)   *358*
    s43   *358*
    s43(1AA)   *359*
    s43(2A)   *359*
    s44(4)   *359*
    s44(5)   *359*
    s45   *359*
    s47   *359*
    s47(3)   *359*
    s94   *344*
    s96(1)   *346*
    Schedule 1   *345, 353*
    Schedule 4   *346, 356, 357*
    Schedule 5   *347, 349, 354*
    Schedule 6   *355*
    Schedule 8   *343, 347, 348, 353*
    Schedule 9   *343, 350, 352*
    Schedule 9A   *358*
    Schedule 10   *350, 351*

1

Introduction

'Tax' is defined by the *Shorter Oxford English Dictionary* as 'a compulsory contribution to the support of the government, levied on persons, property, income, commodities, transactions etc'.

In the United Kingdom, tax is levied both on the income of persons and on their capital, though there is no all-embracing 'wealth tax'. Rather, the primary methods of taxation can be tabled thus:

Taxes on income

> Income Tax: levied on the income of individuals and trustees, personal representatives and partnerships and on the United Kingdom income of non-resident companies.
> Corporation Tax: levied (inter alia) on the income of companies.

Taxes on capital

> Capital Gains Tax: levied on the chargeable gains made by individuals, trustees, partners and personal representatives on the disposal of capital assets.
> Inheritance Tax: levied on the amount an individual gives away on death, or within the seven years prior to death; also levied on certain events during the subsistence of trusts and in relation to shares in family companies.
> Corporation Tax: levied (inter alia) on the chargeable gains of companies on the disposal of capital assets.

It will be noted that there is no tax imposed merely for 'having' property. That would be a true 'Wealth Tax'. There is, in fact, only one example of such a tax in United Kingdom Revenue Law and that is the 'periodic charge' levied on the trustees of discretionary trusts for Inheritance Tax. All other capital taxes are levied, as the *Shorter Oxford* would say, on 'transactions' or, in certain cases, on 'deemed' transactions. See for example s17 of the Taxation of Chargeable Gains Act 1992 where a gift can be treated as having been a disposal for capital gains tax purposes made at market value, the deemed disposal provisions of s25 where a person becomes non-resident, and the occasions in ss71–73 of the same Act where the relevant events are treated as giving rise to a disposal and reacquisition of trust assets by the trustees.

2

The Taxation of Income of Non-corporate Bodies

2.1 The legislation

2.2 The annual review

2.3 The tax years

2.4 The schedular system of taxation

2.5 The unified system of taxation

2.6 Exemptions from income tax

2.7 Persons exempt from income tax

2.1 The legislation

The principal Act charging income tax is the Income and Corporation Taxes Act (ICTA) 1988. This Act, together with its sister Act, the Taxes Management Act 1970, which deals with administrative and procedural matters, consolidates almost all the previous legislation on the income taxation of corporate and non-corporate bodies – but they by no means contain all the statutory learning on the subject.

Students will find that the annual Finance Acts (see section 2.2) contain provisions which change or add to the wording of the existing sections or schedules of ICTA 1988 and the Taxes Management Act 1970 and become embodied in these Acts. Where entirely new provisions are involved these remain as references to the relevant Finance Act until general consolidation of the legislation takes place. This book therefore will at times refer to the current provisions of ICTA as 'introduced by Finance Act 1996' mainly to highlight the fact that the provisions or changes are of recent origin.

2.2 The annual review

Each year, the Chancellor of the Exchequer makes a Budget speech in which he outlines the fiscal policy of the government for the coming year. It is, however, an oddity of the British tax system that the Statute which implements these budgetary matters also deals (indeed, almost exclusively deals) with the technical tax changes required. That Statute, the Finance Act, is usually given the royal assent in April or May, although many of the changes will have been brought into effect immediately after the Budget speech by the operation of the Provisional Collection of Taxes Act 1968 or by the issue of statutory regulations.

As a result of changes announced during the Budget Speech of 1992, the traditional Springtime Budget and Finance Bill disappeared from 1993 when the annual Budget and Finance Bill were switched to November and December respectively, with the Bill being required to become law by 5 May following.

The November Budget announcements (being primarily for the tax year beginning in the following April) gives rise to the Finance Bill, which in turn becomes the Finance Act of the year following the Budget. The annual Finance Bill is considered clause by clause mainly by a committee of Members of Parliament from all parties, at which time amendments may be proposed and voted upon before being added to the Bill, which in due course is returned to the House of Commons for its final processes before receiving the royal assent. Occasionally the Finance Act will contain law which is brought into effect not on the receipt of the royal assent, but on a date to be determined. The delay provision will be enshrined in the text of the provisions themselves; for example, ss178–199 and Schedule 19 FA 1994 introduced the framework for a complete change in the administration of tax through the introduction of a self-assessment system. However s199 enacted that the changes would take effect

> 'so far as it relates to income tax and capital gains tax ... year 1996–97 and subsequent years of assessment, and (b) so far as it relates to corporation tax ... as respects accounting periods ending on or after the appointed day.'

Section 199(3) then provided that

> 'for the purposes of this chapter the appointed day is such day, not earlier than 1st April 1996, as the Treasury may by order appoint.'

2.3 The tax years

For fiscal purposes, income is measured by reference to the income of the person (if an individual) arising in the relevant 'Year of Assessment', which runs from 6 April of one year to 5 April in the next following calendar year, or, (if a company) by reference to the 'Financial Year', which runs from 1 April in one calendar year to 31 March in the next. The basis of assessment under Schedule E underwent a fundamental change from 1989–90 (see s202A ICTA 1988) with the introduction of a receipts basis.

2.4 The schedular system of taxation

It is an irony of United Kingdom tax law that taxpayers have been burdened with a system of taxation which was of relevance only when introduced in 1799. This is the schedular system, which operates by charging the taxpayer separately on each different source of income. The original intention was to ensure that no one government official would have complete knowledge of a taxpayer's affairs and, for that purpose, 19 different surveyors of taxes would each deal with one of the 19 possible sources of income.

There are now four schedules (A, D, E and F, Schedule B having been abolished by FA 1988 and Schedule C having been abolished by FA 1996), and income is taxable if it falls within one of them. Each schedule has its own system of assessment and method of computation of tax. The rules for each schedule determine how much income is to be treated as being assessable for each tax year by allocating the income of the relevant basis period (eg the income of the previous year) to that year of assessment.

Exclusive nature of schedules

Having been taxed once in respect of certain income, one cannot then be taxed again under another schedule – the schedules are mutually exclusive. So, in *Fry* v *Salisbury House Estate* [1930] AC 432 a limited company owned a building of considerable size in the City of London called Salisbury House. The company let rooms in the building to tenants as offices and it was assessed to tax on that income under Schedule A. The inspector of taxes, however, served an additional notice of assessment on the company having classified the income as Schedule D income. The company appealed against this assessment on the grounds that it would constitute double taxation.

Viscount Dunedin stated:

'... income tax is only one tax, a tax on the income of the person whom it is sought to assess, and that the different Schedules are the modes in which the statute directs this to be levied. In other words there are not five taxes which you might call tax A, B, C, D and E but only one tax.'

He went on to conclude that the rents received by the company

'having been assessed under Schedule A, are, so to speak, exhausted as a source of income ... there is no subsequent possibility of dealing with them under Schedule D'.

The House of Lords agreed with him, and so the company was not liable to tax on the rents under Schedule D in addition to the Schedule A assessment – only the Schedule A assessment was necessary.

The case of *Bye* v *Coren* [1986] STC 393 made it clear that the Revenue is not prevented from making alternative protective assessments but a double charge is to be cancelled (s32 TMA 1970). In *IRC* v *Wilkinson* [1992] STC 454 multiple assessments were held to be alternative and not cumulative, and the Revenue was entitled to select the appropriate tax assessment for the purpose of obtaining judgment for the tax due.

Note: the Revenue is entitled, though, to select under which case of a Schedule the taxpayer is to be charged.

The schedules are as follows:

Schedule A: taxes income from land in the United Kingdom (rents etc).

Schedule B: this has been abolished by s65 and Schedule 6 FA 1988. It formerly taxed the occupation of woodlands in the United Kingdom managed on a commercial basis with a view to the realisation of profits.

Schedule D: is subdivided into Cases:
Case I: taxes profits of a trade, including profits or gains of trading purpose loan relationships of trading companies.
Case II: taxes profits of a profession or vocation.
Case III: taxes interest, annuities or other annual payments including profits or gains from loan relationships of non-trading companies and those of trading companies not falling within Case I.
Case IV: taxes income arising from securities out of the United Kingdom.
Case V: taxes income arising from possessions out of the United Kingdom.
Case VI: taxes any annual profits or gains not falling under any other Case or Schedule.

Schedule E: taxes wages or salaries and other 'emoluments' from offices or employments. It, too, is subdivided, this time into three Cases based on the residence status of the employee.

Schedule F: taxes United Kingdom company dividends.

Note: income taxable under Schedule C (the profits from public revenue dividends, payable in the United Kingdom, eg United Kingdom Government Securities) was brought within the charge to tax under Schedule D Case III by the Finance Act 1996.

A full Table of Schedules appears overleaf.

Table of Schedules
(All references in the table are to ICTA 1988)

Note: the following table should be read in conjunction with Notes 1 and 2 at the end of the table, in connection with the changes to the basis of assessment of income under Schedule A and Schedule D.

Schedule	Income assessable	Deductions allowed	Normal basis of assessment
A (See Note 1) Up to 1994–95	Rents etc from land (s15(1))	All reasonable expenses (eg repairs) but *not* improvements (ss25–28)	Rent due less expenses *paid* in tax year (s15(2) and ss21–22)
From 1995–96	Profits or gains from United Kingdom land (s15 via FA 1995 s39 and Schedule 6)	Deduction rules as for Schedule D Case I (s21, s74 via FA 1995 s39(2) and Schedule 6). Interest allowable as deduction 1995–96 onwards (s355(1) deleted by FA 1995 s42)	Profits or gains arising in the tax year, (s15 via FA 1995 s39 and Schedule 6)
D Case I	Profits from trade: including those arising from trading purpose loan relationships (s18)	All expenses incurred wholly and exclusively for the purposes of the trade or profession save for those specifically disallowed by statute (s74(a))	Profits of accounting period ending in year of assessment (s60 to s64) (see Note 2)
D Case II	Profits of a profession or vocation (s18)	As with Schedule D Case I (s74(a))	As with Schedule D Case I (s60 to s64) (see Note 2)
D Case III	Interest annuities and other annual payments (s18(3), s66(1)). Profits or gains from non-trading loan relationships s18(3A) Profits from Public Revenue dividends payable in the United Kingdom s18(3)(c)	None	Income arising in tax year (s64) (see Note 2) Profits arising in tax year
D Case IV	Income from foreign securities (s18(3), s66(1)) Income from foreign possessions (eg trades carried on wholly abroad) (s18(3))	None

Depends on type of income. If rent, as Schedule A; if business profits, as Schedule D Cases I and II (s65(2), s65(1)(a)) | Income arising in tax year (s65, s66(1)) (see Note 2) D Case V Income arising in tax year (s65(1)) (see Note 2) |

Schedule	Income assessable	Deductions allowed	Normal basis of assessment
D Case VI	Any annual profits or gains not caught by any other Schedule or Case (s18(3))	Depends on type of income	Income of current tax year (s69)
E	Earnings from an office or employment		
E Case I	Employee resident and ordinarily resident (s19, s131)	In each of Cases I, II and III, all travelling expenses wholly and exclusively incurred in the performance of the duties of the office or employment and all other expenses wholly exclusively and necessarily so incurred (s198)	(I) Emoluments received in the tax year (s202A)
E Case II	Employee either not resident, or, if resident, not ordinarily resident (s19, s131)		(II) Emoluments for United Kingdom duties received in the tax year (s202A, s132, s192)
E Case III	Employee resident, in respect of certain income not caught by Cases I or II (s19, s131)		(III) Emoluments in the United Kingdom in the tax year (s202A, s132)
F	Dividends and other distributions by United Kingdom companies (s20)	None	On dividends plus tax credit received in tax year (s20(1) para 2)

Notes

1. The changes to the Schedule A system of tax from 1995–96 apply only for *income tax* purposes. The old rules continue to apply for *corporation tax* purposes. See Chapter 4 for further details of the changes.
2. FA 1994 contained provisions in ss200–208 which by the year of assessment 1996–97 changed the normal basis of assessment under Schedule D Cases I to V inclusive from profits or income of the previous year to those of the current year as well as introducing a system of self-assessment (see Chapter 24). However, new businesses or other sources of income commencing from 6 April 1994 became subject to the new current year basis from the start. (See Chapter 6 for further details.)
3. The charge to tax under Schedule E is not confined to income falling within the three cases. Part V (ss131–207) ICTA 1988 contains provisions further to s19, including in particular the charge to tax on payments under s148. (See *Nichols* v *Gibson* [1996] STC 1008, discussed in Chapter 8, section 8.6)
4. See *Fry* v *Salisbury House Estate* [1930] AC 432, above and discussed in Chapter 4.

2.5 The unified system of taxation

The present system of charging income tax, brought into force in 1973–74, is known as the unified system of personal taxation. Prior to that date, income tax was levied at a high 'standard rate' which was reduced if the relevant income was earned income. When the individual's income exceeded a certain figure, a separate tax, known as 'surtax', was levied in the following tax year.

Income tax is now charged at graduated rates. Originally there was an additional rate payable in respect of investment income – that is to say income other than earned income – in excess of a certain level, but this was abolished in respect of individuals by FA 1984. The additional rate remains relevant for income of discretionary and accumulation settlements but is referred to as the 'rate applicable to trusts'.

2.6 Exemptions from income tax

It should not be considered that all income is subject to income tax. There are a considerable number of exemptions, the most important of which are:

1. scholarship and grant income (s331 ICTA 1988);
2. interest and bonuses on National Savings Certificates (s46 ICTA 1988);
3. SAYE terminal bonuses (s326 ICTA 1988);
4. the first £70 on ordinary accounts with the National Savings Bank (ie Post Office) (s325 ICTA 1988);
5. interest or bonuses payable on a deposit account in respect of the period when it is a tax-exempt special savings account 'TESSA' (s326A ICTA 1988);
6. interest on personal injuries awards (s329A ICTA 1988);
7. dividends payable under an approved personal equity plan (PEP).

2.7 Persons exempt from income tax

1. Generally speaking, the Crown is not liable to tax. However, it was announced by the Prime Minister in the House of Commons, on 11 February 1993, that following discussions between the Treasury, the Inland Revenue and the Royal Household new tax arrangements would be introduced for the Queen and the Prince of Wales. With effect from 6 April 1993 the Queen became liable, in respect of her personal income and gains, etc, from all sources, to income tax, capital gains tax and inheritance tax. The Prince of Wales's existing liability to all taxes has been extended to include income from the Duchy of Cornwall.
2. Charities are exempt, under s505, from a considerable number of charges to income tax. Certain forms of trading income of charities are, however, subject to tax.
3. The income of approved pension funds is exempt from tax.

3

Total Income

3.1 Method of charging tax

3.2 Investment and savings income

3.3 Computation of total income

3.4 Relief for interest paid: ss353–379 ICTA 1988

3.5 Charges on income

3.6 Personal reliefs

3.7 The taxation of married couples

3.1 Method of charging tax

Under the present system, income tax is charged at graduated rates: these are referred to as 'lower rate' tax, 'basic rate' tax and 'higher rate' tax.

The rates of tax for 1997–98 are as follows:

£	Rate
1 – 4,100	20%
4,101 – 26,100	23%
26,101 and over	40%

Accordingly, the lower rate is 20 per cent; the 'basic rate' is 23 per cent; and the 'higher rate' is 40 per cent, all charged upon an individual's total income (see section 3.3). However certain income from 'savings' is now charged at the lower rate of tax (see section 3.2), except where the individual is liable to tax at the higher rate of 40 per cent. For a non-higher rate payer any income from savings, as defined in the legislation, will be taxed at 20 per cent, in addition to taxing the first £4,100 of other chargeable income at a 20 per cent rate. Thus, if an individual has a taxable income of £10,000 of which £1,000 comes from savings income, tax will be charged on the first £5,100 at 20 per cent, and the remaining income will be taxed at 23 per cent. The lower rate of tax also applies to personal representatives and the trustees of interest in possession trusts. The system is designed to ensure that the payer of the savings income either taxes it (by deducting tax from it) or is taxed on it (by assessment or otherwise) at 20 per cent before payment – see s4(1A) ICTA 1988.

3.2 Investment and savings income

Individuals, personal representatives and trustees of interest in possession trusts are no longer liable to additional rate tax on investment income. Discretionary and accumulation and maintenance trusts are still liable to a special rate of tax under ss686 and 687 of the Income and Corporation Taxes Act 1988. The special rate is referred to in these sections as 'the rate applicable to trusts', and amounts to the total of the basic rate of tax (currently 23 per cent) and an additional rate of 11 per cent so that the income of these trusts is taxed at a total rate of 34 per cent.

'Investment income' was defined by s32(3) of the 1971 Finance Act (now repealed) as 'any income other than earned income', 'earned income' is defined in its turn by s833 ICTA 1988. Examples of investment income for these purposes were:

1. dividends;
2. income arising to beneficiaries under a trust;
3. bank interest;
4. rents from furnished lettings.

'Savings income', for the purpose of applying the lower rate of tax referred to in section 3.1, is defined by the new s1A ICTA 1988 (introduced by the Finance Act 1996) as:

> '(a) any income chargeable under Case III of Schedule D other than
>   i) relevant annuities and other annual payments that are not interest; and
>   ii) amounts so chargeable by virtue of s119 or s120;
> (b) any income chargeable under Schedule F; and
> (c) subject to subsection (4) [below], any equivalent foreign income.'

'Savings income', for the purpose of applying the charge to tax at the lower rate under s1A ICTA 1988, therefore includes a dividend interest and purchased life annuities.

Examples of earned income are:

1. salaries and wages;
2. pensions in respect of past employment;
3. profits immediately derived by an individual from the carrying on or exercise by him of his trade, profession or vocation either as an individual or, in the case of a partnership, as a partner personally acting therein. So a sleeping partner receives investment income, *not* earned income.

3.3 Computation of total income

The importance of the schedular system lies in its identification of chargeable income and in determining what income from a particular source is to be brought into charge in any year of assessment. Once that has been done, the computation of the person's 'total income' is made – a computation needed for the purposes of higher rate tax.

'Total income' is defined by s835 ICTA 1988 as 'the total income of that person from all sources'. In practice it means the sum of all chargeable income less expenses and charges on that income to the extent that they are permitted under the Income Tax Acts. It is necessary, however, to consider the following situations in more detail to determine the amount to be included as income, or whether an amount is deductible in full, or is restricted to relief at a lower percentage. The remainder of section 3.3 deals with particular items of income, section 3.4 deals with the deductibility of interest and section 3.5 deals with charges on income to be deducted in arriving at 'total income'.

Building society and bank interest

Interest paid by banks and building societies to their investors is normally paid under deduction of lower rate tax at source. For the purpose of computing total income, the figure to be included is the interest before deduction of tax. Persons not liable to tax may receive their interest gross, so as to avoid the need for tax repayment claims, under regulations set out in Statutory Instruments 1990/2231 for building societies and 1990/2232 for banking concerns. National Savings accounts continue to pay interest without deduction of tax.

The 1990 regulations replace the system of composite rate tax which prevented non-taxpayers from reclaiming the tax deducted from interest: ss477A and 480A ICTA 1988 inserted by s30 of the Finance Act 1990.

Dividends from companies under Schedule F

When an individual receives a dividend from a United Kingdom resident company, that distribution will carry a 'tax credit'. That will cover the individual's liability to lower rate tax (non-taxpayers being able to claim a refund) – see s231(3) ICTA 1988 – but the dividend must again be 'grossed up' by adding the amount of the tax credit to the dividend amount and including the total sum in the calculation of total income (see para 2 of Schedule F, ss20(1) and 835(6) ICTA 1988.

Since 1993–94 individuals, other than those liable to tax at the higher rate, have been taxed at only the lower rate in respect of dividends. As outlined in sections 3.1 and 3.2, this is extended to other income from 'savings'. Section 207A ICTA 1988, which provided for the special rate in respect of dividends, was repealed as a result of the new s1A, which was introduced to deal with the combined provisions relating to all savings income, under the Finance Act 1996. This provision ensures (for the administrative convenience of avoiding additional assessments for many taxpayers) that the tax credit received on dividends or deducted from other savings income is enough to satisfy the tax due in all cases other than those of higher rate tax individuals. As will be seen from the illustration in section 3.5, the 'gross' equivalent of an £8,000 dividend is £10,000 with a tax credit calculated at a quarter of the net dividend amounting to £2,000, equivalent to the lower rate tax of 20 per cent of the gross taxable dividend.

Trust income

A beneficiary includes in his total income the sum he receives from the trust, grossed up at the basic rate of tax. The lower rate tax will have been borne by the trustees of most trusts (see s1A(1)(a) and s1A(2), other than discretionary trusts (to which s686 applies), and the beneficiary is entitled to have that tax credited against his own liability, so if he is not liable to tax, because of an excess of personal reliefs (see section 3.6), he can make a repayment claim on the Revenue. Income distributed from a discretionary trust will have borne tax at both basic and additional rate tax. The gross amount before tax is included in the beneficiary's total income and he is entitled to a tax credit for both basic and additional rates of tax (see s687(2) ICTA 1988).

3.4 Relief for interest paid: ss353–379 ICTA 1988

When a person pays interest on a loan, the general rule is that the interest paid is *not* deductible in arriving at total income. There are, however, a few very important exceptions.

The provisions governing relief for payments of interest are contained in s353 ICTA 1988. Relief under is obtained only if the interest satisfies the specific purposes and other conditions imposed by ss354–368. The purposes are set out below. Interest on overdrafts and interest in excess of a reasonable commercial rate are not eligible for relief (s353(3)).

Loan for the purchase of land

1995–96 and subsequent years – let property

As stated in the table of schedules and in the notes to that table in Chapter 2, section 2.4 (and see Chapter 4 for further details), profits from letting of property for individuals, partnerships, trustees and others liable to income tax are to be taxed in the same way as business profits. In fact the new legislation in the Finance Act 1995 s39(2) et seq refers to the 'Schedule A business'. Hitherto no interest relief on property loans was available for income tax purposes unless it satisfied the 'main residence' or 'commercial let' conditions in s355(1) ICTA 1988. That relief, where due, was given against total income and not, for example, as a deduction in calculating the taxable income from the letting. Because the new test for deduction of expenses against 'Schedule A business' income is s74 of ICTA 1988 (as it is for all allowable business expenditure), any interest payments satisfying the 'wholly and exclusively' tests of s74 will qualify for a deduction against the rents etc under the new Schedule A regime. The 'commercial let' provisions of s354(1)(b) are therefore redundant and were repealed by s42(1) FA 1995.

Property other than let property, and let property for years up to 1994–95 inclusive

Interest is eligible for relief if paid on a loan applied in purchasing an interest or estate in land in the United Kingdom or Ireland, and if either:

1. at the time the interest was paid the land (which for the purposes of these provisions includes a caravan or houseboat) was used as the only or main residence of the borrower or of a dependent relative (occupying rent-free and for no other consideration) or of a former or separated spouse of his (the relief for loans on property for dependent relatives and former or separated spouses applies only to loans taken out before 6 April 1988); or
2. the land is let at a commercial rent for more than 26 weeks and for the rest of the time is available for letting or used as in (1) above or is undergoing repairs.

(See ss354–5 ICTA 1988.)

Main residences

It is important to note that although interest relief for the purchase of a 'main residence' was available under s354(1)(a) as a deduction against total income, that is no longer the case. Section 81 of FA 1994 introduced a new s369(1A) ICTA 1988 so that relief is given at the 'applicable percentage', which for 1994–95 was 20 per cent but from 1995–96 was reduced to 15 per cent. Therefore, in total income calculations such interest should be excluded entirely and only brought into account if it is necessary to calculate the actual amount of tax due.

In most cases the 15 per cent relief is given under the MIRAS (Mortgage Interest Relief at Source) scheme at the time when the borrower makes the payment of interest to the bank or building society: (ss369–379 ICTA 1988). If the loan only qualifies under para (1) above, relief is restricted to a loan or loans in an amount not exceeding in aggregate £30,000: s357 ICTA 1988, s71 FA 1990.

Prior to FA 1988, where two or more unmarried persons jointly purchased a residence, each separately qualified for relief in respect of a loan up to £30,000. Now, in respect of interest paid on loans taken out on or after 1 August 1988, the interest relief is restricted to a 'residence' basis. The 'qualifying maximum' of £30,000 applies to each residence, not each borrower. Where two or more persons are borrowers the mortgage interest relief is divided proportionately between them (ss356A, B and C ICTA 1988).

Under s355(1A) ICTA 1988, interest on a main residence loan continues to be eligible for relief for a period of 12 months (extendable under s355(2)) after the property ceases to be a main residence and is put up for sale. The relief is due whether or not a second main residence loan is taken out (see s371) or the taxpayer moves into rented property.

Where two borrowers marry the limit of £30,000 comes into force immediately, so that from the date of marriage each has a limit of £15,000 on his or her MIRAS relief. Section 356B allows a husband and wife who are not separated to jointly elect who will benefit from the tax relief available in respect of the interest payments made on their qualifying loan. This choice is called an 'allocation of interest election'.

Note: if, on a divorce, a person is required to pay a lump sum to his spouse and he discharges his liability by raising a loan on the security of the property, the interest will *not* qualify under ss353–4 since the loan would not have been taken out in order to purchase the property.

Since loans taken out for improvement of property no longer qualify for tax relief, a taxpayer with an existing loan which includes the cost of improvement of his property should not remortgage his property as the new loan will not be regarded as replacing a loan which currently qualifies for tax relief. The taxpayer would forfeit future tax relief on that element of the loan. He would continue to receive tax relief on the amount which reflects the *purchase* of the property.

Meaning of 'only or main residence'
The meaning of 'only or main residence' in para (1) came under scrutiny in the case of *Frost* v *Feltham* [1981] STC 115 where Nourse J said that 'main' meant 'principal or more important' residence. He went on to say that a property could be one's main residence even if a person spent very little time there – giving the example of a person who had both a town and a country residence. There would have been no difficulty had Mr Feltham been an employed person; he was, however, a tenant of a brewery company living over the public house of which he was the landlord. The house which he claimed was his only or main residence was a country cottage where he and his wife went for holidays and to which they intended eventually to retire. Under s356, interest paid on a loan is eligible for relief if the monies are used to purchase a property to be used in due course as the taxpayer's only or main residence if, at the time the interest is paid, he resides in job-related accommodation. 'Job-related' has the meaning laid down by s145 – see Chapter 8, section 8.5. Relief is also available for self-employed persons required to live in job-related accommodation, such as Mr Feltham.

Loan to acquire an interest in a close company
Section 360 provides that interest on such a loan is eligible for relief if the borrower uses the loan to acquire a material interest (more than 5 per cent) in the company or lends money to the company for use in its business. If the individual works 'for the

greater part of his time in the actual management or conduct of the company or of an associated company' relief is still available for the acquisition of less than 5 per cent of the ordinary share capital. Section 360(3A) restricts this relief if the borrower or his spouse claims Enterprise Investment Scheme relief for the acquisition of those shares.

In general, the material interest test exists where the taxpayer and his associates together control more than 5 per cent of the company or would be entitled to receive more than 5 per cent of the assets in the event of the company being wound up. Interest relief is not allowed where the close company is a close investment-holding company (s13A). All of the general conditions must be satisfied at the time when the interest is paid.

Loan to acquire an interest in a co-operative

Section 361 provides that interest on such a loan is eligible for relief if the borrower has, from the time of the loan to the payment of the interest, worked for the greater part of his time as an employee of the co-operative.

Loan to acquire an interest in a partnership

Section 362 provides that interest on a loan is eligible for relief if the individual uses the money to buy a share in a partnership or to contribute to partnership capital.

Loan to acquire machinery or plant: s359

If an individual takes out a loan to buy plant and machinery to use in his employment or for use by a partnership of which he is a member, interest is eligible for relief for the first four years of the loan.

Interest on a loan to pay Inheritance Tax is eligible for relief if the borrowers are personal representatives: s364.

Interest is eligible for relief on a loan taken out by a person of 65 or more to purchase a life annuity, secured on land in the United Kingdom or Ireland: s365. The £30,000 limit applies here as in 'Main residences' above.

Where interest is paid on a loan which was used for the purposes of a business, it may be deducted as a business expense in computing the profits of the trade.

3.5 Charges on income

In certain circumstances, other payments made by a person can be deducted in computing his total income. These are known as 'charges on income'. Formerly, payments such as covenanted sums paid by parents to adult children attending university and maintenance payments, whether by agreement or court order, qualified as 'charges on income', that is, to be deducted by the payer in computing his/her liability to income tax (subject to the deduction of tax at source), and instead were treated as the payee's income. The range of payments falling to be treated in this way was greatly reduced by s347A ICTA 1988, introduced by s36 FA 1988 which provides for many former charges on income, in particular the two mentioned above, to cease to be either a deduction for the payer or taxable income of the payee. Such payments fall out of the tax system. The new rules apply to individuals only.

The most significant charge on income remaining unaffected by s347A is now the covenanted payment to charity.

Covenanted payments to charity

When a person makes a payment under a deed of covenant to a charity this is an 'annual payment' falling within Schedule D Case III. Such payments will be made after deduction of tax. Section 835(6)(b) permits the whole payment to be deducted in arriving at the payer's total income.

Example
Adrian has the following income in 1997–98:

	£	£
Dividend from United Kingdom Company	8,000	
Add: tax credit (¼)	2,000	10,000
Deduct:		
Covenanted income to his favourite charity		
(£1,500 actually paid: £500 tax deducted)		2,000
Total Income		£8,000

3.6 Personal reliefs

Having computed his 'total income' for the year of assessment, the individual may claim to make deductions of personal reliefs from that figure to determine his final 'taxable income', which is the sum on which income tax is actually levied. If personal reliefs exceed total income, the excess is lost, for it cannot be carried forward to the following year.

The reliefs available are as follows:

Personal allowance: s257(1) ICTA 1988

Every individual is entitled to a certain amount of tax free income. This is called the personal allowance. For 1997–98 the personal allowance is £4,045.

A married man may also claim the married couple's allowance if:

1. He is a married man whose wife is living with him, s257A(1) ICTA 1988; or
2. He and his wife ceased to live together before 6 April 1990 but he has continued wholly to maintain her and he is not entitled to deduct sums paid to her as maintenance when computing his total income: s257F(1) ICTA 1988.

So if a married couple are separated, and the husband maintains his wife under a court order or under a deed of separation, then he can only claim a personal allowance – but so can she.

The married couple's allowance for 1997–98 is £1,830. In addition, under s257B ICTA 1988 this allowance is transferable to the wife to the extent that the husband cannot use the allowance because his income is too low.

In the year of marriage the married man receives the married couple's allowance minus one-twelfth of that allowance for each complete month of the tax year which has elapsed before the marriage. In 1997–98 one-twelfth of the excess is £152.50. Accordingly, a man who married on 6 August 1997 will calculate his married allowance as follows:

£1,830 – (4/12 x £1,830)
= £1,830 – £610
= £1,220

Additional personal relief for one-parent families and others in respect of children: s259 ICTA 1988

This relief, which is equivalent to the married couple's allowance (currently £1,830), is available for:

1. an individual who is not entitled to the married couple's allowance, or
2. any married man who is entitled to the married couple's allowance but whose wife is totally incapacitated by mental or physical infirmity throughout that year,

provided that they have a child under the age of 18 in full-time education resident with them. This relief is therefore effectively available to widows, widowers and others to whom the married person's relief is not available, and to single parents and divorced parents if they have a child with them.

Note: as from 1989–90 s259(4A) ICTA 1988 prevents an unmarried couple who are living together from each claiming this relief in respect of their children. Section 259(4A) ensures that they can only make one claim in respect of the youngest of their qualifying children.

Widow's bereavement allowance: s262 ICTA 1988

A widow (but not a widower) may, in the tax year of her spouse's death, claim:

1. any of the married couple's allowance under s257A(1) ICTA 1988 which remained unused at the date of her husband's death; and
2. her widow's bereavement allowance of an amount equal to that specified in s257A(1) ICTA 1988 for the year of his death and the following tax year if she has not remarried by the start of that year, and
3. the additional relief under s259 if she has a qualifying child living with her after her husband's death.

Note: if a married couple are living together and the wife dies the husband gets the married couple's allowance for the year. He does not receive a widower's bereavement allowance.

Reliefs for blind persons: s265 ICTA 1988

The amount of the blind person's allowance for 1997–98 is £1,280. To claim this relief the individual must be a registered blind person for the whole or part of the year of assessment.

Age exemption: s257(2) and (3), s257A(2) and (3) ICTA 1988

If an individual is aged 65 or more the personal allowance is increased to £5,220 and the married couple's allowance is increased to £3,185. If the individual is over 74, these sums are increased to £5,400 and £3,225 respectively. However these allowances are reduced or lost entirely if the individual's income exceeds £15,600 in 1997–98.

Entitlement to personal allowances

Under s278 ICTA 1988, the entitlement to personal allowances is normally restricted to individuals who are residents of the United Kingdom. Under s278(2) reliefs are extended to commonwealth citizens, citizens of the Republic of Ireland, former Crown servants, Isle of Man and Channel Islands residents and former United Kingdom residents now residing abroad for health reasons. In addition to these categories certain double taxation agreements between the United Kingdom and other countries provide, within the treaty, for personal allowances to be made available to non-residents who are taxable in the other country on the same basis as they are made avaiable to resident individuals. Not every double taxation treaty which the United Kingdom has concluded allows for the granting of personal allowances to residents of the other country.

Section 145 of the Finance Act 1996 extended the entitlement to personal allowances to *nationals* of all of the member states of the European Economic Area, which therefore includes not only the member states of the European Union, but those of Iceland, Liechtenstein and Norway. Therefore, this provision will grant personal allowances to *nationals* of these countries, irrespective of whether they are *resident* in the respective member state or not.

3.7 The taxation of married couples

The method of taxing married couples changed dramatically from 6 April 1990, as a result of ss31–35 and Schedule 3 FA 1988.

Pre 6 April 1990 – Method of taxing married couples

Until the end of the tax year 1989–90 s279 ICTA 1988 treated the income of a woman living with her husband as his income for income tax purposes. The husband was responsible for completing his and his wife's tax returns and was liable to pay the tax on the couple's combined income.

Post 6 April 1990 – Method of taxing married couples

Under the independent taxation rules that came into force on 6 April 1990 a husband and wife will:

1. be taxed independently, each on their own income;
2. each has to take responsibility for his or her own tax affairs. Thus each will have to file his or her own tax returns and meet his or her own personal tax liability.

From 6 April 1990 the income of the wife has not been treated as the income of her husband for tax purposes (s279 ICTA 1988 was repealed by s31 FA 1988 with effect from 6 April 1990). Instead the income of both spouses are separately aggregated and separately taxed.

Each spouse is entitled to a personal allowance: s257(1) ICTA 1988. In addition the husband is entitled to a married couple's allowance: s257A(1). The wife can claim this married couple's allowance to the extent that her husband is unable to use it because his income is too low: s257B. In the 1992 Budget, the Chancellor announced proposals to enable a husband and wife to elect how to allocate the married couple's allowance between them from 6 April 1993. See Schedule 5 of the Finance (No 2) Act 1992.

Sections 282A and 282B ICTA 1988 apply where investment income arises from property held in the joint names of a husband and wife who are living together. Section 282A states that such investment income is to be attributed to husband and wife in equal shares unless they specify otherwise.

Note: s282A(4) states that s282A(1) does not apply to earned income or partnership income.

Sections 257D–F ICTA 1988 contain transitional relief to assist married couples in their move from the old rules for taxing husband and wife as one unit to the new rules for taxing husband and wife independently.

Examples

1. Method of taxing the income of married couples post 6 April 1990

During 1997–98 Godfrey had earnings of £25,000 and investment income of £12,000. His wife Wendy also worked during 1997–98 and her earnings were £15,000. She had investment income of her own of £8,000 made up of dividends and other savings income during that tax year.

The computation of Godfrey's and Wendy's tax liability would be:

Godfrey's income	£	£
G's earnings		25,000
G's investment income		12,000
		37,000
Godfrey's allowances		
Personal allowance	4,045	
Married couple's allowance	1,830	
		5,875
		£31,125
Tax		
4,100 @ 20%		820
4,101 – 26,100 @ 23%		5,060
The remainder (£5,025) at 40%		2,010
		£7,890

Wendy's income	£	£
W's earnings		15,000
W's investment income		8,000
		23,000
Wendy's allowances		
Personal allowance	4,045	
		4,045
		£18,955

(Note: As taxable income of £18,955 is below the higher rate limit, all savings income is taxed at 20%).

Tax	
8,000 @ 20%	1,600
4,100 @ 20%	820
£6,855 @ 23%	1,576
	£3,996

Thus the total tax liability for G and W is £11,886 but G is liable for his tax bill of £7,890 and W is liable for her tax bill of £3,996.

2. Method of taxing the income of married couples post 6 April 1990

During 1997–98 Richard had earnings of £4,000. His wife Elizabeth also worked during 1997–98 and her earnings were £18,000. She also had investment income during that year of £4,000.

The computation of Richard and Elizabeth's tax liability would be:

Richard's income	£	£
R's earnings		4,000
Richard's allowances		
Personal allowance	4,045	
Married couple's allowance	1,830	
		5,875
		£1,875

Richard has unused married couple's allowance of £1,875 and he is not liable to tax on his income. Under s257B ICTA 1988 Richard can transfer the unused personal allowance to Elizabeth:

Elizabeth's income	£	£
E's earnings		18,000
E's investment income		4,000
		22,000
Elizabeth's allowances		
Personal allowance	4,045	
Married couple's allowance	1,875	
(transferred from Richard)		
		5,920
		16,080
Tax		
4,000 @ 20% (savings income)		800
4,100 @ 20%		820
7,980 @ 23%		1,835
		£3,455

The total tax bill for Richard and Elizabeth for 1996–97 is therefore £3,455 Richard is not liable to pay any tax, while Elizabeth is liable to meet her tax bill of £3,455.

In the above example, if Elizabeth paid mortgage interest qualifying for relief under MIRAS of £2,000, she would deduct income tax relief of £2,000 at 15 per cent = £300, from the final tax bill of £3,455. It should be noted that the mortgage relief is not deducted from the income of £22,000 since this is not a deduction from total income but is now a relief in terms of tax payable.

On the other hand, if she paid a covenated payment to charity amounting to £1,000, this would be deducted from the income of £22,000, before setting out the personal allowances in the calculation above.

4

Schedule A

4.1 The new Schedule A (post 6 April 1995)

4.2 Section 15 ICTA 1988 (old Schedule A rules)

4.3 Business and trading considerations

4.4 The 'Schedule A business'

4.5 Basis of assessment: s22

4.6 Allowable expenditure and capital allowances (new Schedule A)

4.7 Expenditure incurred in void period (old Schedule A rules)

4.8 Premiums: ss34–49 ICTA 1988 and capital gains tax

4.9 Charge on assignment of a lease at an undervalue

4.10 Allowances for losses

4.11 Income from furnished lettings

4.12 Foreign element

4.13 Anti-avoidance provisions of s33A ICTA 1988

4.1 The new Schedule A (post 6 April 1995)

Income tax

In considering the current statute and existing case law relating to the taxing of income from property under Schedule A for *income tax purposes*, regard has to be had to the fact that the entire system has altered with effect from April 1995. The changes were principally made to facilitate the introduction of a general self-assessment system for income tax, covering income taxable under all schedules. The previous Schedule A system distinguished between the profits, losses and expenses according to the type of lease under which they arose. The new system (as provided for in the revised form of s21 of the Income and Corporation Taxes Act 1988, introduced by s39(2) of the Finance Act 1995) generally amalgamates all types of property receipts, provided that they arise in the United Kingdom, and introduces the concept of all such income arising from a 'Schedule A business', with expenditure deductible according to the existing business profits rules under Schedule D (s74 ICTA 1988).

Corporation tax

The changes do not affect the computation of Schedule A income for corporation tax purposes, and the basis of assessment of income under Schedule A follows the former rules. This will continue to give rise to a payments and rent receivable basis as opposed to the change to accruals basis for income tax. The two sets of legislation will therefore co-exist where relevant, and in this respect the reforms will create as many problems as they are intended to cure.

Note: throughout this chapter therefore reference is made to the 'old Schedule A rules' to indicate the pre-1995/96 and Corporation Tax rules and the 'new Schedule A rules' as being those for income tax purposes from 1995/96 onwards, to distinguish the two regimes.

4.2 Section 15 ICTA 1988 (old Schedule A rules)

This section charges tax under Schedule A in respect of:

> 'the annual profits or gains arising in respect of any ...
> 1. rents under leases of land in the United Kingdom;
> 2. rent charges;
> 3. payments for easements and other rights over land'.

There was a relevant decision in *McClure* v *Petre* [1988] STC 749: that receipts from tipping rights were capital and not income. A contractor dumped soil from a motorway construction site into a field and a disused railway cutting and the receipt was held to be from the disposal of an asset inherent in the land which once realised could not be repeated. It may be that, with the more liberal deduction system of the new Schedule A in comparison with capital gains tax, such an argument may not be run by taxpayers in the future. It is also difficult to see why such receipts are not 'receipts' from the exploitation etc of land etc under the new Schedule A.

Since the tax is only charged on the *profits or gains* it is clear that the landlord can make deductions in respect of certain expenses.

The following income is NOT assessed under Schedule A.

1. income from land outside the United Kingdom;
2. income from furnished lettings (usually charged under Schedule D, Case VI, with an option to be charged instead under Schedule A).

Deductions under old Schedule A rules

Section 25 sets out the general rules as to the deductions which can be made by a landlord in computing the profits and gains liable to Schedule A income tax. He may deduct payments:

1. in respect of maintenance, repairs, insurance and management (see *Southern* v *Aldwych Properties Ltd* [1940] 2 KB 266);
2. in respect of services provided by him otherwise than by way of maintenance or repairs, being services which he was obliged to provide but in respect of which he received no consideration (for example, where a mansion block of flats has hot water and central heating supplied in respect of which the landlord levies no separate 'service charges', relying instead on a larger rent to cover the costs);
3. in respect of rates;
4. in respect of rents to a superior landlord.

He may not, however, deduct interest charges directly from his rental income (s25(2) ICTA 1988). Instead he must seek to deduct them from his total income as 'charges on income': See Chapter 3, section 3.4, 'relief for interest paid'. Nor may he deduct any expenditure attributable to a time when he was himself in occupation. So, since it would appear that the principle of *Law Shipping Co Ltd* v *IRC* (1924) 12 TC 621 will apply, no deductions can be made for the cost of repairs effected to put property into a fit state to let as a result of dilapidation during the landlord's occupation. This is also the case if the landlord buys a property cheaply because of its run-down state and then expends money in repairing it. Such expense is considered to be a capital expense and not deductible.

Revised s15 ICTA 1988 (new Schedule A rules)

The new version of the Schedule A set out in subsection (1) of s15 as applied to income tax now reads:

> 'Tax under this Schedule shall be charged on the annual profits or gains arising from any business carried on for the exploitation, as a source of rents or other receipts, of any estate, interest or rights in or over any land in the United Kingdom.'

It then goes on to include, in addition to profits and gains,

> 'any transaction entered into for the exploitation, as a source of rents or other receipts, of any estate, interest or rights in or over any land in the United Kingdom'

as having 'been entered into in the course of such a business ...', so that, apart from annual profits, the proceeds of single transactions giving rise to income payments are within the scope of the charge to tax, unless specifically excluded.

Although income from property outside the United Kingdom is not taxed under Schedule A, the income is computed according to the new Schedule A rules, but is taxed under Schedule D Case V – s65(2A) and (2B) ICTA 1988.

4.3 Business and trading considerations

In *Griffiths* v *Jackson and Pearman* [1983] STC 184, the taxpayers were accountants who ran a subsidiary business of acquiring properties, which they converted into flats and let on a furnished short-term basis to students. They also provided various services of a relatively minor nature. The Revenue assessed them to tax under Schedule D Case VI; the taxpayers argued that they were carrying on a trade chargeable to tax under Schedule D Case I. Vinelott J held that it was a fundamental principle of English tax law that profit derived from the exercise of property rights by the owner of land was not trading income but chargeable under Schedule A or Schedule D Case VI. The existence of the services had no effect on this, although the taxpayers might have charged a separate fee in respect of such services which itself would have been trading income.

Contrast the position of hotel keepers whose profits are considered to be sufficiently distanced from the property rights of the owner – being received from a variety of services, only one of which is the right to occupy a room – as to be somewhere between a lease and a licence: if the owner of property exploits his rights without parting with occupation, he may be chargeable under Schedule D Case I as carrying on a trade.

In *Gittos* v *Barclay* (1985) 55 TC 633, the taxpayer's wife ran a business of letting furnished holiday accommodation. Goulding J held that the General Commissioners were entitled to conclude that this was not a trade, so the income was liable to tax under Schedule D Case VI. The effect of this was that the income was investment income, aggregable with her husband's, and the taxpayer would not be able to claim the benefit of certain Capital Gains Tax reliefs, such as roll-over relief (s115 of the Capital Gains Tax Act 1979, now s152 of the Taxation of Chargeable Gains Act 1992) and business retirement relief (ss163–164 and Schedule 6 TCGA 1992). This manner of assessment (which had become universal for seaside landladies) was reversed by s50 and Schedule 11 FA 1984 (now ss503–4 ICTA 1988) with retrospective effect to 6 April 1982. Thenceforward such income was to be treated as earned income if it was derived from the commercial letting of furnished holiday accommodation, whether chargeable under Schedule A or Schedule D Case VI. Furthermore, roll-over relief and retirement relief would be granted in respect of property used for that purpose.

4.4 The 'Schedule A business'

Fundamental changes to the Schedule A rules were introduced by FA 1995 with effect from 6 April 1995. The changes apply only for income tax and not for corporation tax purposes. By ss39–42 and Schedule 6 FA 1995, all income from property, including premiums and furnished lettings (see section 4.10), will be assessed as a 'Schedule A business' – s39(2) FA 1995 – with the rules for income and expenditure the same as for Schedule D business income.

'Business' has not been defined under the new legislation ('Schedule A business' in s832(1) ICTA 1988 as imported by Schedule 6 para 28 FA 1995 is stated as being a business whose profits or gains are chargeable to tax under Schedule A). It appears that the exhaustive scope of the receipts to be included under Schedule A may make such a consideration unnecessary. The deeming of all taxable receipts to be part of a Schedule A business dictates that it will not be necessary to find a 'business' activity before determining whether or not its receipts are within the scope of the new provisions. Such considerations have for example been necessary in other tax areas such as value added tax, since the United Kingdom legislation requires that for the supplies to be taxable they must be 'made by a taxable person in the course or furtherance of any business carried on by him' (s1 Value Added Tax Act 1994 – see Chapter 25).

Where the point does become relevant is in determining whether the carrying on of a Schedule A business will enable the person to qualify for tax reliefs which are conditional upon the carrying on of a business or trading activity:

1. Retirement relief for capital gains tax purposes – see Chapter 19 and Schedule 6 TCGA 1992 – is due on a 'disposal of business assets' (s163 TCGA 1992).
2. Roll-over relief under s152 TCGA 1992 – see Chapter 19 – although carrying a heading of 'replacement of business assets', requires the carrying on of a trade and not a business as a precondition.
3. Relief for gifts of business assets under s165 TCGA 1992 requires the carrying on of a 'trade, profession or vocation' for gains on the disposal of 'business assets' by way of gift to be deferred.
4. Business property relief for inheritance tax purposes (see Chapter 22) operates in respect of 'relevant business property' defined in s105(1)(a) of the Inheritance Tax Act 1984 as inter alia 'property consisting of a business or an interest in a business' but excludes in s105(3) business activities of 'dealing in ... land or buildings ...'.
5. A 'trade, profession or vocation' is also required for the purpose of claiming loss relief (s380 ICTA 1988) (see Chapter 6) against general (ie total) income as opposed to being relieved only against income or profits of the same or similar enterprise.

As the provisions of Schedule 6 para 36 FA 1995 deem only those Schedule A businesses whose activities consist of the letting of furnished holiday accommodation to be treated as a trade for s503 ICTA 1988 and therefore also for capital gains tax purposes, there is no scope for any of the reliefs mentioned in (1) to (5) above. It should be noted, however, that by paragraphs 22 to 25 of Schedule 6 FA 1995 some of the special deductions applicable to employee aspects of businesses have been specifically applied to the new Schedule A business.

The principal distinction between passive and active occupation or ownership of property remains even under the new regime, so the decisions in the above cases remain relevant. It is interesting to note that the case of *Fry* v *Salisbury House Estate* [1930] AC 432 referred to in Chapter 2, on the exclusive nature of the schedules, concerned an even older version of Schedule A than that which the 1995 regime replaced. At that time the measure of an assessment under Schedule A was the 'annual value' of the property which was taken to reflect the rental receivable. It is, however, useful to refer to in connection with the distinction between the nature of letting receipts and profits from other related activities.

4.5 Basis of assessment: s22

Current year basis (old Schedule A rules)

For income tax purposes in the years prior to 1995/96 tax was charged under Schedule A on a current year basis and was due on 1 January of the year of assessment. Accordingly, payment was due before it could be calculated precisely. This was effected in practice by requiring the taxpayer to pay an estimated amount which was adjusted after the end of the tax year (5 April) when the final profits were known. The estimate was made by assuming that all Schedule A income and expenditure would be as in the previous year of assessment. This estimate would be adjusted and reduced if the taxpayer could show that his Schedule A was likely to be less because, for example, he had ceased to own a property.

Schedule A was charged by reference to the rents, etc, to which a person *became entitled* in a year of assessment. So a person would be charged tax on unpaid rent unless:

1. He could establish that he has taken reasonable steps to collect the rent; or
2. He had waived the unpaid rent without consideration in order to prevent hardship (s41 ICTA 1988).

If the lost rent was subsequently recovered, the landlord had to inform the Revenue within six months. The Revenue then had six years in which to reopen the assessment for any year affected.

Example
Rent of £10,000 per annum due on 1 January 1996, under the old Schedule A regime, would have been taxed wholly in 1995–96 – the year in which payment fell due – whereas under the new system the assessment would be £2,500 for 1995–96 and the balance of £7,500 would be taken into account in 1996–97, together with the relevant portion of rent falling due in that year.

Scope/limitations under the new basis

Under paragraph 2 of the new Schedule A set out in the revised s15 ICTA 1988, the new provisions do not apply to property-related interest receipts, commercially managed woodlands or mines/quarries income. The letting of tied premises continues to be Schedule D Case I income under s98 ICTA 1988.

Paragraphs 3 and 4 include furnished letting income and income from permanently moored houseboats and fixed caravans within the new Schedule A business regime.

Payment of tax under the new self assessment rules
Having changed the basis of assessment under Schedule A for years 1995/96 onwards, the new regime was therefore in place for the commencement of self assessment in 1996/97. Whereas tax under Schedule A was, as explained above, normally payable within the year in which the income was assessed, under self assessment the position has changed. In common with income tax payable under the other Schedules, tax due on rental income will for the most part become due on the 31 January during, and any balance on 31 January following, the year of assessment. For 1996/97, therefore, the tax becomes due on the 31 January 1997 with subsequent adjustments the following year as necessary – see Chapter 24.

4.6 Allowable expenditure and capital allowances (new Schedule A)

Allowable expenditure and interest relief

Deductions (including interest relief currently governed by ss353–358 ICTA 1988) will need to satisfy only the 'wholly and exclusively' and other tests of s74 ICTA 1988 to be allowable, and income tax will be paid on the profits as calculated for other business purposes. This means that the accruals basis replaces the current rule of assessing Schedule A income to which one becomes entitled in the year of assessment. This also means that the provisions of ss33 and 33A ICTA 1988 are no longer required for income tax purposes since they have the effect of an accruals basis calculation as now required for Schedule A income tax purposes. They remain relevant for corporation tax.

Interest relief, which previously was restricted under s354 to loans to purchase property, will in future be due for all relevant business borrowing, such as maintenance and repairs.

Interest on qualifying loans under the MIRAS scheme (s369) may be deducted in calculating Schedule A profits, under a new s375A option available from Schedule 6 para 18 FA 1995.

Allowance for pre-letting expenditure under s401 ICTA 1988 is now applicable – it formerly required a 'trade, profession or vocation', and only furnished holiday lettings meeting the tests of s503 were treated as a trade. However, a new s401(1B) was added by Schedule 6 para 20 FA 1995 to extend this relief to all Schedule A businesses within the charge to income tax. This will probably be sufficient to deal with expenditure during 'void periods', which previously posed a difficulty since all expenditure had to be related to a lease period before it could be considered deductible. Now it appears either that the 'Schedule A business' is treated as continuous even if all letting activities are suspended, or that it ceases and restarts with pre-commencement expenditure being brought into account; particularly also with the adoption of the new accruals basis in calculating profits, there is less scope for avoidance or undesirable manipulation.

Capital allowances

As for most tax purposes, expenditure of a capital nature is excluded from being deducted in arriving at the taxable profit and a 'capital allowance' is given instead. The allowance is generally calculated on a 'reducing balance' basis which involves calculating the first year's allowance as a percentage of the qualifying capital cost and taking the allowance as an expense against the profit. All following years' allowances are given on the balance left out of the starting capital cost figure after deducting the allowances which have been taken in past years.

For Schedule A purposes, no allowance can be given for capital items of machinery, plant or fixtures supplied with a domestic dwelling (see below, however, for alternative practice) but for other let properties expenditure on machinery or plant (for example vehicles, equipment, computers, furniture, fixtures, lifts, heating and air conditioning) would qualify for the 25 per cent reducing balance allowance. Expenditure on industrial and agricultural buildings will qualify for a 4 per cent allowance each year but calculated always on the original cost and not on the reducing balance. Expenditure on certain hotels qualifies for a 4 per cent reducing balance allowance. Expenditure attributable to the cost of land does not qualify for any allowance.

Section 221 FA 1994 changed the basis on which relief for capital allowances for all income tax purposes is given, in most cases from 1997–98 onwards. (New businesses starting from 6 April 1994 are affected immediately.) Allowances will cease to be given as a deduction from the income or profit being taxed but will become a business expense to be deducted in calculating the actual amount of income or profit assessable. Under Schedule 6 para 8 FA 1995 such allowances will be given as business deductions from 1995–96 onwards except where relief has been or can be obtained under the existing leased plant provisions of s61 of the Capital Allowances Act 1990. Since capital allowances cannot be given for domestic dwellings expenditure – s61 CAA 1990 – the practice of allowing a deduction for wear and tear in furnished letting calculations, normally at 10 per cent of the rent received, or on a renewals basis, will continue.

4.7 Expenditure incurred in void period (old Schedule A rules)

Usually the landlord can only deduct expenses incurred during the currency of a lease. He is, however, also allowed to deduct expenditure incurred in a 'void period' (that is to say, a period when the property is occupied either by the landlord or a tenant) if either:

1. that void period was preceded by a period when the property was let at a full rent; or
2. the period began when the landlord bought the property and ended when a lease at a full rent was granted (ie without any intermediate occupation by the landlord).

4.8 Premiums: ss34–39 ICTA 1988 and capital gains tax

The existing rules under s34 ICTA 1988 for calculating premiums treated as rent paid or received are mostly unchanged but now substitute references to Schedule A treatment for income or deductions rather than to Schedule D Case VI in appropriate cases (Schedule 6 para 9 FA 1995).

It would be very easy to avoid paying Schedule A income tax if, instead of letting properties at rack rents, the landlord were to let them at low rents in consideration of the payment of capital sums, so that capital gains tax would be payable instead and capital gains tax reliefs would be available. Section 34 provides, therefore, that where the payment of a premium is required under a lease not exceeding 50 years, the premium itself is to be treated, at least in part, as rent.

'Premium' is widely defined as including any sum, whether payable to the immediate or a superior landlord, 'or to a person connected with either of them': s24. Section 34 restricts the application of the lease premium provisions to leases of 50 years or less since it considers leases of greater duration as capital assets. Correspondingly, the closer a lease approaches to 50 years, the more it comes to resemble a long lease and the less the premium is brought into account as rent. Section 34, in effect, provides that a 2 per cent reduction is to be made for each complete year that the lease lasts in excess of the first. Thus if A is required to pay a premium of £1,000 for an 18-month lease, the whole £1,000 is treated as rent. If, however, he were to pay £20,000 for a 31-year lease, 30 x 2% = 60% would fall out of charge under Schedule A, leaving only £8,000 to be taxed as income.

The sum thus found taxable is, as a general rule, all to be brought into charge in the one tax year. Section 34(8) provides, though, that if the premium is payable by instalments the sum found to be due may itself be paid in instalments, provided that the landlord can show that he would otherwise suffer hardship. The payments of tax can be spread over the shorter of two periods: that during which the instalments are to be paid, or eight years.

Deemed premiums

It is not possible to avoid the s34 charge by the payment of 'concealed premiums'.

In order to counteract such attempts at avoidance of tax, the following provisions exist:

1. If the provisions of a lease are such that it is unlikely to run its full term, the s34(1) discounting is to be computed as if its term were the anticipated shorter period. (On the other hand, if the provisions of the lease are such that it is likely to exceed the term specified, the discounting is computed by reference to the longer period: s38 ICTA 1988.)

2. If the tenant is required by the lease to effect improvements (not merely repairs), then the landlord is treated as receiving a premium equal to the excess in the value of his reversionary interest immediately after the beginning of the lease over what it would have been in the absence of the provision.

   Example
   X grants a lease to Y for ten years subject to a term that he install central heating. Without these terms, X's freehold reversion at the beginning of the lease would have been £10,000; because of it, he could immediately sell the reversion for £18,000. Accordingly, he is treated as receiving a premium of £8,000 – of which 8,000 x (100-18)% = £6,560 will be treated as rent.

3. Payments by the tenant for the commutation of rent, or variation or waiver of a term of a lease, are treated as premiums taxable in the year of receipt. Discounting is available, the period for which the alteration is effective in each case being the deemed duration of the lease of the purposes of s34(1).

Top-slicing relief

It used to be thought unjust that the Revenue was able to treat a premium for a lease of many years as rental income arising in one year and thus impose high rates of tax on that premium, and so 'top-slicing' relief was available. This relief did not avoid the tax all arising in one year; what it did was reduce the effective rate of tax. However, when FA 1988 introduced a single higher rate of tax for both income and capital gains the need for 'top-slicing' relief disappeared, so the relief was withdrawn with effect from 6 April 1988.

Lease premiums and capital gains tax

Schedule 8 TCGA 1992 provides extended and complex rules for dealing with the liability of lease premiums to capital gains tax. In very simple terms, where the lease is granted for a term of 50 years or more it is not a wasting asset, so no Schedule A liability arises in respect of any premium paid (s34 ICTA 1988), but the whole premium will be liable to capital gains tax. Where, however, Schedule A tax is applicable in respect of part of a premium paid on a lease for a term of less than 50 years, capital gains tax is chargeable on the untaxed part.

4.9 Charge on assignment of a lease at an undervalue

Tax under this heading has been switched from a charge under Schedule D Case VI to being included for profits purposes under Schedule A (Schedule 6 para 10 FA 1995).

Section 35 ICTA 1988 prevents an easy method of avoiding the Schedule A income tax charge on the granting of a lease. As s34 only applies to a premium paid on the grant of a lease and not on its assignment, it used to be common for a landlord to grant a lease to an associate for little or no consideration, ie at an undervalue. The associate then assigned the lease to a real tenant for full market value. Section 35 imposes a charge on the associate by reference to the amount that the landlord could have charged but did not – in other words, the excess of the consideration on the assignment over the premium (if any) paid on the grant of the lease. The associate pays tax on the excess under Schedule D Case VI, discounted by reference to the original term of the lease.

If a series of these transactions occurs, gradually building up to market value, each assignor is charged in the same way on his 'profit' on the transaction.

Example 1
A grants B a lease of Blackacre for 21 years in 1996 for £1 plus a peppercorn rent – a lease for which he could have obtained £20,000. A's Schedule A liability on the premium is 60p (£1 x (100-40)%).

B assigns the lease to C for £10,001. He is chargeable under Schedule D Case VI on £6,000 (£10,000 x (100-40)%).

C assigns it to D for £15,001. He is chargeable under Schedule D Case VI on £3,000 (£5,000 x (100-40)%).

Where a conveyance of land provides for its future re-conveyance at a lower price than that originally charged, the difference is treated as a premium on a lease whose term runs from the original conveyance to the date of possible reconveyance. The transactions are, of course, no more than a disguised lease.

Example 2
A sells land to B for £30,000 with a right to call for a reconveyance after 11 years at a price of £12,000. This is treated for Schedule A purposes as a lease for 11 years for a premium of £18,000. Taking into account the discounting provisions, the rental portion is £18,000 x (100-20)% = £14,400.

4.10 Allowances for losses

The new rules for taxation of income from Schedule A businesses beginning in 1995/96 removed some of the restrictions on the use of losses arising from the renting of property. Under the previous rules losses were segregated according to the type of lease under which the property was let and distinguished between those under which the landlord fulfiled the obligation to repair the property and those under which the tenant was obliged to carry out the repairs and, furthermore, those which were not let at a full rent were treated as a separate category. In general, losses could not be transferred and set off against profits arising under a different type of lease. The exception to this was that losses arising under leases under which the tenant carried out the repairing obligations and which were also let at full market rent could be set off against profits from properties under which the landlord carried out the repairing obligation, and again which were let at full rent.

Under the new Schedule A losses are freely transferable between properties let on a commercial basis. An allowable loss cannot arise from properties not let on a commercial basis, eg at a nominal rent to a relative. The losses allowable under Schedule A may not be set off against the taxpayer's general income except where the loss is represented by capital allowances on equipment leased to a trading tenant. Loss relief claims may also arise in respect of capital allowances for furnished holiday lettings (s379(2) and (9) ICTA 1988). Where allowable losses do arise they may be set off against general income of the year of the loss or against general income in the year following that in which the loss was made.

Losses arising through expenditure and the maintenance or repair of agricultural land or buildings may be set off against general income in the same manner as that explained above in relation to capital allowances.

4.11 Income from furnished lettings

Furnished lettings were normally assessed under Schedule D Case VI. However, an election could be made for such part of the rent which relates to the use of the property rather than to the use of the fittings, fixtures and furniture etc to be assessed under Schedule A. This enabled the landlord to make better use of the loss relief available under Schedule A.

Letting a room

Exemption from tax on the letting of rooms in one's own home was granted for rents up to £4,250 per annum by Schedule 10 para 6 FA (No 2) 1992. This is retained under the new Schedule A regime, but rents in excess of £4,250 are/may be included in full. An election under Schedule 10 para 11 FA (No 2) 1992 to treat only the excess as profit (but not subject to any deductions or capital allowances) remains. The effect of this is that, for example, if rent amounted to £6,000 per annum, an election could be made for a taxable profit of £1,750. It is therefore obviously best to elect for this method of assessment where the expenses on the property do not exceed £4,250.

Furnished holiday lettings

The activities of holiday lettings which satisfy the tests laid down in ss503 and 504 ICTA 1988 have been treated as trading activities; they continue to be so treated under the new regime but are now assessed under Schedule A as opposed to the previous Schedule D Case VI treatment.

4.12 Foreign element

Non-residents

The charge of tax under Schedule A is in respect of all United Kingdom property. Where the property is owned by a non-resident tax will be collected either by withholding it from the rent paid by the tenant or letting agent to the landlord or by self-assessment where the non-resident landlord has received approval from the Inland Revenue for the submission of self-assessment returns.

Where there is an obligation to deduct tax from the rents, this arises under the Taxation of Income from Land (Non-Resident Landlords) Regulations 1995 (SI 1995/2902). The letting agent or, where there is no letting agent, the tenant is obliged to deduct tax from the payment of rent and make payment to the Inland Revenue. The amount to be paid over is tax at the basic rate of 23 per cent of the rent payable less a deduction for expenses, providing those expenses are deductible under the Schedule A rules.

Section 40 FA 1995 introduced a new s42A into ICTA 1988, reflecting the fact that non-residents may apply for self-assessment as opposed to having tax withheld at source on payment of rents. Under self-assessment, if granted, rents could be paid gross by the tenant or letting agent. An application for self-assessment by a non-resident landlord in general would be approved by the Inland Revenue FICO Office, provided that there was a history of compliance with tax obligations within the United Kingdom

Under s82 ICTA 1988 interest paid to non-residents is not deductible as a business expense except for foreign currency loans payable outside the United Kingdom. Special provision was made in Schedule 6 para 13 FA 1995, amending s82 to ensure that such interest is allowed under Schedule A.

Overseas property

Section 41 FA 1995 amends the Case V treatment of overseas property income under s65 ICTA 1988 and adds a new s65A, so that the taxable profits are calculated according to the new 'Schedule A business' principles without – under s41(2) – being aggregated with United Kingdom source income for the purpose of setting off losses and expenses. An exception to the normal rule is to exclude overseas travel costs from deduction under s74 ICTA 1988, even if the 'wholly and exclusively' test is satisfied.

There are also transitional provisions for 1995–96 and 1996–97, due to the switch from the previous year Schedule D Case V basis to the current year basis, and the Schedule A loss relief provisions of s379A ICTA 1988 brought in by Schedule 16 para 19 FA 1995 do not apply to overseas property for years up to 1997–98 inclusive. For these years it is necessary to keep each overseas property separate.

Under the new s65(2A) profits are calculated in the same manner as for United Kingdom property, giving interest relief on the same principles; this reverses by statute the decision in *Ockenden* v *Mackley* [1982] STC 513; [1982] 1 WLR 787, in which a deduction for interest on non-United Kingdom property was disallowed.

4.13 Anti-avoidance provisions of s33A ICTA 1988

Section 33A ICTA (inserted by FA 1992) contains anti-avoidance provisions to prevent manipulation by taxpayers of the rules for charging rent to corporation tax and provides that where rent is payable in arrears between 'connected persons' in a chargeable period, the payer shall be charged on the rent which has actually accrued in that period and not on the rent which the payee was entitled to receive in the period.

Section 839 ICTA 1988 applies to determine if persons are connected. This applies whether the rent is paid directly between the connected persons or indirectly via a third party: s33B ICTA 1988. The person making the payment must be entitled to a deduction in respect of the rents for the purposes of computing his profits or gains for tax purposes.

5

The Taxation of Woodlands

5.1 Introduction

5.2 The old system: Schedule B

5.3 The new system: FA 1988

5.1 Introduction

Woodlands used to be one of the most attractive forms of investment as a result of the generous treatment which used to be afforded to their owners for the purposes of income tax, capital gains tax and inheritance tax.

5.2 The old system: Schedule B

The substantial income tax advantages previously attaching to commercial woodlands were removed by the Finance Act 1988. Formerly a taxpayer occupying woodlands in the United Kingdom, which were managed on a commercial basis with a view to the realisation of profits, was chargeable in respect of one third of the gross annual value of those woodlands. Actual profits were irrelevant to this charge, as were the losses incurred in expenditure on the woodlands. Taxpayers enjoyed an election for assessment under Schedule D Case I which permitted them more favourable loss treatment but removed the advantageous basis of assessment. To counteract this, taxpayers made the election for Schedule D early on in the life of their woodlands, thereby ensuring favourable loss treatment, but immediately before profits were realised they transferred the woodlands to their spouses, a trust or a company so that the favourable Schedule B basis of assessment arose once again, thereby ensuring that the profits realised largely escaped tax.

5.3 The new system: FA 1988

From 6 April 1988 the charge on the commercial occupation of woodlands was abolished by s65 and Schedule 6 FA 1988. These wholly remove commercially managed woodlands from the scope of income tax and corporation tax.

The new Schedule A provisions applicable from 6 April 1995 (see Chapter 4) continue to exclude commercially managed woodlands from the scope of its charge to income tax (see paragraph 2 of the revised s15 ICTA 1988).

6

Schedule D Cases I and II: Profits of a Trade, Profession or Vocation

6.1 The scope of the charge: s18 ICTA 1988

6.2 What constitutes 'trading'

6.3 The badges of trade

6.4 Special cases

6.5 The computation of profits

6.6 Trading receipts

6.7 Trading stock

6.8 Trading expenses: revenue and capital

6.9 1996–97 – Fundamental changes to the Schedule D basis of assessment (also applicable to new businesses 1994–95 onwards)

6.10 The basis of assessment (pre-FA 1994 changes)

6.11 Losses

6.12 Losses under the new Schedule D current year basis of assessment

6.13 Post-cessation receipts

6.1 The scope of the charge: s18 ICTA 1988

Tax under Schedule D Cases I and II is charged on the profits or gains of a trade (Case I) and of a profession or a vocation (Case II) carried on wholly or partly in the United Kingdom.

Of these three sources of income, only 'trade' is defined by statute, s832(1) of the Income and Corporation Taxes Act 1988 providing that:

'"Trade" includes every trade, manufacture, adventure or concern in the nature of trade.'

As to the others, a judicial definition of 'profession' was offered by Scrutton LJ in *IRC* v *Maxse* [1919] 1 KB 647:

> 'It involves the idea of an occupation requiring either purely intellectual skill or manual skill controlled by the intellectual skill of the operator.'

The former sort of occupation is exemplified by the barrister and solicitor, the latter by the surgeon.

In *Partridge* v *Mallandaine* (1886) 2 TC 179, Denman J defined 'vocation' as 'analogous to a "calling"': it means the way in which a person passes his life.' In that case professional bookmakers were held to have a vocation; more usual examples would be those of an author, a sculptor or an artist.

As a general rule, it matters little whether a profit falls within Case I or Case II; the few distinctions will be noted as they arise. It is much more important to decide whether a profit on the sale of an asset is a trading profit, thereby falling within the change to income tax under Schedule D Case I, or a capital gain, subject only to capital gains tax.

6.2 What constitutes 'trading'

It is very difficult to define exactly what 'trade' is. Usually one has to investigate carefully the circumstances of the transaction in question and decide whether the elements that one finds together constitute a trade. The best judicial pronouncement on this matter is that of Lord Wilberforce in *Ransom* v *Higgs* (1974) 50 TC 1:

> ' "Trade" cannot be precisely defined, but certain characteristics can be identified which trade usually has. Equally, some indications can be found which prevent a profit from being regarded as the profit of a trade. Sometimes the question whether an activity is to be found to be a trade becomes a matter of degree, or frequency, or organisation, even of intention and in such cases it is for the fact-finding body to decide whether a line is passed ... Trade involves, normally, the exchange of goods or services for reward – not of all services, since some qualify as a profession or vocation or employment, but there must be something the trade offers to provide by way of business. Trade, moreover, presupposes a customer ... you must trade with someone. The 'mutuality' cases (see below) are in part based on this ... Then there are elements or characteristics which prevent a trade being found, even though a profit has been made the realisation of a capital asset, the isolated transaction (which may yet be a trade) ... Although these are general characteristics which one cannot state in terms of essential prerequisites, they are useful bench marks, so when one is faced with a novel set of facts, the best one can do is to try them as tests in order to see how near to, or far from, the norm these facts are.'

What Lord Wilberforce was referring to was what the 1955 Royal Commission on Taxable Profits and Income called the six badges of trade:

1. the subject matter of the realisation;
2. the length of the period of ownership;

3. the frequency of similar transactions;
4. supplementary work on the assets sold;
5. the reason for the sale;
6. the taxpayer's motives.

It is important to bear in mind that the decision as to whether a trade is being carried on and whether a transaction is an 'adventure in the nature of a trade' is a question based on facts and one which itself becomes a question of fact. As such it is a decision properly to be taken by the Commissioners hearing the appeal, against whose decision there is no further avenue of appeal: see s56 of the Taxes Management Act 1970). The only exception to this rule would be on the basis of the decision in *Edwards* v *Bairstow & Harrison* [1956] AC 14 (see Chapter 24, section 24.3).

6.3 The badges of trade

The subject matter of the realisation

The first question one should ask when determining whether or not a transaction was trading is: what options were open to the taxpayer? In other words, what else could he have done with the asset? If the only thing possible was a re-sale, the transaction will have been trading, or an adventure in the nature of trade.

For example, in *Martin* v *Lowry* [1927] AC 312 the taxpayer bought 45 million yards of surplus government aircraft linen after World War I; he was held to be trading when he sold them at a profit. In *Rutledge* v *IRC* (1929) 14 TC 490 the taxpayer bought and sold one million rolls of toilet paper. He was held to have carried out an adventure in the nature of trade, and so was chargeable under Schedule D Case I. In *Wisdom* v *Chamberlain* (1969) 45 TC 92, the taxpayer bought silver bullion as a hedge against devaluation and inflation. When he sold at a profit, he was held to be chargeable under Case I. Silver locked away in a bank vault produces no income and has no aesthetic value. Its utility lies in its ability to hold, and to increase, its value, so it was only by selling it that it could fulfil its function. Another benchmark used by the Court of Appeal was the fact that the silver was bought with money borrowed at interest – so that it would have to be sold at a profit if the taxpayer was not to make a loss.

The length of the period of ownership

The essence of trading is the 'fast buck', so the longer the period of ownership, the more likely it is that a gain on disposal will be a capital gain. In *IRC* v *Reinhold* (1953) 34 TC 389 it was held that the intention to sell an asset *some* day at a profit, and in the meantime to hold it as an income-producing investment, was not sufficient to stamp the eventual sale as a trading transaction. The Revenue would have to go further and show a continuing commercial intention.

The frequency of similar transactions

Repetition is a strong indication that a person is trading. If you sell one house, you may be doing no more than making a capital gain; if you do it ten times in as many years, it is likely that you are (and have from the first been) trading. The oddest example of this is *Pickford* v *Quirke* (1927) 13 TC 251. There, the taxpayer on four different occasions asset-stripped spinning companies, by buying shares, liquidating the company and selling its assets to a new company. On each occasion he did so in combination with a different set of 'partners'. He alone was held to be trading simply because he had repeated the exercise.

Supplementary work on the assets sold

The fact that a person, rather than merely buying and selling an asset, carries out work in order to adapt it into a different asset, using his own skill, can be the crucial step, elevating an otherwise isolated capital transaction into an adventure in the nature of trade. So, in *IRC* v *Livingston* (1927) 11 TC 538 three tradesmen joined forces to purchase and to convert a cargo vessel into a steam drifter which they then sold. The proceeds of sale were held to be proceeds of an adventure in the nature of trade, since though what they had done might not have been enough to make them persons carrying on the business of shipbuilders, it had all the characteristics of, and was in the nature of, that trade.

The reason for the sale

If the taxpayer can prove that he did not want to sell, but was forced by unforeseen circumstances to do so, this mitigates strongly against there being a charge under Case I. The leading case on the topic is *Simmons* v *IRC* [1980] STC 350 where the taxpayer had bought properties for investment purposes and with the intention of floating a public investment company, but finding the market going against him, had to sell up and did so at a profit. The House of Lords decided that he was not trading. Lord Wilberforce said:

> 'A permanent investment may be sold in order to acquire another investment thought to be more satisfactory; that does not involve an operation of trade, whether the first investment was sold at a profit or a loss ... Frustration of a plan for investment which compels realisation, even if foreseen as a possibility merely cannot give rise to an intention to trade.'

The taxpayer's motives

The Royal Commission said:

> 'There are cases in which the purpose of the transaction of purchase and sale is clearly discernible. Motive is never irrelevant in any of these cases ... it can be inferred from surrounding circumstances in the absence of direct evidence of the seller's intention and even if necessary, in the face of his own evidence.'

Determination of a taxpayer's motive thus becomes important in determining whether to label an ambiguous asset as an investment or as trading stock. Consider, for example, the property in *IRC* v *Reinhold* (above), and see also the cases of *Overseas Containers (Finance) Ltd* v *Stoker* [1989] STC 364 and *Ensign Tankers (Leasing) Ltd* v *Stokes* [1992] STC 226. In *Overseas Containers* Sir Nicolas Browne-Wilkinson VC stressed that a trading transaction must have a commercial purpose and consequently if the *sole* purpose of a transaction is to obtain a fiscal advantage, it is impossible to find a commercial purpose and so it cannot be a trading transaction. Sir Peter Millett in *Ensign Tankers (Leasing) Ltd*, while claiming to be in agreement with the Vice-Chancellor, still maintained that:

> 'The purpose or object of a transaction must not be confused with the motive of the taxpayer in entering into it.'

However, close reading of Millett J's judgment leaves one unable to draw an effective distinction between motive and purpose. Indeed, as Vivien Shrubsall argued in her note in 1990 *British Tax Review* 52, the distinction between 'purpose' and 'notice' is unwarranted.

6.4 Special cases

Mutual trading

Lord Wilberforce said in *Ransom* v *Higgs* (1974) 50 TC 1 (see section 6.2) that trading involved a bilateral element; you must trade with someone. Difficulties arise, however, when a group of persons join together and contribute to some activity for their common benefit: for example, where they subscribe to a golf club. At the end of the year there may be some money left over, which is shared between the participants. Is that 'profit' from the activity and so liable to income tax under Schedule D Case I? The answer, as it was elegantly put in one article on the topic, is that it depends on whether the sum paid back is a return *of* or a return *on* the contribution. If the former, it is not taxable; if the latter, it is.

It will be a return of the contribution if all the members make similar contributions for similar benefits. This was not the case in *Fletcher* v *IRC* [1972] AC 414 where a swimming club which allowed hotels to be 'members' so that the latter's guests could use the facilities was held to be trading with them, since they did not have ordinary membership rights and paid 'membership fees' by reference to the number of guests that each hotel had.

This case and *Carlisle and Silloth Golf Club* v *Smith* (1913) 6 TC 198 also indicate that when a non-member pays to use the facilities, the mutuality principle does not *to that extent* operate, so the club will be held to be trading with him.

Illegal trading

If a transaction otherwise satisfies all the criteria of a trading activity, the mere fact that it happens to be illegal does not prevent the Revenue imposing a charge to income tax under Schedule D Case I. For an example of this, see *Mann v Nash* (1932) 16 TC 532.

The Revenue, for instance, has no hesitation in assessing receipts from prostitution as trading income, although more often it will assess them under Schedule D Case VI: see *IRC v Aken* [1988] STC 69. This is not to say, however, that a charge to income tax under Schedule D Case I can be imposed in respect of any crime; the criminal activity must have the 'badges of trade'. For example, a burglar who kept all that he stole would not be trading, merely stealing.

Farming: s53 ICTA 1988

Section 53(1) provides that all farming and market gardening is to be treated as the carrying on of a trade, chargeable under Schedule D Case I and s53(2) treats all farming carried on by a person or partnership as one single trade irrespective of the number of farming operations. Section 53(3) extends this also to any occupation of land which is managed on a commercial basis with a view to the realisation of profits *other than* the occupation of woodlands.

Property dealing

A distinction has to be drawn between the realisation of real property held as an investment, or as the vendor's private residence, and a transaction amounting to an adventure or concern in the nature of trade. See, for example, *Simmons v IRC* [1980] STC 350 (see section 6.3 'The circumstances responsible for the realisation'). On occasion, when the Revenue has failed to bring a sale of land within Schedule D Case I, it has sought to instead impose a charge under the 'sweeping-up' provisions of Schedule D Case VI. Any such attempt will fail. As was said in *Jones v Leeming* (1930) 15 TC 333:

> '... in the case of isolated transactions of purchase and resale of property there is really no middle course open. It is either an adventure in the nature of trade, or simply a case of sale and resale of property.'

6.5 The computation of profits

Tax under Schedule D Cases I and II is charged on 'the annual profits or gains arising or accruing from any trade, profession or vocation': s18 ICTA 1988. 'Annual' means arising in a particular year. It does not mean 'recurrent'. Accordingly, one asks: 'Did the profit in question arise in the year (or accounting year) by reference

'Earnings', 'cash' or 'bills delivered' basis

Usually, the profits of a trade must be computed on an 'earnings basis', in other words by bringing into account sums which have been earned, *whether or not* they have been received. Correspondingly, though, one is entitled to deduct sums which are owing, even though they have not been paid. The rule is, however, that one need only bring into charge sums which have been earned, and a sum is not yet earned if the trader has not fulfilled all the conditions which would entitle him to payment – a person cannot be taxed on 'contingent profits'. The leading case on the subject is *Willingale* v *International Commercial Bank* [1978] STC 75. There, the bank purchased a bill at a discount, the discount being available because the borrower who had issued the bill did not have to repay the loan for five years. As each year towards maturity passed, the bill increased in value, and in each year the Revenue sought to tax the current increment in value. It failed because no right to receive any money arose until the bill matured, or was sold on.

One alternative to the earnings basis is the 'cash basis' under which profits are calculated by reference to sums received and not by reference to sums earned. Correspondingly, deductions can only be made of bills paid and not of bills owing. This preferential basis is mainly used by barristers and authors.

The other alternative to the earnings basis is the 'bills delivered basis' under which profits are calculated by deducting bills received from bills sent out during the relevant accounting period. This preferential basis tends to be used by professions who regularly send out bills, eg solicitors and accountants.

6.6 Trading receipts

Not all receipts of a trade are assessable to tax under Schedule D Case I. It is a fundamental rule that income tax is a tax on income and not a tax on capital receipts. That having been said, though, great difficulty can be experienced in determining whether a particular receipt is income or capital.

The basic distinction may be symbolised by the analogy of the fruit tree. A farmer who owns orchards has two forms of assets – the trees and their fruit. One asset, the fruit, is of a revenue nature – when he sells it, he receives income, assessable under Case I. If, however, he were to sell his trees, they would be capital items, giving rise to capital receipts, not assessable under Case I. The capital items generate the revenue items, but are not themselves revenue because it is not the farmer's business to sell them, but to keep them to produce the fruit.

It is to be noted, however, that it is the nature of the business which determines the quality of the receipt. Those same fruit trees would, in the hands of a nurseryman, be revenue items – stock in trade – because it is the business of the nurseryman to sell trees, not fruit. Correspondingly, the nature of the business can also determine the quality of expenditure. The farmer buying saplings is incurring capital expenditure; the nurseryman on the same purchase would have revenue expenditure. This analogy between the fruit trees and the fruit has been cited in numerous cases dating back several decades and has been reaffirmed as the basis on which many decisions have been reached by the courts, including the *Vallambrosa* case referred to in section 6.8.

Do not be misled by the unnecessary nomenclature 'fixed capital' and 'circulating capital' into thinking that sales of either give rise to capital receipts. 'Circulating capital' is little more than another description of stock in trade, and the receipts on its sale are the primary form of income subject to tax under Case I.

An interesting case came before the High Court in 1995, in the form of *Wain* v *Cameron* [1995] STC 555, to determine whether an author's drafts, working papers and manuscripts (but not including copyrights to any works) had been disposed of as part of the proceeds of Professor Wain's profession. It was held that these were part of the fruits of his profession, irrespective of the fact that when created it was not contemplated or known that a source for selling them could be found.

See also *Deeny and Others* v *Gooda Walker Ltd (In Voluntary Liquidation) and Others (Inland Revenue Commissioners as Third Party) and Related Appeals* [1996] STC 299. Here the plaintiffs (Deeny and Others) were awarded damages against the managing and members agents of various Lloyd's Underwriting syndicates (Gooda Walker Ltd and Others) as a result of the agents' failure to exercise due care in the exercise of their functions on the members' ('names') behalf. The issue was whether in determining the amount of the damages regard had to be taken of the tax element, for which the agents sought a reduction in the amounts awarded against them. The agents contended that the names had and would continue to save tax on the sums awarded and that accordingly the amounts awarded against them should be reduced by an amount equivalent to the tax so saved. The House of Lords dismissed the agents' appeal, holding that the business of an underwriting name at Lloyd's consisted of a single business and that the agency agreements were contracts made in the course of that business. The damages received by the names were, therefore, a trading receipt of the business, to be taxed according to ss171 and 184 FA 1993. As no tax saving had or would accrue to the names, no deduction should be made from the amount of damages awarded against the agents. See Chapter 27, sectiom 27.1, for further details.

Examples of capital receipts

Sums received for the restriction of one's activities

In *Higgs* v *Olivier* [1952] Ch 311, following the making of the film of *Henry V*, Olivier entered into a deed of covenant with the film company under which he received £15,000 as consideration for an undertaking not to act in, or participate in the making of, any film for any other person for 18 months. It was held that because the sum came to him not in the ordinary course of the exercise of his profession but as a restriction of his professional activities, it was not taxable. It is important to notice that the £15,000 arose out of a completely separate agreement from the contract to act in the film. If this had not been so, but the agreements had been capable of being read together as aspects of one contract to act, the money would have been found to be income, not capital.

In *IRC* v *Biggar* [1982] STC 677, a dairy farmer received compensation under a scheme of the then European Economic Community which was designed to encourage owners of dairy herds to convert their farm to beef production. The taxpayer sought to contend that, on the authority of *Higgs* v *Olivier*, the compensation was a payment for the restriction of his trading activities and thus not a capital receipt. The Court of Session held that the case was distinguishable since the scheme did not impose a restriction 'capable of being equiparated with sterilisation of capital assets.' The trader continued to farm at full capacity, and only the product changed. In *Higgs*, on the other hand, the taxpayer's 'capital' was his acting capacity and that was temporarily and partially sterilised. It seems, therefore, that it is not enough that the taxpayer agrees not to carry on his trade in the manner to which he has been accustomed – it is also necessary to show that the effect of this agreement is to limit his operations so severely as to expose him to inevitable loss.

Compensation for the sterilisation of assets

In *Glenboig Union Fireclay Co Ltd* v *IRC* (1921) 12 TC 427 (House of Lords) the owners of fireclay fields running under the Caledonian Railway were restrained from working part of these fields on payment of compensation. The compensation was computed as a sum equal to the profits which could have been made had the area been worked out. The House of Lords held that the receipt was a capital, not an income, receipt because what the fireclay company was being compensated for was the 'sterilisation and destruction' of its capital asset – the field itself – and the fact that the compensation was computed by the value of lost profits was irrelevant.

This must be correct, since the disposal of a capital asset of a trader almost always involves the disposal of possible future profits. But this state of affairs must be contrasted with that arising when the capital asset is not destroyed but only rendered temporarily unavailable. Such a case was that of *Burmah Steamship Co Ltd* v *IRC* (1930) 16 TC 67 (Court of Session) where damages paid by ship repairers for late delivery were held to be income in the hands of the shipowners; they were being compensated not for any damage to the capital asset but for profits lost which could have been made – clearly, an income receipt. See also *Donald Fisher* v *Spencer* [1989] STC 256.

Compensation for the loss of profits which would otherwise have been made is itself to be treated as a trading receipt. The extent of this principle was demonstrated by the peculiar case of *Lang* v *Rice* [1984] STC 172. There, a Northern Ireland trader received statutory compensation for the loss of trading profits which he would sustain from the time his premises had been closed owing to bomb damage until they could be reopened. He never recommenced trading and the Revenue claimed that the compensation was, therefore, capital in nature and chargeable to capital gains tax; the taxpayer argued that, being for the loss of profits, the receipt was of an income nature, not subject to capital gains tax nor liable to income tax, since the source of his income (the trade) had ceased. The Court of Appeal (NI) agreed with the trader, who thus received a tax-free benefit; 'post-cessation receipts' are only subject to tax when they are sums arising from the carrying on of a trade 'during any period *before* discontinuance: see ss143 and 144 ICTA 1970.

Compensation for cancellation of business contracts

On rare occasions, compensation paid for the cancellation of a contract has been held to be a capital receipt. One such case was *Van den Berghs* v *Clarks* [1935] AC 431 (House of Lords) where the taxpayer company surrendered its rights under three contracts due to operate for the following 13 years in return for a payment of £45,000. The payment was held to be a capital receipt because

> 'The agreements ... were not ordinary commercial contracts made in the course of carrying on their trade ... on the contrary they related to the whole structure of the appellant's profit-making apparatus.'

Nothing less will do; normally a contract will not have sufficient substance or length of life to be a capital asset, and in such a case all that is lost is profit. What one has to look for is a contract on whose existence the taxpayer company depends – for example, where a manufacturer's goods all go to one retailer.

A further example arose in the case of *Rolfe* v *Nagel* [1982] STC 53 in which a diamond broker was compensated by another broker to whom a client transferred after the former had completed the initial work to have the client accepted by the Diamond Trading Corporation as an approved purchaser, following which the client's broker would receive commission on the client's purchases. The receipt was held by the Court of Appeal to be a trading receipt, and it was noted that it was not the intention behind the payment which was the governing factor but the character of the payment in the hands of the payee. In this case the compensation, which was arrived at following arbitration, was in essence a payment for lost income and therefore taxable as trading income.

6.7 Trading stock

General

Unsold trading stock cannot be ignored when determining the net profits of a trade. To do so would be to reduce the size of those profits artificially, and thus encourage traders at their year's end to contract to buy excessive amounts of stock in order to depress profits even further, as on the earnings basis of accounting, bills invoiced but not paid may still be deducted in the computation of profits.

Accordingly, unsold trading stock is brought in as a *receipt* at the end of one accounting period and then again at the beginning of the next period as an *expense*.

Example
Fred has run a small shop for many years and draws up his accounts to 31 March each year. Extracts from one year's accounts are as follows:

Receipts	£	Expenditure	£
Sales	125,000	Opening stock	50,000
Closing stock	90,000	Rent and rates	10,000
		Wages	25,000
		Stock bought	100,000
	£215,000		£185,000
Profit:	£30,000		

The closing stock of £90,000 will become the opening stock of the following accounting period and will be brought in on the expenditure side of the accounts.

If the trading stock was not so treated, Fred's accounts would look like this:

Receipts	£	Expenditure	£
Sales	125,000	Rent and rates	10,000
		Wages	25,000
		Stock bought	100,000
	£125,000		£135,000

Making a loss of £10,000

Nevertheless, in bringing his stock into account, the trader may value each individual item of stock at its cost or its market value, whichever is the lower. Furthermore, he may pick and choose, bringing one in at cost and another at market value, if it is advantageous for him so to do: *IRC v Cock, Russell and Co Ltd* (1949) 29 TC 387.

'Market value' is usually taken to mean the best price available in the trader's selling market: thus, if a wholesaler, in the wholesale market; if a retailer, in the retail market. This supposedly is the result of *BSC Footwear Ltd v Ridgway* (1971) 47 TC 495. The ratio of that case was that while a trader might adopt a market value from a market in which he continued to trade in the item to be valued (whether by buying or selling), a retailer could not rely on a notional wholesale price of an item he would not buy again.

In addition, a trader may not take an item at cost, say, in the closing stock and at market value in the opening stock figure of the next accounting period. The closing stock figure of the earlier period must be taken as the opening stock figure of the later.

Work in progress

Work in progress has to be allocated a value on the profit side of the accounts of a manufacturer for the reason given above: that to ignore it would be to depress profits artificially. There are two methods of valuing work in progress: the 'direct cost' method and the 'on-cost' method. The direct cost method values the work in progress by reference to the costs attributable to the particular item – the costs of the parts used and of the wages of the person employed in making it – but leaves out of account overheads such as the rent of the factory, heating and lighting. The on-cost method attributes a proportion of these to the item as well.

The Revenue prefers the on-cost method, since it brings profits into charge more quickly, and argued in the House of Lords in *Duple Motor Bodies Ltd* v *Ostime* (1961) 39 TC 537 that it was the only correct method of valuation. The House refused to say that either method was invariably correct.

Valuation of stock and work in progress on the discontinuance of a trade

Section 100 ICTA 1988 provides that when a trade is permanently discontinued, any trading stock then belonging to the trade is to be brought into account as if it had been sold in the open market at the date of discontinuance. This is to prevent abuse of the rule that realisation of assets after the discontinuance of the trade does not per se constitute trading: *IRC* v *Nelson and Sons* (1939) 22 TC 716.

There are two exceptions to this:

1. when the stock is sold to a person who purchases it for use as his stock in trade. In this case, the tax take will be unaffected by a sale at an undervalue, since the stock will be brought into the new trader's accounts at the same undervalue: s100(1)(a);
2. when the discontinuance is caused by the death of an individual trader: s102(2).

Section 101 contains very similar provisions which apply when there is work in progress at the discontinuance of a profession or vocation and for accountancy reasons it is necessary to take a valuation of that work. This would be the case, for example, where the accounts had been drawn up on an earnings basis, but not if they had been drawn on a cash basis. The work in progress is valued at the price which would be paid for it on a transfer between persons at arm's length. Again, the exceptions to this are:

1. where it is sold to a person who will bring it in as work in progress of his profession or vocation; and
2. where discontinuance occurs as the result of the death of a single individual exercising a profession or vocation.

Section 770 ICTA 1988 and the rule in Sharkey v Wernher

A trader is entitled to sell his stock in trade on any terms he pleases, so long as he sells in the ordinary course of his business. The Revenue cannot force a trader to sell at the maximum possible profit, nor can he be taxed on profit foregone on a sale at an undervalue. There are, however, two exceptions to this:

Section 770

If the trader *sells* at an undervalue to an associated person, market value is substituted unless the purchaser will bring the cost in as revenue expenditure, in which case there will be no loss to the Exchequer. So s770(1) applies to sales by a United Kingdom trader to a foreign associate, and to sales by a United Kingdom trader to a United Kingdom non-trading associate. If the trader *buys* stock in trade at an overvalue from an associate, market value is substituted, unless the associate is itself a United Kingdom trader, when the overvalue will increase its chargeable profits. Section 770 will primarily apply to sales by a non-resident associate to a United Kingdom trader and is, therefore, principally an attempt to prevent profits improperly being diverted abroad and taxed at a lower rate. The section applies not only to sales but to matters such as the rate of interest charged on loans made between connected companies, and to the recharging of group management expenses between the individual companies in the group.

The matters arising under this section are referred to as 'transfer pricing'. Before adjustments can be made by the Inland Revenue under this section a formal direction has to be made by the Board of Inland Revenue under s770(d). A dispute arose under the *Glaxo* case (*Glaxo Group Ltd* v *IRC* [1996] STC 191) as to whether the Board of Inland Revenue's direction had to be given effect by an assessment raised specifically for that purpose. It was held that it was sufficient to adjust existing open assessments to increase the profits to be subjected to additional tax. In the *Glaxo* case assessments were open, and therefore not finalised, and covered a period of some 20 years. The unsuccessful argument was that the Inland Revenue was out of the normal six-year time limit for making adjustments under the transfer pricing provisions of s770.

The rule in *Sharkey* v *Wernher*

The rule is that where a trader disposes of part of his stock in trade otherwise than in the course of his trade, in particular for his own use, enjoyment or recreation, he must bring the market value of the stock so utilised as a trading receipt. The classic example is that of the restaurateur who provides the wedding breakfast for his daughter's wedding. The cost of wages, food and wine will have been brought in on one side of his accounts already, and some figure must be entered as a counterbalance. The House of Lords decided that that figure should include a profit element, and not merely offset the costs.

It is the amount of this profit element which is the important fact emerging from

Sharkey v Wernher [1956] AC 58. In some senses it is strange to find that a person is taxed on a theoretical profit made as it were from himself when it is accepted that, for example, no taxable profit can arise from activities carried on by members of a club among themselves, even in regard to the purchase and sale of goods. In this case the respective adjustments were made between two activities of Lady Wernher, one taxable within Schedule D and the other not so taxable. The carrying on of horse racing and training was not a business – although for value added tax purposes it has now been accepted as such in order to permit within the United Kingdom a reclamation of value added tax similar to that allowed in other European Union states. It is difficult to see, therefore, where the profit is or why it should be felt that there would otherwise be a loss of tax, although it can be argued that the Exchequer loses through the trader not putting that taxable profit into some other person's hand. However, the same principle is true of members drinking and eating in clubs at reduced prices as opposed to doing so in restaurants and bars.

Another facet of the case is that the adjustment made at cost accorded with current accounting principles. Contrast this with the cases of *Gallagher v Jones, Threlfall v Jones* [1993] STC 537 (discussed in section 6.8), which were founded on applying accountancy principles. However, the provisions of s82 and Schedule 12 FA 1997, in relation to finance lessors, continue a trend towards the adoption of acceptable accounting methods as a basis for assessment to tax. Similarly, the corporate loan relationships regime, discussed in Chapter 16, section 16.5, relies on the use of figures produced in the company accounts, as opposed to figures governed by tax statute, for the amounts to be taken into account each year.

Sharkey v *Wernher* has been considered in many later cases. The important glosses on the decision are:

1. That it does not apply to Schedule D Case II – professional men do not have stock in trade. See *Mason v Innes* [1967] Ch 1079 (Court of Appeal) where Hammond Innes transferred the copyright in *The Doomed Oasis* to his father shortly before the book was published, having deducted revenue expenditure in respect of it over the previous three years.
2. That if the asset transferred never became part of the trader's stock in trade, the rule cannot apply – *Petrotim Securities Ltd v Ayres* (1963) 41 TC 389. If *Petrotim* applies, of course, there is no need for *Sharkey* v *Wernher*, since no deductions will have been allowable in respect of the purchase.
3. If a trader obtains his opening stock on non-trading terms, the corollary of *Sharkey* v *Wernher* is that market value may be brought in as his 'opening costs'. If, however, the transaction under which he obtained his stock was not one susceptible to *Sharkey* v *Wernher* but part of a commercial deal, then it is the actual purchase price, if any, which must be used: see *Jacgilden (Weston Hall) Ltd v Castle* (1969) 45 TC 685.

6.8 Trading expenses: revenue and capital

Expenditure, to be deductible, must:

1. be revenue expenditure, not capital expenditure; and
2. satisfy the rules imposed by ss74 and 577 ICTA 1988.

If expenditure is capital in nature, the trader will have to rely on the much more limited system of capital allowances (see Chapter 7 below).

Capital and revenue expenditure

Over the years, the distinctions between capital and revenue expenditure have become less of a practical problem than in earlier years. Many of the leading cases were brought at a time prior to the introduction of capital gains tax when capital profits were not taxed, and therefore the recipient of the profit had a substantial interest in pursuing a claim for treatment on capital account. The decisions do however continue to provide the framework for determining the revenue or capital nature of expenditure. (See also 'trading receipts' at section 6.6 above.)

1. *Vallambrosa Rubber Co Ltd* v *Farmer* (1910) 5 TC 529 held that capital expenditure is a thing which is spent once and for all, and income expenditure is something which is going to recur every year.
2. *British Insulated and Helsby Cables Ltd* v *Atherton* (1925) 10 TC 155 pointed out that some single payments could still be revenue expenditure, 'but when an expenditure is made, not only once and for all, but with a view to bringing into existence an asset or an advantage for the enduring benefit of the trade' it is most likely to be a capital expense.
3. *Tucker* v *Granada Motorway Services Ltd* [1979] STC 393 (House of Lords) held that the nature of the payment was not to be judged by the subjective test of the intentions of those who actually made the payment, but by the nature and effect of the payment made, and the benefits the payer received in return – thus putting in doubt the words 'but with a view to' in the *British Insulated* case above. See also *Walker* v *Joint Credit Card Co Ltd* [1982] STC 427.
4. In *Lawson* v *Johnson Matthey plc* [1992] STC 466 Lord Goff stated:

    'It is important to observe that the payment does not become a revenue payment simply because the taxpayer company paid the money with the purpose of preserving its platinum trade from collapse ... The question is rather whether on a true analysis of the transaction, the payment is to be characterised as a payment of a capital nature. That characterisation does not depend upon the motive or purpose of the taxpayer.'

    Although the company argued that the payment was made to protect the business, it was held that it was actually made to conclude the sale of the subsidiary's shares to the Bank of England and was therefore a capital transaction. The Bank had declined to complete the rescue operation unless the parent company injected the payment to enable the company to meet its existing debts.

The primary forms of *revenue* expenditure incurred by a trader are, of course, the costs of purchasing raw materials or stock in trade, staff wages and the overheads of maintaining a building in which to carry on business. The cost of buying the building would be capital expenditure and thus not deductible.

Recent examples of the application of these principles are *Whitehead v Tubbs Elastic Ltd* [1984] STC 1, where a payment to secure the removal of various onerous conditions attached to a loan was held to be capital expenditure because it secured a clearly identifiable and enduring advantage which was itself capital in nature (because it enabled the company to utilise its capital assets in a way which would not otherwise have been possible), and *Bolton v International Drilling Ltd* [1983] STC 70, where a payment made by a company to obtain the release of a call option over one of its capital assets was also held to be capital:

> 'The payment was made to secure for IDC the income-earning potential [of the oilrig] for the period of its useful life [ten years] ... the payment was clearly a capital payment ... securing an enduring advantage.'

Similarly, in *Beauchamp v FW Woolworth plc* [1987] STC 279, Hoffmann J held that an exchange loss on a five-year Swiss franc loan was itself a capital loss since the loan was 'an accretion to the taxpayer company's capital and not merely a temporary accommodation.' This decision of Hoffmann J was upheld by the House of Lords in [1989] STC 510.

In the decision of the Privy Council in *Wharf Properties Ltd v CIR* [1997] STC 351, dealing with Hong Kong tax legislation, some of the dicta are potentially important in establishing the dividing line between capital and revenue expenditure and, as such, equally applicable in a UK tax context. Lord Hoffmann indicated that whether a payment constituted a capital or revenue expense depended on the purpose for which it was paid, and that the fact that the expense in question might take the form of recurring and periodic payments did not necessarily mean that it must be a revenue expense. It may be that the Revenue will in the future, on the basis of this decision, seek to enquire more closely into the deductibility of salaries or other recurrent payments where they can identify some underlying 'capital' purpose for which the payments are made. See Chapter 27, section 27.1, for further details.

What revenue expenditure is deductible?

As has already been said, revenue expenditure incurred for the purposes of a trade or business is generally deductible, income tax being levied under Cases I and II of Schedule D on profits, not on receipts. Section 74 ICTA 1988, however, lays down some general rules as to what is *not* deductible and also denies relief for certain specific items of expenditure.

The general rules
Section 74(a) provides that no sum shall be deducted in computing profits in respect of:

> 'any disbursements or expenses, not being money wholly and exclusively laid out or expended for the purposes of the trade, profession or vocation'.

The problem which has confronted the courts in respect of s74(a) is whether expenditure which has two consequences, only one of which is a benefit to the trade, satisfies the 'wholly and exclusively' requirement. A distinction can apparently be drawn between 'wholly' and 'exclusively': 'wholly' refers merely to quantum, 'exclusively' more to motive.

Example
Compare the two conditions in case where £20 is spent on petrol:

1. If half the petrol is used for business purposes, and half for private purposes, £10 may be deducted in the profit and loss account as the whole of that £10 was used exclusively for business purposes.
2. If the taxpayer uses the petrol to take him to Edinburgh where he both conducts business and has a holiday at the Festival, no part of the £20 may be deducted for tax purposes since none of the expenditure would be related exclusively to business: see *Bowden* v *Russell and Russell* (1965) 42 TC 301 (Chancery Division).

What is the position where expenditure is incurred solely for business purposes and yet offers an ancillary – perhaps even a personal – advantage? Reference must now be made to the decision of the House of Lords in *Mallalieu* v *Drummond* [1983] STC 665, which concerned expenditure incurred by a lady barrister on clothes for wear in court in compliance with guidelines laid down by the Bar Council. The taxpayer sought to deduct this expenditure when computing the profits of her profession because it had been necessitated by the requirements of her profession, and not by considerations of warmth and decency. Her claim was rejected by the House of Lords.

Lord Brightman said that the words in s74(a) meant that the expenditure had to be incurred 'to serve the purposes of the profession', in the sense of enabling a person to carry on and earn profits in the profession; the particular words did not refer to 'the purposes' of the taxpayer. Accordingly, the taxpayer's 'object' (or motive) in making the expenditure had to be discovered. If at the time it was incurred the expenditure was to serve two purposes, it was immaterial to the application of s74(a) that the business purpose predominated. The taxpayer's object in making the expenditure had to be distinguished from the effect of making the expenditure; that is to say, it could be made exclusively to serve the purposes of the business yet confer a private advantage. That did not necessarily preclude the exclusivity of the business purposes. It was inescapable that one object (albeit not a conscious motive) in making the expenditure was the provision of clothing that the taxpayer needed as a human being. His Lordship added:

'I reject the notion that the object of a taxpayer is inevitably limited to the particular conscious motive in mind at the moment of expenditure.'

The conscious motive was, of course, of vital significance.

See also *Watkis v Ashford, Sparkes and Harward* [1985] STC 451 where:

1. The cost of meals provided at partners' meetings was not deductible when computing partnership profits; but
2. The cost of the food, drink and accommodation at the Annual Conference was.

The expenditure on accommodation in (2), Nourse J said, was not to meet the needs of the partners as human beings as they all had homes where they could have spent the night; hence, the business purpose was the exclusive purpose and the private benefit purely incidental. The expenditure on food and drinks fell within the general Inland Revenue practice of usually allowing in full hotel bills if reasonable in amount where 'travelling occupations' were concerned.

A decision on s74(a) is *MacKinlay v Arthur Young McClelland Moores* [1990] 1 All ER 45. The partnership, which had some 100 partners (200 by the time of the hearing), offered removal grants to partners and employees who were required to relocate at the request of the firm. While no objection was raised by the Revenue to the deduction of payments made to the employees in the computation of partnership profits, the sums paid to the partners were disallowed. Although the taxpayers were unsuccessful before Vinelott J, their appeal to the Court of Appeal was upheld, but it was later reversed in the House of Lords, which held that there was a duality of purpose in the expenditure relating to the partners since it also related to the setting up of their private homes in addition to fulfilling the partnership needs of relocating the business.

Section 74(b) disallows:

'any disbursements of expenses of maintenance of the parties, their families or establishments, or any sums expended for any other domestic or private purposes distinct from the purposes of the trade, profession or vocation'.

Bowden v Russell and Russell (see above) would be an example of an expense also disallowable under s74(b). It is difficult, however, to imagine a case falling under s74(b) which does not also fall under s74(a) unless s74(b) uses an *objective* test – which, in any event, now seems partly true in the case of s74(a).

Specific items of expenditure

Travelling expenses. The cost of travelling on business is a deductible expense. A distinction must be drawn, however, between travelling *to* work which is not deductible – *Newsom v Robertson* (1952) 33 TC 452 (Court of Appeal) – and travelling *in the course of* one's work, which is. If one's home is also one's office, travelling from there on business will be deductible: *Horton v Young* (1971) 47 TC 60 (Court of Appeal).

Travelling from one place of business to another is generally deductible; it will not, though, be so if it takes place in the course of travelling from home to the second place of work, and the stop at the first office is no more than a break in the journey: *Sargent* v *Barnes* [1978] STC 322 (Chancery Division).

Rent: s74(c). Rent paid for business premises is deductible, even if they are temporarily unused. Only a proportion (generally not exceeding two-thirds of the rent) may be deducted if the premises are partly used for domestic purposes.

Prima facie, premiums paid for leases are non-deductible capital expenditure but s87 ICTA 1988 allows a trader to deduct a proportion of a premium which is taxable in the recipient's hands under Schedule A. The proportion which may be deducted during the currency of the lease (and so long as the premises remain business premises) is:

$$\frac{\text{chargeable slice of premium}}{\text{number of years of lease}}$$

Improvements and repairs: s74(d). A deduction is allowed in respect of the expense of repairs to business premises, provided that the expenditure is revenue, not capital, expenditure. Repairs are usually revenue, and improvements capital. Exceptionally, however, it has been decided that if a trader purchases a capital item at a low cost because of its state of disrepair, any repairs done to it to put it into shape are capital expenses and not deductible: *Law Shipping Co Ltd* v *IRC* (1924) 12 TC 621 (Court of Session). It is necessary to stress, however, that if the state of disrepair has *not* affected the price of the asset, the expense of putting it right is revenue expenditure – *Odeon Associated Cinemas* v *Jones* (1971) 48 TC 257 (Court of Appeal).

Damages. No loss can be deducted unless it is connected with or has arisen out of the trade, profession or vocation (s74(e)). This was taken to extremes in the case of *Strong & Co of Romsey Ltd* v *Woodfield* (1906) 5 TC 215 (House of Lords) where a brewery company sought to deduct the cost of damages which it had to pay in respect of injuries sustained by visitors at one of its public houses when the chimney fell in. The House of Lords held that it was not enough that the loss was remotely connected with the trade, but that this was too remote, falling upon the brewery company in their character as householders, rather than as traders. It is thought unlikely that the case would be decided the same way today.

Fines. Fines incurred by the trader for breaches of the law committed in the course of trading are not deductible: *Alexander von Glehn* v *IRC* (1920) 12 TC 232. In that case the fine was incurred by the taxpayer for inadvertently trading with the enemy in time of war. If such a fine is not deductible, it must follow that no fine can ever be.

Compensation payments. Payments made by a company to get rid of a director or an employee are deductible if the payments were made in the interest of the business: *Mitchell* v *BW Noble Ltd* (1927) 11 TC 372 (Court of Appeal).

Payments in excess of the statutory redundancy amounts, made to employees to secure the orderly run down of business prior to closure, were held to be for the purpose of the trade: *O'Keefe* v *Southport Printers Ltd* [1984] STC 443, and see ss90 and 579 ICTA 1988. Excessive 'golden handshakes' are sometimes also disallowed, not being wholly and exclusively for the purposes of the business.

For a case where a compensation payment was held to be capital expenditure, see *Whitehead* v *Tubbs Elastic Ltd* [1984] STC 1 (discussed above).

Bad debts: s74(j). Traders usually being taxed on an 'earnings' basis will probably pay tax on an unpaid invoice before it is discovered that the debt is bad. The trader is allowed, therefore, to deduct the amount of such debts as are found to be bad. When, however, a bad debt is unforeseeably paid off, it is treated as a receipt of the year of payment.

Interest: s74(n). Interest paid as a business expense is deductible when paid to a United Kingdom resident, but if interest is paid to a non-resident at more than a reasonable commercial rate it is disallowed and, for company payers, treated as a distribution on which ACT is chargeable – s209(2)(d) ICTA 1988. Section 82 requires that interest paid to non-residents must be paid after deduction of tax under s349 ICTA 1988 if it is to be deductible (see Chapter 14).

Interest paid by a company prior to 1 April 1996, however, was not deductible from profits but was treated as a charge on income. From that date, however, interest paid by a compnay is treated as a deduction in arriving at the profits: see Chapter 16, section 16.5 on 'Interest payments by companies'.

Pensions. Pensions, like wages, are deductible if it can be shown that the expenditure was incurred wholly and exclusively for the purposes of the business.

Business entertainment expenses/other miscellaneous expenditure. Section 577 contains the provisions denying any deduction of business entertainment expenses and disallowance of expenditure on which capital allowances might otherwise be due. Mixed sums paid to employees from which entertainment expenses and other expenses are paid are allowed in the trader's accounts, but the entertainment element is disallowed to the employee and therefore taxed upon him. Staff entertainment is allowed. Gifts costing more than £10 and all food, drink and tobacco items are disallowed under the provisions.

Sections 577A, 579, 588, 589, 589A and B contain provisions concerning the deductibility or denial of deduction for crime-related expenditure, redundancy, training and counselling services.

Pre-trading expenditure (s401 ICTA 1988). In addition to the expenditure rules governed by s74, s401 allows relief for expenditure incurred before the commencement of trading, and if the relevant expense would have been allowable if incurred during the conduct of the business it is allowable if incurred up to seven years before the commencement of trading. Relief is given by treating the expenditure as incurred on the first day of trading.

Class 4 National Insurance contributions. Prior to being repealed by s147(1) Finance Act 1996, with effect from 1996/97, s617(5) ICTA 1988 enabled individuals carrying on a trade, profession or vocation to obtain a measure of relief in respect of their graduated contributions. They could deduct one-half of any amount (as finally settled) when computing *total income* (that is to say, the amount is not deducted when computing Schedule D Case I and Case II profits).

When is revenue expenditure deductible for tax purposes? The application of accountancy principles

The matter of when expenditure incurred is deductible from taxable profits has been examined in the cases of *Gallagher v Jones, Threlfall v Jones* in the Court of Appeal ([1993] STC 537). The Court of Appeal overruled the conclusion reached in the High Court and held that expenditure should be deductible in the periods to which it would be allocated by acceptable accounting principles. In these cases, involving finance leases, there were clear accountancy principles laid down in the Statement of Standard Accounting Practices, SSAP 21 by the Accounting Standards Board. The taxpayers sought to deduct for tax purposes initial bulk payments which according to the SSAP should be spread over the rental periods to which they relate. The taxpayers had sought to rely on the decision in *Vallambrosa Rubber Co Ltd v Farmer* (1910) 5TC 529 (above) to deduct revenue expenditure when it was incurred, but the House of Lords rejected this approach, applying the dicta in *Odeon Associated Cinemas* v *Jones* (above). In the *Vallambrosa* case the Master of the Rolls, Sir Thomas Beeching, stated that the decision in favour of a deduction for expenditure in any one year (despite known lack of yield from the rubber trees for six years) did not lay down any general overriding principle.

This matter of the application of accountancy principles in the area of taxation was further explored before the courts in:

1. *Johnston* v *Britannia Airways Ltd* [1994] STC 763, where the decision supported the precept that sound accounting principles were better placed than judge-made rules to determine how items of expenditure were to be provided for – in this case by way of current provision for future engine overhauls.
2. *Vodafone Cellular Ltd* v *Shaw* [1997] STC 734, where it was held that expenditure to discharge an onerous trading agreement (which, following the decision in *Van den Berghs Ltd* v *Clark* [1935] AC 431; 19 TC 390, was a

revenue payment and receipt) was not for the benefit of the trade of the company meeting the payment (the payment having been paid for another company in the group) and therefore not deductible under s74 ICTA 1988 'for the purposes of the trade ...'.
3. *Stone & Temple Ltd* v *Waters* [1995] STC 1, where payment to protect investment was held to be on capital account.

It is important to reflect on the issues involved in the sequence of cases between *Southern Railway of Peru* v *Owen* [1957] AC 334 and the more recent *Gallagher, Vallambrosa Rubber* and *Britannia Airways* cases.

Southern Railway established the principle that no allowance could be made for tax purposes for any amount set aside in accounts (ie provisions) unless those amounts were sufficiently specific or accurate. Lord Radcliffe spoke in favour of accounting practices taking precedence over any judge-made rule for ascertaining the measure of profit for tax purposes.

In *Vallambrosa* no new ground was established, the issue being whether expenditure was properly deductible in any particular year. Hence it merely held that the expenditure was properly part of the expenditure to be deducted in arriving at the year's profits.

In *Gallagher* the decision was to give preference to accounting principles but only in circumstances where there were not two or more possible accounting practices.

In *Britannia Airways* there were several possible accounting methods of making provision in the accounts for the expense required to overhaul engines – either beginning immediately from when a new engine was installed (accruals basis), incurring the overhaul cost and writing it off over the succeeding flying miles during which it would be utilised, or deducting the full cost as and when incurred (ie in one sum in the year it arose). The latter was held not to provide a true basis for the statement of annual profits, and the Court of Appeal totally rejected the High Court approach which had supported this view. In the absence of any legal basis for supporting either of the remaining possibilities, the Court decided that the Special Commissioner had correctly held that proper and accepted accounting techniques were being adopted in applying the accruals basis.

Having said that, the Court really did not take the matter further than accepting that the facts had been properly decided upon by the Commissioners and that no error of law had occurred. It provided no real assistance for cases where optional accounting techniques could apply except to submit to further finding of facts by the Commissioners. However, subsequent legislation has seen the concept of applying acceptable accounting principles to determine the tax treatment in specific areas. Of particular relevance are the areas of foreign exchange gains and losses in FA 1993, interest and other receipts and payments from 'loan relationships' of companies in the FA 1996 (see Chapter 16, section 16.5). In addition, s82 and Schedule 12 FA 1997 deal with the treatment of payments under finance leases – in direct consequence of the issues raised in *Gallagher* v *Jones, Threlfall* v *Jones*.

6.9 1996–97 – Fundamental changes to the Schedule D basis of assessment (also applicable to new businesses 1994–95 onwards)

As will be explained in section 6.10, the rules for determining the amount to be assessed under Schedule D Cases I and II are particularly complex, especially as regards the opening and closing years of a business. From 1996–97, and for new businesses (from 6 April 1994 onwards) it has changed to a simple 'current year' basis. In any one year the profits taxed are the profits of the 12-month accounting period ending in that tax year, with no adjustment required in the opening and closing years other than the single amount of overlap relief (see example under 'Opening years' in section 6.10) and no double assessing or disregard of any period's results, which could happen under the prevailing system. The changes were required before the introduction of a new self-assessment system (see Chapter 24) as it was felt that the complex adjustments and calculations required would make the self-assessment system unworkable. Current year basis is being applied throughout Schedule D's Cases.

Sections 200–205 FA 1994 amend (in most cases from 1996–97 onwards) ss60–63 ICTA 1988 with regard to the previous year's profits being the normal basis of assessment under Schedule D Cases I and II, but for new businesses beginning from 6 April 1994 onwards the new provisions became effective immediately. From 1996–97 the previous year basis is discarded in favour of a current year basis, and the opening and closing years' adjustments of ss61–63 will no longer be required to the same extent. Under the new rules the opening and closing adjustments are much simplified. Where the accounting period is other than 31 March or 5 April new businesses will have an 'overlap' period where profits in at least part of the commencement year are also assessed in year two. Relief for this overlap profit is available on cessation of trade, on a change of accounting date, or when losses arise. For businesses affected by the transitional rules (see below) for 1997–98, the overlap is the profit of that part of the 1997 account period falling before 5 April: see the example in 'Opening years' in section 6.10.

Transitional provisions apply to avoid undue abnormalities either in favour of (through strategic planning) or against taxpayers, so the first year's assessment under the new rules is an average of the previous 24 months' profits ending in 1996–97 tax year. The following year, 1997–98, will be based on the profits of the year ending in 1997–98, and so on for future years. The basis period for the final year of assessment is the full period from the end of the penultimate year's basis period: see the example in 'Closing years' in section 6.10.

6.10 The basis of assessment (pre-FA 1994 changes)

The normal basis on which profits under Case I and Case II of Schedule D have historically been assessed is the preceding year basis, laid down by s60 ICTA 1988, under which the assessment for the current year was based on the profits of the accounting period ending in the preceding year of assessment.

Example
A trader makes up his accounts to 5 May each year, and has done so for many years. For the year of assessment 1994–95, he will be charged on the profits arising in his accounting period ending in the preceding year of assessment, 1993–94, in other words on the profits arising in the period from 6 May 1992 to 5 May 1993.

Opening and closing years

The preceding year basis is unavailable in the opening and closing years of a trade. There are, therefore, special rules applicable in these cases.

Opening years
Assessments made on a new business are as follows:

First year: s61(1). The assessment is on the actual profits arising from the date of commencement to the following 5 April. In practice, the profits of the first accounting period will be apportioned:

John starts trading on 6 May 1991 and has profits in his first accounting period, to 5 May 1992, of £7,200. His first year of assessment is, of course, 1991–92, and 6 May 1991 – 5 April 1992 is a period of 11 months. He will be assessed on:

$$\frac{11}{12} \times £7{,}200 = £6{,}600$$

Second year: s61(3). For the second year of trading a person is charged on the profits of his first 12 months. This will normally be the profits of his first accounting period. So with John, above, the assessment for his second year, 1992–93, will be £7,200.

Third year: s60. In the third year of assessment of trade, the taxpayer is assessed on the usual preceding year basis (see above). In John's case, for 1993–94 he will be taxed on the profits of the accounting period ending in 1992–93, ie on 5 May 1992, so that will again be on the first accounting period's profits of £7,200.

This system of assessment is highly beneficial when profits keep rising. If, however, this is not the case and, after a good first year, profits fall, it will be possible for the trader to elect for a special basis of assessment for the two years following the year of commencement, ie years two and three (s62). The election has the effect of bringing into assessment in each year the actual profits of that year. Such an election must be made in respect of both years and cannot be for one year only. Notice is given in writing to the Inspector of Taxes at any time within seven years after the end of the second year of assessment, and may be revoked at any time within six years after the end of the third year of assessment. So a provisional claim can be made after the end of year two, and revoked, if necessary, after the end of year three.

To continue with John, whose profits are:

		£
Year 1:	To 5 May 1992:	7,200
Year 2:	To 5 May 1993:	4,800
Year 3:	To 5 May 1994:	12,000

His profits on the usual basis have already been described. Tabulated in full, they run:

1991–92:	s61(1) actual basis $\frac{11}{12}$ x £7,200	=	£6,600
1992–93:	s61(3): first 12 months	=	£7,200
1993–94:	s60(1): preceding year basis	=	£7,200
1994–95:	s60(1): preceding year basis	=	£4,800
1995–96:	s60(1): preceding year basis	=	£12,000

On the special basis, they would run:

1991–92:   s61(1) actual basis: $\frac{11}{12}$ x £7,200 = £6,600

(this is never affected)

1992–93:   s62(1): actual basis: $\frac{1}{12}$x £7,200 + $\frac{11}{12}$ x £4,800
= £600 + £4,400   =   £5,000

1993–94:   s62(1): actual basis: $\frac{1}{12}$x £4,800 + $\frac{11}{12}$ x £12,000
= £400 + £11,000   =   £11,400

1994–95:   s60(1): preceding year basis: =   £4,800
1995–96:   s60(1): preceding year basis: =   £12,000

In this example, on the normal basis John would be assessed on:

£6,600 + £7,200 + £7,200 = £21,000

and on the special basis would be assessed on:

£6,600 + £5,000 + £11,400 = £23,000

so the normal basis would be more beneficial. This is because of the substantial rise in profits in year three. Accordingly, John might well have elected for s62 treatment at the end of year two only to have to revoke it by the end of year three.

Example (under the 'new business' rules from 1994)

Assume profits as in the first example in the above paragraph for a business commencing 6 May 1994:

		£
Year 1	ending 5 May 1995	7,200
Year 2	ending 5 May 1996	4,800
Year 3	ending 5 May 1997	12,000

Assessments would be as follows:

1994–95	$\frac{11}{12}$ × £7,200	£6,600
1995–96	12 months in year	£7,200
1996–97	12 months in year	£4,800
1997–98	12 months in year	£12,000

There is no subsequent adjustment to actual basis for the second and third years under s61(1) and the overlap profit amounts to £6,600, being the profits taken into account twice from the first accounting period.

Closing years (old rules)

When a business is permanently discontinued, the basis of assessment under the old rules is:

1. final year: the actual profits from 6 April until the date of discontinuance: s63(1)(a);
2. penultimate year: preceding year basis: s60(1);
3. ante-penultimate year: preceding year basis: s60(1).

The Revenue may, however, by s63(1)(b), reassess the penultimate and ante-penultimate years on an actual basis, if to do so would bring more profits into charge to tax. As with the taxpayer's election under s62, the Revenue must apply the election to *both* years.

In the case of *Baylis* v *Roberts* [1989] STC 693 the taxpayer and his wife, on ceasing business, were taxed by the Revenue under the forerunner of s63(1) on a current year basis. The taxpayer argued that the words in s63(1), viz 'he may be charged', conferred a discretion on the inspector of taxes as to whether to make additional assessments, and that the inspector had failed to exercise that discretion. The court found against the taxpayer by holding that s63(1), properly construed, did not confer any discretion on the inspector. He is required by s63(1) to tax the penultimate and ante-penultimate years on a current year basis if it would increase the tax yield.

Example

Walter makes up his accounts each year to 5 July. He ceases to trade on 5 October 1994. His profits for the past few years were as follows:

	£
Year ending 5 July 1991:	18,000
Year ending 5 July 1992:	21,000
Year ending 5 July 1993:	15,000
Year ending 5 July 1994:	30,000
6 July 1994 – 5 October 1994:	4,800

On the normal basis, his assessments will be:

Final year: 1994–95 – s63(1)(a): profits from 6 April 1994 to 5 October 1994:

$= \frac{3}{12} \times £30,000 + £4,800$ = £12,300

Penultimate year: 1993–94: s60: preceding year basis:

= £21,000

Ante-penultimate year: 1992–93: s60: preceding year basis:

= £18,000

The Revenue will, however, make a reassessment if the profits brought into charge will be greater by using s63(1)(b):

Final year: 1994–95: the same = £12,300

Penultimate year: 1993–94: s63(1)(b): actual basis:

$\frac{9}{12} \times £30,000 + \frac{3}{12} \times £15,000$ = £26,250

Ante-penultimate year: 1992–93: s63(1)(b): actual basis:

$\frac{9}{12} \times £15,000 \times \frac{3}{12} \times £21,000$ = £16,500

The total profits brought into charge in the two preceding years on each basis are, therefore:

Normal s60 basis: £21,000 + £18,000 = £39,000
Special s63(1)(b) basis: £26,250 + £16,500 = £42,750

The Revenue will, therefore, make use of s63(1)(b) to reassess.

Example (under the 'current year' basis applicable from 1996–97)

Assuming the results of the business in the above example relate to a business ceasing to trade on 31 October 1999 with identical profits as stated but for years ending 1996 to 1999 respectively, the assessments would become:

Final year: 1999–2000:
profits from 6 July 1998 to 5 Oct 1999:

Year to 5 July 1999	=	£30,000
6 July to 5 Oct 1999	=	£4,800
TOTAL ASSESSMENT	=	£34,800 (less any overlap relief brought forward)

Penultimate year: 1998–99:
Year to 5 July 1998 = £15,000

Ante-penultimate year: 1997–98:
Year to 5 July 1997 = £21,000

Change of ownership

Section 63 applies where a trade has actually been discontinued. Another consequence of discontinuance of the trade is that ss100–102 ICTA 1988 relating to the accounting treatment of stock in trade and work in progress will apply. Section 113(1) ICTA 1988 generates the same consequences, though, when there is a change in the persons carrying on a trade by deeming there to be a permanent discontinuance of the trade in those circumstances. For a discussion on the circumstances in which this deemed discontinuance can be avoided see Chapter 10, section 10.3).

Section 113 can, however, have consequences for the purchaser too. The purchaser may already have been carrying on a similar business to that of the vendor. If there is no succession to the trade of the vendor, but merely a purchase of the assets of the business, profits for these assets will be assessed, together with the purchaser's other profits, on a continuing preceding year basis. If, however, s113 applies, because the purchaser is considered to have succeeded to the vendor's business (which is a question of fact), the deemed discontinuance will mean that s61 – the assessment provisions relating to the opening years – will apply to the profits from the purchased business, while the purchaser's other profits will be assessed under s60. Of course, if the purchaser had no other business, s61 would apply anyway.

6.11 Losses

Note: unless otherwise stated the following text does not reflect the changes in loss relief which apply under the new current year basis of assessment applicable from 6 April 1996 to existing businesses and to new businesses set up after 6 April 1994 (see section 6.12).

A loss arises in a trade where trading receipts are exceeded by trading expenditure. When this occurs in a business which has been carried on for some years, there will be a nil assessment in the year of assessment in which the accounting period in question ended: s60.

There are several other forms of relief available in respect of the loss. The losses may be:

1. set off against other income of the year of assessment or of the last preceding year (s380(1)(a) and (b) respectively);
2. carried forward to set off against future profits from the same trade (s385);
3. carried back and set off against the profits of the three years of assessment preceding that of discontinuance (s388), if the loss occurs in the twelve months preceding the discontinuance of the trade;
4. carried forward and set off against the income derived from shares in a company to which the trade has been transferred in return for such shares (s386).
5. carried back and set off against other income if incurred in the first four years of assessment in which the trade is carried on (s381);
6. set off against the trader's capital gains (s64 FA 1991);
7. restricted if they are farming and market gardening losses (s397).

Losses under s380

Where any person sustains a loss in any trade, profession, employment or vocation, he may make a claim for relief from income tax on any of his income up to the amount of the loss. Any unrelieved loss may be carried forward under s385 or s386. He may also set it off against the income of the last preceding year of assessment (s380(1)(b)). However, he cannot claim relief for part only of the loss under s380.

In *Butt v Haxby* [1983] STC 239, the trader tried to get the best of both worlds by setting off only part of a trading loss under s380 (thereby seeking to make use of his personal allowances in respect of the rest of his profits and saving the loss for future years – or, in this case, past years) and the rest under s381. Vinelott J held that nothing in s381 allowed s380 to be limited to part of a loss; s380 alone applied, therefore, and the taxpayer's income of the year in question entirely absorbed the loss, to the disadvantage of the taxpayer. The rule thus is that one may choose which reliefs one wishes to apply, and, between s380 and s381, in which order one wishes them to be applied, but one is not allowed to make partial use of a relief.

Section 384 further provides that no relief is available under s380 unless it can be shown that, in the year in which the loss was sustained, the trade was being carried on on a commercial basis with a view to the realisation of profits. This prevents the 'hobby trader' from obtaining loss relief in respect of his hobby year after year.

Section 397 is even harsher where farming and market gardening are concerned; no loss relief is available under s80 in respect of either type of trade if losses have been sustained in the trade in each of the prior five years.

By s117 ICTA 1988 the relief given by s380 has also been restricted in its application to losses incurred by limited partners. Hitherto, limited partners could relieve trading losses in full under s380, but they are now restricted to an amount equal to the capital contributed (that is to say, the capital risked) to the partnership.

This reverses the decision of the Court of Appeal in *Reed* v *Young* [1986] STC 285. Nevertheless, losses accruing to limited partners may, without limit, be carried forward under s385 and set against future trading profits.

Section 401 ICTA 1988 allows relief for expenditure incurred before the commencement of trading, and if the relevant expense would have been allowable if incurred during the conduct of the business it is allowable if incurred up to seven years before the commencement of trading. Relief is given by treating the expenditure as a loss under s380 ICTA 1988 for the first year of trading.

Relief under s385

If losses cannot be set off completely under s380 they may indefinitely be carried forward and set off against *profits of the same trade* in subsequent years of assessment: see the case of *Rolls Royce Motors Ltd v Bamford* [1976] STC 162; (1951) TC 319 where heavy losses incurred in the aero engine divisions of the company could not be set off against the reconstructed motor vehicles activities, which had been carried on both before and then simultaneously with the aero engine activities. It was held that although the combined activities of these and other divisions were carried on as one trade, 'that trade' – as s385 denotes – was not the same one being carried on in the years when the company sought to claim the loss relief.

Special relief under s387

Where a person makes an annual payment taxable under s349 ICTA 1988 as being paid out of capital – there being insufficient profits out of which to pay it – and the payment was made wholly and exclusively for the purposes of his trade, s387 allows him to treat the gross sum as a loss incurred in the trade, and to carry it forward under s385 or s386. The provision is necessary since, being a charge on income, the payment cannot be deducted in computing profits, but only in calculating the charge to tax; accordingly, it would not, without more, be treated as a loss.

Relief under s388

When a trade is discontinued, losses sustained in the last 12 months of the trade can be set off against the profits (if any) made in the business in the three years of assessment preceding the year of assessment in which the discontinuance occurs. The losses are set off against the profits of the most recent year first, and so on backwards. This reduces the amount of interest, or 'repayment supplement' as it is called, that the Revenue has to pay on the returned tax.

Relief under s386

Very often an individual who has been trading for some years decides to convert his business into a close company. This is done by exchanging the business for shares in the company and amounts to the cessation of the trade by the businessman and the commencement of a new trade by the company. If there are unrelieved losses in the previous trade these would, without more, remain unrelieved, since s385 (and, indeed, s380) only allow losses to be set off where the individual continues to carry on the trade.

To avoid this anomaly, s386 allows *the individual* to set off past trading losses from the business transferred *against income he derives from the company* (whether in the form of dividend, salary or otherwise) subject to the following conditions:

1. The consideration for the transfer must have been wholly or mainly the allotment of shares in the company.
2. The taxpayer must have remained the beneficial owner of the shares acquired on incorporation throughout the year of assessment to which the claim relates. In practice, the Revenue concedes relief where the taxpayer retains at least 80 per cent of the shares.
3. Tthe company must have carried on the business transferred throughout that year.

The loss must be set first against earned, and only then against unearned, income.
Note: it is *not* the company which obtains the benefit of the losses.

Relief for losses in the early years

Section 381 provides an extension of relief for individuals who incur losses in their first years of entering a trade or profession as a proprietor or partner. The relief is available in respect of losses sustained in any of the first four years of assessment in which the individual carries on the trade. The relief is given by allowing the individual to deduct the loss from his general income arising in the three years of assessment preceding that in which the loss is sustained, and is set against the earliest year first. As with s380, the relief is only available if the trade is carried on on a commercial basis with a view to the realisation of profit.

Set-off of trading losses against capital gains

Under s72 FA 1991, where a person has trading losses and has made a claim for a year of assessment for relief under s380 he may elect to have an amount, 'the relevant amount', set off against his liability to capital gains tax for the year. The 'relevant amount' is so much of the trading loss which cannot be set against the claimant's income for the year and which has not already been taken into account for the purpose of giving relief for any other year.

The amount which may be treated as an allowable loss for capital gains tax purposes is restricted to the amount on which the claimant would ordinarily be chargeable to capital gains tax, ie the extent of his gains. Making such a claim has the effect of using the losses in preference to the annual exemption for capital gains and before personal reliefs.

Farming and market gardening losses

Section 397 ICTA 1988 sets out the conditions under which relief for farming and market gardening losses incurred by both individuals and companies is granted (see Chapter 16, section 16.6).

6.12 Losses under the new Schedule D current year basis of assessment

Section 380 ICTA 1988

Relief for trading losses against general taxable income is available against the income of the year of the loss or of the previous tax year, even if the trade was not carried on in that previous year (see s380(1)(a) and (b)). As before, no partial claims are permitted. The claim of a current year is given in priority to a claim carried back.

Section 381 ICTA 1988

The carry-back for losses of the first four years against income of the previous three years will now be the loss for the basis period ending in the year and not of the actual tax year. Where relief has been given for part of the basis period due to the overlap in the first year, then the second period's loss is reduced by the amount of that loss to avoid double relief.

Section 385 ICTA 1988

The carry-forward provisions for relief against future profits of the same trade remain unchanged.

Section 388 ICTA 1988

Terminal loss relief for the last 12 months' deficit against the same business's profits of the preceding three years continues, but with relief also now available in the exceptional circumstances where profits are assessable in the final year.

Section 72 FA 1971

This relief continues, with relief against chargeable gains of the year, in addition to total income, for s380 losses.

Sections 386 and 387 ICTA 1988

Carry-forward reliefs under s386 and s387 ICTA 1988 continue unchanged. For partnership losses see Chapter 10.

6.13 Post-cessation receipts

For income tax to be chargeable there has to be a *source* from which that income arose which is still in existence. Where profits are chargeable under Schedule D Case I or II, that source will be the trade or profession. Accordingly, the rule used to be that once the taxpayer had discontinued his business, any sums he thereafter received escaped tax. This did not cause substantial loss to the Treasury where the taxpayer's profits were computed on an 'earnings' basis, since most post-cessation receipts would already have been taxed in the year they were earned. The exceptions would have been:

1. sums not due before discontinuance;
2. sums not ascertained before discontinuance; and
3. bad debts found to be good after discontinuance.

This was not the case where the profits were computed on some other basis, such as the 'cash' basis. Members of the Bar nearing the end of their careers would leave enormous sums of money outstanding, to be received tax-free after, say, their appointment to the Bench. The 'cash' basis is but one form of 'conventional basis' – so called because it is available by convention.

Nowadays, ss103 and 104 ICTA 1988 bring into charge these otherwise untaxed receipts – usually under Schedule D Case VI. Section 103 catches the following situations:

1. where the profits were before discontinuance computed on an earnings basis, all sums not brought into account before discontinuance.
2. where profits were computed on a conventional basis, all sums not brought into charge *other* than those which would already have been brought into account had they been computed on a earnings basis.

Thus s103 catches those sums which were not due or ascertained before discontinuance and bad debts satisfied after cessation. It does not catch, on a bills delivered basis of accounting, sums which were invoiced but not paid prior to discontinuance. These are, instead, now caught by s104.

Any sums which are chargeable as post-cessation receipts are assessable under Case VI in the year of assessment of receipt and are treated as earned income, if they would have been such if received prior to cessation. It is possible to elect, however, to treat these sums as Case I or Case II income, arising at the date of discontinuance, if they are received within six years of cessation. One might wish to treat a post-cessation receipt as Case I or II income arising at the date of discontinuance if doing so means that a lower rate of tax will be applicable to such income, either because one's total income for that year was lower or because tax rates have risen in the intervening period.

7

Capital Allowances

7.1 Introduction

7.2 Allowances on plant and machinery: CAA 1990

7.3 Allowances on security assets

7.4 Allowances on expenditure on stands at sports grounds

7.5 Industrial buildings allowances

7.1 Introduction

It has been explained in Chapter 6, section 6.8, that only revenue expenditure can be deducted in computing profits. As a result a system of capital allowances was created by the legislature so that expenses incurred in the acquisition of a capital asset could be deductible when determining one's trading profits. It should be noted that only certain types of capital expenditure qualify for allowances, and the size of the allowance depends on the type of capital expenditure incurred.

The present system of capital allowances originated with the Income Tax Act 1945; the legislation was consolidated in the Capital Allowances Act 1968 and added to, inter alia, by the Taxes Act 1970, the Finance Act 1971 and the Finance Act 1972. Important changes in the system were made by the Finance Acts of 1984 and 1985. In particular, FA 1984 introduced a phased withdrawal of first year allowances and initial allowances for both plant and machinery and industrial buildings. The capital allowances legislation has now been consolidated into the Capital Allowances Act 1990.

7.2 Allowances on plant and machinery: CAA 1990

There are two entirely separate questions to be asked:

1. What are 'plant' and 'machinery'?
2. What is the system of allowance available?

'Plant'

There is no statutory definition of 'plant', but following s117 FA 1994 a new Schedule AA1 was introduced into CAA 1990 which excludes from the definition of 'plant' land, buildings and fixed structures, other than those items which case law decisions have already held to be plant. Those items are listed in the new schedule and will continue to qualify. Similarly items for which specific statutory provision is made (eg expenditure on safety at football grounds) will continue to qualify. For the most part, therefore, one has to look to decided cases for the meaning of 'plant' and 'machinery'.

The classic definition of 'plant' is to be found in *Yarmouth* v *France* (1887) 19 QBD 647 (Divisional Court):

> '... in its ordinary sense, it includes whatever apparatus is used by a business man, for carrying on his business – not his stock in trade which he buys or makes for sale; but all goods and chattels, fixed or moveable, live or dead, which he keeps for permanent employment in his trade.'

In *Hampton* v *Fortes Autogrill Ltd* [1980] STC 80 (Chancery Division), Fox J said that, in determining whether something is plant, the test is a *functional* test – does the item perform a function in the actual carrying out of the trade? In *Munby* v *Furlong* (1977) 50 TC 491 (Court of Appeal) a barrister's books were held to be plant. In *Cooke* v *Beach Station Caravans Ltd* (1974) 49 TC 514 (Chancery Division) a swimming pool at a holiday camp was held to be plant; the business of the trader was to provide amenities to holiday-makers, and the swimming pool performed a positive function in this. Most difficulty has been encountered in trying to decide whether a building can be plant. Here, before the introduction of s117 FA 1994 mentioned above, one had to ask whether the building performed the function of plant or was merely part of the setting in which the trade was carried on. A dry dock was held to be plant in *IRC* v *Barclay, Curle and Co Ltd* (1969) 45 TC 221 (House of Lords), and in *Schofield* v *R and H Hall Ltd* (1974) 49 TC 538 a grain silo was held to be plant in a trade of grain importing because the silo did much more than merely hold the grain. In *Thomas* v *Reynolds* [1987] STC 135 a partnership of professional tennis coaches was denied allowances in respect of an inflatable cover which housed two hard courts and enabled the courts to be used during the winter, as this was merely a passive 'setting' in which the business was carried on. A similar decision was reached in *Gray* v *Seymours Garden Centre* [1995] STC 706 where a planetarium was held by the Commissioners to be no more than part of the setting for selling plants, despite having some environmental attributes necessary to keep the plants in a saleable condition. The Court of Appeal upheld this approach, referring to Fox LJ's statement that:

> '... the fact that a building in which a business is carried on is, by its construction, particularly well-suited to the business, or indeed was specially built for that purpose, does not make it plant.'

The decision in *Gray* v *Seymours Garden Centre* was applied in *Attwood* v *Anduff Car Wash Ltd* [1996] STC 110, in which the company claimed capital allowances for car wash halls on a number of sites laid out to a specific design system under which four vehicles could be treated at any one time. It was held that the buildings provided only a housing for the car wash cleaning machinery and control equipment and that they were therefore not plant.

If the taxpayers in either *Thomas* v *Reynolds* or *Gray* v *Seymours Garden Centre* had also provided evidence that the cover created an atmosphere peculiarly suitable for playing tennis or actually growing the plants, the decision might well have been otherwise. Such was the approach adopted by the House of Lords in *IRC* v *Scottish & Newcastle Breweries* [1982] STC 296 where expenditure incurred on electric light fittings, wall plaques, tapestries, murals and sculptures by a taxpayer company which operated hotels attracted capital allowances. The House of Lords agreed that such expenditure was necessary to create a certain atmosphere which was a function of the hotel trade, and consequently such expenditure should attract capital allowances. Note also *Wimpey International Ltd* v *Warland*; *Associated Restaurants Ltd* v *Warland* [1989] STC 273, and *Carr* v *Sayer* [1992] STC 396.

Following FA (No 2) 1992 computer software was recognised as machinery or plant, under a new s67A CAA 1990. The new Schedule AA1 introduced into CAA 1990 by s117 FA 1994, which excludes land, buildings and fixed structures from the definition of 'plant', does not affect existing qualifying items decided by case law or provided for by statute.

In *Bradley* v *London Electricity plc* [1996] STC 1054, reversing the finding of the Special Commissioner, the High Court held that the structure of a substation did not perform any 'plant like' functions and that the expenditure relating to its construction did not qualify for capital allowances under the provisions relating to machinery and plant. See Chapter 27, section 27.2, for further details.

The available allowances

First year allowances used to be available as a capital allowance on plant and machinery purchased after 26 October 1970 and before 1 April 1986, but these allowances were abolished from 1 April 1986, save for expenditure incurred before 1 April 1987. However, as a temporary measure, first year capital allowances at a rate of 40 per cent were reintroduced for expenditure between 1 November 1992 and 31 October 1993 only. The first year allowance was in place of the writing down allowance of 25 per cent, the remaining balance being written off at 25 per cent in the normal way. No further relaxation of the first year allowance has since been made.

The basic capital allowance is a writing down allowance (WDA) which constitutes a depreciating allowance of 25 per cent of the qualifying expenditure attributable to the plant and/or machinery purchased wholly and exclusively for the purpose of the trade, such allowances being claimed against the profits of the basis period (s160 CAA 1990). Thus for those taxpayers who pay income tax the basis period is the year of assessment, and for those who pay corporation tax the basis period is the accounting period (s161 CAA 1990).

Note: s102 and Schedule 13 FA 1990 set out new rules for claims by companies to capital allowances in respect of accounting periods ending after the commencement of the pay and file scheme for assessing and collecting corporation tax.

Claimants and conditions

The allowances are available to traders (s24 CAA 1990), professions, vocations and employments (s27 CAA 1990), landlords (s32 ICTA 1988) and lessors of furnished holiday lettings (s29 CAA 1990), on capital expenditure for machinery or plant incurred wholly and exclusively for the purpose of the trade and in consequence of which expenditure the machinery or plant 'belongs' to the trader (s24(1)(b) CAA 1990).

'Belonging' requirement: s24(1)(b) CAA 1990

The 'belonging' requirement was at the centre of *Stokes* v *Costain Property Investments Ltd* [1984] STC 204, which concerned items (inter alia, lifts and central heating) that were acknowledged to be machinery or plant but became part of a building in which the claimant developer had a lease interest. Since they had become landlord's fixtures under land law, they no longer belonged to the developer, and therefore the test of s24(1) was not satisfied. This decision led to the provisions of ss51–59 CAA 1990 under which fixtures can be treated as belonging to a person other than the landlord. Where this involves leasing, one has to distinguish between the leasing of fixtures or plant as a distinct matter from the leasing of the land or building. Only where they can be separated can the landlord's fixtures problem be overcome.

In *Melluish* v *BMI (No 3)* [1995] STC 964 the need for items to 'belong' to the claimant for capital allowances purposes was again examined. Leased assets in homes owned by the local authority were held to be fixtures of the building and did not continue to belong to the lessor. The homes were let to council tenants, with the effect that there was no right of possession for the claimant company. See below re revised provisions regarding fixtures leasing following this decision.

Capital allowances on fixtures and fixtures leasing

Capital allowances on fixtures

The Finance Act 1997 provisions were originally announced in a press release on 24 July 1996 and deal with the entitlement to capital allowances where a building is purchased with fixtures already installed. Part of the proposals will allow the purchaser and seller to agree an apportionment for the purpose of their respective tax assessments, without involving the Inland Revenue in the process. This will apply only where the seller has been claiming capital allowances. The rules will also provide that a purchaser of a building in which fixtures are already installed cannot claim capital allowances on the fixtures on a higher amount than the price at which those fixtures were treated as sold for capital allowance purposes by the last previous owner of the building to claim allowances on the fixtures (whether that person is the purchaser's immediate vendor or not). Since the sale price (or 'disposal value') of such previous owner for capital allowance purposes cannot normally exceed the cost to him of the fixtures, this will mean that a purchaser's allowances will be 'capped' by reference to the cost of the fixtures to the last previous owner of the building to claim allowances.

Fixtures leasing
The intention to introduce provisions (now reflected in s86 and Schedule 16 FA 1997), which amend and augment the existing provisions of ss51 to 59 CAA 1990, was announced in a press release on 24 July 1996. These provisions change the law so as to ensure that equipment lessors will no longer be able to obtain capital allowances where they lease 'fixtures' to non-taxpaying lessees such as local authorities as in the *BMI (No 3)* case (above). The legislation will operate to reverse in part the House of Lords' decision in the case which confirmed that, under the existing law, equipment lessors may obtain allowances where they lease fixtures to tax-exempt lessees just as much as where their lessees are taxpayers. In both cases it was possible to make an election under s53 CAA 1990 to treat the fixtures as 'belonging' to the lessor and thereby to ensure that the lessor is entitled to allowances. Under the new legislation it will no longer be possible for an equipment lessor to make a s53 election unless the final lessee uses the fixtures for the purposes of a trade, or for a non-trading leasing activity, is subject to UK tax on the profits of that trade or other activity, and would have obtained capital allowances itself had it incurred the capital expenditure on the fixtures. This new rule applies to any fixture on which all the lessor's expenditure was incurred on or after 24 July 1996.

Method of giving allowances

Allowances for income tax purposes (but not for corporation tax purposes) have historically been given as a *deduction from the profits* assessed, as opposed to being a deduction *in calculating the actual profits themselves*. Section 211 FA 1994 changed the basis on which relief for capital allowances for income tax purposes is given, in most cases from 1997–98 onwards, with the introduction of a new s140 CAA 1990. New businesses starting from 6 April 1994 were affected immediately. Allowances cease to be given as a deduction from the income or profit being taxed (formerly under s140(2) CAA 1990) but become an expense taken like any other trading expense, to be deducted in calculating the actual amount of income or profit assessable. Balancing charges are now treated as trading receipts.

Example
X, a trader, purchased an asset in year one which cost £2,000. The asset attracted capital allowances and so:

In year one its capital allowance = 25 per cent of £2,000 = £500.
In year two X's capital allowance = 25 per cent of £(2,000 – 500) = £375.
In year three X's capital allowance = 25 per cent of £ (1,500 – 375) = £281.25 etc.

Generally ss24–25 CAA 1990 give WDAs by reference to a 'pool' of qualifying expenditure. Thus all plant and machinery used in the trade is placed in one pool and the WDA is applied to the value of the pool. The qualifying expenditure of the 'pool' alters as items of plant and machinery are bought and sold. When an asset is purchased it joins the 'pool' and the price paid for the asset is added to the qualifying expenditure of the pool. When an asset in the pool is sold the price received for the asset is subtracted from the qualifying expenditure of the pool. This is called the 'balancing adjustment', although it should be noted that if the consideration received for the asset on sale exceeds its acquisition cost the 'profit' made on sale becomes subject to capital gains tax.

Example
Mary, a trader, makes up her accounts to 31 December each year. She purchased asset one in 1997 for £5,000 and purchased asset two in 1998 for £2,000, and she sold asset one in 1999 for £2,500.

	£
Assessment year 1997/98	POOL
Purchase asset 1	5,000.00
WDA 25% of £5,000	(1,250.00)
Qualifying expenditure on 6.4.98	3,750.00
Assessment year 1998/99	
Qualifying expenditure on 6.4.98	3,750.00
Purchase asset 2	2,000.00
	5,750.00
WDA 25% of £5750	(1,437.50)
Qualifying expenditure on 6.4.99	4,312.50
Assessment year 1999/2000	
Qualifying expenditure on 6.4.99	4,312.50
Sale of asset 1	(2,500.00)
	1,812.50
WDA 25% of £1,812.50	(453.13)
Qualifying expenditure on 6.4.2000	1,359.38

However, certain assets do not fall within the general pool – they are pooled separately.

Basis period

As illustrated in the example above, the basis on which capital allowances are claimed is according to the additions or the sales made in the accounting period which forms the basis of assessment for the income tax year in question.

Short life assets – ss37–38 CAA 1990

For assets acquired after 31 March 1986 a taxpayer can elect within two years of acquiring the asset for that asset – short life asset – not to be placed within the general pool of assets. Such election tends not to be available for assets with a working life of less than five years. For a list of the specific assets to which this 'short life asset' election cannot apply see s38 CAA 1990. Examples of such assets in s38 include ships, motor cars, certain leased items, etc.

The main advantage of not putting these 'short life' assets into the general pool is that if the asset is disposed of within a short period the disposal will trigger an immediate balancing allowance or charge instead of simply altering the overall qualifying expenditure of the general pool.

Long life assets

Finance Act 1997 Schedule 14 inserts new ss38A to 38H into CAA 1990, providing for the reduction in machinery and plant capital allowances on businesses incurring major expenditure on long life assets. Long life assets are those with a useful economic life expectancy of 25 years or more – s38A(2)(a). The provisions apply only to those businesses which incur expenditure of £100,000 or more on long life assets in any accounting period – s38D. The provisions exclude expenditure relating to machinery or plant installed as fixtures in a dwelling house, retail shop, showroom or office building, nor to motor cars, ships, certain railway assets – s38B. The writing down allowances for long life assets is reduced from the current 25 per cent to a 6 per cent allowance – s38F. The major impact will clearly be on very long life assets such as aircraft, pipelines, chemical plant, power station equipment and other infrastructure assets. Expenditure which falls within the new rules will be taken into a separate pool for plant and machinery allowance purposes, but where the expenditure could alternatively qualify for industrial buildings allowances, it will be open to the taxpayer to claim IBAs instead. Anti-avoidance provisions will prevent the acceleration of allowances by sale at less than tax written down value.

Assets used partly for business and partly for non-business purposes – s79 CAA 1990

These assets are kept outside the taxpayer's general pool, and the WDA available for them is governed by s79 CAA 1990. Ships, cars and leased assets also have specific provisions in CAA 1990 which govern the method of both pooling such assets and allocating them a WDA. For ships see ss30–33, for expensive cars see ss34–36, and for leased assets and inexpensive cars see ss39–50.

7.3 Allowances on security assets

Section 71 CAA 1990 provides for a capital allowance in respect of the expenditure involved in the provision of security assets. There are again two separate questions to be asked:

1. In what circumstances is the allowance available?
2. What is the system of allowance available?

Security assets

The relief applies where:

1. an individual or a partnership of individuals carries on a trade, profession or vocation;
2. expenditure is incurred by the individual or partnership in connection with the provision for, or use by the individual or any of the individuals of, a security asset;
3. and where no sum in respect of the expenditure could be deducted in compiling the profits or gains of the trade, profession or vocation for the purposes of Case I or Case II of Schedule D; and
4. where no other provision in CAA 1990 would apply.

The asset must be provided or used to meet a threat which is a special threat to the individual's personal security and arises wholly or mainly by virtue of the particular trade, profession or vocation concerned.

The person incurring the expenditure must have as his sole object the meeting of the threat, and he must intend the asset to be used solely to improve personal physical security. If, however, he intends the asset to be used partly to improve personal physical security, then, provided that the other provisions of the section are met, the allowance is available in part, apportioned appropriately, and according to such proportion of the expenditure as is attributable to the intention of the person incurring it that the asset be used to improve personal physical security. This means that the relief is only available if the sole object of the person incurring the expenditure is to meet the special threat.

The asset, once acquired, may have other uses. It is, however, not clear how it is possible to make an apportionment in proportion to the *expenditure* attributable to a different purpose if the asset is a single indivisible unit and the purpose of its acquisition is *solely* to meet the special threat.

By s72 CAA 1990 a security asset is an asset which improves personal security, but does not include a car, a ship, an aircraft, a dwelling or grounds appurtenant to a dwelling. It does, however, include equipment and structures (such as a wall).

The available allowances

Where the sections apply, ss22–83 (Part II) CAA 1990 apply as if the expenditure were capital expenditure incurred on the provision of machinery or plant wholly and exclusively for the purposes of the trade, profession or vocation concerned, and as if, in consequence of the expenditure being incurred, the machinery or plant belonged to the individual or partnership carrying on the trade, profession or vocation, and as if the disposable value of the machinery or plant were nil (see s71(2)). This means that the writing down allowances (at 25 per cent) can be claimed but no balancing charge arises.

7.4 Allowances on expenditure on stands at sports grounds

Additional requirements in respect of the conditions to be fulfilled for the issue of safety certificates in respect of stands at sports grounds were imposed by legislation in 1987 (the Fire Safety and Safety of Places of Sport Act 1987). Relief has been allowed in respect of expenditure to fulfil such requirements by s70. The relief applies where expenditure within the section was incurred as from 1 January 1989.

Where a person carrying on a trade incurs expenditure in respect of a regulated stand at a sports ground used by him for the purposes of his trade, in taking steps in compliance with or towards the obtaining of a safety certificate, then, if no other capital allowance provision is available in respect of that expenditure, the capital allowance provisions in Chapter 1 Part III FA 1971 (now consolidated in CAA 1990) shall apply as if the expenditure were capital expenditure incurred on the provision of machinery or plant for the purpose of the trade and as if the machinery or plant had, in consequence of his incurring the expenditure, belonged to him, and as if the disposable value of the machinery or plant were nil.

7.5 Industrial buildings allowances

There are again two separate questions to be asked here:

1. What is an industrial building or structure?
2. What is the system of allowances available here?

'Industrial building or structure'

What constitutes an industrial building or structure is defined in s18 CAA 1990 by reference to its use. The most important elements of the definition provided by s18 are:

> '1) "Industrial building or structure" means a building or structure in use:
> a) for the purposes of a trade carried on in a mill, factory or other similar premises; or ...

e) for the purposes of a trade which consists in the manufacture of goods or materials or the subjection of goods or materials to any process, or

f) for the purposes of a trade which consists in the storage:

i) of goods or materials which are to be used in the manufacture of other goods or materials; or

ii) of goods or materials which are to be subjected, in the course of a trade, to any process; or

iii) of goods or materials which, having been manufactured or produced or subjected, in the course of a trade, to any process, have not yet been delivered to any purchaser ...

3) "industrial building or structure" does not include any building or structure in use as, or as part of, a dwelling-house, retail shop, showroom, hotel or office, or for any purpose ancillary to the purposes of a dwelling-house, retail shop, showroom, hotel or office.'

In *Bourne* v *Norwich Crematorium* (1967) 44 TC 164 (Chancery Division), the taxpayers sought capital allowances on their crematorium on the basis that it was an industrial building within s18(1)(e) as a building in use for the purposes of a trade consisting of the subjection of goods or materials to a process. Not surprisingly they did not succeed, since a human body is neither 'goods' nor 'materials', and it was not the purpose of the company to subject the coffins to a process, namely incineration. *Vibroplant Ltd* v *Holland* [1982] STC 164 makes it clear that 'process' involves uniformity of treatment. Accordingly, a building which was used for the repair of plant-hire equipment did not qualify, since the treatment afforded to each piece of equipment depended on the damage suffered. The effect of this case has been limited to some extent by s18(3). The definition of 'process' has been extended to include maintaining or repairing goods or materials, but generally only where those goods or materials belong to a third party – for example, a garage repairing motor cars.

By s161(7) CAA 1990:

'Any reference ... to any building ... shall be construed as including a reference to a part of a building.'

It follows that a part of a building may attract an industrial buildings allowance as being in use as a factory, while the remainder is disqualified on the ground of being a shop or offices. Section 18(7) further provides, though, that where not more than one quarter of the expenditure on a building has been incurred on the construction of the non-qualifying part, an industrial buildings allowance may be granted in respect of the whole of the expenditure, by treating the whole building as an industrial building.

'Allowances available'

Allowances in respect of industrial buildings are available under CAA 1990. Prior to FA 1984 there used to be an initial allowance of 75 per cent. However since 1 April 1986 initial allowances are no longer conferred except in certain special cases, for example qualifying buildings and structures in an enterprise zone – a 100 per cent initial allowance being available in these circumstances if required. (See, however, the note at the end of this section on temporary first year allowances.)

Instead, a taxpayer with a relevant interest (s20 CAA 1990) in the industrial building is entitled to claim a WDA equal to an annual allowance of 4 per cent of the qualifying expenditure of the industrial building so long as the expenditure on the building remains in use for one of the purposes described in s18. If within 25 years of the building first being used the taxpayer's relevant interest in the industrial building is ended as a result of the sale, demolition or destruction of the building then a balancing allowance or balancing charge will arise (s4(1) CAA 1990). The rules for determining the relevant allowance or charge are:

1. Where the sale proceeds equal or exceed the capital expenditure on the building, the balancing charge is equal to the amount of capital allowances – they are 'clawed back'.
2. If the sale proceeds are less than the capital expenditure, then:
   a) if sale proceeds plus allowances made exceed the capital expenditure, the balancing charge is equal to the excess;
   b) if capital expenditure exceeds sale proceeds plus allowances made, a balancing allowance equal to the excess is given.

Examples
1. A Ltd buys an industrial building for £100,000 (ignoring the cost of the site) in April 1987. It sells it in April 1999 for:

   (i) £150,000
   (ii) £ 90,000
   (iii) £ 10,000

   A Ltd's accounting period coincides with the financial year.

Chargeable period

		£
Financial Years 1987 to 1997	writing-down allowance 4% pa x 11	44,000
Financial Year 1998	writing-down allowance 4%	4,000
Total capital allowances given:		£48,000

Sale proceeds (brought into account in financial year 1995)

(i) £150,000. Since these are in excess of the total capital expenditure on the building, s3(4A) CAA 1968 provides that a balancing charge equal to the sum of capital allowances given in respect of the building shall be made, so there is a balancing charge of £48,000 for financial year 1999.
(ii) £90,000. The sale proceeds are less than the capital expenditure on the building, so it would not be right to claw back all the allowances given. One claws back (s3(4B)(a)): £90,000 + £48,000 – £100,000 = £38,000 for financial year 1999. In other words, the taxpayer is allowed to keep £10,000

of the capital allowances he has received – the amount of his capital loss on the building.

(iii) £10,000. In this case, the sum of the sale proceeds plus the capital allowances made in respect of the building are less than the capital expenditure on the building, so a balancing allowance is made: £100,000 – (10,000 + 48,000) = £42,000 for financial year 1999.

2. X bought a factory for the purpose of carrying on his trade in 1994 for £200,000. He sold it in 1997 to Y for £170,000. Y continues to use the factory for his own trade.

   1. X will qualify for a WDA from 1994 to 1996 at a rate of 4 per cent pa on £200,000. Thus in 1997 when X sells the factory the original qualifying expenditure of the asset, viz £200,000, will have been reduced to £176,000 as a consequence of his capital allowance of £24,000.
   2. Thus when X sells the factory to Y he will be able to claim an additional allowance of £[176,000-170,000] = £6,000.

3. Robert bought a building for £100,000 in 1987, and in 1999 it was sold for £60,000.

   1. Robert will qualify for 12 years' WDAs equal to £48,000, making his qualifying expenditure in 1999 amount to £[100,000-48,000] = £52,000.
   2. On the sale of the asset in 1999 Robert will suffer a balancing charge of £8,000 = £[52,000-60,000].

Note: the balancing charge, as explained in section 7.2, will be brought into account as a trading receipt.

For income tax purposes the capital allowances will be set against the trading profits of the taxpayer with the relevant interest who occupies the building for the purposes of a qualifying trade (s9(1) CAA 1990). If however the taxpayer lets the building to another, the allowance will then be set against his Schedule A income (s9(5) CAA 1990). Sections 144–5 deals with the treatment of such allowances for corporation tax purposes.

8

Schedule E

8.1 Scope of the charge

8.2 Basis of the charge

8.3 The meaning of 'emoluments therefrom'

8.4 Basis of assessment

8.5 Statutory treatment of benefits in kind

8.6 Terminal payments

8.7 Payments in respect of restrictive covenants

8.8 Expenses taxable and allowable under Schedule E

8.9 Removal expenses

8.10 Redundancy payments

8.1 Scope of the charge

Section 19 of the Income and Corporation Taxes Act 1988 charges tax under Schedule E on the emoluments from an office or employment. The Schedule is subdivided into three Cases. Cases II and III only apply where a foreign element is involved; Case I applies when a person resident and ordinarily resident in the United Kingdom receives emoluments from an office or employment. A discussion of the foreign element of Schedule E will be found in Chapter 9.

8.2 Basis of the charge

Definition of 'office'

'Office' is not defined by the Taxes Acts. The classic judicial definition is to be found in the judgment of Rowlatt J in *Great Western Railway Co Ltd* v *Bater* [1920] 3 KB 266:

'... a subsisting permanent, substantive position which has an existence independent of the person who fills it, which goes on and is filled in succession by successive holders'.

Thus a director of a company holds an office, as statute demands that a company have directors; accordingly, the post of director has an existence guaranteed by law: see *McMillan* v *Guest* [1942] AC 561.

However, the House of Lords in *Edwards* v *Clinch* [1982] AC 845 has decided that Rowlatt J's definition is too restrictive for modern purposes. There is no need for permanence any more, nor for continuity, but the position must be capable of continuance, of being held by successive incumbents; it need not, however, be capable of permanent or prolonged or indefinite existence. See Scott J's application of this test in *McMenamin* v *Diggles* [1991] STC 419.

Definition of 'employment'

Here again, reference must be made to a definition given by Rowlatt J, on this occasion in *Davies* v *Braithwaite* (1931) 18 TC 198:

'... namely, something analogous to an office, something more than a mere engagement in the carrying on of a profession'.

Better guidance is to be found, though, in the decision of Pennycuick J, who in *Fall* v *Hitchen* [1973] 1 All ER 368 who was willing to draw a distinction along the tort lines of contract for services/contract of service. Other examples of the same test being applied include *Sidey* v *Phillips* [1987] STC 87 and *Walls* v *Sinnett* [1987] STC 236.

Hall v *Lorimer* [1994] STC 23 should also be noted; this concerned the dispute over the employment status of a freelance vision-mixer who worked for many different employers on short-term contracts, each of a few days. He claimed to be self-employed and therefore to be assessable to tax under the more liberal Schedule D regime for allowable expenditure (see Chapter 6). The Revenue lost before the Commissioners, the High Court and the Court of Appeal.

If a person enters into a contract for services, that will give rise to Schedule D liability; if, however, he enters into a contract of service, he will hold an employment taxable under Schedule E. In *Fall* v *Hitchen* a dancer had been engaged under a standard-form contract by the Sadlers Wells Ballet Company for a period of not less than 22 weeks, terminable thereafter by two weeks' notice. He argued that while he would have been an employee for other legal purposes, the ratio of Rowlatt J in the *Braithwaite* case required that he be treated as carrying on his Schedule D Case II profession and the contract of employment as being no more than an incident of that profession. The judge disagreed, holding that it was a contract of service and thus necessarily taxable under Schedule E.

This decision had been foreshadowed by cases such as *Mitchell and Edon* v *Ross* [1962] AC 814 where the House of Lords had held that a professional man with a private practice taxable under Schedule D Case II – a radiologist – could also, as an incident of that profession, hold a part-time hospital appointment taxable under Schedule E. It should be noted that that case also decided that when this was so, expenses incurred in the performance of the Schedule E appointment could not be deducted under the Schedule D rules (which, it will be seen, are rather more generous).

It is of little significance that it may be illegal to enter into a contract of employment of the sort which it is sought to charge; the illegality is merely a factor which must be taken account of in determining whether it is likely that the parties would have intended the contract to be one of employment: *Cooke* v *Blacklaws* [1985] STC 1.

The Inland Revenue has published a booklet setting out the tests which it will normally apply for the purpose of determining the employed or self-employed status of an individual. These include the question of whether the person's own capital is at risk in the venture or not. (See Inland Revenue Booklet IR 56.)

8.3 The meaning of 'emoluments therefrom'

'Emoluments'

Section 131 ICTA 1988 provides that:

> 'Tax under Case I, II or III of Schedule E shall except as hereinafter mentioned be chargeable on the full amount of the emoluments falling under that Case, subject to such deductions only as may be authorised by the Tax Acts, and the expression "emoluments" shall include all salaries, fees, wages, perquisites and profits whatsoever.'

'Includes' in this context has the peculiar fiscal meaning of 'exclusively includes'.

Obviously payments in cash will be classified as emoluments within s131 ICTA 1988. However, the definition of 'emoluments' is wide enough to include benefits in kind. Nevertheless it has always been the judicial view that only a limited category of benefits in kind is caught by the general charging words of s19 ICTA 1988. This led to opportunities for the easy avoidance of tax, with the result that special statutory provisions were introduced, some applying to all employees, others only to certain groups. In considering whether benefits in kind are emoluments for the purpose of s19(1), three cases are paramount:

1. *Tennant* v *Smith* [1892] AC 150. This was the first case in which the House of Lord had to deal with benefits in kind. The House decided that the benefits could be taxed – but only if they could be 'converted into money', turned to 'pecuniary account'. It was not enough that they saved the pocket of the employee. There, the benefit was free lodging on bank premises given to the bank manager in order that business could be transacted out of normal banking hours and to ensure the security of the bank. Clearly, the manager could not make money out of the premises by sale or letting, so he was not subject to income tax in respect of the benefit (whatever that might have been).

2. *Wilkins* v *Rogerson* [1961] Ch 133. In this case, the Court of Appeal decided that if a benefit in kind could be turned to pecuniary account, the sum to be treated as part of the employee's emoluments was the amount into which it could be turned – sometimes known as the 'secondhand value' of the benefit.

   It was this decision that formed the basis of most avoidance schemes: it is common knowledge that many items diminish in value as soon as they leave the showroom. This being so, if your employee wanted a hi-fi worth £1,000 whose secondhand value on leaving the shop was £400, far better to give it to him (and let £400 be treated as part of his emoluments) than to pay him an extra £1,500 or £2,000.

3. *Nicoll* v *Austin* (1935) 19 TC 531. In this case Finlay J held that if an employee incurs a debt and his employer discharges that debt, a sum equal to the amount so discharged is treated as part of his emolument.

'Therefrom'

It is not sufficient that a payment be connected with the office in some vague way. This was exemplified by the case of *Hochstrasser* v *Mayes* (1959) 38 TC 673 where the House of Lords approved a dictum of Upjohn J that:

> '... not every payment made to an employee is necessarily made to him as a profit from his employment ... the authorities show that to be a profit arising from the employment, the payment must be made in reference to the services the employee renders by virtue of his office, and it must be something in the nature of a reward for services past, present and future.'

This is sometimes expressed by saying that the employment must be the causa causans and not merely the causa sine qua non of the benefit.

In *Hamblett* v *Godfrey* [1987] STC 60 the taxpayer was an employee at the Government Communications Headquarters (GCHQ). The government decided to withdraw trade union membership rights as well as rights under the Employment Protection Acts. Staff who wished to remain at GCHQ after this variation in their rights were paid £1,000 each in recognition of the loss of the rights. The Court of Appeal held that the payment was a taxable emolument from the employment even the employee was under no more than a moral obligation to remain after receiving the payment. Purchas LJ referred to *Hochstrasser* v *Mayes* and said that it was important to note that the test in that case looked not only at the performance of the duties of the employment but also at the status of being an employee 'in return for *acting as* or *being* an employee'. In the GCHQ case the rights for the loss of which compensation was expressed to have been paid were inextricably tied to the fact of the taxpayer's employment – if the employment had not existed, neither would have the rights. He accordingly felt that the payments were 'therefrom' in the *Hochstrasser* sense. Neill LJ held that the payments were 'therefrom' since the rights were rights which had been enjoyed within the employer/employee relationship; their removal involved a change in the conditions of service and the payment was in recognition of that change. Accordingly, the source of the payment was the employment and the payment was referrable to the employment and to nothing else.

Similarly, in the House of Lords decision in *Shilton* v *Wilmshurst* [1991] STC 88 Lord Templeman stated that:

'... section 181 TA 1970 (now s19(1) ICTA 1988) is not confined to "emoluments from the employer" but embraces all "emoluments from employment"; the section must therefore comprehend an emolument provided by a third party, a person who is not the employer. Section 181 is not limited to emoluments provided in the course of employment; ... The result is that an emolument "from employment" means an emolument "from or becoming an employee". The authorities are consistent with this analysis and are concerned to distinguish in each case between an emolument which is derived "from being or becoming an employee" on the one hand, and an emolument which is attributable to something else on the other hand ...'

See also the Privy Council decision in *Glynn* v *Commissioner of Inland Revenue* [1990] STC 227.

It should be noted that the causa causans/causa sine qua non distinction is true of emoluments falling with s131(1); however, the Court of Appeal in *Wicks* v *Firth* [1983] AC 214 indicated that it did not apply to the statutory provisions which brought into charge certain otherwise non-taxable benefits using the wording 'where by reason of his employment a benefit is provided'. The words 'by reason of his employment' signified that the employment merely had to be a cause of the provision of the benefit, not the causa causans.

Two areas of great difficulty exist, however. The first is: when will a benefit provided by an employer *not* be taxable? and the second: when will a benefit provided by a third party be an emolument from a person's employment?

The first problem has already been touched on above. The taxpayer will have to show that there was some other reason for making the payment than the good services he has performed or, indeed, the existence of the employment status. The easiest way to escape from the charge is to show that the employer had made a personal gift to the employee, one related to his personal circumstances: for example, where the employer helps out an employee going through a difficult financial period. But the taxpayer need not show that it was a personal gift; as Megarry J said in *Pritchard* v *Arundale* [1971] 3 All ER 1011, that is no more than an *example* of a transaction which will not fall within the taxable category of remuneration for services. There are others; a payment may, for example, be part of a purely commercial transaction not connected with his status as an employee, as where the employer buys an asset from an employee.

Schedule E imposes a charge to tax not only on the 'emoluments' of employment, as defined in s131 and not only on items falling under the three cases in s19, but also taxes payments falling within the other charging sections such as termination payments under s148 and payments for entering into restrictive covenants as in s313 (see sections 8.6 and 8.7). The point was emphasised in *Nichols* v *Gibson* [1996] STC 1008, where a payment of compensation for loss of office which the former employee received in a year when he was no longer resident or ordinarily resident in the UK was held to be taxable under s148 ICTA 1988.

Two special categories of payment which historically have posed difficulties in determining whether or not they are taxable under Schedule E are the inducement and the variation cases. The difficulties arise in assessing whether the payments arise 'from the employment' or from the giving up or varying of personal or other rights. To some extent payments arising before or after employment have escaped, without the need to consider whether or not they would be taxable if paid while the employment was still held. The current legislation as found in s19(4A) and s202A enlarge the scope to cover payments related to an employment to be held or which has been held. See also section 8.4.

The 'inducement' cases

The 'inducement' cases are those where a prospective employer pays the prospective employee to induce him to abandon something else to come and work for him. In *Jarrold* v *Boustead* [1964] 3 All ER 76 (Court of Appeal) the taxpayer gave up his status as an amateur Rugby Union player for a 'signing-on fee' of £3,000. By signing on, he lost the benefits attached to his amateur status and the £3,000 was held to be non-taxable compensation for that reason.

In *Pritchard* v *Arundale* (above) the taxpayer gave up his position as senior partner in a firm of chartered accountants to become joint Managing Director of a group of companies. In consideration of undertaking to serve, he was given 4,000 shares. Megarry J held the shares not to be an emolument stressing the following facts:

1. The *Hochstrasser* v *Mayes* test (above) required the connection to be with the services to be rendered; here the consideration was directed to the office, which was not sufficient.
2. The shares, which were given in advance of service would not have been recoverable if the taxpayer had died before entering service: cf *Riley* v *Coglan* (1968) 44 TC 481.
3. The taxpayer had given up something in respect of which compensation was being paid; he would have found it extremely difficult to pick up his former profession. A benefit given up only for the duration of the contract might well have been nothing more than disguised remuneration.

See also, by way of contrast, *Shilton* v *Wilmshurst* (above) where a professional footballer was paid £75,000 by his existing club to agree to be transferred for a fee of £325,000 to another club. He appealed against the Revenue's inclusion of the £75,000 as being an emolument falling within s19 ICTA 1988, contending that it was properly attributable to be taxed instead under s148. The effect of this would have been to afford him relief under s188(4) on £30,000 of the payment on the grounds that it fell to be treated as a payment on termination of employment.

Although he found support in the High Court, the House of Lords held that it was an emolument taxable under the more onerous s19.

The variation cases

If a man genuinely varies or surrenders rights he has against his employers in consideration of the payment of a sum of money, that payment will not be an emolument since it will not be a reward for services but consideration for the variation. The most obvious example of this occurs where an employee is wrongfully dismissed and his employer enters into a compromise whereunder the employee agrees not to sue in consideration of damages. Another example is that of the employee who accepts a lump sum in computation of pension rights – see *Hunter* v *Dewhurst* (1932) 16 TC 605. But beware: the courts are only too ready to treat a payment as an emolument; thus in *Wales* v *Tilley* [1943] AC 386 the Court of Appeal held that an agreement to continue serving an employer at a reduced salary in consideration of a lump sum payment was no more than a contract under which there were two rewards for services – the salary and the lump sum. They were unwilling merely to treat the lump sum as consideration for the variations; all that had happened was a variation in the form of the emolument, however the contract might have been worded.

It should be noted that variations after which the employee continues to perform exactly the same duties as before are treated with most suspicion by the courts. The most recent example of this is *Hamblett* v *Godfrey* [1987] STC 60.

In *McGregor* v *Randall* [1984] STC 223, Scott J held there was overwhelming authority that where an employee is entitled, under his contract of employment, to periodic salary or commission, and he accepts a lump sum in lieu thereof (or part of it), the lump sum so paid is considered to be remuneration in advance for services to be rendered rather than compensation for the loss of the other benefit.

Voluntary payments by third parties

There is nothing in the Taxes Acts which restricts the charge under Schedule E to emoluments provided by an employer. Of course, it is less likely that a third party will reward an employee for the services he renders under his contract of employment – but if he does, the reward is taxable. The way the courts approach this matter can be seen in two sets of cases known as 'the clergy cases' and 'the cricket cases'. In the clergy cases, incumbents of parishes received, by custom, the sums put in the collection plate at Easter. The congregation knew this and contributed accordingly. In *Blakiston* v *Cooper* (1908) 5 TC 347, it was held that the sums collected were taxable because, though they were voluntary, the vicar received them in his capacity as vicar. The same fact is stressed in the cricket case of *Moorhouse* v *Dooland* (1954) 36 TC 1, where, under the terms of his contract, a professional cricketer was entitled to have a collection taken on his behalf every time he scored 50 runs or took a certain number of wickets. Jenkins LJ held that when a voluntary payment was in issue, the test of liability to tax was whether, from the standpoint of the recipient, it accrued to him by virtue of his office; and that, where the recipient's contract of employment entitled him to receive such payments, that was strong evidence that it did.

So the difference between a payment by an employer and a voluntary payment by a third party is that in the former case you consider the matter from the employer's point of view (eg *Laidler* v *Perry* [1966] AC 16; (1965) 42 TC 351), whereas in the latter case, when the payer has little thoughts of 'emoluments therefrom', you consider it from the recipient's point of view.

Two concessions were introduced with effect from 6 April 1987 which are now incorporated in s155(7) ICTA 1988:

Entertainment provided for employees by third parties
Where entertainment is provided for an employee at what is essentially a working occasion the Inland Revenue has long accepted that no tax liability should be imposed on the employee – eg the working business lunch. It is now proposed that employees should also be exempted from tax where entertainment is provided primarily in order to foster business contacts and clients as a means of generating goodwill – for example, seats and receptions at sporting or cultural events. The exemption will *not* apply where the entertainment is procured by some arrangement effected by the employer, or where it is in recognition of some specific service done by the employee in the course of his duties.

Gifts to employees from third parties
Third parties will now be able to make gifts in favour of employees not exceeding £100 per annum in value. As with entertainment, gifts procured by the employer or rewarding some specific service performed in the course of the employee's duties will not be exempted from tax and will also not cover gifts in cash or tips.

The possibility of avoiding tax through the manipulation of third party payments has been addressed in the realm of payments using credit cards, tokens, vouchers etc to the extent that PAYE can now be applied not only to cash payments but also to non-cash payments. The rules apply generally and are not confined to third party payments. Not only do the rules deter such avoidance schemes but also where they continue the cash flow disadvantage to the Inland Revenue is nullified through earlier collection of tax on items which were previously chargeable to tax under Schedule E but for which a direct assessment after the end of the relevant tax year was required. Section 125–30 FA 1994 introduced rules into s203 ICTA 1988 in the form of new ss203B–K for payment of PAYE at the relevant time on, inter alia, payments by intermediaries of the employer, payments to certain contractors, payment in the form of tradeable assets and through the use of non-cash vouchers, credit tokens and cash vouchers. (See also section 8.5.)

8.4 Basis of assessment

Section 37 FA 1989 (now s202A–B ICTA 1988) altered the rules for determining when individuals were liable to pay tax on their Schedule E income. Broadly, under the new rules employees will be taxed on a receipts basis. Thus from 1989–90 s202A ICTA 1988 states that income tax shall be charged under Cases I and II of Schedule E on the full amount of emoluments received in the year in respect of the office or employment. Section 202B offers guidance as to when emoluments are treated as received for s202A purposes.

Under s202B emoluments will be treated as being received on the earlier of the following events:

1. the time when the payment is made of, or on account of, the emoluments;
2. the time when a person becomes entitled to payment of, or on account of, the emoluments;
3. if the holder of the office or employment is a director of a company and sums on account of emoluments are credited to the company's accounts or records, the time the emoluments are so credited;
4. if the holder of the office or employment is a director of the company and the amount of emoluments for the period is determined before that period ends, the time when the period ends; or
5. if the holder of the office or employment is a director of a company and the amount of emoluments for a period is not known until the amount is determined after the period has ended, the time when the amount is determined.

In addition the House of Lords decision in *Bray* v *Best* [1989] 1 All ER 969 has been reversed by statute. In that case the taxpayer formerly employed by G Ltd received sums totalling £18,111 from a trust connected with his employment in the year of assessment following that in which he ceased to be employed by G Ltd. The question arose, on the taxpayer's being assessed to tax under Schedule E in respect of the £18,111, as to which year or years of assessment the emoluments were attributable. The House of Lords held that prima facie emoluments are attributable to the year in which they are received. No circumstances existed in this case for disturbing that presumption. Consequently, the emoluments being attributable to a year of assessment during which the taxpayer occupied no office or employment, they escaped tax. However this case is no longer of benefit since the change to a receipts basis of assessment under Schedule E includes provisions bringing into charge receipts from employment whether or not the office or employment is still held when the amount is received (s202A(2)(b) ICTA 1988).

Section 19(4A) ICTA 1988 (introduced by s36 FA 1989) now states that when emoluments from an office or employment would be for a year of assessment in which a person does not hold an office or employment, then if in that year the office or employment is not yet held, the emoluments will be taxed in the first year in which the office or employment is held; if the office or employment is no longer held, they will be treated as emoluments for the last year in which the office or employment was held.

8.5 Statutory treatment of benefits in kind

Benefits in kind provided for an employee are deemed to be emoluments arising from the employment if the employee is earning £8,500 per annum or above – s154(1) ICTA 1988. As noted in section 8.3 above, other employees are taxable, under the general charging provisions of Schedule E, only on items which are convertible into cash. However, specific further charging provisions apply to all employees in respect of the provision of living accommodation and the use of vouchers and similar facilities which could be used as a substitute for payment in cash.

Statutory provisions applicable to all employees
Section 145 – Living accommodation

Where living accommodation is provided for an employee or a member of his family by reason of his employment (see *Wicks* v *Firth* [1983] STC 25) he is treated as receiving emoluments equal to the value of the accommodation. The value of the accommodation is its annual value under s837, less any amount made good by the employee.

An exception is made under s145(4) for certain forms of accommodation:

1. where it is necessary for the proper performance of the employee's duties that he should reside in the accommodation, eg the bank manager in *Tennant* v *Smith* [1892] AC 150 (section 8.3 above);
2. where the accommodation is provided for the better performance of his duties and it is customary for employers to provide living accommodation to persons in his kind of employment, eg policemen, and waiters and other staff of hotels, it is very hard to establish that provision is 'customary'. In *Vertigan* v *Brady* [1988] STC 91 Knox J said in dismissing the taxpayer's claim that regard should be had to (1) how common a practice of providing accomodation is, (2) how long the practice had endured and (3) whether it found general acceptance with the relevant employers;
3. where he resides in the accommodation as part of special security arrangements, there being a special threat to his security, eg cabinet ministers;
4. where the taxpayer is employed by a local authority and gets a council house on the usual terms.

Section 106 Finance Act 1996 made changes to counter an avoidance scheme which had grown up in the provision of living accommodation for employees. The charge to tax under ss145 and 146 only arose if the benefit was not chargeable to tax under s19 ICTA 1988. By utilising the decision in *Heaton* v *Bell* (1969) 46 TC 211, an option to take a cut in salary in return for the provision of living accommodation would bring the salary reduction into the normal charging rules of Schedule E, in line with the decision in *Heaton*. The amount to be brought into charge was the amount of salary forgone, and therefore it was possible to set up arrangements where the provision of living accommodation was an alternative to a salary difference amounting to much less than the value of the accommodation supplied. In this way, the charging ss145 and 146 could not operate. However, s106 FA 1996 provides that ss145 and 146 will apply by omitting the words 'and is not otherwise made the subject of any charge to him by way of income tax' from s145. A new s146A gives priority to the charge under ss145 and 146 before considering whether any other amount is to be treated as Schedule E emoluments.

Expensive living accommodation provided for an employee

Section 146 provides an additional charge to tax under Schedule E where:

1. Living accommodation is provided to a person by reason of his employment; and
2. He is already caught by s145; and
3. The cost of providing the accommodation exceeds £75,000.

In these circumstances, in *addition* to the charge levied by s145, the employee must pay tax on an amount calculated by reference to the excess of cost to his employer *over* £75,000, and based on the 'official rate' of interest applied to beneficial loans. It should be noted that 'cost' includes improvement expenditure. Unlike the provisions relating to beneficial loans this charge remains based on the rate in force at 6 April and does not fluctuate thereafter (s146(11)).

Example
X occupies, on 6 April 1997, a house which his employer bought for £575,000. He will pay tax on £575,000 − £75,000 = £500,000 x (6.75%) = £33,750. Assume 6.75 per cent (the actual rate in force on 6 April 1997) is the official rate of interest. Since he is liable to tax at 40 per cent, he will thus will be liable to tax (in addition to that already charged under s145 itself) of £13,500.

If the employer bought the property more than six years before its first occupation by that particular employee, the charge will be imposed not by reference to cost price but by its market value when the employee first occupied it.

Sections 141–143: vouchers, cash vouchers and credit tokens

These sections enabled the Revenue to bring into charge vouchers which may be exchanged for goods or services (s141) or for money (s143). The usefulness of vouchers was that they enabled the employee to select the benefit in kind that he wanted from a large selection on offer at a shop in the voucher system, without losing the advantages of *Wilkins* v *Rogerson* [1961] Ch 133 (see section 8.3). It was extremely important, nevertheless, to ensure that the manner in which the transaction had been carried was technically capable of achieving the intended tax saving. If, for example, the employee had contracted to buy an article and the employer had then discharged the debt, *Nicoll* v *Austin* (1935) 19 TC 531 would have applied: see *Richardson* v *Worrall* [1985] STC 693.

Sections 141 and 143 negated the *Wilkins* v *Rogerson* advantage by providing that in determining the sum which enters the emoluments of the employee, one must ignore the value of the benefit which he obtained and treat him as receiving a sum equal to the expense incurred by his employer (less any amount which he made good).

It was found, however, that the voucher provisions had certain shortcomings:

1. They did not apply to season tickets provided by the employer. Such vouchers were not chargeable at common law because they were not 'convertible', and they did not fall within s141 since that applied only to vouchers which were capable of being *exchanged* for goods or services – a season ticket is merely *produced* in order to obtain the services. Accordingly, s141 was amended to include 'transport vouchers' – which are defined as documents, tickets, passes or tokens intended to enable a person to obtain passenger transport services (whether or not in exchange for it).

    It should be noted that employees of passenger transport undertakings are not charged in respect of transport vouchers which they receive, whether for their employer's transport or that of another.

2. They did not apply to credit cards owned by an employer which he lent to an employee. Again, no voucher was *exchanged* in order to obtain benefits.

    On this, though, see *Richardson* v *Worrall* (above), where an employee was held have incurred a debt when purchasing petrol which was then discharged by use of his employer's credit card and as such was held to be a taxable emolument of the employee. There has been some debate as to whether this applies where an employee indicates the use of the card prior to, for example, filling up with petrol and therefore before he incurs any debt to the supplier.

    Accordingly, a new section – s142 – was introduced relating to 'credit tokens'. Credit tokens include any sort of credit card, and the employee is treated as having received a sum equal to the expense incurred by the employer in the provision of the credit token or in its use.

See the end of section 8.3 for inclusion of voucher payments within the PAYE rules. It is important to note that s89 FA 1994 has amended ss141–144 ICTA 1988 to change the quantum of the charge under Schedule E to the amount represented by the expense incurred by the person at whose cost the voucher is supplied, and the charge is the total of the cost of supplying the voucher plus the money and the value of the goods or services for which it can be exchanged.

Statutory provisions applicable to any person who is employed as a director or in employment providing emoluments at the rate of £8,500 pa or more

Sections 153–168

Section 154 provides that where in any year in which a person is employed as a director or in employment providing emoluments at the rate of £8,500 per year or more, there is provided for him or any member of his family a benefit to which the section applies, and the cost of providing the benefit is not otherwise chargeable to tax as his income, an amount equal to the cash equivalent is treated as part of his emoluments. The time when a benefit is 'provided' was determined in *Templeton* v *Jacobs* [1996] STC 991, where a loft conversion for use as an office was contracted for in the tax year before the employment commenced but completed afterwards. The taxpayer contended that the loft conversion was not assessable as a benefit in kind under s154 as it had been provided during the tax year 1990–91, which was before the commencement of his employment with the company. In addition, the employee claimed that even if it were a benefit for that year it fell within the job-related accommodation exemption of s155(2)(b). The court held that in order for a benefit to be regarded as 'provided' for the purposes of s154(1), the benefit had to be available to the taxpayer and, until such times as the benefit was capable of being enjoyed by the taxpayer, there was no relevant benefit for s154 purposes. As to the exemption claimed under s155(2)(b), what was provided for the employee was not 'accommodation' as required by the language of that section. The provision of a loft conversion was therefore a taxable benefit and assessable for the year 1991–92. See Chapter 27, section 27.3, for further details.

Certain benefits in kind are excluded from s154 because they are specially provided for elsewhere by statute. Apart from these, the only benefits which will not fall within s154 are:

1. payments of wages to the employee;
2. pension payments;
3. payments falling within the rule in *Nicoll* v *Austin* (see above).

Section 154 catches other benefits in kind because the secondhand value of a benefit will not be the same as the cost of providing it.

Employees earning £8,500 or more, and directors

This phrase is defined by s167 as amended by s53 Finance Act 1989. Effectively it means:

1. anyone who (taking into account the cash equivalent of benefits in kind) earns more than £8,500. In computing the earnings of the employee for this purpose, the section precludes the deduction of expenditure allowable under s198 ICTA 1988. Once the computation under s167 has been made, however, the expenditure again becomes deductible for the purpose of calculating the employee's net taxable emoluments.

2. any person who, though earning less than £8,500, is a director of the company *unless* he is a full-time working director of the company with less than a 5 per cent shareholding in it.

Thus a lower-paid employee, one earning less than £8,500 per annum, will not fall within the scope of s154, and any benefits in kind will either (not being convertible) not be taxable, or be taxable only on their secondhand value, or be otherwise taxable under specific statutory provision.

The £8,500 threshold has been in force since 1979. In 1989 it was accepted that it was inappropriate to refer to such a wage as being for 'higher-paid employment' and the phrase was therefore deleted.

The cash equivalent of the benefit

This is defined by s156(1) as the amount of the cost of the benefit less so much as is made good by the employee to those providing the benefit. Section 156(2) then further defines what will be deemed to be the cost of the benefit. It states that the cost of the benefit is the amount of any expense incurred in or in connection with its provision, and includes a proper proportion of any expense relating partly to the benefit and partly to other matters.

Pepper v Hart

The meaning of s156(2) was discussed in the case of *Pepper v Hart* [1992] STC 898 which went to the House of Lords for a decision which is important as much, if not more, for its non-tax implications as for its interpretation of s156(2). Those aspects are discussed separately in Chapter 24. In this case the taxpayers constituted the bursar and nine assistant masters at Malvern College. The taxpayers' sons were educated at the school at one-fifth of the fees normally charged. The Special Commissioners found as a fact that during the period when the taxpayers received this benefit in kind the school was not full to capacity and there was no waiting list for places. In addition there was evidence to show that the payment of one fifth of the fees covered the marginal costs to the school of admitting each additional boy. The question for the court was whether the phrase 'cost to the employer of providing the benefit' in s156(1) and (2) meant the marginal cost of the benefit or the average cost of the benefit.

The court held that the taxpayers were liable to pay tax on the average cost to the school of providing a place for each boy. As the taxpayers had only made good the marginal cost of the benefit they were liable to pay additional tax. However the House of Lords disagreed, and to the relief of these taxpayers, and countless others in receipt of in-house benefits, who would have been affected by an adverse decision, it was held that the liability was to be based on only the marginal extra cost of educating the pupils. The House of Lords arrived at this decision only after an interim finding that the courts could take account of a statement by a government minister (made at the time the relevant legislation was introduced, and which would have led to this conclusion) in interpreting the statutory provisions.

It should be noted, however, that such statements can only be relied upon in interpreting legislation where it is 'ambiguous or obscure, or leads to an absurdity' and is not therefore to be applied in interpreting all statutes. However, the number of occasions on which *Pepper* v *Hart* is being relied upon before the courts is increasing and reflects the general complexity of legislation not only in tax law but in other areas of the law.

An employee is allowed a deduction where his employer procures a third party to provide the employee with a benefit and the employee reimburses all or part of the cost which he has incurred. Thus, in a simple example, if an employer buys a hi-fi for his employee for £1,000 and the employee pays back £400, £600 will be treated as part of his emoluments.

Although the benefit provided by the employer may be used wholly, necessarily and exclusively for the purposes of the employee's employment, this does exclude him from an obligation to calculate the cash equivalent of that benefit. Section 156(8) then permits the employee to deduct from the cash equivalent the amount that would have been deductible had he actually incurred the cost of the benefit out of his emoluments. This process casts the burden of proving the deductibility of the item firmly on the employee.

There also appears to be one glaring anomaly: Section 156(3) provides that if the employers buy an asset, but before transferring it it is used or depreciates in value, the cash equivalent is its market value at the date of transfer. There would still seem to be scope for abuse of the system.

One abuse which has long since been eradicated, though, is the loan of the asset to the employee for a period, followed by its eventual transfer when it has diminished in value. Section 156(5) provides that when an asset is put at the disposal of the employee, then the cash equivalent for each year it is so put at his disposal is 20 per cent of its market value when first lent – unless the employer himself is renting the asset for a consideration in excess of 20 per cent, when the larger figure is taken as the cash equivalent of the benefit. Section 156(4) then provides that if, after a period of loan, the asset is transferred to the employee, the cash equivalent is the greater of:

1. its market value at that time; and
2. its original market value less the aggregate of amounts taken account of in the 'loan years'.

Example
John, who was an employee of X Co in April 1993, had, by reason of his employment, two items put at his disposal: a yacht costing £40,000, and a hi-fi costing £5,000. In April 1996, when the yacht is worth £35,000 and the hi-fi £800, the assets are given to him.

The cash equivalents each year are:

	Yacht	Hi-fi
1993–94	£8,000 (£40,000 x 20%)	£1,000 (£5,000 x 20%)
1994–95	£8,000	£1,000
1995–96	£8,000	£1,000
Aggregate amounts:	£24,000	£3,000

In April 1996, assets transferred:

Current market value:	£35,000	£800
Original market value less aggregate amounts under s156(5):	£16,000	£2,000

Accordingly, in 1996–97, the cash equivalents of the transferred assets will be:

Yacht: £35,000   Hi-fi: £2,000

Special types of benefits in kind

Section 155 excludes four sorts of benefit from charge under these provisions:

1. the provision by the employer of business accommodation, business supplies and business services for use by his employees in performing the duties of the employment;
2. provision for the employee of a car parking space at or near his place of work;
3. death or retirement benefits;
4. meals provided by the employer in a canteen used by the staff generally.

Thus the taking of lunch in the directors' dining room is a chargeable benefit in kind.

The Inland Revenue by concession also allows an employer to provide his employees with up to 15p per day of luncheon vouchers free of tax.

Section 165: scholarships

This provision was enacted to reverse the decision of the House of Lords in *Wicks* v *Firth* [1983] STC 25. As a result, scholarship income, which is exempt from tax by virtue of s331 ICTA 1988, is exempt only so far as the recipient is concerned. After 15 March 1983 it is taxable as a benefit in kind in relation to directors and employees if provided by the employer, or any person connected with the employer, for a member of the director's or employee's family or household. Certain exemptions do, however, exist, namely where not more than 25 per cent of the total scholarship payments are provided for members of employees' families by the employer.

Further amendments were made to the predecessor of s165 by FA 1984. The most common example of an employee whose children are afforded scholarship income under a trust fund is the overseas employee of a British firm, and such employees are likely to obtain a 100 per cent deduction from the charge to income tax under Schedule E Case I. In a fund, therefore, where a large number of the employees are in such a position, the non-taxable part of the fund – supposed to consist of payments to children whose parents are not connected with the company which established the fund – will, in fact, be swollen by the payments to children whose fathers work overseas. The amendment made is designed to add such scholarships to the employee side of the equation, where they should rightfully be.

It should also be noted in this context that an employer who pays his employee's children's school fees does not thereby provide them with 'scholarship income' within *Wicks* v *Firth* (above) and s165. Rather he is probably discharging a debt of his employee – which will be caught by *Nicoll* v *Austin* (1935) 19 TC 531 – or, if the children are the persons who, under the contract with the school, are the persons who are obliged to pay the fees, providing a benefit to a relative of an employee earning £8,500 per annum or more. Such a benefit will be directly caught by s154, since such payments are not within the ambit of s331; 'scholarship income' is something which takes the form of a payment to a person attending full-time education by reason of his scholastic achievement.

Car benefits for directors and employees earning £8,500 per annum or more
The provisions relating to car benefits are somewhat complex. In outline, the rules are:

1. If the car is given to the employee outright, s154 applies as usual.
2. If, however, the car is lent to the employee, the special rules contained in ss157 to 159 apply.

Section 158: pooled cars. If an employee is provided with the use of a 'pooled car', there is no charge to tax in respect of it. A 'pooled car' is one:

1. which is made available and used by more than one employee, but must not be used by one to the exclusion of the others;
2. the private use of which made by any of them must be merely incidental to his other use of it;
3. which must not normally be kept overnight on or in the vicinity of any of the employees' homes.

In relation to the incidental private use referred to at 2 above, the Inland Revenue issued a Statement of Practice (SP2/96) setting out its views in respect of private use being incidental to the business use of the car. Where the private use of the car is independent of the business use it is not incidental to it and a charge to tax would therefore arise. In the case where the private use follows from the business use it would be regarded as incidental to it. The statement provides the example of an early morning journey which could not reasonably be undertaken starting from the normal place of work but begins from home – then the journey from home would not be regarded as private use. Private use while away on business would also be treated as incidental but generally within reasonable limits. Where the car is supplied with a driver, a journey from home to work, even while working on confidential papers, will not necessarily be passed as business use.

Cars available for private use: s157. If a car is made available to a director or an employee by reason of his employment (see *Wicks* v *Firth*, above) and is available for his private use, then the cash equivalent to be treated as part of the employee's emoluments is determined by reference to tables set out in Schedule 6 to the Act. 'Private use' is defined by s168(5)(f) as any use otherwise than for business travel, and 'business travel' is defined by s168(5)(c) as 'travelling which a person is necessarily obliged to do in the performance of his duties'. As *Gilbert* v *Hemsley* [1981] STC 703 shows, it will only be in the very rarest of circumstances that an employee who takes his car home will be able to avoid s157. The case also shows that it is necessary for an employer actually to forbid private use for a car not to be available for such use.

Schedule 6, para 1 provides for the cash equivalent of the benefit of private use of a car to be assessed at a maximum of 35 per cent of the price of the car, with reductions dependent upon the extent of the business use. If the car is used preponderantly for business purposes – more than 18,000 miles are travelled on business – the cash equivalent is reduced by two-thirds and by one-third where the business mileage is between 2,500 and 18,000. For cars four or more years old at the end of the year of assessment the car price on which the 35 per cent is calculated is reduced by one-third – Schedule 6, para 5. The cash equivalents have been increased significantly since they were introduced, and such increases have to a great extent reduced the tax efficiency of the provision of company cars.

The cash equivalent of a car falling within s157 covers not only the provision of the car itself but also every other benefit which may be provided in connection with it – such as the cost of repairs, the vehicle excise licence and insurance – other than the provision of a chauffeur and of petrol: s155(1). As from 1994–95 the cash equivalent is based on 35 per cent of the price of the car, reduced by one-third for cars at least four years old. The figure is also reduced by one-third where the business mileage is between 2,500 and 18,000 miles and by two-thirds for 18,000 business miles or more (Schedule 3 FA 1993.) This places a higher level of tax on the infrequent business user.

Cash alternatives to cars. In addition, where an employee was offered a cash alternative to the provision of a car he was taxable on the cash amount instead of the scale benefit, under the principles of the decision in *Heaton* v *Bell* [1970] AC 728, since the benefit is 'convertible'. However, s43 FA 1995 remedies the abuse of this principle which arose where low cash alternatives were offered. The provision takes the charge out of s19 ICTA 1988 as an emolument, and, since it is no longer 'otherwise taxable' (see the wording of s154(b) ICTA 1988), the benefit to be taxed is the normal scale charge. See also the Finance Act 1996 change in the law in relation to living accommodation above.

Car fuel: s158. This section brings into charge the provision of car fuel to an employee in connection with a car made available for his private use and falling within s157. All other possible charges (see *Richardson* v *Worrall* [1985] STC 693 for examples) are overridden in favour of the imposition of a fixed PAYE charge determined by reference to tables set out in the section itself. The charge imposed will vary according to the cylinder capacity of the car. If the employee either makes good the whole of the cost of the fuel which he uses for private purposes, or the fuel is only made available for business travel, no charge to tax is incurred. If, though, the employee only partially reimburses his employer for the cost of providing car fuel for private motoring, no reduction at all is allowed in the cash equivalent – the matter is all or nothing. A lower fuel scale charge for diesel cars was introduced by FA 1992. The car fuel tables continue to be based on the cylinder capacity of the car.

Beneficial loans to directors or employees

Section 160 provides that where a loan is made to an employee at no interest, or at a low rate of interest, then the amount of interest forgone by the employer is treated as an emolument received by the employee. Prior to 1994–95, where the *interest* benefit exceeded £300, tax was charged on the full amount, but if it was less than £300 it was exempt (s161). From 1994–95 onwards no tax is charged where the *loan* does not exceed £5,000, aggregating all relevant loans (s88 FA 1994, amending s161 ICTA 1988). Section 107 Finance Act 1996 allows the aggregation of loans as an option in reporting the cash equivalent to be taxed under s160(IB) ICTA 1988.

Where the taxable loan is for a qualifying purpose (eg purchase of main residence) the reduction in the tax payable in respect of the qualifying portion of the loan (eg £30,000 for main residence purchase loans) must not exceed 20 per cent for 1994–95 and 15 per cent from 1995–96 onwards, to mirror the provisions for interest paid relief under s353 ICTA 1988. (See Chapter 3, 'Total Income', for mortgage interest relief treatment.)

In cases where tax is chargeable under s160, the interest forgone is computed by reference to an official interest rate published from time to time by the Treasury. As at 6 April 1997 the rate stood at 6.75 per cent. The amount assessed to tax for the year varies with each change in the official rate of interest during the year, in accordance with the provisions set out in Schedule 7 paras 4 and 5 ICTA 1988.

Where the employer later writes off the loan, or part of the loan, otherwise than on the death of the employee, the amount so written off is treated as an emolument received in the year written off, even if the employee has by then ceased to be in the service of the employer. In such a case the Revenue merely needs to establish that the loan was outstanding at some period when the taxpayer was employed as a director or employee earning £8,500 per annum or more.

Employee shareholdings

Section 162 provides that where a person employed or about to be employed at a level of £8,500 pa or more, or a person connected with him, acquires shares at an undervalue in a company (whether in the employing company or not) in pursuance of a right or opportunity available by reason of his employment, then:

1. Section 160 (beneficial loan arrangements) applies as if the employee had the benefit of an interest-free loan equal to so much of the market value of the benefit as is not already chargeable as an emolument of the employee (that is, market value of shares less so much as has been made good by the employee). Generally, the provision of shares at an undervalue *will* be chargeable to tax (at common law under the rule in *Weight* v *Salmon* (1935) 19 TC 174 or under ss77–89 FA 1988, or under s135 ICTA 1988) and s162 will not apply. Section 162 will be applicable, though, if the transfer fell outside the scope of tax under, say, *Pritchard* v *Arundale* [1971] 3 All ER 1011 (see section 8.3). This notional loan carries on until the employee pays full value for the shares, sells them, or dies.
2. There are exceptions for shares acquired under Inland Revenue approved employee share schemes (see Schedule 9 ICTA 1988).
3. When the employee sells the shares, he is treated as receiving an emolument in an amount equal to the difference between the sale proceeds and what (if anything) he paid for the shares.

Provision for employee of care for child

Broadly, s155A ICTA 1988 (introduced by s21 FA 1990) states that s154 ICTA 1988 does not apply to a benefit consisting in the provision for the employee of care for the child if:

1. the child is a child for whom the employee has parental responsibility or is a foster child whom the employee maintains;
2. the care is provided on premises which are not domestic premises.

Mobile and car telephones

Where a mobile telephone is made available to an employee by reason of his employment and is available for private use, then the employee is treated as receiving as emolument the cash equivalent of the benefit. By s159A ICTA 1988 (inserted by s30 FA 1991) this cash equivalent is £200 for each mobile phone so made available. If, however, the employee does not use the mobile telephone for private use, or he is required to pay to the person providing the mobile telephone the full cost of private calls, then the cash equivalent of the benefit is nil.

8.6 Terminal payments

A sum paid to an employee or office holder on the termination of his employment or in consideration of a variation in the terms of his employment is dealt with as follows:

1. Where the sum is received as a result of a prior arrangement, for example under the contract of service, any sum received on the termination of his employment is treated as deferred remuneration and is taxable under s19: *Dale* v *De Soissons* (1950) 32 TC 18 and *Williams* v *Simmonds* (1981) 55 TC 17.
2. If the payment is made in anticipation of future services it is treated as advance remuneration and, once again, taxed under Schedule E: *Wales* v *Tilley* [1943] AC 386 and *McGregor* v *Randall* [1984] STC 223, and see section 8.3.
3. If neither (1) nor (2) above applies, the payment is likely only to be taxable under s148, which charges:

   'any payment (not otherwise chargeable to tax) which is made whether in pursuance of any legal obligation or not, either directly or indirectly in consideration or in consequence of, or otherwise in connection with, the termination of the holding of the office, or any change in its functions or emoluments ... '.

   Thus the section catches *all* payments: for example, damages in settlement of an employee's claim for wrongful dismissal.

   In *Nichols* v *Gibson* [1996] STC 1008 a payment of compensation for loss of office which the former employee received in a year when he was no longer resident or ordinarily resident in the United Kingdom was held to be taxable under s148 ICTA 1988. The Commissioners' decision, upheld by the High Court and the Court of Appeal, was that the payment was taxable under what is now s148 ICTA 1988, and that this section imposed a charge to tax under Schedule E independently of the charge under s19. In other words, the charge under Schedule E is not confined to what falls within the three cases of s19. The s148 charge includes past holders of an office or employment, so that being non-resident by being absent from the United Kingdom from 1 April and remaining out of the United Kingdom for a whole tax year was not sufficient to avoid tax on the payment. The effect of s148 was that, although the taxpayer was not within any of the three cases of Schedule E, he was nevertheless taxable under Schedule E as a result of his residence status at the time of receipt.
4. Section 188 provides certain exemptions and reliefs in respect of payments falling within s187, but if a payment is taxable under s19, the s188 reliefs are *not* available. The exempted payments are:

   - those made on the termination of the employment by the death or injury of the holder;
   - sums chargeable under s313 ICTA 1988 (restrictive covenants: see below);
   - benefits paid under approved retirement benefits schemes.

Even if a payment is taxable under s148, a certain amount of relief is afforded by s188(4) in respect of payments received after 5 April 1988, as the first £30,000 is tax free, although the excess over £30,000 is charged to tax in the usual way. See *Shilton* v *Wilmshurst* [1991] STC 88, discussed in section 8.3, where a claim for relief under this section was unsuccessful.

One of the main difficulties in practice is that the making of an agreement for a payment on termination of employment renders it fully taxable. Commercial reality dictates that trusting that compensation will be duly paid means risking more than the tax relief. The timing and implementation of any such negotiations is therefore of paramount importance.

8.7 Payments in respect of restrictive covenants

A payment made as consideration for the giving of a restrictive covenant in connection with the holding of an office or employment would not be taxable unless the Revenue could prove that the sum paid was nothing more than disguised remuneration: *Beak* v *Robson* [1943] AC 352. This is, of course, because the restrictive covenant and not the employment would be the causa causans of the payment. The recent decision of the Court of Appeal in *Hamblett* v *Godfrey* [1987] STC 60 must be considered carefully for its application in this area – it seems that it will apply if the covenant relates directly to the relationship of employer and employee, whereas:

> 'Purely by way of contrast ... if for instance the employers had for some reason best known to themselves objected to some social or other activity which their employees or some of them enjoyed, such as joining a golf club ... then a payment made by an employer to recognise the voluntary or, indeed, the compulsory withdrawal if the employer had sufficient influence with the committee of the golf club concerned, then that I can readily acknowledge would be a payment made to a person who was an employee but was not made in circumstances which would satisfy section (19); that is that the payment must arise "therefrom".' (Purchas LJ)

Section 73 FA 1988 amended s313 ICTA 1988 and now provides a simplified new regime for such payments. Such payments now fall to be treated as emoluments in the usual way.

On 4 April 1996 the Inland Revenue published a Statement of Practice (SP 3/96) clarifying its view over the tax position in respect of undertakings made by employees as part of the financial package on termination of employment. The statement confirms that sums paid in settlement of claims which the employee could have pursued in law would be regarded as having no value for the purpose of any charge under s313.

8.8 Expenses taxable and allowable under Schedule E

Expenses received by employees, whether by means of a general expense allowance or reimbursement, are deemed to be emoluments arising from the employment, if the employee is earning £8,500 per annum or above – s153(1) ICTA 1988. There are no provisions for taxing true expenses paid to employees earning below that threshold. For those whose expenses are taxable there are provisions for claiming deductions under s198 against the taxable amounts for those expenses which the employee incurs. However, the tests under s198 are very strict and only those which have been incurred 'wholly, exclusively and necessarily in the performance of the duties of the employment' may be deducted. All limbs of the test must be satisfied. The same tests apply to employees who claim deductions of expenses which have been reimbursed to them.

Prior arrangements may be entered into between the employer and the Inland Revenue to treat the expenses paid to employees as covered by a 'dispensation' so that the process of of lodging claims for expenses is avoided. Such a dispensation will be granted if the Inland Revenue is satisfied that the scope of expenses paid to or for employees will not ultimately give rise to any loss of tax if the process of assessing and counter claiming were adhered to in full.

Section 198 ICTA 1988 determines what expenses an employee can deduct from his emoluments taxable under Schedule E. It falls into three parts; the holder of the office or employment may deduct:

1. the expenses of travelling in the performance of the duties of the office which he is necessarily obliged to incur and defray out of his emoluments;
2. the expenses of keeping and maintaining a horse to enable him to perform the duties of his office;
3. expenses which he incurs wholly, exclusively and necessarily in the performance of the duties of the office.

Travelling expenses

The wording of the section is 'is necessarily obliged to incur ... the expenses of travelling in the performance of the duties of the office'. The first case to arrive at the House of Lords was *Ricketts* v *Colquhoun* [1926] AC 1, where the House produced a interpretation so restrictive that it has made the section difficult to apply ever since. The ratio of the case can be described in the words of Lord Blanesburgh:

> 'The language of this section points to the expenses with which it is concerned as being confined to those which *each and every occupant* of the particular office is necessarily obliged to incur in the performance of his duties ...'

Thus Mr Ricketts could not deduct the expenses of travelling from his London practice to the courts in Portsmouth where he held a part-time appointment as a Recorder. It becomes clear that, as a general rule at least, travelling from home to work is not travelling in the performance of the duties of the office. After all, it might have been possible to appoint a person who lived closer – a barrister who lived in Portsmouth.

Subsequently, however, the House of Lords slightly modified its approach. In *Pook* v *Owen* [1969] TR 113 a GP held a part-time appointment as an obstetrician at a hospital 15 miles away. He was reimbursed part of the cost of travelling to the hospital but had to pay the rest himself. The House, by a majority in each case, held that the reimbursement was not an emolument, and that his own travelling expenditure was a deductible expense. Although the ratio of their Lordships is not clear, it would appear to be that his duties began as soon as he left home; he would receive a telephone call and give instructions before setting out. Thus it could be said that his home was also a place of work, and during his journey between the two places of work he was travelling in the performance of the duties of the office.

There still remained the Revenue argument that his journey *distance* was personal to himself. It was established, however, that the particular job could only be filled by a GP who would have to travel and, as Lord Wilberforce said:

> 'Section 198 is drafted in an objective form so as to distinguish between expenses which arise from the nature of the office and those which arise from the personal choice of the taxpayer. But this does not mean that no expenses can ever be deductible unless precisely those expenses must necessarily have been incurred by each and every office holder. The objective factor must relate to their nature, not to their amount.'

Before turning to a third case, it is necessary to refer to one particular statutory provision: s153. The section provides that where a person is employed as a director, or in employment earning £8,500 or more per annum, and is paid sums in respect of expenses, those sums shall be treated as part of his emoluments. The effect of the section is to require employees subject to s153 to bring any reimbursement of expenses into charge as an emolument and to justify the deduction of the actual expense itself under s198.

It was the precursor to this section that gave rise to a third case, *Taylor* v *Provan* [1975] AC 194. It would appear that the ratio of the case is that when a person is genuinely required to perform the duties of his office in two separate places, then any travelling expenses incurred in moving between them are deductible. Mr Provan was the only person in the world who was an expert in brewery take-overs; he lived in North America and worked for Allied Breweries in the United Kingdom. He was not paid, doing it as a 'hobby', but had the title of director; although he was only part-time, he fell foul of s153 and was required to bring the reimbursements of his transatlantic travel into charge under s191 and justify deductions under s198.

The House of Lords held that since the terms of his contract were that he was to perform as many of the duties of his office as he could in North America, only coming to England when absolutely necessary, the transatlantic travel was in the performance of the duties of the office. It may be that the ratio was, alternatively, that Mr Provan had a 'travelling occupation' – such as a travelling salesman has – where one of the duties of the employment is physically to travel.

Especially interesting are Lord Reid's comments about the second part of the s198 rules – the horse. Compare Vinelott J in *Perrons* v *Spackman* [1981] STC 739.

In 1995, the High Court decided in *Miners* v *Atkinson* [1997] STC 58 that a director who incorporated a company from his home address could not deduct the cost of travel from there to a client's premises. In this particular case he had worked at the client's premises under a contract initially up to one year but which was extended for several years thereafter. In delivering her judgment Arden J relied on *Horton* v *Young, Pook* v *Owen* and *Taylor* v *Provan* (above) and although the special commissioner had found that the taxpayer worked from his home address, his duties as a director were not necessarily carried out from there. These findings of fact were not disturbed by the High Court decision but the case therefore fell on the 'necessarily' aspect of s198 not being satisfied.

Section 62 of the Finance Act 1997 provides some relaxation of the travelling expenses rule. The section, amending s198 ICTA 1988, allows, from 1997/98 onwards, the additional cost of travelling from home direct to a site other than the normal place of employment. This eases the position highlighted in the travelling expenses cases referred to above.

Using own car for business travel

On 29 March 1996 the Inland Revenue published a new leaflet IR 125 which, among other things, extends the option of taking a fixed tax-free mileage allowance in accordance with the scales set out in the Fixed Profit Car Scheme previously adopted for civil service employees only. Any reimbursement of amounts up to this scale will not be taxed under Schedule E, and if no reimbursement is made and the expense satisfies the qualifying conditions in s198, as explained above, the employee may deduct an amount equivalent to the scale set out under this scheme.

Other expenses

These are even more difficult to deduct. It is vital to show that the expenses are wholly, exclusively and necessarily incurred for the purposes of the office: see Vaisey J in *Lomax* v *Newton* (1953) 34 TC 558. The rules to be deduced from the cases are:

1. It is not enough that one's employers require one to incur the expense because they feel it is desirable for the employee to do the things on which the money is spent. It must be shown that the money is spent in the performance of the duties of the office – *Brown* v *Bullock* (1961) 40 TC 1.
2. Expenses incurred to put one in a position to perform the duties of the office are not deductible. Thus in *Lupton* v *Potts* [1969] 1 WLR 1749 an articled clerk was not able to deduct the cost of his Part II solicitors' examinations. This was the argument pursued by the Revenue in the cases of *Fitzpatrick* v *IRC (No 2)*; *Smith* v *Abbott* [1994] STC 237, both concerning groups of journalists. The Revenue eventually won in each case, but not before the cases reached the House

of Lords. In the *Abbott* case a finding of fact by the Commissioners that there was a requirement to incur the expense of newspapers purchased by the taxpayers, and for which they were reimbursed, was sufficient for the Court of Appeal to hold in favour of the taxpayer (Mr Abbott, who was alone among the five in losing in the High Court) and to dismiss the Revenue's appeals against the High Court judgment in favour of Mr Abbott's four colleagues. Although the amount reimbursed was acknowledged to be taxable, the expense was held to be incurred not as preparatory to, but 'in', the performance of the duties of the employment.

However, the House of Lords decided that the Commissioners had erred in law and ruled that the expenses, although a requirement, were to enable the journalists to perform their employment duties better and were not incurred 'in the performance' of those duties. See also *Wilcock* v *Eve* [1995] STC 18 concerning payment for loss of the opportunity to exercise a share option.
3. United Kingdom resident individuals are now given relief as a set-off against income for payments made by themselves with regard to qualifying vocational training schemes under s31 FA 1991.

8.9 Removal expenses

Where an employee receives from his employer assistance with or reimbursement of removal expenses in the course of changing or taking up employment, Schedule 11A ICTA 1988 has applied since 1993–94, so the expenses are not emoluments within s19 insofar as they are qualifying expenses. The qualifying expenses (as listed in Schedule 11A) are however subject to a current limit of £8,000 – Schedule 11A para 24(9). This replaces the tax-free treatment of more liberal amounts under extra-statutory concession. Interest on a 'beneficial loan' from an employer may also be included within the £8,000 limit.

8.10 Redundancy payments

Payments made under the government's statutory redundancy scheme, whereby redundant employees are entitled to a fixed amount dependent upon their length of service, are not taxable as provided for in s579 ICTA 1988.

Other payments arising on the occasion of redundancy may be taxable as emoluments if they are not made to directly compensate the employee for the loss of employment or related rights. The requirement, particularly in the light of the cases considered below, is to establish the precise nature of each payment and, having regard to the circumstances in which it is made, the precise purpose to which each payment is attached. True redundancy payments can become blurred with other termination of employment payments. Each individual case and set of circumstances giving rise to the payment, as to whether it is occasioned more by retirement, dismissal or on unacceptable changes in the employment, needs to be examined.

It had been considered, following *Dale* v *de Soissons* [1950] 2 All ER 460, that the existence of contractual rights to payments in these circumstances necessarily made them taxable as emoluments. This was put in some doubt following *Mairs* v *Haughey* [1993] 3 WLR 393. This case held that the redundancy payments, even if contractual and non-statutory (and not therefore already exempt under s579) were not emoluments of the employment nor for acting as an employee. Therefore by applying the test in *Hochstrasser* v *Mayes* (1959) 38 TC 673, the payments were not emoluments for the purpose of s19 ICTA 1988. The practice in this area had been based on the Inland Revenue's Statement of Practice SP 1/81 which was revised (SP 1/94 dated 17 february 1994) following the decision. In assessing the nature of the payments it could be argued that while all employments will inevitably end, not all will end in redundancy and therefore that payments made in the latter are purely contingent on some external cause.

In *Allan* v *IRC, Cullen* v *IRC* [1994] STC 943, two related Scottish cases heard before the Court of Session, employees were informed of impending redundancy and that they were to be paid supplementary redundancy payments in addition to payments under the statutory scheme. In the event, certain employees including Mr Allan and Mrs Cullen were re-engaged by the company's new owners but still received the same redundancy payments as those who were not re-employed.

It was held that the payments could not be said to be made in anticipation of the loss of employment and were therefore to be treated as emoluments of the employment and taxable under s19 ICTA 1988.

9

The Foreign Element of Schedules D and E

9.1 Domicile, residence and ordinary residence

9.2 Foreign element of Schedule D Cases I and II

9.3 Schedule D Cases IV and V

9.4 The foreign basis of computation under Schedule D

9.5 The foreign element of Schedule E

9.1 Domicile, residence and ordinary residence

This Chapter is concerned with the circumstances in which income arising outside the United Kingdom is liable to United Kingdom income tax and also with the circumstances in which foreigners are liable to tax in the United Kingdom. The Inland Revenue published a Consultative Document entitled *Residence in the United Kingdom – the Scope of United Kingdom Taxation for Individuals* in 1988, but in the end decided against making any major changes in the law. However, FA 1995 made important changes to the taxing of non-residents liable to tax through a branch or agency. The existing provisions in ss78–85 Taxes Management Act 1970 are replaced, but the principles established by case law concerning the exercise of trade in the United Kingdom are not enshrined in the new legislation. They are left to apply as before (See section 9.2.)

There are three 'connecting factors' whose existence or non-existence can be decisive in determining liability to tax:

1. domicile;
2. residence;
3. ordinary residence.

Domicile

Domicile is not, save in the case of Inheritance Tax, a word with a special meaning for tax purposes. Accordingly, it bears the meaning usually attributed to it in the context of Conflict of Laws. Reference should be made to books such as Dicey & Morris *The Conflict of Laws* for an exact definition. A person's domicile means the country where he has his permanent home or to which he intends to return.

The three essential categories of domicile are:

1. domicile of origin;
2. domicile of choice; and
3. domicile of dependency.

Domicile of origin is that acquired at birth. Domicile of choice is that acquired through complete abandonment of the domicile of origin. Domicile of dependency is principally that acquired through marriage. In 1992 a Reform of the Law of Domicile Bill was presented to Parliament but in 1996 the government announced that it had no immediate intention of making any change in the law.

There are provisions in s207 of the Income and Corporation Taxes Act 1988 and s9(2) of the Taxation of Chargeable Gains Act 1992 for resolving disputes on domicile and ordinary residence.

Residence

'Residence' does, however, have a technical tax meaning. The rules which exist are partly statutory and partly imposed by the Inland Revenue, which has adopted those judicial decisions which favour it. On this basis, a taxpayer is said to be resident in the United Kingdom in any tax year if:

1. He spends six months (183 days) or more in the United Kingdom during the tax year. Days of arrival and departure are, in practice, ignored. This applies even if the taxpayer is only temporarily in the United Kingdom: see s336(1) ICTA 1988.
2. He spends regular 'substantial' periods in the United Kingdom in several consecutive years. The Revenue interprets 'substantial' as meaning visits averaging three months or more each year for four years or more: see Inland Revenue pamphlet IR 20.
3. He maintains a place of abode in the United Kingdom and visits the United Kingdom for one day at least in the tax year: see *Cooper* v *Cadwalader* (1904) 5 TC 107; *Loewenstein* v *De Salis* (1926) 10 TC 424; and IR 20. However, the Finance Act 1993 disapplies the place of abode test in determining the residence status of those whose presence in the United Kingdom is for a temporary purpose only. This will affect the application of s336 ICTA 1988 and s9 TCGA 1992.

If, however, the person works full time in a trade, profession or vocation, no part of which is carried on outside the United Kingdom, or in an office or employment, all the duties of which are carried on outside the United Kingdom, this rule does not apply: s335(1) and (2) ICTA 1988. In determining whether this rule has been satisfied, the performance of duties (ie Schedule E duties only) in the United

Kingdom which are 'merely incidental' to the person's other duties can be ignored. This is a very restrictive rule, though: see *Robson* v *Dixon* [1972] 3 All ER 671.

There are no provisions in the Income Tax Acts for residence to be determined other than on a full income tax year basis. Strictly, therefore, income tax years may not be split between periods of residence and of non-residence. However, the position is covered in practice by an extra-statutory concession, A11, a revised version of which was issued on 29 January 1996. The concession allows for separate periods where an individual comes to the United Kingdom to take up permanent residence or to stay for a period of at least two years.

Similarly, the concession applies to split the tax year if the individual leaves the United Kingdom, having been resident here, for the purpose of taking up permanent residence abroad. In the year of arrival in the United Kingdom, the concession is not applied where a person ordinarily resident in the United Kingdom left for intended permanent residence abroad, but returned to the United Kingdom to reside here before the end of the next tax year. The concession is available where an individual goes abroad for full-time employment covering at least one income tax year and does not visit the United Kingdom for 183 days or more in any tax year or for an average of 91 days or more over a period of absence up to four years. In these circumstances the limit of a non-resident's liability to income tax under s128 FA 1995 has no relevance since that section applies only to complete income tax years of non-residence.

The Inland Revenue issued an interpretation statement (see Issue no 6 *Inland Revenue Tax Bulletin* February 1993) explaining its understanding of the meaning of 'full-time employment' for the purpose of s335 ICTA 1988. Where people are in other than 35–40 hours per week employment, the Revenue will recognise, for example, several concurrent part-time jobs, the aggregation of several jobs within the same group, and the fact that there may be an absence of a formal structure in certain types of occupation.

Note: *Inland Revenue Tax Bulletins* are available from the Inland Revenue, Finance Division, Barrington Road, Worthing, West Sussex BN12 4XH.

Ordinary residence

Clearly, 'ordinary residence' is a narrower term than mere 'residence': not all persons who are resident in the United Kingdom are also ordinarily resident. Neither, however, will a person who is ordinarily resident in the United Kingdom *necessarily* be resident here – though almost always it will be the case that he is. One definition of the phrase was given by Viscount Sumner in *IRC* v *Lysaght* [1928] AC 234:

> 'I think the converse to ordinarily is extraordinarily and that part of the regular order of a man's life, adopted voluntarily and for settled purposes, is not extraordinary.'

In *R* v *Barnet LBC, ex parte Shah* [1983] 2 AC 309, Lord Scarman, delivering the leading speech, observed that in *Lysaght* and in *Levene* v *IRC* [1928] AC 217 the

House of Lords had given the words 'ordinary residence', in their tax context, their natural and ordinary meaning as words of common usage in the English language. He took the phrase to mean an abode which an individual had adopted 'voluntarily and for settled purposes as part of the regular order of his life for the time being, whether of short or of long duration'. This might be for a limited period so long as 'the purpose of living where one does has a sufficient degree of continuity to be properly described as settled'. (Quoted in *Reed* v *Clark* [1985] STC 323: see section 9.2.)

Thus it would seem that a man might go abroad for a tax year, having lived in the United Kingdom for many years and intending to do so again after his sojourn abroad, and, though not resident in the United Kingdom during that year, would still remain ordinarily resident (see, again, *Reed* v *Clark*, below). See also *Nichols* v *Gibson* [1996] STC 1008 in Chapter 8, section 8.6, where the taxpayer sought unsuccessfully to exploit the change of residence position.

The residence of companies

Companies do not have a domicile, even for tax purposes. Since, however, some connecting factor is necessary in order to establish tax liability, residence has become that factor. The topic is difficult, and the judicial pronouncements conflict. Moreover, some statutory guidance has been offered by the Finance Act 1988. The following principles appear, however, to form the basis of the modern law on the subject:

1. Under s66(1) FA 1988 a company incorporated in the United Kingdom is to be regarded as resident there for tax purposes. Where this rule applies it excludes the operation of any other rule of law for determining the tax residence of the company.
2. A company which is not incorporated in the United Kingdom may nevertheless be resident there if its central management and control exists there: *De Beers Consolidated Mines Ltd* v *Howe* [1906] AC 455.
3. That place of central management is *not* where the directors are resident: *John Hood and Co Ltd* v *Magee* (1918) 7 TC 327. Thus if the directors carry on the administration of the company from Jersey and hold all board meetings there, the fact that they fly over from the United Kingdom to do so each time will not prevent the company, being resident in Jersey and not in the United Kingdom. Historically the main test of where the place of central management of a company was located, was where the company's Board of Directors met. With greater ease of transport and communication, this is no longer considered an effective test on its own merits. One now has to look at where the real decisions as to the operation of the company are taken on a day-to-day basis – ie the place of effective management.
4. As *De Beers* said, it is the place where the central management is *actually* carried on and not the place where it *ought* to be carried on which is vital: see *Unit*

Construction Co Ltd v *Bullock* (1959) 38 TC 712, where, contrary to the rules contained in the Articles of Association, the central management of a Kenyan company's affairs was carried on in the United Kingdom by the parent company and not by the Kenyan Board of Directors. Accordingly, the company was resident in the United Kingdom.
5. Factors which are usually irrelevant are:

   – the place where the company trades;
   – the residence of the shareholders;
   – the country of registration (as opposed to incorporation) of the company.

9.2 Foreign element of Schedule D Cases I and II

Section 18 ICTA 1988 provides, inter alia, that income tax is charged in respect of the annual profits or gains arising or accruing:

1. to a *resident* of the United Kingdom from any trade, profession or vocation *whether carried on in the United Kingdom or elsewhere*;
2. to any person *not* resident in the United Kingdom ... from any trade, profession or vocation *exercised within the United Kingdom*.

Clearly, the rule which can at once be derived from this is that Schedule D Cases I and II do not catch the income of a non-resident derived from a business exercised wholly outside the United Kingdom.

Residents

The width of s18 is apparent in the words 'whether carried on in the United Kingdom or elsewhere' and would appear to bring into charge the profits a person makes from a business carried on wholly abroad. This possibility has, however, been negated by judicial decisions, in particular, by *Colquhoun* v *Brooks* (1889) 2 TC 490 which decided that Cases I and II are only applicable to businesses which are carried on partly abroad *and* partly in the United Kingdom. Where a resident carries on a business *wholly* abroad, the Revenue has to look to Case V instead.

The scope of *Colquhoun* v *Brooks* itself has, however, been restricted to a certain extent by subsequent case law. Although it is relatively easy for a person who carries on trade abroad in partnership with non-residents to show that Case I cannot apply, it is much more difficult for a sole trader to do so. Indeed, in *Ogilvie* v *Kitton* (1908) 5 TC 338 the court went so far as to decide that the profits accruing to the sole owner of a business which traded entirely in Toronto, Canada, were still liable under Case I, because although he exercised no control over the day-to-day management of the business, yet he had sufficient control over the direction of the business from Scotland for the business to be considered to be trading in the United Kingdom.

The meaning of the term 'trading in the United Kingdom' essentially is that the economic activities from which profits are obtained are carried on in the United Kingdom: see *Erichsen* v *Last* (1881) 4 TC 422 (re the place where contracts are made) and *Firestone Tyre and Rubber Co Ltd* v *Lewellin* [1957] 1 All ER 561 (re an American company trading in the United Kingdom and being assessed through its subsidiary as its agent).

In *Reed* v *Clark* [1985] STC 323 the court held that a taxpayer, who was a British subject, domiciled in England, and hitherto resident and ordinarily resident in the United Kingdom, was not resident there in the year 1978–79 within the contemplation of s18, and could not be regarded as having left the United Kingdom for the purposes of 'occasional residence abroad' within s334, notwithstanding that he lived in the United States of America throughout the relevant year of assessment to avoid liability to income tax. Because his income under Schedule D was based on a previous year basis, Mr Clark could not be assessed as a non-resident in his year of absence.

As far as Case II is concerned, great difficulty will always be encountered by a professional person who seeks to convince a court that he carries on entirely separate activities outside the United Kingdom from those carried on within the United Kingdom, so as to prove that he exercises two separate professions; see, for example, *Davies* v *Braithwaite* (1931) 18 TC 198. Nevertheless, a successful attempt to achieve this was made in *Padmore* v *IRC* [1987] STC 36 in which Peter Gibson J held that it was possible for a partnership to have a residence, as much as a company or an individual, with the consequence that the taxpayer escaped tax on profits from a Jersey patent agency in accordance with the Jersey Double Tax Convention. The effects of this result were countered by legislation which can now be found in s112(4) and (5) ICTA 1988.

Non-residents

A non-resident is liable to pay United Kingdom income tax on profits from a business exercised within the United Kingdom. The distinction which has to be made is that between trading *within* the United Kingdom and trading *with* the United Kingdom. In the early cases, the courts held that the place where the contract was made was all important. Thus in *Erichsen* v *Last* (above) Brett LJ said:

> '... wherever profitable contracts are habitually made in England by or for a foreigner with persons in England, because these persons are in England, to do something for, or supply something to those persons, such foreigners are exercising a profitable trade in England, even though everything done by or supplied by them in order to fulfil their part of the contract is done abroad. The profit arises to them from the contract they make.'

This is still the rule as far as contracts of sale are concerned: the courts have, however, been less happy to apply this rule alone in the more complex world of manufacturing. In this case the rule is: where do the operations take place from which the profits in substance arise? See *Firestone Tyre Co Ltd* v *Llewellin* (1957) 37

TC 111. The decisions in these cases are still relevant under the post Finance Act 1995 regime (see below).

Most non-residents trading in the United Kingdom do so through a branch or agency in the United Kingdom – for an example, see *Hafton Properties Ltd* v *McHugh* [1987] STC 16 (especially the decision of the Special Commissioners, upheld by Peter Gibson J). See below for the current provisions relating to the liability of branches and agents which were introduced with effect from 1996–97.

Post Finance Act 1995 – non-residents and their representatives

As noted in section 9.1, there are new provisions governing the method of taxing non-residents in receipt of income via a branch or an agency. Sections 78–85 TMA 1970 are replaced, and the regime introduced by ss126–129 and Schedule 23 FA 1995 has brought in the concept of a United Kingdom representative on whom the relevant tax liability falls. A branch or an agency is a non-resident's United Kingdom representative for these purposes. There is now a limit imposed on the extent of that liability, it being confined mainly to the income which is not subject to tax at source. This was previously limited in the same way, but only by Inland Revenue extra-statutory concession. Under the new rules it has full statutory force. As explained in the section on residence in section 9.1, this limitation on liability applies only to complete income tax years and not to split years comprising periods of non-residence and residence.

Additionally, the United Kingdom members of a partnership are collectively deemed to be the United Kingdom representative of a non-resident, contrary to the individual responsibility which partners now face under the self-assessment rules for their shares of United Kingdom partnership income (s125 FA 1995).

Agents in receipt of income for non-residents in the exercise of investment management transactions, or those acting as brokers or who are not acting as the regular agent of the non-resident, are excluded from assessment as the United Kingdom representative (s127 FA 1995).

The provisions of the former s83 (see above) allowing for the retention of monies to pay taxes are now confined to 'independent agents' (Schedule 23 paragraph 7 FA 1995).

The new provisions were introduced to meet the changing situation regarding self-assessment, which are also available to non-residents. (See Chapter 4 for the changes affecting tax on property income paid to non-residents.)

9.3 Schedule D Cases IV and V

Schedule D Case IV charges tax in respect of income 'arising from *securities* out of the United Kingdom'; Case V, in respect of income 'arising from *possessions* out of the United Kingdom, not being income consisting of emoluments of any office or employment'.

'Securities' means debts or claims the payment of which has in some way been secured; surprisingly, it does not include stocks or shares. Debentures, however, are embraced by Case IV, since they are secured by a floating charge: see *Williams* v *Singer* [1921] 1 AC 41.

'Possessions', though, has a much wider meaning, catching all forms of income not falling within Case IV – other than income from foreign employments. See, once again, *Colquhoun* v *Brooks* (1889) 2 TC 490. Thus it covers payments made under a discretionary trust: *Drummond* v *Collins* [1915] AC 1011. Most importantly, however, it brings into charge income from foreign trades.

Income from property situated outside the United Kingdom is taxed under Case V of Schedule D, the profits and losses of which are calculated in the same manner as those for a Schedule A rental business (see Chapter 4). Income is charged on the current year basis – the profits of the year ended 5 April 1998 are charged to tax for the tax year 1997/98. The tax year 1997/98 is the first year of the new current year basis where the property was let before the 5 April 1994. Properties first let after that date became subject to the current year basis immediately.

Cases IV and V apply, of course, only to persons who are resident in the United Kingdom.

9.4 The foreign basis of computation under Schedule D

Cases I and II

The charge under s18 ICTA 1988 is imposed on the full amount arising of the profits or gains, whether or not remitted to the United Kingdom. The usual rules of assessment will apply to the income.

Cases IV and V

Section 65(1) ICTA 1988 charges tax on the full amount of the income arising in the current year of assessment, whether or not remitted to the United Kingdom (but this is now subject to change: see 'The new current year basis of assessment', below).

There are, however, certain exceptions to this:

Section 65(2) ICTA 1988
Where the income which is chargeable on an arising basis is a foreign pension, s65(2) allows a 10 per cent deduction, without restriction, from the amount to be brought into charge.

Certain taxpayers still chargeable on the remittance basis
A 'remittance' basis of assessment brings into charge in a year of assessment only so much of the income as is *remitted* to the United Kingdom. Section 65 ICTA 1988

goes into great detail as to when income is remitted or to be treated as remitted to the United Kingdom. The general rule is that if sums spent here are in some way derived from the income, or if property brought into the country was purchased with the income, then the income is to be treated as remitted.

The current rules are most easily set out in a table as follows:

Types of income	Investment income	Foreign pensions	Foreign trades
Taxpayer resident, ordinarily resident, and domiciled United Kingdom	Full amount arising	Amount arising minus 10%	Full amount arising
Taxpayer resident, ordinarily resident but *not* domiciled in United Kingdom	Remittances	Remittances	Remittances
Taxpayer resident, *not* ordinarily resident but domiciled in United Kingdom	Remittances	Remittances	Remittances
Taxpayer resident, but not ordinarily resident and not domiciled in United Kingdom	Remittances	Remittances	Remittances

The new current year basis of assessment

In common with the fundamental changes affecting the rest of Schedule D (see Chapter 6), the basis of assessment under Cases IV and V is switching to the current year one. By s207 FA 1994, ss65–67 ICTA 1988, which provide for the previous year's profits being the normal basis of assessment under Schedule D Cases IV and V, will be amended from 1997–98, but for new sources, beginning from 6 April 1994 onwards, the new provisions are effective immediately.

From 1997–98 the previous year's basis will be discarded in favour of a current year basis, and the opening and closing years' adjustments of ss65–67 will no longer be required. Income will in future be assessed strictly on the actual income of the fiscal year.

9.5 The foreign element of Schedule E

As mentioned in the preceding chapter, Schedule E is divided into three Cases, which reflect differing territorial restrictions:

Case I

Case I applies to persons who are both resident and ordinarily resident in the United Kingdom. It applies to *all* emoluments.

Case II

Case II applies to persons who are:

1. resident but not ordinarily resident;
2. not resident but ordinarily resident;
3. neither resident nor ordinarily resident.

In short it applies to non-residents and to those who, if resident, are not ordinarily resident. It applies only to emoluments for the period in question in respect of duties performed in the United Kingdom.

Case III

Case III applies to persons who are:

1. resident but not ordinarily resident;
2. resident and ordinarily resident.

It does not overlap with Cases I or II, however, but only applies to certain special types of income excluded from these Cases (s131(2)):

1. foreign emoluments for duties performed outside the United Kingdom by a person resident but not ordinarily resident;
2. foreign emoluments for duties wholly performed outside the United Kingdom by one both resident and ordinarily resident;
3. emoluments for duties performed outside the United Kingdom by one resident but not ordinarily resident in the United Kingdom.

Case III catches emoluments which are remitted to the United Kingdom in the year of assessment. Section 65 rules apply to determine what has been remitted or is to be treated as remitted. 'Foreign emoluments' are emoluments earned by a person who is not *domiciled* in the United Kingdom from an office or employment with any person not *resident* in the United Kingdom.

Certain reductions are available:

1. in respect of emoluments earned in jobs involving a certain amount of time spent out of the United Kingdom;
2. in respect of foreign emoluments.

Persons resident and ordinarily resident in the United Kingdom

Such persons are chargeable under Case I in all but one instance (foreign emoluments for duties wholly performed outside the United Kingdom: Case III). Unless the emoluments are foreign emoluments, the whole of the income is chargeable to tax.

Duties performed outside the United Kingdom

Section 193 ICTA 1988 affords certain relief in respect of earnings from work done abroad.

The 100 per cent deduction: s193(1) ICTA 1988. If the taxpayer can accumulate a 'qualifying period' of at least 365 days, then a 100 per cent deduction is permitted from all his emoluments from the office in that period; thus, there will be no tax charged in respect of them. A 'qualifying period' is a period consisting either wholly of days of absence from the United Kingdom, or partly of days of absence and partly of days of presence: Schedule 12 para 3 ICTA 1988. A 'day of absence' means a day on which the taxpayer was absent from the United Kingdom at midnight: see *Hoye* v *Forsdyke* [1981] STC 711.

Days of presence in the United Kingdom can be added to days of absence if:

1. after the days of presence there are more days of absence;
2. the days of presence in the qualifying period do not exceed 62 in all;
3. the days of presence do not exceed more than one sixth of the whole period.

The 365 days are built up gradually, and these three rules must be satisfied in relation to each period.

The ability to link one period with a previous period applies only where the employee remains resident and ordinarily resident in the United Kingdom throughout the combined periods (or became so prior to 6 April 1992): see *Inland Revenue Statement of Practice* SP18/91 6 December 1991.

Example
Fred, a person resident, ordinarily resident and domiciled in the United Kingdom, goes to work for Smith (France) Ltd. He spends 90 days in France, 10 in England, 80 in France, 10 in England, 70 in France, 40 in England and 70 in France. The whole period qualifies because:

1. there are only 60 days of presence in the whole period;
2. $90 + 10 + 80 = 180$ days; $10 < \frac{1}{6}$ of 180
   $180 + 10 + 70 = 260$ days; $10 + 10 = 20 < \frac{1}{6}$ of 260
   $260 + 40 + 70 = 370$ days; $10 + 10 + 40 = 60 < \frac{1}{6}$ of 370

If however, the period were to be reversed, so that it went:

70(F); 40(E); 70(F); 10(E); 80(F); 10(E); 90(F)

then Fred would not qualify for a 100 per cent reduction since his first period would run:

70 + 40 + 70 = 180 days; 40 > ⅙ of 180.

Accordingly, the first 110 days could not be connected with the remaining 260.

Schedule 12 para 1A ICTA 1988, introduced in 1992, provides that the exemption applies to emoluments after all allowable deductions so that the deductions are not capable of reducing any other chargeable income.

Persons resident but not ordinarily resident in the United Kingdom

Such persons will find emoluments chargeable either under Case II or under Case III.

1. Where the duties are performed *wholly* in the United Kingdom, all the emoluments are chargeable under Case II, with reductions for foreign emoluments (see above) where available.
2. Where the duties are performed *wholly outside* the United Kingdom, the *only* emoluments chargeable are those *remitted* to the United Kingdom which fall within Case III.
3. Where the duties are performed partly within and partly outside the United Kingdom, emoluments attributable to duties performed *within* the United Kingdom are chargeable under Case II; those attributable to duties performed outside the United Kingdom are chargeable under Case III if remitted.

Persons not resident in the United Kingdom

1. If the duties are performed wholly within the United Kingdom, then the emoluments will be susceptible to United Kingdom income tax and chargeable under Case II. Foreign emoluments may obtain a reduction where this is still available.
2. If the duties are wholly performed outside the United Kingdom the emoluments will not be susceptible to United Kingdom income tax – Case III only applies to *residents*.
3. If the duties are performed partly within and partly outside the United Kingdom, only those emoluments attributable to duties performed within the United Kingdom will be susceptible to United Kingdom income tax and chargeable under Case II.

Such persons will find that some emoluments are susceptible to United Kingdom income tax and that these are chargeable under Case II.

Setting all this out in tabular form:

Table A: Employees domiciled in the United Kingdom

Type of individual	Duties performed		
	Wholly in the United Kingdom	Partly in, partly out of the United Kingdom	Wholly outside the United Kingdom
Resident and ordinarily resident in the United Kingdom	Taxable in full	Long absences – reduced by 100% – Section 193(1) ICTA 1988	
Resident but not ordinarily resident in the United Kingdom	Taxable under Case II in full	Earnings related to UK duties – taxable under Case II in full overseas earnings – Case III remittance basis	Remittance basis under Case III
Not resident in the United Kingdom	As above	As above	No assessment

Table B: Employees not domiciled in the United Kingdom

Type of individual	Duties performed		
	Wholly in the United Kingdom	Partly in, partly out of the United Kingdom	Wholly outside the United Kingdom

If employed by a United Kingdom resident employer, use Table A in all cases. If employed by a non-resident employer the emoluments are 'foreign emoluments', in which case –

Resident and ordinarily resident in the United Kingdom	Case I	a) United Kingdom earnings – Case I b) overseas earnings – Case III remittance basis	Remittance basis only – Schedule E Case III
Resident but not ordinarily resident in the United Kingdom	Case II on all (United Kingdom) earnings	a) Case II on UK earnings b) Case III remittance basis	Remittance basis only under Schedule E Case III
Not resident in the United Kingdom	Case II	Case II on UK earnings. Overseas earnings not chargeable	Not chargeable

10

Partnership Taxation

10.1 Introduction

10.2 Existence of a partnership

10.3 Mode of assessment and liability for tax

10.4 Change of partners

10.5 Partnership losses

10.6 Partnership retirement annuities

10.7 Partnerships controlled abroad or trading abroad

10.1 Introduction

Two very important changes have taken place which fundamentally alter the historical basis on which partnerships have been taxed in the United Kingdom. The phasing out of the 'previous year basis' (see Chapter 6) for all assessment under Schedule D is combined with the introduction of 'self-assessment' (see Chapter 24) to change both the amount on which and the administrative arrangements under which partnerships (as well as other income tax payers) are assessed. For partnerships the new rules go one step further in ending the joint and several liability of partners for the total partnership tax and replacing this with individual liability (through self-assessment) for tax on one's own 'total income' (see Chapter 3), which includes the allocated share of income from a partnership. Nourse J's statement from *Reed* v *Young* [1984] STC 38 (see below) illustrates the problems which have surrounded partnership taxation in the past. Under the previous year basis it was a recurrent anomaly that a partner was paying tax on a portion of profits different from what he was actually earning in any tax year where the partnership sharing ratio had changed as a result of incoming or retiring partners or other agreed changes in profit-sharing ratios. The changes which affect partnerships can be found in the Finance Acts 1994, ss184–189, and 1995, s117.

10.2 Existence of a partnership

In order for the special rules relating to the taxation of a partnership to apply, a partnership according to the rules of general law must exist. Section 1 of the Partnership Act 1890 defines 'partnership' as 'the relation which subsists between persons carrying on business in common with a view to profit'. Thus neither a body of trustees nor a members' club will normally be a partnership.

The difficulty is, however, that partnership merely describes a special relationship existing between separate persons; a partnership in England is not a separate legal entity as a company is – it is merely a collection of individuals. The Taxes Acts, however, ignore this to a certain extent, assessing the profits of a business carried on by a partnership jointly on the partnership rather than on the persons comprising it.

It should be noted, however, that capital gains tax arising on the disposal of partnership assets is charged on the partners separately.

10.3 Mode of assessment and liability for tax

Section 117 FA 1995 provides that on the introduction of self-assessment from 1996–97 onwards there will no longer be a combined partnership assessment on the total profits of the partnership. Instead, each partner's share of the profits will be taxed on him, since self-assessment provides for one assessment on each individual incorporating total income from all sources.

The result of this change is that a partnership is no longer to be treated as distinct from the partners who are the members of the partnership (see the amended form of s111 of the Income and Corporation Taxes Act 1988 as introduced by s117 FA 1995). Partners are to be individually assessed on their total incomes, including the share of partnership profits, ending the historical system of the global partnership assessment with allocation of the total tax bill among the constituent partners, where the legal liability for payment was a joint and several one for the total amount assessed.

Pre-FA 1995 form of s111 ICTA 1988

Section 111 ICTA 1988, in the form which applied before FA 1995 changes, provided that:

> 'Where a trade or profession is carried on by two or more persons jointly, income tax in respect thereof shall be computed and stated jointly, and in one sum, and shall be separate and distinct from any other tax chargeable on those persons or any of them, and a joint assessment shall be made in the partnership name.'

Thus the liability for paying the tax was placed on the partnership, rather than each partner being directly liable for his portion alone. As with individuals, in general the assessment was based on the profits arising in the accounting period ending in the preceding year of assessment, but those profits were divided among the partners for total income purposes according to the profit-sharing ratios of the current year of assessment. Each partner's personal allowances were then deducted from that partner's respective share of profit before tax was calculated at each partner's rate and the result combined in one global assessment.

The matter was discussed by Nourse J in *Reed* v *Young* [1984] STC 38, at p57:

> 'It has long been settled that partnership income is taxed on an artificial basis. An assessment in the partnership name is made on the partners, who are jointly liable to the Revenue for the whole of any tax which may be payable. There must then be an apportionment of the income between the partners so as to arrive at each individual's income. The partnership is not taxed on the income of the year of assessment, but on that of the previous year. That income is known as the statutory income. The income of a partner for any year is deemed to be the share of the statutory income to which he is entitled during that year (see *Lewis* v *IRC* [1933] 2 KB 557).'

Revised provisions of ICTA 1988 s111

As mentioned above, s117 FA 1995 introduced a new form of wording for partnership taxation into ICTA 1988, the principal changes being reflected in the following:

> '(1) Where a trade or profession is carried on by persons in partnership, the partnership shall not, unless the contrary intention appears, be treated for the purposes of the Tax Acts as an entity which is separate and distinct from those persons.
> (2) So long as a trade or profession is carried on by persons in partnership, and any of those persons is chargeable to income tax, the profits or gains or losses arising from the trade or profession ... shall be computed ... as if (a) the person were an individual; ...
> (3) A person's share in the profits or gains or losses ... for any period ... shall be determined according to the interests of the partners during that period.'

It will be noted from subs(2) above that partnerships comprised wholly of companies are not affected by the changes.

Computing the partnership assessment

Because of the special treatment meted out to partnership income, it is necessary to determine what, exactly, that income is. The rules were, and still remain after FA 1995 changes, as follows:

1. Salaries paid to partners are not to be deducted in computing profits, because a partner is not, if he *is* a partner, an employee: *Stekel* v *Ellice* [1973] 1 WLR 191. Accordingly, any salary will form part of the profits given to him, and be taken into account in determining the profit-sharing ratios.
2. Similarly, interest paid to a partner on the capital he has contributed to the partnership is treated as an attribution to the partner of profits and is earned income – see the example below.

3. If the partnership rents property from one of the partners, that will not be a mere attribution of profits by reference to capital contributed to the partnership, since the property will not be partnership property. The rent will, therefore, be deductible in computing the profits of the partnership; it will not be added to the partner's profits in determining the profit-sharing ratios but will be Schedule A income of the individual partner to be included in the total income return for self-assessment purposes.

Each partner is entitled to have personal reliefs due to him set off against his share of the partnership profits. This would reduce not only his own share of tax but also the partnership's joint liability to tax.

If the reliefs are not exhausted after being utilised in this way, the excess may be set off either against the partner's other general income or against his share of the firm's liability in respect of investment income.

Example

V, W and X have been in partnership for several years. Their profit-sharing agreement is as follows:

		V	W	X
		£	£	£
Interest on capital		400	200	100
Salaries		NIL	600	1,000
Balance of profits:	Until 31.3.1995	1/3	1/3	1/3
	After 31.3.1995	2/5	2/5	1/5

They draw up their accounts to 31 March each year. Their adjusted profit for tax purposes for the year ending 31 March 1995 was £32,300. Therefore, £2,300 of the profit is taken in the form of interest and salaries, leaving £30,000 to be shared further among the partners in their respective sharing ratios.

Note: the interest part of the allocation is still earned income for all purposes and not investment income. It is merely a mechanism in sharing out the partnership profits.

The *actual* division of profits was:

	V	W	X
	£	£	£
Interest	400	200	100
Salary	NIL	600	1,000
Balance of profits	10,000	10,000	10,000
	10,400	10,800	11,100

These profits would be brought into charge (on the old preceding year basis) in the Year of Assessment 1995-96. They would be divided for tax purposes, however, by reference to the profit-sharing ratio current in 1995-96 and not that current when they were earned. Under the current year basis, the basis period and the allocation year will coincide. Thus the profits for the year to 31 March 1998 will be assessed for the year 1997–98 (and not 1998–99) and allocated according to the partnership agreement sharing ratio for the year ended 31 March 1998.

	V	W	X
	£	£	£
Interest on capital	400	200	100
Salaries	NIL	600	1,000
Balance 2:2:1	12,000	12,000	6,000
	12,400	12,800	7,100

Under the historical system, each partner's personal allowances would be deducted from each of the above figures and the tax calculated on each balance at each partner's rate of tax, giving three tax amounts which would be aggregated to give the total partnership tax. Under the new rules, each of these amounts would be the subject of a separate assessment on each partner for which he alone would be liable for payment. Thus under the old system, if partner X had personal allowances of £7,100 or more no tax would be due on his share, but he remained potentially liable for the partnership's total tax.

Basis of assessment for existing partnerships continuing beyond 5 April 1997

The following shows the effects of both self-assessment and the change to current years basis of assessment where a pre 5 April 1994 partnership continues to trade after 5 April 1997:

1995–96
– Assessed on profits of previous year
– Composite assessment on partnership
– Allocate to partners on sharing ratios for tax year 1995–96

1996–97
– Assessed on year's average of profits for 24 months ending in 1996–97 tax year
– Composite assessment on partnership
– Allocate to partners on sharing ratios for tax year 1996–97

1997–98
– Assessed on profits of accounting year ended in 1997–98
– Each partner self-assessed
– Share on which self-assessed is that of the accounting year

Basis of assessment on cessation of partnership

Where a partnership ceases, each partner is assessed on his share of profits in the final year, based on the profits from the end of the accounting period which formed the basis of assessment for the year preceding the final year, up to the date of cessation – eg a partnership whose accounts year ends annually on 31 August will be assessed for 1997/98 on profits for the year ended 31 August 1997. If it ceases on 30 September 1998, the taxable profits for each partner for 1998/99 will be those for the period from 1 September 1997 to 30 September 1998. If the partnership continues, but a partner retires on 30 September 1998, he will be taxed for 1998/99 on the same 13-month period mentioned above, whereas continuing partners will be taxed on their share of profits for the year ended 31 August 1998.

10.4 Change of partners

When partnerships are assessed on the current year basis under the new rules, changes in the composition of the partnership will not make the same impact as before. Because the profits of the basis period will be taxed in the same year in which they are earned (see section 10.3), it will only remain to tax any departing partner on his share of profits from the end of the last accounting period to the date on which he leaves. New partners joining will be taxed on their share of the profits of the first accounting period in which they join, subject to the adjustment for the opening tax year. In effect they are treated as commencing a new business when they join an existing partnership and are assessed on the same principles as any other new sole business (see Chapter 6). Where at least one partner remains after a change, the partnership is treated as continuing, and current year basis will automatically apply – s113(2). Under the old rules, s113(2) made it necessary for the continuing partners to sign an election if they wished to opt for continuation treatment. Now s113(2) makes it automatic. There are transitional arrangements for changes in existing partnerships which occur before 5 April 1997.

The 'historical position on changes of partners', and 'election for continuation', as described below, continue to apply to changes in partnerships up until that date. The combined effect could be, for example, that in 1996/97 the partnership is assessed on the transitional profits on a continuing basis, on one year's average profits for the 24 months ending in the 1996/97 tax year (see section 10.3). The resulting assessment, if a continuation election is in force, would mean part of this assessment being allocated to the outgoing or incoming partner according to his profit-shared ratio for 1996/97. Similarly, if no continuation election is made, the partnership would be treated as ceasing at the changeover date and the Revenue would be in a position to readjust the preceding two years' assessments under the normal cessation rules.

Historical position on changes of partners (pre-current year basis only)

Section 113 ICTA 1988 provides that where there is a change in the persons carrying on a business chargeable under Schedule D Case I or II, tax is to be computed as if the business were discontinued, and a new business begun, at the date of the change. Thus the old partners are subject to the closing year rules (s63

ICTA 1988) and the new partners are subject to the opening year rules (s61 ICTA 1988).

Under s61(4) ICTA 1988, on a change in partnership where the discontinuance and recommencement provisions of ss61 and 62 apply (because the partners do not make an election, as discussed below, under s113), then the new partnership is assessed on the actual profits of each year of assessment for the year of the change and for the subsequent three income tax years (s61(4)). Therefore in the year of commencement of the new partnership, and in the second, third and fourth years, the partnership is assessed on its current profits earned in those years. In the fifth and sixth year of assessment the partnership reverts to the preceding year basis for assessment, although the partnership can elect for the current year basis of assessment to apply to these additional two years also (s62 ICTA 1988).

Election for continuation – s113(2) ICTA 1988 (pre-current year basis only)

If at least one person who was engaged in carrying on the trade prior to the change continues to be so engaged afterwards, an election can be made under s113(2) that s113(1) should not apply, in which case no discontinuance will occur. Such an election must be made by all the partners old and new (or by the personal representatives of a deceased partner) within two years of the change. In this case the basis of assessment for the partners continues to be the preceding year basis. Consequently, the new partners will be assessed on the profits earned by the old parternship.

Although other matters, such as capital allowances, have to be taken into account, as a general rule, where the profits of the partnership are increasing year by year it is preferable to make the election, since this will continue assessments on a preceding year basis, delaying the assessment on the increasing profits for as long as possible. If, however, profits are decreasing it will be preferable to accept the deemed discontinuance under s113(1). In this case the rules for the assessment of profits in the opening and closing years of a business will apply and the tax charge will be reduced.

Where an election has been made under s113(2), and within two years of the date of that change there is an actual discontinuance, or a change occurs in respect of which no continuation election is made (so that a discontinuance is treated as having taken place), then the Revenue can apply s63(1)(b), if it so wishes, to revise the assessments for the penultimate and pre-penultimate years, substituting an actual basis, thereby affecting taxpayers who are not partners at the time of the second change. See above for the new rules on change of partners and revised s113(2).

10.5 Partnership losses

If a partnership sustains a loss it is divided among the partners in exactly the same way that a profit would be. Each partner may then claim to make use of his share of the loss, independently of the others. For example, one partner may claim to set his part off against his general income under s380, and another to carry it forward under s385.

Note: see Chapter 6, section 6.11, for restrictions imposed by s117 ICTA 1988 on a limited partner's ability to relieve trading losses in full under ss380 and 381. There is no such restriction under s385 on losses carried forward for relief against the limited partner's future share of profits from the limited partnership trade. Compare the previous position in *Reed* v *Young* [1986] STC 285.

10.6 Partnership retirement annuities

Section 682 provides that when a person ceases to be a member of a partnership, whether through age, ill health or death, and under the partnership agreement annual payments are made for his benefit, or for the benefit of his widow or dependants, these payments will, subject to a limit explained below, be treated as earned income. The limit is 50 per cent of the ex-partner's average share for tax purposes of the partnership profits for those three years in which the assessable profits of the partnership were highest out of the last seven years in which the partner was engaged full-time in the business.

The above provisions relate to payments by the partnership or successor. Under rules in effect prior to 1988 the self-employed could effect their own arrangements for additional pension under 'retirement annuity contracts' with the insurance offices. Tax relief was given on the contributions under limits which varied with age. These contracts are no longer available, having been superseded by personal pension contracts following a major review of pension arrangements for both the employed and the self-employed. The tax relief provisions can be found in s630 onwards ICTA 1988, and the allowable percentages in s640.

10.7 Partnerships controlled abroad or trading abroad

A partnership carrying on part of its business in the United Kingdom, but controlled or managed abroad, is assessable only to the extent of its business there: s112 ICTA 1988. In this situation the partnership is only liable on the profits made from trading *within* the United Kingdom, on which tax will be chargeable under Schedule D Case I. The profits earned abroad will be apportioned according to the profit-sharing ratio of the partnership, and the shares accruing to partners resident in the United Kingdom will be Case V income in their hands.

For a recent example in which this was utilised to avoid tax see *Padmore* v *IRC* [1989] STC 493. The future effects of the decision were reversed by s112(4) and (5) ICTA 1988.

However, it was held that since a Jersey resident partnership was exempt from United Kingdom tax, as a consequence of the terms of the United Kingdom/Jersey double taxation agreement, the exemption extended to United Kingdom resident partners on their share of the partnership income. The s112 provisions limit the exemption to non-United Kingdom residents.

11

Schedule D Case VI

11.1 Scope of the charge

11.2 'Annual' profits

11.3 Furnished lettings

11.4 Computation of income

11.1 Scope of the charge

Section 18 of the Income and Corporation Taxes Act 1988 provides that tax is charged under Schedule D Case VI 'in respect of any annual profits or gains not falling under any other Case of Schedule D, and not charged by virtue of Schedule A, B, C or E'.

It will also be found that tax is charged under Case VI by many provisions of the Taxes Acts: for example, post-cessation receipts and in many cases where a charge to tax is imposed by an anti-avoidance provision. For instance, the tax benefit of a 'transaction in securities' (s703(3) ICTA 1988), transfers of assets abroad (s740(4)) and the capital profit derived from what were previously called 'artificial transactions in land' (s776(3)) are deemed to be taxable amounts falling within Schedule D Case VI. Similarly the settlement anti-avoidance provisions of s660A–G dictate that any resulting charge on the settlor (under s660C) will be under Schedule D Case VI.

Thus Schedule D Case VI is designed to catch all types of income not otherwise charged to income tax. Even so, there are some types of receipts which Case VI does not cover:

1. Capital receipts. Capital profits are not assessable under Case VI, other than those deemed to be income by the anti-avoidance legislation mentioned above, but will fall instead under the charge to Capital Gains Tax.

2. Profits resembling trading profits. If a profit looks like a trading profit, it will either be caught by Schedule D Case I, being a profit arising from an adventure in the nature of trade, or be a capital receipt. It cannot, however, be a Case VI receipt.

3. Ejusdem generis. A profit which is not 'ejusdem generis' with annual profits and

gains of the five preceding Cases of Schedule D cannot fall within Case VI. It can only be within Case VI if it is in the nature of an annual profit or gain and if it is not caught by the other cases of Schedule D, for example as trading income.

The case which illustrates all these points is *Jones* v *Leeming* [1930] AC 415, where Lawrence LJ said in the Court of Appeal:

> 'I have the greatest difficulty in seeing how an isolated transaction of this kind, if it be not an adventure in the nature of trade, can be a transaction ejusdem generis with such an adventure and therefore fall within Case VI ... In the case of an isolated transaction of purchase and resale of property, there is really no middle course open. It is either an adventure in the nature of trade, or else it is simply a case of sale and resale of property.'

The Revenue also failed in its appeal in the House of Lords, where Lord Macmillan said:

> 'The transaction being thus excluded from charge under Case I, it was maintained that it fell within Case VI, which subjects to tax any annual profits or gains not falling under any of the preceding Cases and not charged by virtue of any other Schedule. The difficulty which here confronts the Crown is that the profit made by the respondent was the result of an isolated transaction of sale but not of a transaction of sale by way of trade and it is not easy to see how the profit on an isolated sale which is not a trading transaction can be other than a capital accretion and so outside the category of annual profits or gains. The case of *Cooper v Stubbs* on which the Attorney-General relied, differs widely in its facts from the present case. The court was there dealing with the profits of transactions in cotton "futures" extending over a considerable number of years and involving numerous transactions in each year, but which the Commissioners had found not to be profits resulting from the carrying on of the trade. As Lord Justice Warrington and Lord Justice Atkin (as they then were) pointed out, the profits made were plainly "annual profits or gains". Consequently if they were not otherwise charged they necessarily fell under Case VI.
>
> I am content to hold that the profits of the particular transaction here in question were not annual profits or gains within the meaning of Case VI. The result is that in my opinion the appeal of the Crown fails and should be dismissed ...'

11.2 'Annual' profits

Section 18 ICTA 1988 provides that Case VI is charged on 'annual profits'. The word 'annual' does not, however, require that the profit be recurrent. An isolated transaction may be chargeable, subject to the *Jones* v *Leeming* point. There is, though, no Case II equivalent of an adventure in the nature of trade, so adventures in the nature of a profession or vocation will fall within Case VI.

Thus in *Hobbs* v *Hussey* [1942] 1 KB 491 the appellant sold the serial rights in his life story to a newspaper for £1,500. He claimed that what he had sold was the *copyright* in those stories, and thus he had made nothing but a capital gain. Lawrence J held that what had occurred was not the sale of property but the performance of services; as he was not an author by profession, his revenue profits needs must fall within Case VI.

11.3 Furnished lettings

Prior to 6 April 1995 furnished letting income was assessed to tax under Case VI, but it is now taxed wholly under the new Schedule A described in Chapter 4, with deductions claimed under the revised 'Schedule A business' rules.

11.4 Computation of income

Tax under Case VI is charged on the full amount of profits or gains received in the year of assessment, ie on a current year basis. The 'profits' will be the excess of the receipts over the expenses incurred in earning them.

Schedule D Case VI losses

One of the disadvantages of finding that a source of income has to be treated as being within Schedule D Case VI is that if it gives rise to a loss in any year, then the loss can only be used up against other income which is similarly chargeable under Case VI (s392 ICTA 1988). There was an exception for furnished holiday lettings which, although assessable under Case VI up to 5 April 1995, were treated as producing trading losses relieved under s380 et seq, by virtue of s503. From 6 April 1995 furnished holiday lettings are assessable under Schedule A (see Chapter 4).

Case VI income is investment income.

12

Schedule D Case III

12.1 Introduction

12.2 Definitions

12.3 Collection of the tax

12.4 Section 349(2) and (3) ICTA 1988 and interest payments

12.5 Sections 348–9 and 347A–B ICTA 1988: annuities and other annual payments

12.6 Tax-free payments

12.7 Purchased life annuities

12.1 Introduction

The charge to income tax under Schedule D Case III is imposed by s18(3) of the Income and Corporation Taxes Act 1988:

> 'Case III – tax in respect of:
> 1. any interest of money whether yearly or otherwise, or any annuity or other annual payment ... ;
> 2. all discounts;
> 3. income from securities bearing interest payable out of the public revenue.'

Note: with effect from 6 April 1996 Schedule C was abolished and income previously charged under that schedule became chargeable under Schedule D Case III.

For corporation tax purposes in regard to accounting periods ending after 31 March 1996, s18(3) is redefined to include 'profits and gains arising from loan relationships'. The effect of the new provisions, brought in by the Finance Act (FA) 1996, are that both capital and revenue profits from corporate and government securities are charged as income for corporation tax purposes. In addition, where this income might previously have been assessed under Case V because of a foreign source, it too becomes subject to the new 'loan relationships' regime under Schedule D Case III. However, the loan relationship profits and losses of trading companies, entered into for trading purposes are Schedule D Case I receipts or expenses.

It should be noted at the outset that ss347A and 347B ICTA 1988 ensure that most legal obligations to make annual payments entered into by individuals on or after 15 March 1988 have been taken outside the charge to tax under Schedule D Case III.

The only exceptions to this rule are provided by s347A(2) ICTA 1988, and they are:

1. payments of interest;
2. covenanted payments to charity;
3. bona fide commercial payments made in connection with a person's trade, profession or vocation; and
4. payments falling within s125 ICTA 1988.

In relation to Schedule D Case III, one may often (as in ss348, 349 and 835) have to consider its provisions from the point of view of the payer of the interest, annuity or other annual payment etc (for the purpose of a relief or charge) where the provisions concern payments which in the hands of the recipient are taxed under Case III. Indeed, most of the leading cases referred to below (see section 12.2) concerned the payers of interest or sums considered to be interest, and in order to establish whether they should withhold tax from the payments the courts were required to determine whether or not the payments were in fact interest in nature.

12.2 Definitions

Interest

'Interest' has been described by Rowlatt J as 'payment by time for the use of money': *Bennett* v *Ogston* (1930) 15 TC 374. A gloss was put on this by Megarry J in *Re Euro Hotel (Belgravia) Ltd* [1975] 3 All ER 1075, where he said:

> 'Interest is, in general terms, the return or consideration or compensation for the use or retention by one person of a sum of money belonging to, in a colloquial sense, or owed to, another.'

In this case the company financing the costs of a development on which it was to take a lease on completion of the development was to be paid 'interest' once the construction costs reached a certain level. It was held that the payments were not interest since, although they represented sums calculated by reference to a sum of money (as opposed to any other variable), that sum of money did not itself represent an amount due and owing from party to another. In the absence of this criterion, the test for interest failed. From Megarry J's statement, the sum in question could be due to a third party in the transaction and would still be 'interest' in nature, if it was a sum owing.

Another leading case is *Chevron Petroleum (UK) Ltd* v *BP Petroleum Development Ltd* [1981] STC 689, in which a payment made to adjust the ratios in which each of these two companies had contributed to the cost of oilfield developments included an 'interest factor': an adjustment for the fact that one had effectively borne part of the contribution due by the other. The interest factor element of the payment was adjudged to be interest.

The four tests to be satisfied from these three leading cases are:

1. Is the payment calculated by reference to a sum of money?
2. Is that sum of money due from one person to another?
3. Is the payment calculated by reference to a period for which the sum in (2) is outstanding?
4. Does it represent 'payment by time for the use of money' or 'compensation for delay in payment'?

Annual interest and short interest

'Annual interest' means interest on an obligation which is intended to mature in a year or more. Anything else is 'short interest'.

There is an obligation under s349 ICTA 1988 to deduct tax on payment of 'annual interest'. The distinction between annual and short interest is therefore important in determining whether the interest falls within the requirement to deduct tax on payment.

The obligation referred to above relates to interest payments by companies, partnerships which have at least one company as a partner and to all payments of interest, whether by companies, partnerships or individuals, where the lender has his 'usual place of abode' outside the United Kingdom.

Even where the interest is 'annual' there are several instances where the obligation to deduct tax is to be ignored. Under s349(3) interest paid *to* a bank on an advance is paid gross, providing the bank is within the charge to United Kingdom corporation tax. All interest paid *by* a bank in the ordinary course of its business is paid without deduction of tax. Interest on quoted Eurobonds is also paid without deduction of tax.

For a case drawing a distinction between 'annual interest' and 'short interest' see *Cairns* v *MacDiarmid* [1983] STC 178 where Sir John Donaldson MR said that it depends on the intention of the parties. In this case it was intended that the loan would be repaid immediately after it was drawn down. So interest paid on a mortgage providing (as mortgages usually do) a facility for possible repayment after six months will still be annual interest if the parties intend that it may have to be paid from year to year and it is calculated on an annual rate.

Neither Megarry J's nor Rowlatt J's definition of interest is exhaustive, but they are considered to be sufficient to deal with the ordinary case. In other complex financing arrangements, further analysis is likely to be required. Interest does not only arise where a person uses someone else's money for a continuing consideration but also where he pays by time for the availability of money: for example, 'I will pay you £500 per day if you maintain £100,000 ready for my immediate use.' Even if the payer does not draw down any of the available sum, he is still paying interest on the money which has been at his disposal. See also the decision of Vinelott J in *Peracha v Miley (Inspector of Taxes)* [1990] STC 512, where it was held that interest added to a bank deposit secured against loans was assessable on the taxpayer.

Payment by reference to a notional, but non-existent, sum is not payment of interest.

Annuity

The usual definition of 'annuity' is that offered by Watson B in *Foley v Fletcher* (1858) 28 LJ Ex 100:

> 'An annuity means where an income is purchased with a sum of money and the capital has gone and has ceased to exist, the principal having been converted into an annuity.'

Most annuities will be investment income, being a return on capital invested, but retirement annuities derived from arrangements for retirement from employment or business will, provided that the limits are not exceeded, be regarded as earned income: see section 12.7.

Other annual payments

It is not possible to give a definition of 'other annual payments'; rather, it is necessary to state those characteristics which a payment must have if it is to fall into this category:

1. The payment must be ejusdem generis with 'interest' and 'annuities': *IRC v Whitworth Park Coal Co Ltd* [1958] Ch 792. In that case a sum paid to a trader for having to wait for compensation on the nationalisation of his coal mine was held not to be an annual payment.
2. The payment must be made under a binding legal obligation, eg a court order, a will, a contract or a deed of covenant. There must not, however, be consideration moving from the payee to the payer.
3. The payment must have the quality of recurrence: *Moss Empires Ltd v IRC* [1937] AC 785. In that case a company guaranteed that if another company's profits fell below a certain level the first company would make available a sufficient sum to enable specified dividends to be paid. The House of Lords held that the fact that the payments were dependent on the performance of the other company, and thus were contingent and variable, was irrelevant. The important point was that the liability to make payments *could* arise in successive fiscal years. There is no requirement, therefore, that the payments be of a set amount; either that must be so, or the size of the payment must be calculated by reference to a fixed formula.
4. The payment must be 'income per se' or 'pure income profit'. This means that the payment must all be taxable and must not be subject to any deduction in respect of revenue expenditure; see *Earl Howe v IRC* [1919] 2 KB 415, in which

Scrutton LJ said that a yearly payment to a garage proprietor for the hire of a motor car would not be Case III income in the hands of the proprietor, even though it was an annual payment, because the sum was, in the hands of the recipient, nothing more than an element in the ascertainment of his profits.

See also *Campbell* v *IRC* [1970] AC 77, where the owners of a school covenanted to make payments to the Trustees of an educational trust on the 'understanding' that the Trustees would apply the money in the purchase of the school's business. The scheme was nothing more than an elaborate device to enable the school to reclaim the tax charged on its profits; as will be seen, such payments are made after deduction of tax which is retained by the payer if his income has already been taxed. The payee can then reclaim the tax paid on his behalf if he is not taxable – which is so in the case of a registered charity.

The House of Lords held that the 'understanding' amounted to a contractual obligation of the trustees; the scheme was therefore ineffective, since the covenantors got something in return for making the payments – their money back – with the consequence that the covenanted income was not pure income profit, and also, the bargain being that the covenantees had to hand the money back, nothing passed either way other than the price of a capital asset. If a vendor of an asset provides the purchase money, he makes capital payments, not falling within Case III. What is particularly important about the decision of the House is that their Lordships held that there was no magic in a covenantor receiving something from the covenantee as a result of the making of the covenanted payment; what had to be shown was that that which was received was sufficient to prevent the covenantee from obtaining 'pure income profit'.

This having been said, it can be very difficult to distinguish a capital payment from either an income payment or a mixed payment of capital and income. This is especially so where a sum of money is being paid in instalments. For example, if property is sold at a price of £20,000, to be paid in ten equal instalments of £2,000, these instalments will be capital payments. But if there were no original price and the property were sold in these equal instalments over ten years, the court might well conclude that there must be some element of interest to compensate for the time the vendor was being made to wait for his money.

The high-water mark of these 'dissection' cases was *Vestey* v *IRC* [1962] Ch 861. In *Vestey* the market value of shares sold (£2 million) was less than the agreed sale price payable by annual instalments (£5.5 million). It was held that each instalment, other than the first, carried an interest element. Having regard to the respective share values, the challenge to the contention that the payments were non interest bearing was almost inevitable. The decision of Cross J was resiled from to a certain extent by the House of Lords in *IRC* v *Church Commissioners* [1977] AC 329, where it was said that dissection *is* permissible where the parties first agree on a lump sum price and then agree that instalments should be paid which in aggregate exceed the lump sum, the excess then being interest falling under Case III. The House was, however, unwilling to speculate that anything less than this might justify dissection, 'explaining' *Vestey* on the basis that its facts fell into the category of an agreed sum payable by instalments which was greater in aggregate than the value of shares sold. The House of Lords did not wholly approve of the reasoning to warrant apportionment of interest in all cases involving a deferred purchase price.

Discounts

Ditchfield v *Sharp* [1983] STC 590 is a case which provides an indication of the modern meaning of the word 'discount'. It refers to the dictionary meaning of

> 'the deduction made from the amount of a bill of exchange or promissory note by one who gives value for it before it is due'.

This is basically what a discount is. The case then applied these rules far outside the usual discounting transactions of the City of London, thereby proving that if someone purchases a chose in action for less than its 'redemption value', then, even though the transaction is far removed from the sphere of banking, that purchase may still be chargeable under Schedule D Case III. What is taxed is the difference between what was given and what is finally received.

The problem one faces is determining whether something is a discount or a 'premium': that is, a sum which is payable on the return of money lent in excess of the amount given but which is not interest, not being paid by time. A premium will, except in special cases, be capital. The leading case on the distinction between a discount and a premium is *Lomax* v *Dixon (Peter) Ltd* (1943) 25 TC 353, 367. It is very much a question of fact: if a proper rate of interest was given, the extra sum demanded in addition will be a premium; if no, or inadequate, interest is given, the transaction will be one of discounting.

In order to counteract the conversion into capital of what should be income received on a loan to a company in a case where a premium is to be taken, special provisions relating to 'deep discount securities' were introduced by s36 and Schedule 9 FA 1984. These provisions, which were contained in Schedule 4 ICTA 1988 but were replaced by new provision in FA 1996.

For income tax purposes Schedule 13 of FA 1996 provides for the treatment of both interest and realised discount on sale, transfer or redemption of securities to be taxed as income. Thus, where the face value of the security is greater than the issue price, the 'capital' profit realised is also subject to tax as income under Schedule D Case III. For this purpose, Schedule 13, para 3(1) defines that a security is a 'relevant discounted security' if '(a) taking the security as at the time of its issue, and (b) assuming redemption in accordance with its terms, the amount payable on redemption is an amount involving a deep gain ...'. Company shares, most gilt-edged securities and indexed securites are the principle exemptions from the provisions.

For corporation tax payers, the deep discount security provisions are replaced by the FA 1996 'loan relationship' provisions taxing both interest and capital profit from non-trading loan relationships as income, under Schedule D Case III – see Chapter 16.

12.3 Collection of the tax

The basis of assessment

Section 206 FA 1994 amends ss64–67 ICTA 1988, with regard to the previous year's profits being the normal basis of assessment under Schedule D Case III, from 1997–98, but for new sources from 6 April 1994 onwards the new provisions are effective immediately.

From 1997–98 the previous year basis will be discarded in favour of a current year basis, and the opening and closing years' adjustments of ss66 and 67 will no longer be required. Interest will in future be assessed strictly on the income of the fiscal year. In addition all income under Schedule D Case III is, for income tax payers, subject to tax by s1A(2)(a) at only the lower (and not basic) rate of tax, but where an individual is liable to tax at the higher rate the income is taxed at that higher rate as the top slice of income. Where tax is to be deducted at source from Case III income, s4(1A) restricts the deduction to tax at the lower rate.

Prior to the above changes, ss64 and 66–67 ICTA 1988 made provisions whereby the Inland Revenue could assess a taxpayer in respect of Case III income. Until the FA 1994 current year provisions apply (either from 1997–98, or earlier if a new source is being assessed) the following rules apply:

1. Section 64: generally, assessments are made on the full amount of the income arising in the preceding year of assessment. It should be noted that:
   – The period in question is the preceding year of assessment itself, *not* some accounting period ending in that year.
   – The word used is 'arising': income does not 'arise' until it is either paid to the taxpayer or credited to his account: *IRC v Whitworth Park Coal Co Ltd* (1959) 38 TC 531, and see also *Parkside Leasing v Smith* [1985] STC 63.
2. When income first arises from a fresh source, s66 provides that the basis of assessment is:
   – in the year of assessment when the income first arises: on the *full* amount of income in that year;
   – in the second year: on the actual income of that second year;
   – in the third year: on the income arising in the preceding year (the second year); but the taxpayer has the option to remain on the current year basis for the third year.

   If the FA 1994 current year provisions are in operation, this section ceases to have effect.
3. When the income from the source ceases, s67 provides that income of the final

year of assessment should be on the actual basis: the Revenue is entitled to adjust the assessment of the penultimate year to an actual basis as well, if this would bring more income into charge. If the FA 1994 current year provisions are in operation, this section ceases to have effect.

The direct assessment provisions above are combined with the deduction of tax at source provisions of ss348 and 349 to provide the comprehensive system of collecting tax under Schedule D Case III. A deduction from total income (see Chapter 3) is available for payments made under deduction of tax (s835 ICTA 1988). Deduction applies to all payments which are Case III income in the hands of the recipient, other than interest. A deduction is denied, by reason of s347A, for most annual payments, including maintenance payments, by taking them outside the charging provisions of Case III. Deductions for interest is governed by s353 et seq (see Chapter 3, section 3.4).

12.4 Section 349(2) and (3) ICTA 1988 and interest payments

Interest is excluded from the operation of ss348 and 349(1) ICTA 1988 – see below. Instead, s349(2) and (3) apply, providing that where any yearly interest chargeable under Case III is paid, the general rule is that it is to be paid gross. The exceptions to this system of gross payment, as confirmed in s349(3) are:

1. interest paid by a company on its own behalf;
2. interest paid by a partnership of which a company is a member; and
3. interest paid to a person not resident in the United Kingdom – even if paid by an individual.

In all these cases, *unless* the interest is paid by a bank in the ordinary course of its business or is paid to a bank in respect of an advance and at the time of payment of the interest the bank is within the charge to United Kingdom corporation tax, the interest is to be paid under deduction of tax. Prior to the passing of the Finance Act 1996, there was a further requirement that the bank had to be carrying on a 'bona fide banking business in the United Kingdom'. The Inland Revenue had to approve institutions for this purpose. Following the Finance Act 1996, a 'bank', for full purposes of the Taxes Acts, means:

1. the Bank of England;
2. an institution authorised under the Banking Act 1987;
3. a relevant European institution; or
4. a relevant international organisation which is designated as a bank for the purposes of that provision by an order made by the Treasury.

(On the meaning of a bank carrying on a bona fide banking business in the United Kingdom, see *UDT* v *Kirkwood* [1966] 2 QB 431.) The above was and still is particularly relevant in planning the financing of a transaction and in deciding whether the finance will be set up via a bank or a non-bank company. The need to retain tax on payment of the interest affects the cash flow of the arrangements. Bank interest is paid gross, unless paid on certain deposit accounts.

The system of composite rate tax was abolished from 6 April 1991 by s30 and Schedule 5 FA 1990 (see Chapter 3, section 3.3). Interest paid on building society accounts and bank deposit accounts is now paid net of lower rate tax: ss477A and 480A ICTA 1988. Non-taxpayers may either reclaim tax deducted from the Inland Revenue or complete a certificate allowing interest to be paid to them gross. Higher-rate taxpayers must enter the gross amount of interest from which tax has been deducted at the basic rate in their total income, for the purposes of computation. If the interest is not 'yearly interest' but 'short interest', it is always paid gross.

Note: s28 FA 1990 inserted s326A ICTA 1988. This section states that when interest is paid from a tax-exempt special saving account (TESSA) that interest shall be paid gross and disregarded for all purposes of the Income Tax Acts.

12.5 Sections 348–9 and 347A–B ICTA 1988: annuities and other annual payments

Taxing annuities; taxing annual payments pre 15 March 1988 or within ICTA 1988 s347A

(For the law governing the taxation of maintenance payments see Chapter 15 'Matrimonial Taxation'. Prior to the Finance Act 1988 these were treated as annual payments and within the charge to tax under Case III. For most purposes now they are neither.)

In the situations where annuities (whether or not entered into before 15 March 1988), annual payments entered into on or before 15 March 1988, and annual payments entered into after 15 March 1988, which fall within s347A(2), have to be taxed, Case III income tax is collected via the mechanism of deduction of tax at source. Sections 348–350 ICTA 1988 deal with this form of collection of tax. Section 348 applies where the Case III income is paid wholly out of the profits or gains of the taxpayer which are brought into charge to income tax. This means that profits assessable to tax exceed the payments made. Sections 349–50 apply where the payer does not pay some or all of the Case III income out of profits and gains liable to income tax.

Section 348
Section 348 provides that where an annuity or other annual payment charged with tax under Case III of Schedule D, not being interest, is payable wholly out of profits or gains brought into charge to income tax, then:

1. The payer is charged to tax on the whole of his income, without regard to the

Sections 348–9 and 347A–B ICTA 1988: annuities and other annual payments 145

annuity or annual payment. Thus as far as basic-rate tax is concerned, if Y earns £10,000 but has covenanted to pay £1,000 per annum to X, Y's income is £10,000 not £9,000.
2. But the payer is entitled on making the payment to deduct and retain out of it a sum equal to the income tax thereon. Section 4 ICTA 1988 provides that 'income tax' means 'income tax at the basic rate'; thus if Y, having an income of £10,000, entered into a covenant in January 1988 (ie pre 15 March 1988) to pay X £1,000 per annum, Y can deduct and retain 23 per cent (basic-rate tax) of the £1,000 and need only pay £770. The effect, of course, is that Y has only paid basic-rate tax on £9,000 of his £10,000 income; he has diverted that extra £1,000 to X.
3. The payee must accept that his legal entitlement to £1,000 has been satisfied by the payment of £770: s348(1)(c). He is treated as having paid basic-rate tax on the whole £1,000: s348(1)(d). If he is not liable to tax (eg having unused personal allowances or being a charity) then he may make a repayment claim on the Revenue for the tax deducted.

If none of the anti-avoidance provisions contained in Part XV ICTA 1988 applies (see Chapter 14, 'Anti-avoidance Settlements'), then the gross amount of income will form part of the payee's total income and he will be liable to higher-rate tax in excess of the 23 per cent paid on his behalf. If it does form part of the payee's total income, it will not form part of the payer's: see s835(6)(b) ICTA 1988.

Example
A, who earns £1,000 and has personal allowances of £4,045, entered into a covenant in May 1997 (in other words, the covenant is post March 1988 but falls within s347A(2) ICTA 1988) to pay £1,000 per annum to B, a charity. The situation would be:

1. A uses s348 to deduct and retain £230, paying £770 over to B.
2. B, being a charity, could then reclaim £230 from the Revenue.

If this were so, the Revenue would end up £230 out of pocket. For this reason, two special provisions have to be considered:

1. Section 3 ICTA 1988 provides that where a person is assessable and chargeable to income tax on property, profits or gains out of which he makes an annual payment, he is liable to basic-rate tax on that amount.
2. Section 276 ICTA 1988 provides that where a person makes an annual payment out of his income, he may *not* claim to set off any personal reliefs against that income.

Accordingly, what actually happens is:

1. A deducts £230, paying B £770.
2. A is made liable to basic-rate tax on the income of £1,000 by s3.

3. A is not then permitted to treat the covenanted income as a charge on income under s835(6)(b) because of the s3 rule.
4. Section 276 prevents him from claiming to set off his personal reliefs against the £1,000; he must, therefore, pay £230 income tax to the Revenue. He effectively uses the sum deducted to discharge this liability.
5. B can reclaim £230 from the Revenue, deemed to have been paid on its behalf: s505(1) ICTA 1988.

Thus there can never be a case where the payer pays no tax on income transferred to a payee, yet the payee can make a claim on the Revenue.

Section 349
Under s349(1) where an annuity or other annual payment chargeable with income tax under Case III, not being interest (see section 12.4 for the treatment of interest under s349(2) and (3)), is not payable or not wholly payable out of profits or gains brought into charge to income tax, then the payer:

1. must deduct basic-rate tax from the payment; and
2. is assessable and chargeable with income tax at the basic rate on so much as is not made out of profits or gains brought into charge to tax.

If, therefore, in the above example A had covenanted to pay B £2,000, £1,000 would have been paid out of income and £1,000 out of capital. Section 349 would have applied instead, and he would have been required to deduct basic-rate tax from the payment. The Revenue would therefore have received £480 from A (under a combination of ss3, 276 and 349), and B would then have been able to make a repayment claim.

When a deduction has been made under s349, then, assuming that none of the anti-avoidance provisions apply, the gross income will form part of the payee's total income: s835(6)(b) ICTA 1988.

Which section applies?
The rule that if the payer has income out of which the annual payment *could* be paid, s348 applies rather than s349, even though the payment may actually have been made out of capital: *IRC v Plummer* [1980] AC 896. If, however, the payer has restricted himself, for other legal reasons, to pay out of capital, then the general principle is overridden and s349 applies: see *Chancery Lane Safe Deposit and Offices Ltd v IRC* (1965) 43 TC 83. Section 349 will always apply to a company since companies do not pay income tax.

The distinction between s348 and s349 was explained by Viscount Simonds in *IRC v Whitworth Park Coal Co* [1961] AC 31:

> 'It is plain that between them [ss348 and 349] are intended to cover all cases of annual payments etc. made by a taxpayer. Under both there is provision for deducting tax when making the payment, but the purpose is quite different according to whether or not the

money which is paid has already borne tax. If it has, then the Crown has no interest because the same money is not to be taxed twice, and the authority to deduct tax is for the purpose of enabling the taxpayer to recoup himself when he has already paid tax on the money which he now has to pay away; and the payee has to submit to this deduction of tax because it ought in the end to fall on him. But if the money has not borne tax, then the Crown has an interest in the money because the money becomes on payment a part of the taxable income of the payee. So the payer is bound to deduct tax and to pay it to the Revenue. [Section 349] operates not as an authority to deduct tax but as an obligation to do so, and to account to the Revenue for the tax deducted, and the whole purpose of [s349] appears to me to be to enable the Revenue to recover from the payer tax which is really due from the payee.'

Payments made late

Section 4 ICTA 1988 further provides that the basic rate to be used when making a deduction from a payment is:

1. the rate in force for the year in which the payment becomes due, if made out of profits or gains brought into the charge to income tax (ie under s349); and
2. the rate in force for the year of payment in any other case (ie under s348).

The position was explained by Vinelott J in *IRC* v *Crawley* [1987] STC 147:

'Sections 348 and 349 in conjunction with s4, on the one hand, and s835, on the other hand, are complementary sections, or as Counsel for the Crown put it, two sides of a single coin. The payer on making an annual payment deducts tax at the rate in force at the date when the payment becomes due or at the date of payment according to whether the payment is or is not made out of profits or gains brought into the charge to tax. In estimating the total income of the payee the income is deemed to be the income of the year by reference to which tax was deducted. So when payment is made out of profits or gains brought into charge to tax the payment is part of the payee's total income even though that may have been more than six years before the time when the payment was made.'

Failure to deduct tax

As between the payer and payee. The general rule is that an overpayment of this sort cannot be recovered, being a payment made under a mistake of law. Exceptions to this exist, though:

1. Where the payments are made by instalments during a tax year, failure to deduct tax from the earlier instalments can be relieved by greater deductions from the later instalments of that year.
2. When the basic rate of tax is increased by the latest Finance Act, so that earlier payments have suffered under-deductions, an adjustment can be made in the first instalment following the passing of the Act. If no further instalment is due, the under-deduction can be recovered as a debt.
3. If the mistake was not one of law but one of fact, the mistake is rectifiable, and the excess can be recovered.

The inability of the payer to recoup an earlier failure to withhold tax from a payment of rent to an overseas landlord (s349(1)(c)) was upheld in the case of *Tenbry Investments Ltd v Peugeot Talbot Motor Co Ltd* [1992] STC 791.

As between the parties and the Revenue. Under s348(1)(a), the whole of the profits or gains will already have been brought into charge, so that the failure to deduct does not cause loss to the Revenue. Under s349, the Revenue has a choice: it can either enforce s350(1) against the payer, or go against the payee. It may not adopt the latter course, however, if the payee has received a net sum, the failure being that of the payer – to account rather than to deduct. In such circumstances, the Revenue must look to the payer.

Taxing annual payments post 15 March 1988, not within s347A(2) ICTA 1988

Section 347A ICTA 1988 states that annual payments entered into after 15 March 1988 will cease to constitute charges on the income of the payer. Thus the payer cannot deduct the annual payment for the purpose of computing his liability to income tax and so is subject to income tax on his total income.

He must then pay the annual payment to the payee out of his taxed income; ss348 and 349 do not apply. The payment is not taxable in the hands of the payee and does not form part of his income.

Example

In January 1995, X with an income of £40,000, entered into a deed of covenant to pay £2,000 pa to his son Y. Y earns £2,500 pa.

1. X is therefore liable to pay tax on his total income of £40,000. For the tax year 1997–98:

   X's taxable income (less personal allowances) will be £(40,000 – 4,045) = £35,955.
   The first £4,100 of his income will be taxed at 20 per cent = £820.
   The next £22,000 of his income will be taxed at 23 per cent = £5,060.
   The remainder (£9,855) will be taxed at 40 per cent = 3,942 – Total £9,822.
   This leaves him with income after tax of £30,178.

2. He will make the annual payment out of his net income of £30,178. The annual payment will be gross, leaving him with net of tax income of £28,178.

3. Y will receive a payment of £2,000 gross which will not constitute income liable to tax in his hands. Thus, as Y's income is below the level of his personal allowance, he will pay no tax.

12.6 Tax-free payments

Section 106(2) TMA 1970

Section 106(2) of the Taxes Management Act 1970 renders void every agreement for the payment of interest, rent or other annual payment in full which does not allow for any deduction of income tax in all cases where the deduction is directed by the Taxes Acts.

The effect of the section is to strike out the offending clause but not to nullify the whole agreement to make payments. Thus if A agrees to pay B £100 free of tax, B will not be able to recover £100 from A, but will be entitled to £75, or whatever the net payment after deduction of tax might be.

Section 106(2) applies only to 'agreements'. It has been held that it does not, therefore, apply either to wills or to court orders, but it will apply to covenants, to separation agreements pre-15 March 1988, and to contracts.

The problem with s106 is that it makes it difficult for a covenantor to ensure that the covenantee will receive the same net sum each year, since the basic rate of tax is variable at the whim of Parliament. A formula has been devised, however, which overcomes this problem. One covenants to pay:

'Such a sum as, after deduction of tax at the basic rate for the time being in force, will leave £X.'

On this basis, it is the gross sum which will vary; the net sum will remain constant.

There have in fact been occasions when the court has construed the phrase 'I promise to pay £X free of income tax' as a promise to pay 'such a sum as will, after deduction of basic-rate tax, leave £X': see *Ferguson* v *IRC* [1970] AC 412. The matter is of importance: if £X is £1,000, then, on the construction that the parties intended to ignore s106(2), the payee receives a net sum of £770; on the *Ferguson* construction, the payee receives a net sum of £1,000, corresponding to a gross sum of £1,298.70.

A direction under a will to pay an annuity 'free of tax' will be construed as a direction to pay free of *all* tax to which the annuitant will be liable as a result of the receipt of the payment, whether that tax be at the basic rate or the higher rate – so the Court of Appeal decided in *Re Reckitt* [1932] 2 Ch 144. Presumably, in determining the sum to be paid to the annuitant, one has to treat it as the highest part of his income.

If, on the other hand, a direction is made under a will that the income of a trust fund is to be paid 'free of income tax' to a person who is not liable at the basic rate, then the trustees will begin by paying him the specified amount and paying to the Revenue the tax deemed to have been deducted from the notional gross amount; the payee will then reclaim the whole or a part of the tax paid and will thus end up with more than the testator intended.

Thus if a testator directs that £1,000 be paid to his daughter 'free of income tax', she having unused personal reliefs available, the daughter will be treated as having received a net amount of £1,000 corresponding to a gross amount of some £1,299 and will be able to recover the excess £299. She cannot, however, keep all the excess. Romer J, in *Re Pettitt* [1922] 2 Ch 765, held that in these circumstances the payee must return to the trustees, for the benefit of the residuary legatees, the proportion of the recovered tax equivalent to the proportion of her total income consisting of the annuity. Thus, if she were to have income after tax of £1,500, £1,000 of which was the annuity, she would have to repay two-thirds of the recovered tax to the trustees. This amount returned to the trustees would then be treated as additional income on which they would also be liable to tax!

Payments under court orders entered into pre 15 March 1988

As has already been stated, a court order is not an agreement and so is not subject to s106(2) TMA 1970. This fact is taken notice of by the courts, which will sometimes direct, as a general rule, that the respondent pay £X 'less tax'; this enables the payer to deduct tax under s348 or s349 for pre 15 March 1988 arrangements.

If, however, the court orders a person to pay £X 'tax free', that is merely an order to pay such a sum as after deduction of tax at the *basic* rate will leave £X. In such a case, if the payee is not liable to income tax, the rule in *Re Pettitt* will *not* apply: *Jefferson v Jefferson* [1956] P 136. For in this sort of case the husband would have entered the gross sum as a charge on his income, and would thereby already have been afforded relief. Accordingly, the wife would retain all the tax recovered.

12.7 Purchased life annuities

Section 656 ICTA 1988 provides that the capital element in each instalment of a purchased life annuity shall be exempt from income tax. The capital element is determined by dividing the purchase price of the annuity by the number of years' life expectancy of the annuitant, calculated at the date of the purchase. This element remains a constant amount throughout the life of the annuitant, even if that exceeds the expectancy. Income tax is then charged under Schedule D Case III on the excess.

Certain purchased annuities are excepted from s656:

1. Annuities for a fixed term: part of these will, without the assistance of s656, be treated as capital.
2. Annuities granted in consideration of payments satisfying either s266 ICTA 1988 or the retirement annuity relief provision: s619 ICTA 1988. In these cases, the original payments will not have been capital payments but payments of income.
3. Annuities purchased under a direction in a will.
4. Annuities purchased under a sponsored superannuation scheme: these have their own special tax regime, outside the scope of this textbook.

13

Trust Income

13.1 Introduction

13.2 The taxation of the trustee

13.3 The scope of the charge on the trustees

13.4 The taxation of the beneficiary

13.5 Sections 686 and 687 ICTA 1988

13.6 Payments out of capital treated as income

13.7 Income tax and the administration of an estate

13.1 Introduction

The taxation of trust income falls into two distinct parts: the taxation of trustees receiving income, and the taxation of the beneficiary who receives income from the trustee. The problems arising from the existence of stringent anti-avoidance provisions (now contained in Part XV of the Income and Corporation Taxes Act 1988) are dealt with in Chapter 14. These provisions were substantially simplified by the Finance Act 1995, which introduced a new Chapter 1A into ICTA 1988.

13.2 The taxation of the trustee

There is no provision of the Income Tax Acts which specifically states that trustees are liable to income tax in their capacity of trustees. There are, however, certain indications that trustees are so liable.

Sections 15 and 18 ICTA 1988, for example, deal with the liability of persons to tax under Schedule A and Schedule D respectively. Each says:

'Income tax under Schedule (A/D) shall be charged on and paid by the persons receiving or entitled to the income in respect of which tax is directed by the Income Tax Acts to be charged.'

Similarly, there are special provisions in the Taxes Management Act 1970 which are directed towards specific situations involving nominees or trustees: ss72 and 73, for example.

In *Williams* v *Singer* [1921] 1 AC 65, Viscount Cave said:

> 'And even apart from these special provisions, I am not prepared to deny that there are many cases in which a trustee in receipt of trust income may be chargeable with the tax upon such income. For instance, a trustee carrying on a trade for the benefit of creditors or beneficiaries, a trustee for charitable purposes, or a trustee who is under an obligation to apply the trust income in satisfaction of charges or to accumulate it for future distribution, appears to come within this category ...
>
> ... if the Income Tax Acts are examined, it will be found that the person charged with the tax is neither the trustee nor the beneficiary as such, but the person in actual receipt and control of the income which it is sought to reach. The object of the Acts is to secure for the State a proportion of the profits chargeable, and this end is attained (speaking generally) by the simple and effective expedient of taxing the profits where they are found. If the beneficiary receives them he is liable to be assessed upon them. If the trustee receives and controls them, he is primarily so liable. If they are under the control of a guardian or committee for a person not sui juris or of an agent or receiver for persons resident abroad, they are taxed in his hands.'

The rules, as further explained by *Reid's Trustees* v *IRC* (1929) 14 TC 512, appear to be:

1. If trustees *receive* income, they are liable to income tax on the income received: *Reid's Trustees* v *IRC*.
2. If, however, the trustees do not receive income, but it accrues beneficially to a foreign beneficiary, the trustees are not to be charged as having been in receipt or control of the monies: *Williams* v *Singer*.
3. If the trustees do not receive income, but direct the payer to forward it to the appropriate beneficiary, and the trustees make a return of the name, address and profits of the beneficiary, s76 TMA 1970 exempts the trustees from tax: *Williams* v *Singer*.

In *Dawson* v *IRC* [1989] 2 All ER 289 there was a discretionary trust under which all of the beneficiaries were resident outside the United Kingdom and all but one of the trustees were resident outside the United Kingdom. Consequently all the administration of the trust was also done outside the United Kingdom. The Inland Revenue attempted to tax the single trustee who was resident in the United Kingdom. The outcome was that the United Kingdom trustee was not chargeable to tax on the trust's foreign income, not being the person receiving or entitled to receive it. Section 110 FA 1989, enacted following this case, ensures that if one of the trustees is a United Kingdom resident, any trust where the settlor was resident, ordinarily resident or domiciled in the United Kingdom when he provided funds to the trust is treated as a United Kingdom resident settlement.

The House of Lords held unanimously that a United Kingdom resident trustee was not chargeable to Schedule D income tax on income of overseas settled property that was not remitted to the United Kingdom where there were other trustees of the settlement resident abroad. Lord Keith stated that trust income accrued to trustees jointly and thus did not arise or accrue to the resident trustee alone. Thus the resident trustee was not liable to charge under s108 ICTA 1988.

The residency of trustees has now been put into statutory form. Section 110 FA 1989 states that where the trustees of a settlement include at least one who is not resident in the United Kingdom and at least one who is, then for all purposes of the Income Tax Acts:

1. If the settlor (or any one of the settlors) is at the relevant time resident ordinarily resident or domiciled in the United Kingdom then the trustee or trustees not resident in the United Kingdom shall be treated as resident there; and
2. otherwise, the trustee or trustees resident in the United Kingdom shall be treated as not resident there (but as resident outside the United Kingdom).

13.3 The scope of the charge on the trustees

Trustees, in their official capacity, are not 'individuals'. Accordingly, by virtue of s1(2) ICTA 1988, they are only liable to basic-rate tax and not to higher rate tax. This accords with the common law: see *IRC* v *Countess of Longford* [1928] AC 252.

There is an exception to this rule: s686 ICTA 1988 provides that most discretionary trusts are liable to additional tax (see section 13.5).

Note: the lower rate band under s1 ICTA 1988 does not apply to trusts but only to individuals. However, the provisions of s1A(1) and (2) under which income from savings, which includes all income taxable under Schedule D Case III and Schedule F, do apply to limit the rate at which trust income of this nature is taxed to the lower rate. As noted above, income of discretionary trusts will of course suffer tax under s686 at the special rate applicable to trusts, currently 34 per cent.

With effect from 1996/97, trustees are within the self-assessment regime (see Chapter 24) and are therefore liable (unless they elect otherwise) to calculate tax due on the trust income and gains when submitting the Trust Tax Return.

13.4 The taxation of the beneficiary

Trust income which has passed into the hands of the beneficiaries will already have borne tax normally at the lower rate under s1A, either because it was income paid under deduction of tax, or because the trustees paid lower-rate tax under the Schedule or Case appropriate to its source. Most but not all trust income will fall into the category taxed at lower rate under s1A.

Thereafter, either there will be one or more beneficiaries entitled to the income, or the trustees will have to exercise a discretion to accumulate the income or to allocate it to various beneficiaries.

Where there is a beneficiary with a vested right to income

The House of Lords in *Baker* v *Archer-Shee* [1927] AC 844 decided that

> 'in considering sums which are placed in the hands of trustees for the purpose of paying income to beneficiaries, for the purpose of the Income Tax Acts you may eliminate the trustees. This income is the income of the beneficiaries.'

Accordingly, where an individual beneficiary has a vested life interest in a trust fund comprised of shareholdings his income will be Schedule F dividend income; if the trust fund is deposited at a bank, his income will be Case III bank interest. On receiving this income the trustees will pay tax at 20 per cent on that income in a representative capacity – on behalf of the beneficiary.

Example

In June 1995 Sam, the settlor, settled trust property on trust for Richard for life, remainder to Tom absolutely. Richard was 25 years old and his marginal rate of income tax was 40 per cent.

In 1997–98 the income produced by the trust property was £10,000 and all sums were received by the trustees. The trustees paid tax at 20 per cent on the income, ie £2,000, and the remaining sum, ie £8,000, was paid to Richard at his request.

Richard therefore received £8,000 from the trustees. However that sum up is grossed up in order to calculate his tax liability:

$$\pounds 8{,}000 \text{ grossed up at a 20\% tax rate} = \frac{\pounds 8{,}000 \times 100}{80} = \pounds 10{,}000$$

	£	£
Richard's gross income from trust fund		10,000
Tax liability at 40%		4,000
Tax credit for tax trustees paid		2,000
Tax Richard still owes to the Inland Revenue		2,000

If the trustees in any one year fail to pay over to the beneficiary the income to which he is entitled, the gross amount of income will still enter into his total income for the appropriate year. This problem arose in *Hamilton-Russell's Executors* v *IRC* [1943] 1 All ER 474, where trustees accumulated income arising under a trust fund in which the deceased had had a life interest for many years. Eventually he had directed the trustees to hand over the accumulations. The Revenue successfully sought to charge the beneficiary with surtax on the income, relating it back to the years in which the income was received by the trustees. The beneficiary's argument that the trustees had capitalised the income by accumulating it failed because the income was already his before it was accumulated.

Where the beneficiary does not have a vested life interest but is merely entitled to an annuity, the rule in *Baker* v *Archer-Shee* does not apply; instead, the annuity will fall under Schedule D Case III. If the annuity is, say, of £1,000 per annum, and is payable under 'existing obligation' within s36(3) FA 1988, the trustees will apply s348 and pay over £770. The annuitant will then sort out his own tax affairs in the usual way – reclaiming the tax if he is not liable to income tax, or paying higher-rate tax on the gross amount if his income is of sufficient size.

It must be realised, however, that the rule in *Baker* v *Archer-Shee* only applies if the beneficiary has a vested interest in the income of the trust fund. If, therefore, the beneficiary's right to receive income which has arisen is contingent on the exercise of the discretion of the trustees, or if it is liable to be divested by some later event, the Revenue cannot look on the beneficiary as being the person entitled (for s59 ICTA 1988 purposes) to the income without actual receipt of it, and the beneficiary will not be liable to income tax *until* the income has irrevocably become his.

This most often is the case with infant beneficiaries. Section 31 of the Trustee Act 1925 provides:

'*Maintenance, advancement and protective trusts*
31(1) Where any property is held by trustees in trust for any person for any interest whatsoever, whether vested or contingent, then subject to any prior interests or charges affecting that property:
  i) during the infancy of any such person, if his interest so long continues, the trustees may, at their sole discretion, pay to his parent or guardian, if any, or otherwise apply for or towards his maintenance, education, or benefit, the whole or such part, if any, of the income of that property as may, in all the circumstances, be reasonable, whether or not there is –
  a) any other fund applicable to the same purpose; or
  b) any person bound by law to provide for his maintenance or education; and
  ii) if such person on attaining the age of eighteen years has not a vested interest in such income, the trustees shall thenceforth pay the income of that property and of any accretion thereto under subsection (2) of this section to him, until he either attains a vested interest therein or dies, or until failure of his interest;
Provided that, in deciding whether the whole or any part of the income of the property is during a minority to be paid or applied for the purposes aforesaid, the trustees shall have regard to the age of the infant and his requirements and generally to the circumstances of the case, and in particular to what other income, if any, is applicable for the same purposes; and where trustees have notice that the income of more than one fund is applicable for those purposes, then, so far as practicable, unless the entire income of the funds is paid or applied as aforesaid or the court otherwise directs, a proportionate part only of the income of each fund shall be so paid or applied.
(2) During the infancy of any such person, if his interest so long continues, the trustees shall accumulate all the residue of that income in the way of compound interest by investing the same and the resulting income thereof from time to time in authorised investments, and shall hold those accumulations as follows:
  i) If any such person –
  a) attains the age of eighteen years, or marries under that age, and his interest in such income during his infancy or until his marriage is a vested interest or;
  b) on attaining the age of eighteen years or on marriage under that age becomes entitled to the property from which such income arose in fee simple, absolute or determinable, or absolutely, or for an entailed interest;
  the trustees shall hold the accumulations in trust for such person absolutely, but without prejudice to any provision with respect thereto contained in any settlement by

him made under any statutory powers during his infancy, and so that the receipt of such person after marriage, and though still an infant, shall be a good discharge; and

ii) In any other case the trustees shall, notwithstanding that such person had a vested interest in such income, hold the accumulations as an accretion to the capital of the property from which such accumulations arose, and as one fund with such capital for all purposes, and so that, if such property is settled land, such accumulations shall be held upon the same trusts as if the same were capital money arising therefrom; but the trustees may, at any time during the infancy of such person if his interest so long continues, apply those accumulations, or any part thereof, as if they were income arising in the then current year.

(3) This section applies in the case of a contingent interest only if the limitation or trust carries the intermediate income of the property.'

The effect of the section is to prevent any infant from having a vested interest in the income of the trust fund, whatever may be the actual limitations imposed by the Trust Deed. As a consequence, there is much judicial learning on whether the interest an infant does get is sufficient to charge him on income arising which the trustees are entitled to accumulate. To answer this, it is necessary to describe the consequence of the section in detail. It must be realised that it is possible to exclude the operation of the section (s69(2) ICTA 1925).

First, it converts all trusts in which an infant has an interest which is not expectant on another interest held by an adult into an accumulation and maintenance trust (s31(1)(i) and (2)). This is so whether the infant's interest is contingent, vested or even vested and absolute. Accordingly, the trustees *must* accumulate such income as they do not decide to expend on the maintenance, education or benefit of the infant beneficiary. This, of course, can have the effect of divesting an infant of the otherwise vested right to receive the income of the trust fund.

Secondly, if an infant on attaining the age of 18 does not become entitled to a vested interest in income (for example, because the trust is 'To A on attaining 30'), s31(1)(ii) requires the trustees, nevertheless, thenceforward to pay him the income from his prospective share – thereby giving him a vested interest in the income.

Thirdly, it deals with the accumulations which arise during infancy:

1. If the beneficiary on attaining 18 or marrying becomes entitled to the property from which the income arose; or
2. If the beneficiary attains 18 or marries under that age *and* during infancy his interest was vested,

then on attaining 18 or marrying he will become entitled to the accumulations (which will, by then, be capital): s31(2)(i).

In any other event, however, the accumulations are held as an accretion to capital and the beneficiary will only be entitled to the income from the accretions and not to the accretions themselves.

The income tax consequences of this are:

1. The only infant beneficiary who is liable to higher-rate tax on undistributed trust

income is one who has a vested and absolute interest in personalty, for even if such an infant were to die before attaining 18, the accumulations would pass as part of his estate to his personal representatives. (Realty is excluded because of the provisions of s51(3) of the Administration of Estates Act 1925; this renders an absolute interest of an infant in realty contingent: if the infant dies before marriage or reaching 18, the property passes as if he had merely an entailed interest.)

2. If an infant has, apart from the operation of s31, merely a vested interest in income and not in the capital, he is not liable to income tax on undistributed income, since his interest in the accumulations is vested but defeasible – if he dies before attaining 18 or marrying, s31(2)(i) will never apply and the accumulations will pass to the person entitled to the capital: see *Stanley* v *IRC* [1944] 1 KB 255. It cannot, therefore, be said that he is absolutely and indefeasibly entitled to the trust income as it arises. When, eventually, he reaches 18, s31(2)(i) requires the trustees to give him the accumulations. But at this stage no charge to income tax can be levied in respect of what is, by now, capital.
3. If an infant who does not have a vested interest in capital receives income from the trustee, or if sums are paid on his behalf, for his maintenance, education or benefit, then, to the extent of such payments, the infant will become liable to income tax. In such circumstances s687 ICTA 1988 will apply (see section 13.5), and the grossed-up amount of the receipt (or payment) will enter the beneficiary's total income.
4. When an infant whose interest is contingent on his attaining an age in excess of 18 reaches that age, s31(1)(ii) will give him a vested interest in income. Thereafter, he will be liable to income tax in respect of the income of the trust fund, whether he receives it or not: *Hamilton-Russell's Executors* v *IRC* [1943] 1 All ER 474.

13.5 Sections 686 and 687 ICTA 1988

Section 686

Section 686 imposes an additional tax charge on trustees who hold settled property on trusts containing some element of discretion. It reads:

> '1) So far as income arising to trustees is income to which this section applies, it shall be chargeable to income tax at the rate applicable to trusts, instead of at the basic rate or, in accordance with s1A, at the lower rate.
> '2) This section applies to income arising to trustees in any year of assessment so far as it:
> (a) is income which is to be accumulated or which is payable at the discretion of the trustees or any other person (whether or not the trustees have power to accumulate it).'

Section 686(1A) determines the 'rate applicable to trusts' as being the basic rate and additional rate in force for that year. Under s832 the additional rate for 1996–97 is 10 per cent, making a total of 34 per cent.

Reference should be made to the interpretation of s686(2)(a) of Vinelott J in *IRC v Berrill* [1981] STC 784:

> 'The words "income which is payable at the discretion of the trustees" are as easily applied to income which trustees have power to withhold from a beneficiary entitled in default of the exercise of the power as to income which they have power to apply or which they are bound to apply pursuant to a mandatory discretionary trust.'

Accordingly, the section applies to every sort of discretionary trust, save those *specifically* set out in s686(2)(b)(c) and (d). So it applies:

1. to trusts where the trustees have absolute discretion to select beneficiaries from among a class (and perhaps also to accumulate some or all of the income);
2. where the beneficiaries are specified and their entitlement is fixed but the trustees have power to accumulate (eg one-third each to A, B and C but subject to the power of the trustees to accumulate), and to every shade of discretionary trust in between.

To return to the section:

> '(b) is not, (before being distributed), either the income of any person other than the trustees, or treated for any of the purposes of the Income Tax Acts as the income of a settlor.'

The types of trust (b) is considering are:

1. trusts where an infant has an absolute vested interest but s31(1)(i) ICTA 1925 directs an accumulation;
2. trusts to which the anti-avoidance provisions, contained in Chapter 14 below, apply.

In these cases there is no need to apply s686 since the beneficiary (or settlor) will automatically be susceptible to higher-rate tax even though the trust income is not distributable.

> '(c) is not income arising under
> i) a trust established for charitable purposes only; or
> ii) an approved Company Pension Scheme.
> (d) exceeds the income applied in defraying the expenses of the trustees in that year which are properly chargeable to income (or would be so chargeable but for any express provision of the trust.)'

This is a concession; usually one cannot deduct the expenses of the trustees in determining what is the income of the beneficiary. This is logical, considering the rule in *Baker v Archer-Shee* [1927] AC 844 that a beneficiary with a vested interest in income is entitled to the income as it arises, not after the trustees have dealt with it. Here, the rate applicable to trusts is only chargeable on the remainder. However, if only part of the income of a non-resident trust is chargeable to United Kingdom tax, the deduction for management expenses is correspondingly reduced (s686(2A)).

On the effect of s686(2)(d) see *Carver* v *Duncan* [1984] STC 556 – on its true construction, the subsection only permits the deduction of expenses which would be chargeable on income according to general law, and one cannot deduct expenses which the trust instrument specifically provides should so be chargeable by way of derogation from the usual rules.

Section 687

Section 687 ensures that income paid to a beneficiary which has suffered tax at the rate applicable to trusts is treated as income in his hands, with a tax credit of the full amount of tax suffered. This applies provided that the legislation does not treat the income as belonging to the settlor under the anti-avoidance sections (see s660A et seq ICTA 1988, and Chapter 14 below).

Example 1
In 1997–98, trustees of a discretionary trust receive from land rental profits of £10,000. The income is chargeable at the rate applicable to trusts (34 per cent). Since trustees have no personal allowances, tax of £3,400 must be paid to the Revenue, leaving £6,600 which can be distributed.

Of this, the trustees decide to accumulate £5,840 and to distribute £660 to X, an infant with unused personal allowances of £4,045 and no other income. Under s687(2), the £660 is treated as a net sum corresponding to a gross sum of £1,000 (this corresponds to the idea that trustees pay tax in a representative capacity). The £1,000 enters (or, in this case, forms) X's total income for the year of assessment. He is treated as having paid £230 basic-rate and £110 additional-rate tax on that income.

The trustees are liable to pay the £340 tax on his behalf under s687(2)(b), but they can set against that liability the £340 tax they have already paid, thus cancelling it out. X is able to make a repayment claim on the Revenue for the full £340, since his personal reliefs of £4,045 cancel out his liability to basic-rate tax on the £1,000.

The remaining £5,840 will be capitalised. When it is paid out at a future date to beneficiaries, no more income tax will be payable (unless it is converted back into income under the special rules set out below) simply because it will be capital. This seemingly beneficial result will be contrary to the interests of the trust if the beneficiaries have, or will have, liabilities to income tax at rates below 34 per cent. No repayment claim will be possible since personal allowances do not apply to capital payments, and s687 is expressly restricted to payments of income.

Example 2
X settles property on trust for such of his nephew and nieces as the trustees in their absolute discretion shall determine. X has one nephew, Philip, and two nieces, Susan and Mary. Philip receives no income, Mary pays tax at 23 per cent marginal rate, and Susan pays tax at 40 per cent marginal rate.

In the tax year 1997–98 the trust property produces income of £10,000. The

160   Trust Income

trustees receive this income into their hands. The trustees must pay 'tax at the rate applicable to trusts' on this income. Thus the trustees pay tax at 34 per cent and will send £3,400 to the Revenue: s686 ICTA 1988.

The trustees are left with £6,600 in their hands. They decide to pay £660 to Philip, £1,320 to Mary and nothing to Susan.

Examination of Philip's tax position: under s687(2) the £660 received by Philip is treated as a sum received net of tax. One must gross up the sum at the rate applicable to trusts in order to determine what sum Philip is deemed to receive:

$$= \frac{£660 \times 100}{66} = £1,000$$

The £1,000 therefore enters Philip's total income for the year 1997–98. He is treated as having paid £340 in tax and as Philip receives no income during 1997–98 he is not liable to pay any tax. He can reclaim the tax that the trustees paid on his behalf.

Examination of Mary's tax position: similarly, the £1,320 received by Mary is treated as a sum received net of tax. It has to be grossed up in order to determine the sum that Mary is deemed to receive:

$$= \frac{£1,320 \times 100}{66} = £2,000$$

The £2,000 is part of Mary's taxable income for the year 1997–98. She will have to pay tax at 23 per cent on this slice of income – £460. However she has a tax credit in respect of the tax that the trustees paid on her behalf. This tax credit constitutes £680 – 34 per cent of £2,000. She can therefore reclaim the difference of £220 (£680 less £460).

If one examines the position of the trustees at the end of 1997–98 one finds that they received £10,000 in income, on which they paid tax of £3,400. They were left with £6,600 after tax, of which they distributed £1,320 to Mary and £660 to Philip. They decided to capitalise the remaining sum, £4,620 – in other words, they accumulated it. When they pay this capitalised sum out at a future date to beneficiaries, no income tax will be payable (unless it is converted back into income – see section 13.6). This will be disadvantageous to the beneficiaries if some or all of them would have been able to receive the trust income in the year 1997–98 and recovered some or all of the tax paid by the trustees.

Obviously no advantage would have been gained by paying trust income to Susan because she would simply have had to pay additional tax at 6 per cent. This is because her marginal rate of tax is 40 per cent and thus she would only obtain credit for the 34 per cent tax that the trustees had paid.

However, if money had been paid to Mary while she remained paying a 23 per cent marginal rate of tax, she would have been able to recover 11 per cent of the tax that the trustees had paid on her behalf. Similarly, if the money had been paid to Philip while he remained a non-taxpayer, he could have recovered all the tax that the trustees had paid on his behalf. Moreover, even when he became a 23 per cent taxpayer he would still have been able to recover 11 per cent of the tax – like Mary.

However, as the trustees decided to capitalise the income, the opportunity for the beneficiaries to recover the tax paid by trustees is lost. This is because s687(2) ICTA 1988 is expressly restricted to payments of income.

13.6 Payments out of capital treated as income

The general rule, as set out in section 13.5, is that when income has been capitalised it is capital, and when paid out to beneficiaries it retains that character and is capital in their hands too. The courts have on occasion, however, decided that capital payments can be transformed into income taxable in the hands of the beneficiary.

The first case in which this occurred was *Brodie's Will Trustees* v *IRC* (1933) 17 TC 432. There, Finlay J considered the case of trustees who were directed on the testator's death to pay an annuity of £4,000 per annum to his widow. It was directed that any deficiency in the trust income of the year should not cause the annuity to abate, but the trustees were to raise and pay out of capital such a sum as when added to the income would make £4,000: 'my intention being' the testator said 'that the income payable to my wife during her life shall in no case be less that £4,000 a year'. The trustees had to have recourse to the capital of the fund in six successive years. Finlay J held that, though paid out of capital, the payments themselves were income in the hands of the widow and so all fell to be taxed under Case III. Clearly the provisions of the will made this a very strong case; as was said in *Stevenson* v *Wishart* [1987] STC 266, the testator was simply directing an annuity of £4,000 per annum.

The decision was followed and extended by the Court of Appeal in *Cunard's Trustees* v *IRC* [1946] 1 All ER 159. There trustees held a fund on trust to pay the income thereof to the settlor's sister, and were empowered, if the income of the fund was insufficient to enable her to live in a freehold property which she was permitted to occupy under the will

> 'in the same degree of comfort as she now lives there with me to apply such portion of the capital of my residuary estate *by way of addition to the income* as they shall think fit'.

The Court of Appeal held that the payments, being made for an income purpose, were income in the hands of the beneficiary, even though there was no obligation on the trustees to make good the deficiency.

Both cases, it will be noted, were strongly in the Revenue's favour; in both, capital was paid *in substitution for* and *as* income. It was also in the Revenue's favour that the capital payments were repeatedly made. The cases were summed up in *Stevenson* in this way:

> 'In the *Brodie* and *Cunard* cases, the payments out of capital were in augmentation of an income interest, and their nature as income was determined accordingly.'

In *Stevenson* itself, the facts were not of this kind; nor was there any express gift of an annuity, where the source of the payment in satisfaction will necessarily be wholly irrelevant. The Court of Appeal stated that the fact that payments were made periodically out of capital or for personal maintenance did not mean that they were *necessarily* income. They gave the following examples of what would *not* be a payment of income out of capital:

1. Where property was held in trust for a beneficiary contingently on attaining the age of 30. If the trustees exercised their statutory power of advancement to make regular annual payments of capital to the beneficiary they would be capital and nothing else – all that would be happening was that the beneficiary was getting what was presumptively his or hers in advance of the vesting date. This would also be the case if those payments were paid specifically for the purpose of funding his school fees or for some other 'income purpose'.
2. If a beneficiary is only the object of a power to appoint capital, a one-off payment of, say, £40,000 because he or she was without adequate income for her maintenance would not be income – and the repetition of the payment in the following year would put the Revenue in no stronger position to argue 'income'.

The Revenue in *Stevenson* contended that the matter was different on the facts of the case, given the size, recurrence and purpose of the payments, and that one had to apply Finlay J's test of the 'reality' of the thing. In a period between May 1978 and April 1980, the trustees had made a large number of payments amounting in toto to some £90,000, under a power to appoint out of capital, in order to maintain an elderly and sick beneficiary in a nursing home. The court said:

> 'Applying the test of the "reality" of the matter, the position was this. Mrs Henwood was a woman of very advanced age who needed nursing home care. That was exceedingly expensive. It seems to me quite unreal to regard it as an ordinary income expense. Certainly it involved day-to-day maintenance expenditure, but it was expenditure on such a scale that it cannot be regarded as normal. Between 10 May 1978 and 14 April 1980, the payments amounted to £90,000. That was the sort of expenditure which, if it is to be met at all, is in practice either met from the patient's own capital or from family capital ... In short, the obvious source to meet such expenditure was capital ... There is nothing in the present case which indicates that the payments were of an income nature except their recurrence. I do not think that is sufficient. The trustees were disposing of capital in exercise of a power over capital. They did not create a recurring interest in property. If, in exercise of a power over capital they choose to make at their discretion regular payments of capital to deal with the special problems of Mrs Henwood's last years rather than release a single sum to her of a large amount that does not seem to me to create an income interest.'

While this case dealt a severe blow to the Revenue in its desire to extend the application of the *Cunard* principle, it left certain questions unanswered – in particular, is the Revenue entitled to assess trustees under s687 ICTA 1988, as releasing income, if they make regular payments out of capital by discretion but for everyday income purposes, rather than for the sort of emergency facing Mrs

Henwood? That is to say, was Knox J, at first instance, correct in drawing the distinction between cases where the trustees had given the beneficiary an interest entitling her to future payments (of an income nature) and ones where future payments remained at the discretion of the trustees? Some trace of this appears in Fox LJ's final words, when he said:

> 'In my opinion Lord Greene's words in *Cunard*, "... the purpose was an income purpose and nothing else", have no application to the present case. The words have to be read in their context. Lord Greene had, only a few lines previously, referred to the fact that the payments were to be made "by way of addition to the income" (which was the wording of the will). It seems to me that the 'income purpose' in *Cunard* was primarily identified by these words. There is no similar provision here.
>
> The result, in my opinion, is that there is nothing in the present case which indicates that the payments were of an income nature except their recurrence. I do not think that is sufficient.'

and concluded

> 'In my opinion, Knox J came to the correct conclusion. I would dismiss the appeal.'

13.7 Income tax and the administration of an estate

The personal representatives

Income arising during the course of the administration of an estate is treated as income of the personal representatives (PRs) in their representative capacity. Personal representatives are only liable to basic-rate tax, and unlike trustees they are not liable to income tax at the rate applicable to trusts under s686.

The beneficiaries under the will

Sections 695–702 ICTA 1988, which deal with this matter, provide a primary distinction between persons having an absolute interest in residue and persons having a limited interest in residue. A person has an 'absolute interest' in residue, or a part of it, if he would be entitled to the capital of the residue, or part of it, if the residue had been ascertained. He has a 'limited interest' in residue if, in those circumstances, he would be entitled to have the income, but not the capital, paid to him.

Where a beneficiary has a limited interest in residue

A beneficiary who has a right to the income of the residue will, once the residue has been ascertained and the administration is thus complete, be considered to have been entitled to the income of the residue from the date of the testator's death. Until the administration is complete, however, it will not be possible to determine the exact amount of income to which he will be entitled, and not until then will he be entitled to his interest under the will, as beneficiaries in unadministered estates only possess a chose in action enabling them to require the personal representatives to administer the estate: *Commissioner of Stamp Duties (Queensland)* v *Livingston* [1965] AC 694.

For these reasons, the following method of charging tax on the beneficiary have been adopted:

1. Up to 5 April 1995, sums paid to the beneficiary during the period of administration were treated as part of his total income for the year of receipt; the PRs would already have paid basic-rate tax, so the beneficiary would simply be charged at the higher rate, if applicable, on the grossed-up receipts from the PRs. This remains the case for interim payments made after 5 April 1995 also.
2. When the administration was completed prior to 5 April 1995, the sums already paid to the beneficiary were aggregated with any others found due to him and the aggregate was deemed to have accrued to him day by day, during the administration period, in an even flow. The beneficiary would therefore have had new figures for total income during each year of administration, and any necessary adjustments were made.
3. When an administration is completed after 5 April 1995, any sums due to a beneficiary are treated as paid to him in the year in which the administration ends. This change to s695 ICTA 1988 was made by Schedule 18 paragraph 2 FA 1995. When income to be grossed up includes dividends, then since these are only taxable at lower rate they should be grossed up at lower rate and not basic rate (see s701(3A) ICTA 1988).

Where the beneficiary has an absolute interest in residue

A beneficiary who has an absolute interest will be entitled to the capital and the income, so that any sums paid to him during administration could represent either or both. What s696 attempts to do is to impose a system of identification on payments made; this having been carried out, only the income element is included in the beneficiary's total income.

The method of achieving this is as follows:

1. The residuary income of the estate, ie the aggregate income of the PRs from all sources, less management expenses and charges of an income nature (such as interest on legacies), is computed.
2. Any funds paid to the beneficiary during the administration period are treated as income up to the amount of the residuary income; any excess is treated as capital.
3. At the end of the administration period, where this occurred before 5 April 1995, adjustments were necessary to re-apportion the final income over the years of administration. For estates where the administration is completed after 5 April 1995, any sums paid are income for the year of receipt and any sums remaining due after the completion of the administration are income for the year in which the administration ends.

The alterations described above are further illustrations of the changes to the income tax regime to facilitate the introduction of self-assessment (see Chapter 24). This particular one brings a measure of greater certainty than before in ruling out the possibility of provisional assessments which would in the past have been substituted at a later date.

Where neither (a) nor (b) applies
If the residue is held on discretionary trusts, s698(3) provides that the absolute interest system applies to discretionary payments made.

Legacies and annuities
General legacies. Interest is payable on general legacies. However, the legatee may decline to receive the interest, so only the amount of interest actually paid to him is included in his total income assessable under Case III of Schedule D: see *Dewar* v *IRC* [1935] 2 KB 351.

Specific legacies. Interest arising from a specific legacy forms part of the legatee's total income from the date of death unless the will provides otherwise.

An annuity under a will is payable from the date of death and therefore forms part of the annuitant's total income from that date. The annuitant is entitled to have a sum set aside which will produce sufficient income to secure his annuity. Even if the annuity is actually paid out of capital, the sum is treated as forming part of the annuitant's total income and tax is deducted under s349. If the estate is insufficient to provide the annuity fund, the annuitant is generally entitled to receive the actuarial value of the annuity itself. In these circumstances it would be a capital sum received by the annuitant and therefore not included in the annuitant's total income.

14

Settlements – Anti-avoidance

14.1 Introduction

14.2 Chapters 1A and 1B ICTA 1988, ss660A et seq

14.3 Preliminary concepts

14.4 Children's settlements: s660B ICTA 1988

14.5 Section 660A(4) – (9) ICTA 1988

14.6 Other anti-avoidance provisions: ss677 and 678 ICTA 1988

14.1 Introduction

A wealthy person may wish to transfer a portion of his income to another so that it ceases to be his income and becomes the donee's. If the donor's marginal rate of income tax is high and the donee's is low or nil (eg a charity) a considerable reduction may be achieved in the tax payable on the income, with the result that the donor can benefit in a generous fashion a donee to whom he has paid a relatively low amount of taxed income.

The two most commonly used methods of alienating income are:

1. a deed of covenant, promising to make annual payments out of income; and
2. a settlement of income-producing property.

The former method enables the donor to retain the source from which the income flows, while the latter requires him to give away the capital out of which the income is to be made.

14.2 Chapters 1A and 1B ICTA 1988, ss660A et seq

Legislation has been gradually introduced to counteract gross abuses of the opportunity of alienating income. This legislation was contained in the former ss660–685 of the Income and Corporation Taxes Act 1988, the aims of which were threefold:

1. to prevent income from being stored inside a trust, having suffered only the basic rate of income tax, and subsequently re-emerging as capital for the benefit of the settlor, his wife or his immediate family – the 'nuclear family';
2. to minimise the opportunity for diverting income to others members of the family who might be taxable at a lower rate of tax. In most events, however, the restrictions do not extend to grandparents' arrangements in favour of their grandchildren;
3. to prevent short-term manipulations which effectively leave the settlor's economic position unchanged while achieving temporary tax advantages. For example, a man with an abnormally high income in one year is not allowed to reduce his tax liability by covenanting away excess income of that year alone. Short-term planning of this nature, using deeds of covenant, was largely ended by the FA 1988 changes – see s347A ICTA 1988 and Chapter 3, section 3.5. The old provisions of s660 dealing with 'dispositions for short periods', except as re-enacted in s347A(2)(b), are not reflected in the new ss660A et seq.

Replacement of former anti-avoidance provisions of ss660 et seq

With effect from the year 1995–96 the anti-avoidance provisions relating to settlements, which had been gradually added but not necessarily co-ordinated over the years, have been replaced by fewer sections providing substantially the same effect. The repealed provisions were those of ss660–676 and 683–685. The new provisions are ss660A–G. The main change of any substance is that, while the existing provisions excluded certain settlements which existed when they were introduced, the new provisions apply to all settlements, whenever created, and extend the general definition of 'settlement' to include transfer of assets. This latter item was in the past confined to settlements on children.

The new sections were introduced by Schedule 17 of the Finance Act 1995 and are constructed to set out the provisions relating to:

1. settlements where the settlor has retained an interest – s660A;
2. payments to unmarried minor children of the settlor (where not already caught by s660A) – s660B;
3. the mode of assessing the settlor – s660C;
4. adjustments between settlor and trustees – s660D;
5. settlements with more than one settlor – s660E;
6. information powers – s660F;
7. the definition of settlement and settlor – (s660G).

Sections 677 and 678 ICTA 1988 remain in place and, for all purposes of interpreting the meaning of undistributed income throughout the new provisions, s682 remains in force.

The changes in the tax treatment of covenants now contained in s347A (see Chapter 12, section 12.5) cancel the need for further anti-avoidance provisions, and for this reason ss660 and 661 were repealed.

14.3 Preliminary concepts

Settlement

For the purposes of ss660A–682 ICTA 1988 'settlement' is defined by s660G, which provides:

> '... "settlement" includes any disposition, trust, covenant, agreement, arrangement or transfer of assets.'

'Includes' is generally accepted to be exclusionary – if an operation is not covered by one of the terms specified, it is not within the definition. The treatment of a transfer of assets was, prior to the 1995–96 changes, confined to settlements on children. In *Thomas* v *Marshall* [1953] AC 543 a father made absolute gifts to his infant children by transferring money into Post Office accounts opened in their names. The House of Lords held that the transfers were 'settlements' for the purposes of the forerunner of the former s663, so the income arising on the account was to be treated as his for tax purposes.

There are, however, some limitations on the meaning of 'settlement'. In *IRC* v *Plummer* [1980] AC 896 the House of Lords held that a transaction did not fall within the definition of settlement unless it contained an 'element of bounty'. The case concerned a surtax payer who sold a personal annuity to a charity in consideration of the payment to him of a capital sum. The Revenue argued that the scheme was caught by the former s660 so that, far from being (i) a payment falling under what is now s348 and (ii) deductible from his total income, the annuity remained his income. The taxpayer won, because the transaction contained no element of bounty and so fell outside the scope of the anti-avoidance provisions. The effect of the decision has been reversed in subsequent cases by what is now s125 which was introduced in 1977.

Two interesting related cases appeared before the House of Lords in 1993 – *Moodie* v *IRC; Sotnick* v *IRC* [1993] STC 188. They were concerned with self-cancelling annuity schemes identical to those upheld in the *Plummer* case. The Court of Appeal had heard these cases and decided that it was bound by the *Plummer* decision, notwithstanding the later decisions in *WT Ramsay Ltd* v *IRC* and *Furniss* v *Dawson*, under which *Plummer*-type schemes would have failed. The House of Lords held that it was not bound by the decision in *Plummer*, since in that case the court had not been asked to rule on the effectiveness of self-cancelling schemes. Accordingly the decision in *Ramsay* was to be followed, to deny a deduction from total income in respect of the payments.

The word 'bounty' is not, however, a definition – merely 'a judicial gloss descriptive of these classes of cases which are caught by the definition in contrast to those which are not' – per Nourse J in *IRC* v *Levy* [1982] STC 442. Thus in *Chinn* v *Collins* [1981] AC 583, a Capital Gains Tax case, the taxpayer argued that an appointment by trustees of a settlement under a special power did not contain an element of bounty since they were merely agents of the settlor, whose bounty had been exhausted on the creation of the settlement. The House of Lords disagreed, holding that a transaction of this kind would be a settlement since it contained an element of 'derivative bounty' conferred by the special power of appointment. In *IRC* v *Levy*, on the other hand, the taxpayer made an interest-free loan to a company of which he was the sole beneficial shareholder. The Revenue sought to treat that transaction as one falling within s677 (see section 14.6), but Nourse J decided that there was no element of bounty, even though the company got something (the use of the money) for nothing:

> 'The absence of a correlative obligation on the part of him who is at the receiving end of the transaction may be material, but is not conclusive, in determining whether it contains an element of bounty or not.'

The question remains whether *IRC* v *Plummer* reverses earlier cases such as *Yates* v *Starkey* [1951] Ch 465, in which the subject of dispute was the order of another court that a father pay £X per annum to his ex-wife in trust for the children of the marriage. The Court of Appeal refused the father's claim to deduct the gross sum in computing his total income, holding that a court order in that particular form was a 'settlement' within what was s670, notwithstanding that the money was paid under compulsion. In *Harvey* v *Sivyer* [1985] STC 434, Nourse J held that the two decisions were compatible and that the House had not intended to overrule *Yates* v *Starkey*:

> '[Lord Wilberforce] may well have thought that the natural relationship between parent and child was one of such deep affection and concern that there must always be an element of bounty by the parent, even where the provision is on the face of things made under compulsion. That, as it seems to me, may be the reconciliation between the general test and the apparent exception. Furthermore, a parent's settlement is, I think, a typical example of what Lord Roskill had in mind when, in *Chinn* v *Collins*, he referred to those cases where the recipient benefits without any assumption by him of any correlative obligation.'

It should be noted, too, that the House of Lords cited *Yates* v *Starkey* without adverse comment in *Sherdley* v *Sherdley* [1988] AC 213, so its authority appears to be impregnable. In those days, parties to matrimonial proceedings had to be careful not to create a 'settlement' in favour of children. However, the courts became more aware of the difficulties, and orders were worded accordingly. The more recent provisions relating to qualifying maintenance payments in s347B ICTA 1988 largely deal with this problem.

In *Sherdley* the court had to decide whether a divorced father with custody of his children could obtain an order of the court against himself in order to take advantage of the Revenue practice. The House held that this was acceptable but warned:

> 'The Inland Revenue, however, have accepted, since 1953 at least, that, where an order is made against a father for payment of maintenance direct to his children, ... [section 663 of

the 1988 Act does not apply]. It is no doubt open to the Inland Revenue to depart from their previous policy in the matter, and to test, in appropriate tax proceedings, the applicability of [section 663] ... to the situation created by such an order. It seems unlikely, however, having regard to the Attorney-General's letter ... of 1979 ... that the Inland Revenue would now take that course. It is nevertheless right to say that the question of tax law involved has never been decided by the courts, and it would not be appropriate for your Lordships to express any opinion on it in this appeal.'

Clearly, the House had some doubts whether the practice was more than an administrative concession of the Revenue.

For the purposes of conformity with the system of independent matrimonial taxation introduced in 1990–91, s685 ICTA 1988 was amended to provide that outright transfers between spouses are not to be considered settlements; the provision can now be found in s660A(6). Inter-spousal transfers will, however, be treated as settlements if the transfer does not carry a right to the whole of the income which arises from the property transferred. Additionally, such transfers will be settlements if the gift is subject to conditions, or if the property given or any derived property is or will or may become, in any circumstances whatsoever, payable to, or applicable for the benefit of, the donor. 'Settlement' within s660G ICTA 1988 does not include the irrevocable allocation of pension rights by one spouse to the other in accordance with the terms of a statutory scheme (s660A(7)).

The purpose of these amendments is to make a total and outright capital transfer between spouses effective to transfer income and, therefore, income tax liability. Such effect cannot, however, be achieved where the transfer is conditional or such as to allow benefits to revert to the transferor. In this way abuse is stemmed. Similarly, pure income transfers are not effective.

It is suggested that a realistic view must be taken as to the possibility of reversion to the transferor. Such a possibility, however remote, must always exist in relation to inter-spousal transfers and does not in any way facilitate abuse by artificial income or income-producing capital asset transfers. For example, the intestate death of the transferee spouse will result in the passing of the estate to the surviving spouse. A reversion may similarly take place under the will of a spouse or even upon divorce!

In *Young* v *Pearce; Young* v *Scrutton* [1996] STC 743, it was held that the issue of certain preference shares to the wives of the sole shareholders of the company was wholly or substantially a right to income and that the dividends arising on the shares constituted a 'settlement' for the purposes of what is now s660A. It has been suggested that the lack of capital rights on the preference shares contributed to the court's ruling and that if the shareholders had given away part of their existing holdings of ordinary shares, the transaction could have been regarded as an outright gift in which the settlors retained no interest. See Chapter 27, section 27.4, for further details.

Settlor

'Settlor' is defined by s660G as:

> 'any person by whom the settlement was made': 'A person shall be deemed for the purpose of this Chapter to have made a settlement if he has made or entered into the settlement directly or indirectly, and in particular ... if he has provided or undertaken to provide funds directly or indirectly for the purpose of the settlement, or has made with any other person a reciprocal arrangement for that person to make or enter into the settlement.'

The judicial decisions on this topic show that a person is a settlor if funds arrive in a settlement as a result of his acts. The Revenue need not, however, show that there was any mental element involved, even though the subsections say 'for the purpose of'.

In *Mills* v *IRC* [1975] AC 38, Hayley Mills, a child actress, signed documents by which a settlement was created under which trustees were to receive her income and capitalise it without liability to surtax. The House of Lords rejected her counsel's contention that, at the age of 14, she could not have had the mental purpose necessary for the operation of s660A (see below), stating that there was no requisite mental element – merely a physical requirement of provision of funds.

Moreover, the decision in *Butler (Inspector of Taxes)* v *Wildin* [1989] STC 22 illustrates how funds can arrive in a settlement as a result of a reciprocal arrangement between two persons that consequently makes them settlors in respect of the settlement. In *Butler* a company was incorporated by two brothers (the taxpayers) who acted as unpaid directors. The issued share capital of the company was £100 divided into 100 £1 shares that were allotted to the two taxpayers and their four infant children. The company started trading, financed by a bank loan guaranteed by the taxpayers. Dividends were declared on the shares and paid to each shareholder. Each taxpayer then sought repayment of the Advance Corporation Tax (ACT) attributed to the dividends of their respective children on behalf of them. Such repayments were refused.

Vinelott LJ held that the taxpayers were the architects of a reciprocal arrangement to which both had contributed the provision of skills or services, so the company, and so indirectly the children, took the benefit of the development at no risk to themselves. The arrangement contained an element of 'bounty', and so when the dividends were paid the payment was 'by virtue or in consequence of a settlement within the forerunner of s663'. Therefore the income which arose under the settlement – the dividend payments to the four children – should be treated as the income of the taxpayers.

See also Chapter 20, section 20.2, for discussion of the House of Lords' judgment in *Marshall* v *Kerr* [1994] 3 WLR 299.

14.4 Children's settlements: s660B ICTA 1988

Under the revised form of the settlement provisions which apply from 1995–96, the special provisions relating to settlements on children apply only to supplement the more general s660A, which catches all settlements where the settlor retains an interest.

Section 660B provides:

'(1) Income arising under a settlement which does not fall to be treated as income of the settlor under section 660A but which during the life of the settlor is paid to or for the benefit of an unmarried minor child of the settlor in any year of assessment shall be treated for all the purposes of the Taxes Acts as the income of the settlor for that year and not as the income of any other person.'

So if a parent puts money into trust in 1995 from which his 13-year-old son is paid £1,000 per annum for the next ten years, payments made to the child before he attains the age of 18 (or marries) will be treated as the income of the settlor and not as the child's income. For reported cases on children's settlements see *Thomas* v *Marshall* [1953] AC 543 and *Harvey* v *Sivyer* [1985] STC 434.

Section 660D allows the settlor to recover from the trustees (if any) or the child the tax he pays as a result of ss660A and B. Where the settlor does not exercise that right to recover from the trustees, the Inland Revenue will treat the amount foregone as the provision of additional funds into the settlement for the purpose of attributing gains to the settlor – see Schedule 5 para 9(3) of the Taxation of Chargeable Gains Act 1992 and IR Statement of Practice SP5/92 para (f) dated 21 May 1992.

It will be remembered that 'settlor' in s660G includes a person who has made a reciprocal arrangement with another for that other to make or enter into a settlement. Thus if A and B agree that A will covenant to pay £1,000 to B's child, B covenanting likewise in favour of A's, A is a settlor of B's covenant with A's child, so that any income paid to A's child by B will be treated as A's income under s660B.

Section s660B(1) is extended under s660B(2) and (3) to certain accumulation trusts – to settlements under which income or assets representing the income may at any time in the future in any circumstances become payable to a child of the settlor. This ensures that trustees cannot simply accumulate income, paying it out later to the child as capital, and avoiding the operation of s660A. Section 660B also applies to the treatment of any capital sum distributed to an infant beneficiary as income, to the extent that undistributed income (whether accumulated or not) exists within the settlement.

The previous provisions distinguished between revocable and irrevocable settlements. The combined effects of ss660A and B are to treat all accumulated income which exceeds the aggregate of trust revenue expenses, payments already charged by ss660A and B, and payments to beneficiaries other than the settlor's minor unmarried children as the settlor's income, to be taxed under Schedule D Case VI.

Example
X creates a settlement in favour of his three children, A, B and C, who are respectively 18, 16 and 14, and his three nephews, E, F and G. The trusts provide, inter alia, for the income to be accumulated for 21 years, with power in the trustees to pay income to the beneficiaries in such shares (if any) as in their absolute discretion they think fit. Section 660B(2) and (3) would treat any income not payable to the eldest child as the income of the parent. If the intention is to divide the income (of say £3,000) equally among them, the £1,000 to be distributed to A is outside the scope of s660B, but the £1,000 to B and C is caught and is taxed at the settlor's rates.

14.5 Section 660A(4)–(9) ICTA 1988

Section 660A provides that, save in certain exceptional circumstances, income payable under a settlement to any person other than the settlor is to be treated as the settlor's income for the purposes of 'excess liability', and not as the income of any other person. Those exceptional circumstances are contained in s660A(4) to (9):

1. where the settlor has divested himself absolutely of the property from which the income arises, in other words he no longer retains an interest, or where he can only benefit through exceptional circumstances such as the death or bankruptcy of some other person;
2. where the income arises under a settlement made by one party to a marriage in favour of the other (NB *not* in favour of a child of the marriage) by way of provision for the other:
   – after the dissolution or annulment of the marriage; or
   – under an order of the court; or
   – under a separation agreement; or
   – where the parties are separated in such circumstances that the separation is likely to be permanent;
3. where the income relates to annual payments made for bona fide commercial reasons in connection with his trade, profession or vocation;
4. where the income arises from a transfer to a spouse or from the transfer of pension rights to a spouse under an approved pension scheme;
5. where the payments are made in the form of covenanted payments to a charity.

14.6 Other anti-avoidance provisions: ss677 and 678 ICTA 1988

It would be very easy for a settlor to 'milk' the income and capital of a settlement by means other than those described above; for example, he could borrow money from the settlement and never pay it back, or he could lend money to a settlement, instead of giving it outright to trustees, and then extract it again as repayments of a loan. Such devices are the object of ss677 and 678.

For many years the section which preceded s678 suffered from bad drafting, with the consequence that it was a trap for the unwary, catching those whom it was never intended to ensnare but failing to stem the abuses effected by those who took professional advice. Eventually FA 1981 amended the section, introducing what is now s678. Even so the drafting was defective, and amendments were made by FA 1982.

Section 677 applies where any capital sum is paid directly or indirectly in any year of assessment by the trustees of a settlement to the settlor. Section 677(9) defines 'capital sum' as meaning:

1. any sum paid by way of loan or repayment of loan;
2. any sum paid otherwise than as income, being a sum not paid for full consideration;
3. any sum paid to a third party at the direction of the settlor; and
4. any sum otherwise paid or applied for the benefit of the settlor.

Remarkably, one of the easiest ways of avoiding s677 was for the trustees to discharge an obligation of the settlor to pay a third party. This has now been dealt with by s677(10).

The measure of the income deemed to arise to the settlor where s677 applies is determined by reference to the amount of 'available income'. This is the amount of undistributed income (whether or not capitalised) in the hands of the trustees from the relevant year of assessment and from previous years, less any income which has already been treated as the income of the settlor under any other anti-avoidance provision (including s683), and less basic and additional tax for the relevant year on the sums then remaining available to be treated as the settlor's.

Where available income exceeds the capital sum paid to the settlor, the whole of the capital sum, grossed-up at the rates of basic and additional rate tax in force for the year, is treated as the income of the settlor. The settlor is then deemed to have paid basic and additional tax (a total of 34 per cent), so he is only liable to further tax on the sum if he is paying tax at 40 per cent. He may not, however, make a repayment claim. The income is Case VI income.

If the available income is insufficient to treat the whole of the capital sum as income in the settlor's hands, the untaxed portion of the capital sum is carried forward to the next year of assessment and is taxed (or the appropriate proportion of it is taxed) by reference to the available income arising in that year. As a result of this, there will be no available income from previous years. This process can continue for up to ten years of assessment after that in which the capital sum was paid.

There are some restrictions imposed on the above process:

1. If a loan is *wholly* paid off, s677 applies to the capital sum for the year of discharge but not for any following year. Thus if a loan is made in year 1 and paid off in year 2, it can be brought into charge as above in years 1 and 2 but not in years 3 to 11.
2. If a loan has been made and paid off in the past and another loan is made, only the excess of that second loan over the amount of the former loan brought into charge under s677 is taxable. This is because the whole of the undistributed income remaining in the settlement is applicable to the second loan.

Thus if a settlor borrows £10,000 from a settlement, and £5,000 of that has been treated as his income by the time the loan is paid off, and subsequently a second loan of £7,000 is made to him, only £2,000 of that loan can be subjected to s677.

Section 678 extends the idea behind s677 to loans made by close companies with which the settlement is connected. The scheme aimed at here is one whereby the trustees lend money to the company and the company on-lends the money to the settlor. Such a process would be outside the scope of s677, but would have the self-same effect. Accordingly, s678 provides that if trustees of a settlement have paid any sum or transferred any asset to the close company otherwise than for full consideration, within five years of that company paying a capital sum (as defined as in s677) to the settlor, the capital sum is, to the extent that it does not exceed the associated payments made by the trustees, to be treated as a capital sum paid by the trustees to the settlor – and so as falling within s677.

15

Matrimonial Taxation

15.1 Introduction

15.2 Income taxation of married couples living together

15.3 Income tax position of separated couples and maintenance payments

15.4 Mortgage interest relief on separation

15.5 Capital gains tax treatment of married couples

15.6 Capital gains tax on separation

15.7 The disposal of the matrimonial home by one spouse to the other

15.8 Inheritance tax and married couples

15.1 Introduction

This chapter is intended to draw together all the different strands of income tax, capital gains tax and inheritance tax which specially affect married couples. Under the system of independent taxation introduced for married couples with effect from 6 April 1990, spouses are effectively taxed separately, each being entitled to an individual personal relief. Married couples are also taxed separately in respect of the capital gains realised by the respective individual.

Prior to 1990, all income and gains of a wife were taxed at the husband's rate of tax.

15.2 Income taxation of married couples living together

The method of taxing the income of a husband and wife living together post 6 April 1990 has been dealt with above: see Chapter 3, section 3.7.

Personal allowances

Basically, since 6 April 1990 each spouse has been taxed separately, each being entitled under s257(1) of the Income and Corporation Taxes Act 1988 to a personal allowance; the old single personal allowance and the wife's earned income relief were abolished from 6 April 1990. There is now a new married couple's allowance, s257A ICTA 1988, which will prima facie be claimed by the husband but which can be transferred to the wife (under the rules in s257BA) if the allowance remains unused by him. The rules also permit the allowance to be apportioned between the couple as they agree and give a wife a right to make a claim for up to half of the married couple's allowance against her income. From 1995–96, relief for the amount of the married couple's allowance is only given at 15 per cent under s256(2).

Jointly held property

Sections 282A and B deal with the problem of whose income is whose, where income-producing capital is held in the joint names of husband and wife. Generally s282A provides that the income of the property held jointly by the husband and wife shall be regarded as accruing to them in equal shares. However, s282B permits the couple to make a joint declaration for the income of the property to be allocated unequally to them. Such a declaration can only be made if their beneficial shares in the income are the same as their beneficial shares in the property.

Note: s282A does not apply to partnership income or earned income.

As a result of amendments to s685 ICTA 1988, an outright gift of property made by one spouse to another will not be treated as a settlement within s683 ICTA 1988 provided that the recipient spouse receives the right to the whole of the income from the property gifted.

Mortgage interest relief

From 6 April 1990, when a qualifying loan of £30,000 is in the joint names of husband and wife the mortgage interest relief is allocated equally between them. However, both spouses retain the right to make an allocation of interest election, which enables them to share the relief in whatever proportions they choose: s356B ICTA 1988.

Mortgage interest in year of marriage

Where two borrowers marry, the limit of £30,000 comes into force immediately so that from the date of marriage each has a limit of £15,000 on his or her MIRAS relief.

15.3 Income tax position of separated couples and maintenance payments

Except in so far as s257F ICTA 1988 ensured that in the transition from the old to the new system of taxation a married man could still obtain the benefit of s257(1)(a)(ii) ICTA 1988 if he voluntarily and completely maintained his wife and made no deduction for the payments made, the new system of independent taxation does not alter the tax treatment of separated couples because they were already treated as two separate individuals for tax purposes.

Payments under 'existing obligations'

These are obligations entered into before 15 March 1988. Where a husband is maintaining his separated wife under a court order or separation agreement made before that date he can only claim his personal allowance, but he can deduct his maintenance payment from his total income on making a claim under s38 FA 1988 – although from 1988–89 onwards the statutory deduction for maintenance payments was capped at the 1988–89 level.

In addition, by virtue of s257A(1) (s38(5) FA 1988), the recipient of maintenance payments under a pre 15 March 1988 agreement or court order can claim an additional relief in 1990–91 and onwards, equal to the married couple's allowance, if:

1. The payment is made pursuant to an 'existing obligation' (that is, pursuant to an agreement or order made before 15 March 1988); and
2. The payment is made by one of the partners to a marriage (including a dissolved or annulled marriage) either –
   – to or for the benefit of the other party and for the maintenance of the other party, or
   – to the other party for the maintenance by the other party of any child of the family; and
3. The payment is due at a time when –
   – the parties are not a married couple living together, and
   – the party to whom or for whose benefit the payments are made has not remarried; and
4. The payment is within Schedule D Case III (or Case V) and does not fall foul of the anti-avoidance provisions in Part XV ICTA 1988.

Thus the relief is not available for payments made directly to dependent children.

From 1994–95, by s85 FA 1994, maintenance payments made at a time when the recipient child is over 21 years of age are treated in like manner to other such payments, and the relief is only available to the extent that the payments are within the 'qualifying maintenance payments' provisions of s347B. Previously it was possible to obtain full relief for these as annual payments.

Post 14 March 1988 arrangements

If the separation agreement or court order was made on or after 15 March 1988, then the sums payable thereunder will no longer be deductible in computing the liability of the payer, and neither will the payments constitute Schedule D Case III income in the hands of the payee (that is, the sums will represent 'tax-free' income in the payee's hands).

If, however, the payments are 'qualifying maintenance payments' within s347B ICTA 1988, then the payer of the payment is entitled, in place of the former charges on income deduction, to a relief equal to the size of the payment or the size of the married couple's allowance (s257A(1)), whichever is the less (s347B(2) and (3)). A payment is a qualifying maintenance payment if it:

1. is made under a United Kingdom or a European Union State court order or a separation agreement governed by the law of any European Union State; and
2. is made by one of the parties to a marriage (including a dissolved or annulled marriage) either
    - to or for the benefit of the other party and for the maintenance of the other party, or
    - to the other party for the maintenance by the other party of any child of the family; and
3. is done at a time when:
    - the two parties are not a married couple living together, and
    - the party to whom or for whose benefit the payment is made has not remarried, and
4. is not a payment otherwise available for relief or caught with the anti-avoidance provisions.

Thus, as with payments entitling the payee of maintenance under an existing obligation to an additional relief (see above), payments directly to children do not attract the favourable tax treatment in s347B(1) ICTA 1988. The meaning of 'qualifying maintenance payments' is extended by s347B(8)–(12) (see Chapter 12, section 12.5).

15.4 Mortgage interest relief on separation

Formerly a taxpayer was entitled to relief for interest paid on a loan to purchase a property used as the only or main residence of the borrower or his former or separated spouse.

Section 44 FA 1988 now ensures that, with regard to loans made after 5 April 1988, interest payable ceases to be eligible for deduction under s354. But loans entered into before 6 April 1988 remain eligible for relief, provided (broadly) that any interest paid before 6 April 1988 qualified for relief.

15.5 Capital gains tax treatment of married couples

Section 104 FA 1988 introduced the principle of independent taxation to Capital Gains Tax with effect from 1990–91 onwards.

Since 6 April 1990 husbands and wives have been treated as separate individuals for capital gains tax purposes. Thus each is liable for his or her own gains, which will form the top slice of his or her income and be charged at his or her marginal rate of income tax. Each is entitled to an annual exemption of £6,500 for 1997–98.

The mutual offsetting of losses ceased to be available after 6 April 1990. Instead any unused losses arising pre 6 April 1990 can only be carried forward and be set against the gains of the spouse who incurred the losses.

Under s58 TCGA 1992, disposals between spouses continue to take place on a no gain/no loss basis and will not give rise to any capital gains tax liability. See section 15.6 for the application of this principle in cases involving separation and divorce.

15.6 Capital gains tax on separation

TCGA 1992 s58 only applies while a couple are married and living together. Once separation takes place the automatic roll-over relief of s58 is no longer available, although the couple will continue to be 'connected persons' within ss18 and 286 TCGA 1992 until a decree absolute has been pronounced. Accordingly, any inter-spousal disposals which occur before that decree will be deemed irrebuttably to have been made in a transaction otherwise than by way of a bargain at arm's length under s18, and s17 will deem the disposal to have been made for a consideration equal to market value: see *Aspden* v *Hildesley* [1982] STC 206.

As couples have been treated as separate individuals for capital gains tax purposes from 6 April 1990, the fact that a couple separate will not affect their liability for capital gains tax, except with regard to inter-spousal disposals – see above.

15.7 The disposal of the matrimonial home by one spouse to the other

On the breakdown of the marriage, one spouse is likely to leave the matrimonial home for other accommodation. When this occurs, the matrimonial home will cease to be that spouse's residence. It may well be that eventually an order will be made or an agreement reached to transfer the interest in the property to the former spouse. As explained in section 15.8, that will be a chargeable disposal, and if more than three years have elapsed since the spouse left the property the exemption under s223(2) TCGA 1992 would be limited. By concession, No. D6, the Inland Revenue has stated, however, that:

'Where, as a result of the breakdown of a marriage one spouse ceases to occupy his or her matrimonial home and subsequently, a part of a financial settlement disposes of the home, or an interest in it, to the other spouse, (or, if the transfer is after divorce, ex spouse), the home may be regarded for the purposes of s223 as continuing to be a residence of the transferring spouse from the date his (or her) occupation ceases until transfer, provided that it has throughout this period been the other spouse's only or main residence.'

It is also necessary that the spouse who has left has not in the meantime elected that some other property be treated as his or her main residence. The effect of the provision is to avoid any Capital Gains Tax on that particular property.

15.8 Inheritance tax and married couples

There are two specific provisions in inheritance tax dealing with husbands and wives:

1. Section 11 of the Inheritance Tax Act 1984 provides that a disposition made by one party to a marriage in favour of the other is not a transfer of value if it is made for the maintenance of the other. Section 11(6) further provides that 'marriage' includes a former marriage if the disposition in question was made on the occasion of the dissolution or annulment of the marriage or varied a disposition so made. It follows that almost all maintenance orders are outside the scope of IHT, even though they inevitably reduce the value of the disponer's estate.
2. Section 18 states that a transfer of value is an exempt transfer to the extent that the value transferred is attributable to property which becomes comprised in the estate of the transferor's spouse or increases that spouse's estate. This is restricted, though, in cases where the transferor is domiciled in the United Kingdom but the transferee is not; then the section only exempts a lifetime's transfers of value not exceeding £55,000.

It should be noted that s11 takes precedence over s18 – if a disposition is not a transfer of value, s18 cannot apply to it. Section 18 applies whether or not the parties are separated – only once the decree absolute has been pronounced does it cease to apply. In cases where capital assets are to be transferred on the breakdown of a marriage, the parties should ensure either that the transfer precedes the decree absolute or that s10 IHTA 1984 – 'dispositions not intended to confer gratuitous benefit' – applies. The Capital Taxes Office has stated that it anticipates that the latter section will normally apply on a divorce.

The new system of independent taxation for husband and wife does not require any amendments to the inheritance tax provisions because they are already treated as separate individuals for inheritance tax purposes.

16

Corporation Tax

16.1 Introduction

16.2 The charge to corporation tax

16.3 The rate of corporation tax

16.4 Charges on income

16.5 Interest payments by companies (loan relationships)

16.6 Losses

16.7 Reform – the pay and file system and self-assessment

16.1 Introduction

Corporation tax is imposed by s6 of the Income and Corporation Taxes Act 1988 on the profits of companies. 'Company' is defined widely by s832(1) as:

'any body corporate or unincorporated association, but does not include a partnership, local authority or local authority association'.

For an idea of the difficulties which can be encountered with this definition see *Conservative and Unionist Central Office* v *Burrell* [1980] 3 All ER 42.

Corporation tax is, however, subject to certain territorial limitations – s11 provides that companies not resident in the United Kingdom are, as a general rule, not within the charge to it. If, however, a non-resident company carries on trade in the United Kingdom through a branch or agency, it is chargeable to corporation tax on its 'chargeable profits'.

'Chargeable profits' are defined by a combination of s11(2) ICTA 1988 and s10 of the Taxation of Chargeable Gains Act 1992 as:

1. trading income arising directly or indirectly from the branch or agency;
2. income from property or rights held by the branch or agency; and
3. chargeable gains on the disposal of assets situated in the United Kingdom used in or for the purposes of the trade or acquired, used or held for the purposes of the branch or agency.

This is not to say, however, that other income profits of non-resident companies necessarily escape all liability to United Kingdom tax. Section 6(2) only exempts from income tax *income falling within the charge to corporation tax*. Thus non-resident companies will normally be subject to income tax on, for example, income with a United Kingdom source, if they are not trading in the United Kingdom through a branch or an agency. By concession B13, however, interest paid gross to a non-resident is not subjected to taxation. Steps have been taken to ensure that banks are not obliged to operate the MIRAS scheme (which gives tax relief at source on payment of mortgage interest by withholding tax at the time of payment of interest) for non-residents' accounts.

It should be noted that one type of income is always exempt from corporation tax: dividends and other distributions paid by United Kingdom resident companies (s208 ICTA 1988). Given the system of taxation imposed on companies and their distributions, any other course would lead to double taxation.

16.2 The charge to corporation tax

Corporation tax is imposed on both the income profits and the capital gains of companies. Accordingly, companies liable to pay corporation tax are subject neither to income tax nor to capital gains tax.

Section 9 ICTA 1988 provides that the computation and determination of what is or is not to be treated as the income of a company is to be made in accordance with income tax principles. In particular, the computation and the assessment are made under the same Schedules and Cases as apply for income tax, with the proviso that the income so found to be taxable is then aggregated with its chargeable capital gains, to arrive at the total profits.

Section 12(1) ICTA 1988 provides that corporation tax is assessed and charged for any accounting period on the profits of that period. Section 8(3) elaborates:

> 'Corporation tax for any financial year shall be charged on profits arising in that year; but assessments to corporation tax shall be made on a company by reference to accounting periods, and the amount chargeable [after making all proper deductions] of the profits arising in the accounting period shall, where necessary, be apportioned between the financial years in which the accounting period falls.'

Some explanation of this is required:

1. Corporation tax does not rely on 'years of assessment' but on 'financial years'. Section 834(1) explains that the financial year runs from 1 April on year to 31 March the following year; for example, the 'financial year 1997' runs from 1 April 1997 to 31 March 1998.
2. The rates of corporation tax do not slavishly follow those for income tax. Furthermore, subject to relief afforded to companies with small profits, a single rate of corporation tax applies for each financial year. The relevant rates are now:

corporation tax   33 per cent
small companies' rate 23 per cent – financial year 1997
                       24 per cent – financial year 1996

In applying tax to profits of accounting periods, regard has to be paid to changes in the rate of tax. For example, profits amounting to £200,000 for the accounting period ended 31 December 1997, would be charged partly at 24 per cent and partly at 23 per cent, as follows:

Profits from 1.1.97 to 31.3.97 £200,000 x 3/12 = £50,000 @ 24% – Tax £12,000
Profits from 1.4.97 to 31.12.97 £200,000 x 9/12 = 150,000 @ 23% – Tax £34,500
                                                        Total   £46,500

3. The company is charged to tax on its profits of its accounting period, which may not necessarily coincide with a financial year. The profits of that period are apportioned by reference to the respective lengths of the parts of the period falling into each financial year, the appropriate proportion being taxed at the corporation tax rate for the appropriate financial year.

Example
Sparks Ltd, a company resident in the United Kingdom, makes up its accounts each year to 31 December. For the accounting period to 31 December 1997, it has income profits of £2,000,000 but no capital gains. Its liability to tax is calculated as follows:

$\frac{1}{4}$ of its accounting period (1 January–31 March) falls into financial year 1996, and $\frac{3}{4}$ (1 April–31 December) into financial year 1997.

So $\frac{1}{4}$ x £2m = £500,000 is taxed at 33 per cent = £165,000 corporation tax and $\frac{3}{4}$ x £2m = £1,500,000 at 33 per cent = £495,000,

making a total corporation tax liability for that accounting period of £660,000.

Although in the above example the rates of corporation tax are the same, a change of rate in one financial year would affect the tax payable on the proportion of profits which fall into that year. (The rates for years 1989 to 1991 were 35, 34 and 33 per cent respectively.)

Note: if a company makes up its accounts for a period of less than 12 months, corporation tax is assessed and paid on that period's profits.

16.3 The rate of corporation tax

As stated in section 16.2 corporation tax is levied not only on income profits but also on the capital gains of United Kingdom resident companies. Mainstream corporation tax is chargeable on all the profits of a company (including chargeable capital gains). Thus for a financial year a company will pay corporation tax on its profits at 33 per cent unless it is classified as a small company within s13 ICTA 1988. 'Small' means that in the particular financial year under review a company's profits do not exceed the limits discussed below. Therefore the largest public company could be subject in any year to the small companies' rate of corporation tax if it made only a small profit.

Section 13 ICTA 1988, as amended by s59 FA 1997, provides mitigation where a company's profits are not large. Where the profits of a company in its accounting period do not exceed £300,000, the corporation tax rate on its income and capital gains for that period is only 23 per cent. A company's 'profits', for the purpose of applying the small companies' rate, include its United Kingdom dividends (not chargeable to corporation tax), ie franked investment income (FII) (see below), as well as its income profits plus its chargeable gains.

'Franked investment' is defined (s238(1)) as a distribution in respect of which the company is entitled to a tax credit (equivalent to the rate of advance corporation tax – s231) and equals the sum of the distribution and the credit. Thus, if a company received £8,000 of what are known as 'qualifying distributions' it will have FII of £10,000.

Where a company's profits exceed £300,000 but do not exceed £1,500,000, tapering relief is given. In this case it is charged to corporation tax at the general rate in force, but the amount of tax on its income so determined is reduced by a *fraction* of the amount:

$$(M-P) \times \frac{I}{P}$$

where:

M is the 'upper relevant maximum amount' – ie £1,500,000 if a company has no associated companies;

I is the amount of the company's income;

P is the amount of the company's profits.

The small companies' fraction for s13(2) purposes is laid down by s59 FA 1997 as $\frac{1}{40}$ for the financial year 1997; see *Example 2* below for an illustration of its application.

Examples
1. Arri Co Ltd is a company whose accounting period coincides with the financial year. For its accounting period ending on 31 March 1998 (the financial year 1997), its accounts show:
   - dividends received from UK Ltd of £8,000;
   - trading profits of £60,000;
   - chargeable gains of £12,000.

Its profits for the period are, therefore:

	£
FII (£8,000 grossed-up)	10,000
Trading profits	60,000
Taxable chargeable gains	12,000
	£82,000

Since its profits for the period do not exceed the lower relevant maximum amount of £300,000 (it has no associated companies), its profits are only taxable at 23 per cent.

Its corporation tax liability for the period is, therefore:

£72,000 x 23% = £16,560

Note: dividend income, though used to compute profits in s13 ICTA 1988, is not liable to corporation tax – s208.

2. If, however, Arri Co Ltd's accounts showed the following receipts for the financial year 1997:

	£
– dividend income received from UK Ltd	16,000
– trading profits	500,000
– chargeable gains	48,000

its profits, within s13, would be:

	£
FII (£16,000 grossed up)	20,000
trading profits	500,000
chargeable gains	48,000
	£568,000

Accordingly, only tapering relief would be available.

Taking the computation in stages:

1. Corporation tax at 33 per cent on:

	£
trading profits £500,000	165,000
chargeable gains £48,000	15,840
	£180,840

2. $(M - P) \times \dfrac{I}{P}$

$= £1,500,000 - 568,000 \times \dfrac{548,000}{568,000} = £868,598$

3. The corporation tax on Arri Co Ltd's profits is, therefore, reduced by:

$\frac{1}{40}$ × £868,598 = £21,715,

making a net tax bill of £(180,840-21,715) = £159,125.

It will be noticed that the tapering relief does not result in an automatic charge of the first £300,000 of any company's profits at the lower rate, with the $\frac{1}{40}$ relief available for all profits exceeding £300,000 but not exceeding £1,500,000 in respect of any company. The corporation tax charge at the full rate of 33 per cent is reduced, as illustrated by the calculations set out above, but such reductions diminish gradually until the company's profits have reached £1,500,000, at which point the reductions disappear altogether.

Certain anti-avoidance provisions exist to prevent companies with large profits from subdividing into lots of smaller companies to obtain the benefit of the lower rate under s13. If a company has associated companies, the upper and lower relevant maximum amounts (U/L RMA) are divided by one plus the number of such companies, so groups of companies do not benefit unduly over single companies. A company is associated with another company if both are under the control of the same person or persons or if one has control of the other. Thus, if Arri Co Ltd had been associated with Been Ltd in the financial year 1997, the lower relevant maximum amount for each would have been

$\frac{£300,000}{2}$ = £150,000,

and the upper relevant maximum amount for each would have been

$\frac{£1,500,000}{2}$ = £750,000.

To summarise this, for the financial years 1996 and 1997 the relevant rates and sums are:

	1996	1997
Corporation tax rate	33%	33%
Small companies' rate	24%	23%
URMA	£1,500,000	£1,500,000
LRMA	£300,000	£300,000
Small companies' fraction	$\frac{9}{400}$	$\frac{1}{40}$

16.4 Charges on income

Prior to changes introduced by the Finance Act 1996, companies could only obtain a deduction for yearly or annual interest under the form of a charge on income. Such interest payments were not deductible in computing the profits of the company. In respect of interest payments falling after 31 March, 1996, such interest payments are no longer regarded as 'charges on income'. A completely new regime under the term 'loan relationships' was introduced by the Finance Act 1996, and is explained in more detail in section 16.5. Section 337A excludes interest from charges on income or from any other deduction except as provided for under the new loan relationship regime.

Although, as in section 16.2, the general rule is that the computation of income of companies follows the rules laid down for income tax, there are divergences. In particular, the Corporation Tax Acts have their own special system for the treatment of charges on income, to be found in ss338–40 and s249 ICTA 1988. Section 338(1) provides that charges on income are to be deducted from the total profits of the company, rather than at the earlier stage of computing the company's income. This is advantageous, since the charge is thus not merely deductible against the particular source of income from which it arises. Section 338(2), however, provides:

'... no payment which is deductible in computing profits or any description of profits for purposes of corporation tax nor any annuity or other annual payment ... shall be treated as a charge on income.'

The effect of this can be the postponement of such a deductible expense to a future year: see *Wilcock* v *Frigate Investments Ltd* [1982] STC 198.

Also expressly excluded from the definition of charges on income are 'dividends or other distributions' of the company. Section 338(3), following the changes introduced by the Finance Act 1996, as mentioned above, defines 'charges on income' as any annuity or annual payment payable otherwise than in respect of any of the company's loan relationships and any such other payments as mentioned in s348(2), but not including sums which are chargeable under Schedule A. Interest payable by a company (so long as the company is chargeable to corporation tax and not income tax) is therefore not a potential charge on income.

Prior to the 1996 changes, 'short interest', payable in the United Kingdom on an advance from a bank carrying on a bona fide banking business in the United Kingdom (whether charged to revenue or capital) was allowable as a charge on the company's income – s338(3)(b). Short interest paid to a person other than a bank was deductible as a trading expense. Similarly, all 'yearly' interest, whether payable to a bank or not, was a charge on income for this purpose – s338(3)(a).

The remaining provisions of s338 are concerned to limit and restrict the circumstances in which payments are to be treated as charges on income:

1. Any potential charge must have been made out of the company's profits brought into charge to corporation tax: s338(1). It is probable, however, that the rule in *IRC* v *Plummer* [1980] AC 896 is equally applicable to companies, so that if the company has income which is chargeable to corporation tax, it does not matter that it paid the expense out of a capital account.
2. The payment (not being interest) must not be charged to capital: see *Chancery Lane Safe Deposit Co Ltd* v *IRC* (1965) 43 TC 83 (House of Lords), a case

decided when the rule forbade the charging of interest to capital as well. The mischief aimed at is the possibility that, by charging an annual payment to capital, a company could leave itself with a greater sum available for distribution by way of dividend, since its income would not thereby be reduced. If it were to do so it could not really be said that the payment was a charge on *income*: s338(5)(a).

3. The payment must be ultimately borne by the company: s338(5)(a).
4. The payment must be made under a liability incurred for valuable and sufficient consideration: s338(5)(b). The leading case on this point is *Ball* v *National and Grindlay's Bank* (1971) 47 TC 287 (Court of Appeal), in which a company with many overseas employees entered into a deed of covenant with trustees of an educational trust it had established, to pay sums to the trustees to be used to educate the children of such employees. Such a trust was not, of course, charitable, being restricted in its possible beneficiaries. When the company sought to deduct the payments as charges on income, it was found that they fell outside s248 (now s338(5)(b)) because, although they were made to promote good employee relations, the trustees had not in return provided valuable and sufficient consideration.

One might ask why it was that the company did not simply look to deduct the sums paid to the trustees in computing its trading profits, since it was clear that the payments were made wholly and exclusively for the purposes of its trade (being made as one form of indirect remuneration to its employees). The answer lies in s337 ICTA 1988, which provided, before the Finance Act 1996 made yearly interest deductible, in subs(2) that a company may not deduct in computing income from any source:

> '(a) dividends or other distributions;
> (b) any yearly interest of money *or other annual payment* ...'; and
> (3) In computing income from a trade subsection (2)(b) above shall not prevent the deduction of yearly interest payable in the United Kingdom on an advance from a bank carrying on a bona fide banking business in the United Kingdom.'

Thus the yearly payments could not be deducted in computing the profits of the trade and could not be deducted in calculating the company's taxable profits as charges on income.

The only escape from this dilemma in such cases is to ensure that the board of directors resolves every year to make *voluntary* payments to the trustees of a sufficient amount to cover the trust's liabilities for that year. Such amounts will be deductible from trading profits, since they will not be 'annual payments', not being made under a binding legal obligation: see *British Insulated and Helsby Cables Ltd* v *Atherton* [1926] AC 205, *Heather* v *PE Consulting Ltd* [1973] Ch 189, *Jeffs* v *Ringtons Ltd* [1986] STC 144, and *Bott (E)* v *Price* [1987] STC 100.

An exception to the rule that charges on income must be made for valuable and sufficient consideration exists in the case of a 'covenanted donation to charity', which s339(8) defines as:

'a payment under a disposition or covenant made by the company in favour of a body of persons or trusts established for charitable purposes only, whereby the like annual payments (of which the donation is one) become payable for a period which may exceed three years and is not capable of earlier termination under any power exercisable without the consent of the persons for the time being entitled to the payment.'

In such a case the annual payment may be deducted, provided that the other conditions are satisfied.
5. The payment must actually be made in the accounting period: s338(1).
6. Section 338(4) imposes additional rules where the payment is made to a non-resident. In outline, these rules are:
   - the payment must be made under deduction of tax under ss349–350 and the company must account for the tax deducted (since it is not liable to income tax it cannot retain the sums deducted); or
   - the payment is made out of the company's Case IV or Case V income.
7. Under s401(1A), charges on income incurred before the trade, profession or vocation are commenced, are treated as incurred on the first day of trading. This basis applies to those set up after 5 April 1995, prior to which such expenditure was treated as a loss of the year of commencement on which the usual trading loss reliefs could be claimed (see section 16.5).

16.5 Interest payments by companies (loan relationships)

The FA 1996 introduced a significant new regime for the tax treatment of interest payments by companies after 31 March, 1996. The new regime is referred to in the legislation as 'loan relationships' and provides a framework for the tax treatment of all payments of interest and profits or losses arising in respect of debt obligations of companies both as regards the creditor and the debtor. The essence of the new regime is to tax as income all profit whether arising by receipt of interest or increase in value of the loan and to allow as a deduction for corporation tax purposes all interest payments, expenses or losses associated with each loan relationship, whether such interest, expenses or losses arise on capital or revenue account. The deduction under the new system will be taken as a deduction in calculating the profits of the company and not, as was previously the case under s338, as a charge on income (see section 16.4).

Background

For some time the tax authorities were having to react to differing types of financial instruments being marketed by companies raising funds in the financial markets. Securities and bonds would be issued by companies to investors, on terms and including concepts not envisaged when the relevant tax legislation, for the tax treatment of interest etc, was enacted. For example, securities issued at a discount to their nominal value would carry lower than market rates of interest, the remainder being made up on redemption of the security at face value, the investor having paid less than face value for it when issued.

Due to the many variations of this theme, legislation was brought in at various times according to which type of developments in the financial markets were current at the time. The main problems to be addressed on each occasion were how to tax the investor's split receipts and how and when to grant a deduction for the payment of these amounts by the company issuing the securities to raise finance. The distinctions between interest, capital, discount and premiums meant that the tax authorities were continually having to analyse the complexities of each type of instrument to see whether it fell within the taxing or deduction regimes. In the example given above, was the discount from face value of the security deductible by the company as a quasi-interest return to the investor? If so, was it deductible in the year of issue, the year of redemption or was it to be spread over the lifetime of the security? For this reason, specific tax regimes for 'deep discount securities' and 'deep gain securities' grew up alongside the 'accrued income scheme'.

Following a review of the tax treatment of interest focusing on debt instruments issued by corporate or government borrowers, the new 'loan relationships' legislation was enacted in the FA 1996. It has also been referred to, at various stages of the review, as 'gilts and bonds' or 'corporate and government debt' legislation.

Finance Act 1996 loan relationship provisions

The most important features of the loan relationships legislation, which is contained in ss80 to 105 and Schedules 8 to 15 FA 1996, are as follows:

1. 'Loan relationships' includes all corporate or government money debt, but excludes shares and bonds convertible into shares. A relationship arises where a company 'stands ... in the position of a creditor or a debtor as respects any money debt' and 'that debt is one from a transaction for the lending of money': s81 FA 1996.
2. It affects *discounts and premiums* after 31 March 1996 but applies to *interest* for accounting periods ended after 31 March 1996 and therefore encompassed interest payments falling before that date.
3. It applies only to companies, not to individuals or trusts. It applies to all those within the charge to United Kingdom corporation tax and therefore includes all United Kingdom resident companies and branches.
4. It treats all interest receipts, profits and gains of companies arising from loan relationships as income. Where these arise to trading companies and the loan relationship was effected for trading purposes the tax treatment is that of a Schedule D Case I receipt for all interest receipts, profits or gains and a Case I expense for all interest payments or losses. For non-trading companies or for non-trading purpose loan relationships within trading companies, Schedule D Case III treatment applies to all receipts, gains or losses.

5. The amount to be taxed or relieved will normally follow the amount shown in the company accounts. This will normally mean accruing the receipt or payment in accordance with normal accountancy 'accruals basis' guidelines. In addition to actual receipts or losses, financial traders will normally account for all increases and decreases in the value of loans during each accounting period and treat such differences as income or expenses.
6. Connected party loan relationships must be accounted for on the strict accruals basis, irrespective of the company's normal accounting method.
7. Gains or losses on foreign exchange (FOREX) will continue to be treated under the capital gains tax regime of FA 1993.

16.6 Losses

The corporation tax treatment of losses, contained in ss393–396 ICTA 1988, is similar to that afforded to individuals.

The general rule

Section 393 provides the rules which apply to companies continuing to trade:

1. Where a company carrying on a trade incurs a loss in that trade, it may claim to set off that loss against *profits of whatever description* of that accounting period. Section 73 FA 1991 allows a company to roll back trading losses for three years and set them off against profits of any description: s393(2). Special rules apply to apportion the loss where the company's accounting periods fluctuate in length. This ensures that a twelve-month loss cannot be used to cancel out profits of a six-month accounting period.

    Note: s393A(1) allows the loss to be set off against income not only from other sources but also from chargeable gains.

    Section 393A(3) provides certain restrictions on the claiming of s393A(1) loss relief. It does not apply to trades falling within Schedule D Case V, and, more importantly, it must be shown that either the trade was carried on under statutory powers (eg British Steel, British Shipbuilders, British Rail), or for the accounting period in question the trade was carried on on a commercial basis, with a view to the realisation of gain in the trade or in any larger undertaking of which the trade forms part. This latter condition can render deductible losses in a trade which, while unlikely to produce profits itself, may assist the overall creation of profits by the organisation, eg in a research and development activity.

2. A company may also make a claim, in any accounting period in which it carries on a trade in which it incurs a loss, to set off that loss against trading income from the same trade in subsequent accounting periods. *Scorer v Olin Energy* [1985] STC 218 is a good illustration that s177(1) only allows a carry-forward

against profits from the *same* trade, and that losses can only be set off against profits of another trade carried on by the same company to the limited extent allowed by s393(2) effectively, against the profits of that or the previous accounting period. In this case the inspector unwittingly permitted the company to set off losses incurred in a defunct trade against profits from one which was still continuing. Nevertheless, owing to a technicality of the appeal/assessment procedure the Revenue could not retreat from the agreement at a later stage. This latter point was the subject of further appeals which reached the House of Lords. See also *Rolls Royce Motors Ltd v Bamford* discussed at Chapter 6, section 6.11.

If, however, the trading income of a subsequent accounting period is insufficient to exhaust the loss, the company can set off the loss against interest or dividends on investments which would fall to be taken into account as trading receipts but for the fact that they have otherwise been taxed: s393(8).

Note: s393(1) applies to Case V losses, as well as to Case I losses, for the purpose of carrying forward losses, but s393A(1) does not permit either carry-back or set-off against other income of the same period.

If there is an excess of charges on income over the profits against which they are deductible, then, to the extent that they are made wholly and exclusively for the purposes of the trade, they may be treated as s393(1) losses.

Relief for trading losses against general profits of current and preceding accounting periods: s393A

A company may set trading losses against profits, of whatever description, of the same accounting period. This includes capital gains. Where trading losses cannot be relieved against profits in the same accounting period, the company may make a claim to carry the loss back against profits of preceding accounting periods. If the loss in question was incurred in an acounting period ending on or before 31 March 1991, that loss may only be carried back to relieve profits of the preceding accounting period. If the loss was incurred in an accounting period ending after this date the loss may be carried back and set against profits of the preceding three years. The company must carry on the same trade, and losses must be set against profits of a later accounting period first.

Capital losses

While trading losses can be relieved against the income and chargeable gains of companies, there are no provisions for relieving capital losses against anything other than current or future chargeable gains.

Case VI losses

As in the taxation of an individual, Case VI losses can only be set off, or carried forward and set off, against other Case VI profits: s396.

Section 397: farming and market gardening losses

This section, which applies to both companies and individuals (see Chapter 6, section 6.11), in the case of a company prevents losses incurred in a trade of market gardening or farming from deduction under s393(2) if losses were also incurred in each of the accounting periods falling within the previous five years.

Section 397 does not disallow the deduction of a loss:

1. if the claimant can show that the whole of his farming or market gardening activities of the year are of such a nature, and carried on in such a way, as would have justified a reasonable expectation of gain in the future *and* that a competent farmer or market gardener who had carried on the trade from the time when the claimant began could not reasonably have expected the activities to become profitable until some time after the year of claim; or
2. if the trade has not yet been carried on for five years; or
3. if the farming or marketing gardening forms part of, and is ancillary to, a larger trade undertaking.

Equally, it is enough if in any period of five years *one* year is profitable; one then needs merely to ensure that at some stage in the following five years there will be another profitable year, and so on. Usually, unless the business is hopelessly bad, this can be achieved by loading all expenses into one year and avoiding heavy expenditure until the next but one year; the one exception is likely to be where the farm itself has been purchased by means of a 100 per cent loan, and interest rates are rising. In such a case, the interest rates themselves are likely to overwhelm any potential profits.

Company reconstructions without change of ownership

Sections 343 and 344 ICTA 1988 provide that when one company ceases to carry on a trade and another company begins to carry it on, and:

1. on or at any time within two years not less than a three-fourths share in it belongs to the same people as owned interests in it before the takeover of the trade, and
2. the trade is not, within the period taken for comparison, carried on otherwise than by a company within the charge to tax in respect of it,

then the successor company can make use of the losses and allowances of its predecessor as if it were the same company. Correspondingly, however, the predecessor cannot make use of s394 terminal loss relief unless the successor ceases to trade within four years of the succession: s343(6), but see below. The rules then are:

1. if the successor ceases to trade within four years, the predecessor can make use of any loss the successor cannot claim, as if the predecessor had itself incurred it.
2. if the successor ceases to trade within one year, the predecessor can claim ordinary terminal loss relief under s394.

It should be noted that in a case such as this the successor will be restricted in its claims for loss relief to setting brought-forward losses against profits which it makes from carrying on the trade previously carried on by its predecessor – and provisions exist to ensure that profits obtained by expanding or aggregating the trade with another trade of the same sort are apportioned, and loss relief restricted accordingly. Some doubt was raised as to whether the above is still the position, following the repeal of s343(6) FA 1991 and the introduction of the three-year carry-back for losses under the new s393A ICTA 1988.

Group relief and consortium relief

Two companies are members of a group if one is the 75 per cent subsidiary of the other or both are 75 per cent subsidiaries of a third company. The varied meanings of 'a group' for different purposes of the Income Tax Acts is set out in s838 ICTA 1988 and s170 TCGA 1992. The meaning of 'control' for these and certain other corporate provisions is contained in s840 and is discussed in Chapter 18, section 18.6.

If a company which has incurred *trading* losses is a member of a group, within the meaning of s402 ICTA 1988, it may surrender those losses to another member of the group, which may then claim to set off the losses against its total profits for its corresponding accounting period. The claimant company may pay the surrendering company for the losses it surrenders. Any such payment is wholly ignored for tax purposes in the accounts of both companies: s402(6).

Group relief applies not only in respect of trading losses but also to capital allowances and to excesses of management expenses of an investment company falling within s75 ICTA 1988. It is also available in respect of companies which are members of, or owned by, a 'consortium'. A company is owned by a consortium of companies when all the ordinary share capital of the company is directly and beneficially owned by five or fewer companies; those shareholder companies, each of which owns at least five per cent of the share capital of the target company, are themselves the members of the consortium. Where a consortium exists, group relief is available in the case of a surrendering company and a claimant company where either of them is a member of the consortium and the other is:

1. a trading company owned by the consortium which is not a 75 per cent subsidiary of any company (in such a case only pure group relief is available between the 75 per cent owner and its 75 per cent subsidiary); or

2. a trading company which

   - is a 90 per cent subsidiary of a holding company owned by the consortium; and
   - is not a 75 per cent subsidiary of any company other than the holding company; or

3. a holding company owned by the consortium which is not a 75 per cent subsidiary of any company.

In *Imperial Chemicals Industries plc* v *Colmer (Inspector of Taxes)* [1996] STC 352 a consortium involving ICI and the Wellcome Foundation owned all the share capital in CAHH, a holding which was also a UK incorporated company. CAHH owned 100 per cent of the shares in all but one of its 23 subsidiary trading companies, four of which were UK resident, six were resident in other EU Member States and 13 were resident outside the EU. The House of Lords held that the proper and intended interpretation of the words of what is now s413(5) ('references in this Chapter to a company apply only to bodies corporate resident in the United Kingdom') was that it included not only the claimant and surrendering companies but the holding company and the companies whose shares comprised 'wholly or mainly' the shares held by the holding company. Despite reaching the conclusion that the statute as written, both historically and currently, imposed a general requirement of UK residence, the House of Lords have referred the matter to the European Court of Justice before the appeal can finally be determined. See Chapter 27, section 27.5, for further details.

Corresponding accounting periods

In essence, group relief is available only for *current* losses and management expenses etc. Section 408 ICTA 1988 ensures, therefore, that where accounting periods of surrendering and claimant companies do not coincide, but only overlap, the group relief available is likewise restricted. So if 'A' is the period common to the two accounting periods, 'B' is the length of the accounting period of the surrendering company, and 'C' is the length of the accounting period of the claimant company, then:

1. the amount of the loss, etc, which may be set off against the total profits of the claimant company for the corresponding accounting period is restricted to A/B of the loss;
2. this restricted amount may only be set against A/C of the profits of the claimant company for the corresponding period.

In fact, if the claimant company has profits in both of its accounting periods which 'correspond' to that of the surrendering company in which the loss is sustained, there may well be no restriction on relief, but merely on the period for which the loss is available, though this is by no means always so.

Example
X Ltd is the wholly-owned subsidiary of Y Ltd. In X Ltd's accounting period ending on 31 December 1997, it sustains a loss of £120,000. Y Ltd draws up its accounts on 31 March each year and has profits in the periods to 31 March 1997 and 31 March 1998 of £480,000 and £30,000 respectively. X Ltd and Y Ltd agree that the latter company will make a payment to X Ltd of £20,000 for the surrender to it of the whole of its loss. Y Ltd is restricted in the use of the loss as follows:

1. Off-set of loss against profits to 31 March 1997. Since there is only a three-month coincident period, and both accounting periods last 12 months, the figure for A is three and for B and C is 12. So:

    – Of the loss of £120,000, $3/12$, or £30,000, may be set against Y Ltd's available profits
    – Similarly, of Y Ltd's profits of £480,000, only $3/12$, or £120,000, are available to be reduced by group relief.

    Thus the £30,000 reduces the profits of £120,000, and Y Ltd's taxable profits for the period are £450,000. The payment for group relief is ignored, being less than the amount surrendered.

2. Off-set of losses against profits to 31 March 1998. On this occasion, the coincident period is nine months, and each accounting period is 12 months long. A is therefore nine, and B and C are each 12.
3. Of the loss of £120,000, $9/12$, or £90,000, may be set against Y Ltd's available profits.
4. And of Y Ltd's profits of £30,000, $9/12$, or £22,500, may be reduced by group relief.

Thus £67,500 of the loss may not be surrendered, and Y Ltd is liable to corporation tax on £7,500 of its profits for this accounting period.

16.7 Reform – the pay and file system and self-assessment

Pay and file

Commencement
Sections 82–90 and 95 FA (No 2) 1987, together with Schedule 6, inserted new provisions dealing with the reform of corporation tax assessment and collection into the Taxes Management Act 1970. After considerable discussion and consultation the Inland Revenue confirmed in a press release in February 1991 that the new system known as 'pay and file' would be introduced for all accounting periods ending on or after 1 October 1993. In effect, therefore, it applies to annual accounting periods beginning on or after 2 October 1992. The purpose of the new system was to put virtually all of the mechanics of the returning of profits, the calculation of

corporation tax payable and the payment of tax firmly in the hands of the company. The company is responsible for submitting its accounts, calculating the tax due and then 'paying' the due amount.

Payment of corporation tax

Payment is due nine months after the end of the accounting date, and penalties plus interest provisions are brought into effect for failure to comply with either the paying or the filing provisions. The 'file' aspect relates to the completion of the official corporation tax return form – see below. From an administrative point of view the new system should do away with the need for estimated assessments followed by appeals, which in turn involve the Commissioners until they are resolved. Corporation tax therefore falls due nine months after the accounting date and without the issue of any notice of assessment.

Filing corporation tax return forms

A corporation tax return form will be issued by the Inland Revenue and is required to be filed within 12 months of the end of the accounting period, unless it is issued more than nine months after the end of the accounting date.

Self-assessment

The 'pay and file' system was the forerunner to self-assessment, introduced for individuals, partnerships and trustees from 6 April 1996, which is discussed in more detail in Chapter 24, section 24.3. The pay and file provisions are to be extended so that on filing corporation tax returns an additional element is introduced: the return includes a calculation of the tax due and effectively makes the appropriate assessment, which at that point becomes a legally enforceable charge to tax. The inspector will no longer have to make a formal assessment based on the calculation of tax, as is the case under the pay and file arrangements. The statutory provisions for the introduction of self-assessment for companies were contained in ss181–183 FA 1994, subject to commencement on an 'appointed day'. According to an Inland Revenue press release issued on 25 September 1996, self-assessment for companies will be introduced for accounting periods ending on or after an 'appointed day', which will not be before early 1999. The earliest accounting period for which a company could be within self-assessment therefore is one commencing in 1998.

17

Dividends and Distributions of Companies

17.1 Introduction

17.2 'Distribution'

17.3 'Qualifying distribution'

17.4 Set-off of ACT against mainstream corporation tax: s239 ICTA 1988

17.5 Treatment of surplus ACT

17.6 Franked payments made to individuals

17.7 Franked payments made to other companies

17.8 The uses of surplus franked investment income

17.9 Special rules for groups and consortia

17.10 The purchase by a company of its own shares and 'special dividends'

17.1 Introduction

The system of taxing companies and their shareholders on dividends made and received underwent a fundamental change from 6 April 1993. This chapter incorporates both old and new systems for the sake of current completeness.

The primary purpose of the changes was to try to halt the build-up of surplus unrelieved advance corporation tax (ACT) payments, particularly within multinational groups, which at the time of the publication of a consultative paper with the 1993 Budget was said to stand at around £5 billion. The changes for shareholders were a more indirect result of trying to achieve this end.

In the same way that the Revenue is eager to have tax collected at source on its behalf under Schedule D Case III and Schedule E, the system of corporate distributions is geared towards the collection of Schedule F income tax by the company which makes a distribution to its shareholders. As usual it is up to the recipient to adjust matters if he (or it) is not liable to such tax. The system is not framed in terms of deduction of tax on payment, in the same way as interest payments. Instead there is a liability to account for tax on a fraction of the net amount of the dividend or distribution. In outline it is as follows:

1. When a company makes what the legislation calls a 'qualifying distribution' it is required to make to the Revenue an advance payment of corporation tax, known as 'advance corporation tax' (s14 Income and Corporation Taxes Act 1988).
2. The ACT is equal to one quarter of the amount of the distribution. Thus, if a company makes a qualifying distribution of £80,000 to its shareholders, it must pay £20,000 ACT to the Revenue.
3. The individual shareholder who receives a qualifying distribution is liable to Schedule F income tax on the grossed-up sum; thus, if he receives £800, he is liable to Schedule F tax on £1,000. That distribution carries a 'tax credit' equal to the ACT thereon – £200 – and that will satisfy his liability (if any) to lower rate tax under s1A. The £1,000 will be part of his total income under s20(1) para 2 and is investment income rendering him liable to excess liability, if he has sufficient income.

It can be seen that in reality the system is one of accounting for tax at source.

Lower rate of tax on dividends paid to individuals

The tax rate for individuals applicable to company dividends received is set specially at the lower rate of tax under s1A. As from 1996/97, the lower rate of tax was extended to all income from savings. Only if taxpayers are liable to tax at the higher rate is any further tax due from them. As will be seen from the preceding figures, the tax credit of £200 which the shareholder receives is sufficient to meet tax at the lower rate of 20 per cent on the figure of £1,000.

Tax exempt and non-resident shareholders

The credit system will also impact on tax-exempt recipients such as charities and pension funds as well as on non-resident shareholders, particularly on a change of rate of ACT. In the example at (3) above, for 1992/93 when the rate of ACT was one-third the £800 dividend would have carried a tax credit of one-third, ie £266 which would be repayable to the non-liable recipient, while under the new rules the credit is only £200, so that the non-liable recipient's income is effectively reduced by £66 in this instance.

In the same way, non-resident shareholders, who have tax credit benefits only by virtue of the terms of a double tax treaty, would suffer similar reductions in the amounts passed on to them for credit against their tax liabilities in their countries of residence.

17.2 'Distribution'

'Distributions' are defined by ss209–211 ICTA 1988, as subsequently amended. The word includes:

1. Dividends.
2. Capital dividends, such as dividends paid out of the surplus arising on the sale of a capital asset.
3. Any distribution out of assets of the company (whether in cash or otherwise) in respect of shares of the company, unless, or to the extent, that the distribution represents a reduction of capital. So if a preserves manufacturer gave a pound of jam to each shareholder for every share held, that would be a distribution, to be computed by reference to the market value of the assets transferred.

    Exceptionally, distributions made by a company in respect of share capital in a liquidation are not 'distributions' for the purposes of the Corporation Tax Acts and will be taxed only as capital gains accruing to the shareholder on the deemed partial disposal of his shares.
4. Redeemable share capital or any security issued in respect of shares in the company to the extent that it is not properly referable to new consideration. It would otherwise be easy for the company to distribute profits by the redemption for cash of redeemable shares.
5. Any interest payments or other distributions out of the assets of the company in respect of securities of the company which are like shares in the company – for example, a loan made to a company where the consideration for the use of the money lent fluctuates by reference to the company's results; the more the company owes, the more return the lender gets.

    It should be noted that a limitation on this particular case was introduced by s60 of the Finance Act 1982; quite simply, it benefited a bank to convert interest into a qualifying distribution by making a small proportion of it dependent on the company's results, since (at the rates then current) it paid 30 per cent tax at source (which, it will be shown, could on a subsequent distribution, be treated as basic rate tax paid by its shareholders) rather than 52 per cent corporation tax on pure interest. The new provision is intended to prevent this. While the paying company was, on the face of it, worse off, since it obtained no deduction for the distribution paid, it was normally in the position of having excessive allowances, and it benefited to some extent by a reduction in the rate of interest charged by the bank.
6. Transactions connected with the repayment of capital. It has already been stated that a reduction of capital is a payment of capital and not a distribution of income. Where, however, a repayment of share capital is preceded by, or followed by, a bonus issue of shares, the latter event can be treated as a distribution.

    Section 210 provides that where a company repays any share capital, and at or after that repayment issues shares as paid up otherwise than by the receipt of new consideration (ie issues bonus shares), the amount so paid up is to be treated as a distribution, except insofar as it exceeds the amount of share capital repaid. Thus if a company with a share capital of £100,000 repays 25p in the pound, so repaying £25,000 of share capital, and afterwards makes a bonus issue of ordinary shares of one for every two shares held – thus creating £50,000 of new capital – £25,000 of that bonus issue will be treated as a distribution.

There are two exceptions to this rule:

- Where the repaid share capital consisted of fully paid preference shares, such shares partake more of the nature of loans to the company than shares in it.
- Where:
  - the bonus shares are not redeemable bonus shares; and
  - the company is not a close company (see Chapter 18, section 18.1); and
  - the issue of the bonus shares occurs more than ten years after the repayment of capital.

In either case, the subsequent issue of bonus shares will not be treated as a distribution.

Section 211 provides for the reverse case. Where a company issues bonus shares, and the issue does not fall to be treated as a qualifying distribution, and subsequently it makes repayments of share capital, those payments are not to be treated as repayments of share capital (and thus are to be treated as distributions) until the repayments of share capital exceed the paid-up amount of the bonus shares.

There is only one exception in this case. Section 235 does not apply to any repayment of capital made more than ten years after the issue of the bonus shares if:

- it is not made in respect of redeemable share capital; and
- the company is not a close company (see, again, Chapter 18, section 18.1).

Chapter 18 will show that 'distribution' has a wider meaning where close companies are concerned.

17.3 'Qualifying distribution'

This phrase is defined by s14(2) ICTA 1988. Any distribution other than:

1. something which is a distribution by reason only of being bonus redeemable shares or securities, or

2. a distribution of such shares or securities as have been received directly or indirectly by one company (which is now distributing them) from another,

is a qualifying distribution.

Where a company resident in the United Kingdom makes a qualifying distribution, the section provides that it shall be liable to make a payment of ACT at a rate of one quarter of the amount of the distribution. Thus for every £800 distributed to the shareholders the company must pay £200 to the Revenue.

The sum of a qualifying distribution plus the ACT thereon is described as a 'franked payment'. So, if a company makes a qualifying distribution of £800, it makes a franked payment of £1,000 (£800 + £200 ACT).

Unlike mainstream corporation tax (MCT), which is collected not earlier than nine months after the accounting period to which it relates, ACT must be paid over within 14 days of the end of the quarter in which the qualifying distribution was made: Schedule 13 ICTA 1988. Quarters end on 31 March, 30 June, 30 September and 31 December.

17.4 Set-off of ACT against mainstream corporation tax: s239 ICTA 1988

Since ACT is an advance payment of corporation tax, the amount of MCT a company has to pay will be reduced when it has made qualifying distributions in the relevant accounting period.

Provision is made, however, to ensure that the amount of MCT is not excessively reduced by outsized distributions. A company may set off so much ACT as would be payable were it to use its income and chargeable gains taxable for the accounting period in question to make a qualifying distribution and to pay the ACT thereon. In other words, a company can set off a maximum of ACT equal to 20 per cent of the aggregate of its income profits and chargeable gains for the period.

If a company cannot utilise all the ACT it has paid in the accounting period, it has 'surplus ACT', the uses of which are described in section 17.5.

Example

X Co, which makes up its accounts to 31 March each year, has income of £1,600,000 and chargeable gains of £400,000. It pays dividends of £2,800,000 in that period. Its tax liability is as follows, where the rate of MCT is 33 per cent:

ACT liability: ¼ x £2,800,000 = £700,000
MCT: 33% x £2,000,000 = £660,000

Clearly, if there were no restrictions on the set off of ACT, its MCT liability would be wholly erased. The company can, however, only set-off ACT of:

20% x £2,000,000 = £400,000

Its MCT liability is, therefore:

$$£660,000 - £400,000 = £260,000$$

It also has, however, surplus ACT of £300,000 (£700,000 − £400,000).

17.5 Treatment of surplus ACT

Section 239(3) ICTA 1988 provides that where a surplus of ACT arises, a company may elect to roll it back and treat it as ACT arising in accounting periods beginning in the six years prior to that in which it actually arose. The rule is, however, that one treats it as arising in the most recent accounting period first and gradually works one's way backwards. Any surplus which remains can then be carried forward and treated as surplus ACT of future accounting periods in exactly the same way (s239(4)).

By s245 a company is not entitled to roll forward its surplus ACT in either of the two following cases:

1. where, within three years, there has been a change in the ownership of the company and a major change in the company's trade;
2. where, within three years, there has been a change in ownership after the trade has become small or negligible and before it revives.

This rule has as its purpose the prevention of the sale or disposal of companies for the purpose of the transfer of surplus ACT.

By s245B this restriction on the use of surplus ACT applies equally where the surplus ACT is surrendered to a subsidiary both companies subsequently passing into the same ownership. This means that where the surrendering company would have been unable to carry forward surplus ACT, by reason of s245, the subsidiary equally will be unable to carry forward surplus ACT surrendered to it.

Surrender of ACT to subsidiary

Section 240 provides one other method of dealing with surplus ACT: it can be surrendered to a 51 per cent subsidiary. The surrender can be made for a consideration not in excess of the amount surrendered and, to that extent, will be ignored for corporation tax purposes in the accounts of both the subsidiary and the surrendering company. The surrender is not to be made against a subsidiary's liability to corporation tax for any accounting period or any part of an accounting period in which it was not a subsidiary of the surrendering company.

The ACT received by the subsidiary is treated as ACT paid by it, and the subsidiary may set it off under s239 as if it were ACT paid by the subsidiary. The surrendered ACT must be used in preference to any ACT paid by the subsidiary itself.

Only ACT paid by the parent company in respect of dividends (in other words not that paid on any other distributions) may be surrendered in this way. The ACT may not, however, be carried back by the subsidiary and may only be used in the corresponding or future accounting periods (s239(3)) from which it is surrendered.
Note: a subsidiary may not surrender ACT to its parent company – only the reverse is allowed.

Provisions for reducing surplus ACT in companies and groups

Following the introduction in 1993 of the new system of taxing company distributions in respect of both companies and shareholders, the further problem of surplus ACT arising in companies (see section 17.1) was tackled by legislation in FA 1994 which now can be found in ss246A ICTA 1988. The old provisions limited the set-off of ACT not only to the relevant fraction of profits, as illustrated in section 17.4, but also to the ACT attributable to dividends out of profits taxed in the United Kingdom. A company or group with overseas earnings (taxed in that overseas country) might well pay dividends reflecting its combined profits, and while the ACT portion of the United Kingdom source dividend is relieved against MCT, that attributable to the overseas source dividend is left in charge and builds into further surplus year by year.

The new provisions apply to dividends paid on or after 1 July 1994 and introduce two new concepts: 'foreign income dividends' (FIDs), recognising the payment of dividends out of profits earned abroad, and 'international holding companies' (IHCs), which recognise the past problem of creating offshore holding companies through which to pass dividends merely to iron out the differences in rates of recovery of foreign tax in the United Kingdom.

Foreign income dividend measures

Under the FID scheme a company has to elect to treat the dividend as a foreign income dividend (s246A), and there are the initial practical difficulties associated with demonstrating that a dividend has been paid out of foreign taxed profits (ss246J–M) in order to reclaim the ACT attached to it. The initial payment of ACT is not dispensed with and there is no tax credit available to the recipient (s246C). An individual who receives such a dividend is, however, treated as receiving a tax credit equivalent to the lower rate of tax (s246D), so that his liability other than to higher rate tax is satisfied (see section 17.1). Foreign income dividends in the hands of companies are not franked investment income for corporation tax purposes (s246E).

International holding companies

The ACT-free scheme for those companies which satisfy the eligibility test of international holding companies (IHCs) does not carry the dividend identification and ACT payment/reclaim difficulty. No ACT is payable on distributions by companies which satisfy the requirements. If the company (IHC) is wholly owned by a foreign company, or by a foreign company whose shares are listed on the United Kingdom Stock Exchange, or is 80 per cent owned with a 5 per cent minimum interest held by each non-resident non-company shareholder or by foreign-held companies, the main parts of the test are satisfied. IHCs will be able to receive and redistribute profits from foreign subsidiaries without any United Kingdom domestic tax. The relevant provisions are contained in ss246S–Y ICTA 1988.

The European Union parent/subsidiary dividend directive

Much of what has been said above does not apply to dividend payments to related companies based in other European Union Member States. The parent/subsidiary dividend directive has been adopted by virtually all the Member States with a view to achieving the untaxed flow of dividends between groups of companies within the European Union borders. It is achieved either by omitting to withhold tax on payment of a dividend to a shareholder in another Member State or by allowing a full tax credit to the recipient shareholder. As the United Kingdom's system is not a deduction-of-tax one (see section 17.1), it will adopt the latter method. The country where the ultimate recipient is based will tax the dividend and of course will also continue to tax any dividend passing outside the confines of the European Union.

17.6 Franked payments made to individuals

Note: 1. the use of the word 'franked' in the following paragraphs may be literally translated as meaning stamped 'tax paid'; 2. the position of individuals in receipt of dividends after 6 April 1993 has been outlined in section 17.1.

Section 20 ICTA 1988 provides that an individual is liable to Schedule F income tax in respect of all dividends and other distributions made to him by a company resident in the United Kingdom; dividends from non-resident companies will fall within the scope of Schedule D, Case V. Section 20(1) adds that where a distribution carries a tax credit, Schedule F tax is chargeable on the aggregate of the distribution plus the credit, and s231 lays down that qualifying distributions paid to companies and individuals resident in the United Kingdom carry such a credit. That credit is, of course, equal to the amount of the qualifying distribution received by the shareholder.

Non-resident shareholders are not, under s231, entitled to a tax credit (except that for those resident in a country with which the United Kingdom has a double tax treaty, there will be a measure of credit as set out in the treaty). While, though, they will be liable to income tax in respect of any distribution received, s233(1) provides that any such persons are *not* liable to lower rate tax in respect of the distribution, and any higher rate tax is to be reduced by the amount of the basic rate tax inherent in that assessment.

For a restriction on the payment of tax credits see s231(3) and (3A)–(3D) ICTA 1988.

17.7 Franked payments made to other companies

Companies, as has already been explained, are not liable to tax, be it income tax or corporation tax, on distributions from other United Kingdom companies. Most distributions that a company receives, however, will be qualifying distributions in respect of which the companies paying them will have been obliged to account for ACT and which will, as a result, carry tax credits.

United Kingdom resident companies which are exempt from corporation tax (eg charitable corporations) may reclaim the tax credits on qualifying distributions they receive: s231(2) ICTA 1988, and other companies use such distributions to reduce the amount of ACT they have to pay in respect of their own qualifying distributions.

Section 238 ICTA 1988 provides that the aggregate of a qualifying distribution plus the tax credit it carries which is received by a company resident in the United Kingdom is to be known as 'franked investment income' (FII). Thus, if A Ltd makes a qualifying distribution of £80,000, it will have to pay ACT of £20,000. If B Ltd, another company resident in the United Kingdom, holds 10 per cent of the shares in A Ltd, it will be entitled to £8,000 of the distribution, and that sum will carry a tax credit of £2,000. It will accordingly, have FII of £10,000.

Section 241 ICTA 1988 provides that, in any accounting period, a company on making a qualifying distribution need only pay ACT on that distribution where its franked payments (see section 17.3) exceed its FII for the period. When there is such an excess, it need only pay the ACT inherent in that excess.

Example
Taking the example above, B Ltd then pays dividends of £24,000, on which ACT of £6,000 would be payable. It has, therefore, franked payments of £30,000 and franked investment income of £10,000. It must, accordingly, pay ACT but only that inherent in the excess of £20,000, that is to say £4,000 (ie £6,000 – £2,000 = £4,000).

The effect of setting off FII against franked payments is twofold: first, as has already been indicated, it reduces the amount of ACT a company has to pay; secondly, it indirectly increases the amount of MCT the company has to bear, since there will be less ACT available to set off against it. This will not, of course, always be immediately so – FII may go merely to reducing the recipient company's surplus ACT – but it will eventually have that effect. Still, tax postponed is tax saved, so the availability of FII is beneficial.

17.8 The uses of surplus franked investment income

It may happen that a company's FII exceeds its franked payments for an accounting period. When this is so, no ACT will be payable. The surplus of FII, it is provided by s241(3) ICTA 1988, may be carried forward to the next following accounting period and treated as FII arising in that period; if there is still a surplus (or the surplus increases) that, in its turn, is carried on to the next, and so on, until it is finally used up. Unlike ACT, it is never rolled back.

There is, however, an alternative. Section 242 enables a company to release the tax credit in its surplus FII by setting it off against other unrelieved deductible items, namely:

1. trading losses;
2. charges on income;
3. management expenses falling within ss75 or 76 ICTA 1988;
4. certain capital allowances;
5. certain capital losses made on the disposal of unquoted shares in trading companies falling within s573(2) ICTA 1988.

In such a case, the surplus FII is treated as a fund of notional profits which have borne tax at 20 per cent. The company utilises the deductible items available and sets them off against the fund of profits, and it becomes apparent that, owing to the existence of, say, a trading loss, no tax ought to have been paid. The company can then make a claim for the 'repayment' of the tax credit in the FII. The consequences of this procedure are:

1. The amount of surplus FII which can be carried forward to later accounting periods is reduced.
2. The amount of ACT which will be payable in these future periods is increased.
3. The amount of MCT payable in these periods will be reduced by the greater ACT payable on the one hand, but will be increased by the non-availability of the exhausted deductible items on the other.

This will, on the whole, not be beneficial to the company, since those items (eg trading losses) could have been used to reduce the amount of income subject to MCT at 33 per cent, instead of merely releasing the tax credit in the FII. For this reason, balancing adjustments are made in later periods:

1. No adjustment is made in the amount of ACT the company has to pay – having had the benefit of the tax credit, it must later repay it.
2. The amount of ACT so paid which may be set off against MCT is, however, reduced by the amount of the tax credit paid out under s242 ICTA 1988 – this would have happened automatically if the FII had been carried forward: see s244(2).
3. As the company incurs a liability to pay ACT on the excess of franked payments over FII, so it is deemed to have incurred a trading loss, or whatever deductible

item is being utilised, equal to the excess of franked payments over FII: s242(5),(6). The effect of this is to reduce the amount of income liable to MCT, thus reducing the differential.

See Inland Revenue Booklet IR18, paras 118–120, for an example of the operation of the balancing adjustments.

17.9 Special rules for groups and consortia

Just as special rules exist for the surrender of certain deductible items by one member of a group or consortium to another (see 'Group relief and consortium relief' in Chapter 16, section 16.5), so too they do in relation to 'group income'. The rules pertaining to this matter are contained in ss247 and 248 and Schedules 17A and 18 ICTA 1988.

Sections 247 and 248 allow a company receiving dividends from another, both being resident in the United Kingdom, on the election of both to be treated as if such payment was not FII in the hands of the recipient company. The paying company will be treated as if the payments were not franked payments in the hands of the payee company. Dividends falling within the foreign income dividend scheme mentioned above are not eligible for payment free of ACT under a group income election (s247(5A)).

The sections, however, only apply in the following cases:

1. The company paying the dividend is either

    – a 51 per cent subsidiary of the other, or
    – a 51 per cent subsidiary of a company of which the other is also a 51 per cent subsidiary,

    provided that in either case the parent company would be beneficially entitled to more than 50 per cent of any profits available for distribution to equity holders of the subsidiary company, and provided also that the parent company would be beneficially entitled to more than 50 per cent of any assets of the subsidiary company available for distribution to its equity holders on a winding up.
2. The company is a trading or holding company owned by a consortium of which the recipient company is a member, unless it is a 75 per cent subsidiary of any other company, or arrangements of any kind (whether in writing or not) are in existence by virtue of which it could become such a subsidiary. For this purpose, a company is owned by a consortium if 75 per cent or more of the ordinary share capital of the company is beneficially owned between them by companies resident in the United Kingdom of which none

    – beneficially owns less than 5 per cent of that capital,

- would be beneficially entitled to less than 5 per cent of any profits available for distribution to equity holders of the company, or
- would be beneficially entitled to less than 5 per cent of any assets of the company available for distribution to its equity holders on a winding up.

(For the definition of 'beneficially entitled' see *J Sainsbury plc v O'Connor* [1991] STC 318.)

The effect of this is, of course, that the payer does not have to pay ACT on so much of its dividends as are distributed to the recipient company, but, correspondingly, the recipient company cannot reduce its liability to ACT on its own payment of dividends by reference to the group income. It will be noted that group income relief is restricted in application to dividends and does not apply to other forms of distributions.

The group income provisions apply to one other sort of income in addition to dividends: payments of charges on income – that is to say, to interest, annuities and other annual payments falling within ss348–350 ICTA 1988. Usually the company making the payment would have to deduct a sum equal to income tax from the payment. Section 247(4) allows the payment to be made gross when the companies fall into any of the relationships described above, and also in cases where the recipient company is the 51 per cent subsidiary of the payer.

Schedules 17A and 18 introduced certain rules for calculating the relevant percentages of share capital owned where options, etc, are exerciseable on a company's share capital.

17.10 The purchase by a company of its own shares and 'special dividends'

If a company is authorised by its articles of association to purchase its own shares, ss159–181 Companies Act 1985 allow companies to do so. Any payment to a shareholder in excess of a sum paid on the original allotment (nominal capital and premium) of the shares would normally be treated as a distribution, unless the repayment occurs on the winding up of the company – s209(2)(b) ICTA 1988. Section 219 provides an exception to this in a limited number of cases. When s219 applies and shares are bought back the monies received by a shareholder will not be treated as a distribution so that any profit made will be charged to capital gains tax. The purchasing company must not be listed on the official list of a Stock Exchange but shares may be dealt with on the Alternative Investment Market (AIM). It must be either a trading company or the holding company of a trading group.

The vendor of the shares may be an individual, a trustee, the personal representative of a deceased shareholder or a company. He should be resident and, if an individual, ordinarily resident in the UK. Normally, the shares must have been owned for at least 5 years – s220(5). The vendor should either dispose of all his shares in the company or at least 'substantially reduce' his shareholding, which the Revenue consider means that the shareholder should have reduced his fractional interest in the company's issued capital by at least 25 per cent and is not left with a dominant – at least 30 per cent – holding of the issued shares. In calculating these fractions, spouses and associates generally are treated as one person.

The sale of the shares must satisfy the permissible reasons test. First, the purchase by the company must benefit its trade (or that of a 75 per cent subsidiary) and not be part of a scheme designed to enable the shareholders to participate in the company's profits without receiving a dividend or otherwise to avoid tax – s219(1)(a). The second permitted reason for the sale of the shares is where the whole (or substantially the whole) of the proceeds of sale is to be used by the recipient in discharging his inheritance tax liability charged on a death. The money must be so used within two years of the death and it has to be shown that the tax cannot be paid without undue hardship unless the shares are sold back to the company. In this case, the requirements relating to the vendor of the shares do not apply. The inheritance tax need not be owing in respect of the shares.

Whenever a s219 buy-back of shares is proposed, advance clearance can be obtained for the scheme.

If the vendor of the shares is a UK company, and the payment is treated as a distribution, the sum received (less the original subscription price) will be treated as franked investment income in which case, although it will not attract any charge as such (and an ACT credit will be available), it appears that the vendor's gain would be caught in the capital gains legislation.

Special dividends – FA 1997 Schedule 7

As stated above, the payment of any amount in excess of the nominal amount paid on the allotment of shares will be treated as a distribution unless it falls within the own share purchase exception for unquoted trading companies. The main effects of 'distribution treatment' are the payment of ACT by the company and the reclaim of the tax credit generated by the ACT payment. However, a measure, announced on 8 October 1996 and now contained in Schedule 7 of Finance Act 1997, is intended to make unattractive schemes involving the purchase by a company of its own shares for a premium over the subscription price and/or the payment by a company of special dividends in connection with a takeover. With the exception of distributions received by trustees of discretionary trusts, the provisions of Schedule 7 affect all relevant distributions on or after 8 October 1996. Recipients of such payments would be treated as if they had received foreign income dividends in respect of which claims for refund of tax credits are not allowed. The circumstances in which the provisions of Schedule 7 apply are: (1) on the redemption, repayment or purchase of a company's own shares – para 1(2)(a); or (2) on the purchase of rights to acquire its own shares – para 1(2)(b); or (3) where certain features of the distribution are 'referable to' a 'transaction in securities' which means all of the transactions listed in s709(2) ICTA 1988 (subscriptions for, purchases, sales, exchanges, issues of securities and alteration of rights under securities) where a distribution is made following arrangements which can link any of the specified elements of the distribution to such a transaction – para 1(3)(a). The elements in question are: (a) the actual decision to make the distribution; (b) its timing; (c) its form; or (d) its amount – para 1(4).

Exemption from the treatment is granted for distributions made in connection with certain transactions which would otherwise be caught. These are principally pre-sale distributions (providing the distribution is made in the 14-day period prior to the change of ownership of the company) and fixed rate preference share dividends – paras 5 and 6 Schedule 7. The 14-day period of grace under para 5 is thought to be unnecessarily strict, but the Inland Revenue are apparently inclined to the view that it is realistic to assume that it has to be very close to the change of ownership to be regarded as a genuine pre-sale distribution.

As stated above, para 2 Schedule 7 provides for the treatment of Schedule 7 dividends or 'special dividends' to be that governed by the foreign income dividend (FID) regime of s246A et seq, denying the recipient repayment of tax credit while still imposing the initial ACT liability on the paying company. As mentioned in Section 17.5 above, such dividends are not franked investment income in the hands of the recipient company – s246E.

18

Close Companies

18.1 Introduction

18.2 'Close company'

18.3 'Participator'

18.4 'Associate'

18.5 'Loan creditor'

18.6 'Control'

18.7 Extended meaning of 'distribution'

18.8 Loans to participators

18.9 Apportionment of income and chargeable gains

18.10 Small companies' rates are not available to CICs

18.11 Profit distributions by CICs

18.12 Transfer of assets at an undervalue: s125 TCGA 1992

18.1 Introduction

A close company used to provide a vehicle for tax planning, built around the idea of using the close company to store income until it could be brought out subject to lower rates of tax or, preferably, as capital on a liquidation or reduction of capital. In an attempt to check the schemes which proliferated, special provisions were passed which resulted in the tax treatment accorded to close companies differing from the tax treatment accorded to other companies.

These provisions primarily aimed to prevent two main evils: members retaining profits in the company to avoid higher rates of tax, and members extracting profits in a form which would considerably reduce their tax liability. The provisions were therefore of two kinds:

1. penalising the failure to distribute available income to shareholders;
2. extending the definition of 'distribution' to cover various transactions.

Later, the tide has to some extent turned the other way. The legislature has come to realise that its restraints on the close company were such as to stifle genuine endeavour, catching many more than merely those seeking to avoid tax. Section 103 of the Finance Act 1989 abolished ss423–430 of the Income and Corporation Taxes Act 1988 (shortfall apportionment provisions), yet at the same time FA 1989 denied close investment companies (CICs) the favourable rate of corporation tax normally accorded to small companies. However, before the changes introduced by FA 1989 can be discussed it is necessary to define some of the terms to be found in the close company legislation.

All references are to ICTA 1988 unless otherwise stated.

18.2 'Close company'

Broadly speaking, s414 ICTA 1988 states that to be a close company a company must:

1. not be one in which 35 per cent or more of its share capital is held by the public;
2. be resident in the United Kingdom;
3. be under the control of five or fewer participators, or participators who are directors; or participators who together possess or are entitled to acquire:

   - rights entitling them, on a notional winding up, to the greater part of the assets available for distribution among participators, or
   - rights entitling them, on a notional winding up, to the greater part of the assets for distribution among participators, disregarding any rights which any of them or any other person has as a loan creditor.

The assets deemed to be available for distribution are assets which would actually be available for distribution to participators on an actual winding up. The amount a participator would be entitled to receive is calculated on the basis of his interest in the company direct together with any proportionate interest he may have in a participating company.

In determining when a company is under the control of its participators, the rights of the participators' associates are taken into account: s416(6).

18.3 'Participator'

Section 417 provides that a 'participator' is:

1. any person who possesses, or is entitled to acquire, share capital or voting rights in the company; or
2. any loan creditor of the company; or

3. any person who possesses, or is entitled to acquire, a right to receive or participate in distributions of the company; or
4. any person who is entitled to secure that income or assets of the company will be applied directly or indirectly for his benefit.

In short, he is a person who can, in one way or another, participate in the profits or assets of the company.

18.4 'Associate'

Section 417(3) provides that an 'associate', in relation to a participator, is:

1. any relative of the participator; or
2. any partner of the participator; or
3. any trustees of a settlement of which the participator or any relative of the participator, is the settlor; or
4. where the participator is a beneficiary under a will or a trust containing shares in the company, any other beneficiary.

'Relative' means husband or wife, parent or grandparent, child or grandchild, brother or sister.
See section 18.6 for further implications of the interest of associates being taken into account in determining 'control'.

18.5 'Loan creditor'

A 'loan creditor', s417(7) provides, is any creditor in respect of any debt created by the company:

1. for any money borrowed or capital acquired by the company; or
2. for any right to receive income created in favour of the company; or
3. for consideration the value of which to the company was (at the time the debt was incurred) substantially less than the amount of the debt;
   or in respect of any redeemable loan capital issued by the company.

Bankers lending money in the ordinary course of their business are not, however, loan creditors.

18.6 'Control'

Section 416 definition

'Control' of a company for close company lesislation and other purposes mentioned below, is defined by s416. A person is to be taken as having control of a company if he exercises, or is able to exercise, or is entitled to acquire, control, whether direct or indirect, over the company's affairs, and in particular if he possesses, or is entitled to acquire:

1. the greater part of the issued share capital of the company; or
2. the greater part of the voting power of the company; or
3. such part of the share capital of the company as would, if all its income were distributed, entitle him to receive the greater part thereof; or
4. such rights as would, on a winding up, entitle him to receive the greater part of the assets of the company.

Most importantly, s416(6) allows the Revenue to attribute to a participator all the rights and powers of his relatives and other associates (see section 18.4). Thus, if X, his wife, his partner, the trustees of a settlement he has created, and one of his children each have 11 per cent of the shares of Y Co, then Y Co is controlled not by five different people, but by one – X. It is on this basis that the number of participators who control a company is computed.

It should also be noted that s417(5) provides that the word 'director' includes not only persons actually called by that name but also any person at whose behest the directors are accustomed to act and any person who plays a part in the management of the company and who controls at least 20 per cent of the ordinary share capital of the company.

The s416 definition of 'control' is also applied when considering close investment holding companies (s13A), in the context of demergers (s218), enterprise investment scheme (s312) and for connected persons purposes (s839).

Section 840 definition

The provisions of s416 are not applied when determining the circumstances in which companies are regarded as controlled when applying the provisions relating to company distributions – s229(1); advance corporation tax – s240(11); group relief 'arrangements' – s410; company migration – s767(5); transfer pricing/associated companies – ss773 and 774. Although the Capital Allowances Act 1990 contains its own definition in s161(2), the wording exactly mirrors that of s840.

The s840 provisions deem control to occur where there exists the power to secure that a company's affairs can be conducted in accordance with the wishes of those persons either through holding of shares or voting power or through the provisions of the Articles of Association or other agreement or document. This extends to holding of shares or powers exercised through the medium of another company. This definition was considered in *Steele v EVC International NV* [1996] STC 785. See Chapter 27, section 27.6, for further details.

18.7 Extended meaning of 'distribution'

Apart from all the usual types of distribution falling within s209 (see Chapter 17, section 17.2) s418 provides that certain benefits afforded to participators in a close company shall also be treated as distributions (and thus as qualifying distributions in respect of which the company will be liable to pay advance corporation tax (ACT)).

Section 418(2) states:

> 'Subject to subsection (3) below, where a close company incurs expense in, or in connection with the provision for any participator of living or other accommodation, of entertainment, of domestic or other services, or of other benefits or facilities of whatever nature, the company shall be treated as making a distribution to him of an amount equal to such of that expense as is not made good to the company by the participator.'

Clearly, this provision is akin to s154 relating to directors and higher-paid employees. When a clash occurs, the participator also falling within s154, s418 gives way, so that the provision of the benefit is earned income in the hands of the participator, deductible by the company in computing its trading profits, and not liable to ACT. A similar rule applies where the benefit provided is living accommodation falling within s145.

Section 418(4) provides that the amount of the expense incurred by the company is determined by using the cash equivalent rules of s156.

18.8 Loans to participators

It would be easy for a company to avoid having to distribute income by lending its profits to its participators. Such loans would not be subject to ACT in the hands of the company and would not be Schedule F income in the hands of the participator. Clearly, this is a problem likely to be particularly rife in connection with close companies. Section 419 provides, therefore, that where a close company makes a loan to an *individual* who is a participator or an associate of a participator, and does so otherwise than in the ordinary course of its business, the company is required to pay to the Revenue a sum equal to the amount of ACT which would have been payable had the loan been a qualifying distribution. Although equal in amount to ACT, the payment made is not ACT but income tax. Provisions relating to the use of ACT are therefore not applicable to this amount.

'Loan' is given an extended meaning by s419(2) and includes cases where the individual incurs a debt to the close company, and where the company takes an assignment of a debt due by the participator to a third party. Under s420(2), though, the company is permitted to make loans of sums up to £15,000 in aggregate to participators working full-time in the company who do not have material interests in the company – that is to say, who own less than 5 per cent of the shares in it. Such loans may well, of course, fall within s160 'beneficial loan arrangements' where the participator is a director or higher-paid employee (see Chapter 8, section 8.5). No penalty is imposed on the participator by s419. Moreover, when the loan, or a proportion of the loan, is repaid, the company itself will be repaid a corresponding proportion of the tax originally charged. Because of the possibility that it may be repaid, the tax under s419, though like ACT, is *not* ACT and cannot be used to reduce the company's mainstream corporation tax (MCT) liability.

Due to the timing of the reporting of such loans and the raising of the assessment, it would not be unusual to find that the loan had been repaid before an assessment had been raised on the company. The interaction of the penalty and interest provisions of ss88–91 of the Taxes Management Act 1970 in this context were in point. Prior to 1986, if a loan had been repaid the Inland Revenue could not raise an assessment. For returns made after that date a failure to notify the liability was neglect, and interest could be charged. This was illustrated in *Earlspring Properties Ltd v Guest* [1995] STC 479 which set aside the normal provisions of s91 TMA 1970, which cancels out interest where tax is repaid on discharge of an assessment in the case of loans repaid to participators.

The method of accounting for tax on loans to the participators of close companies was changed by s173 Finance Act 1996. Rather than accounting for tax within 14 days of the end of the accounting period in which the loan was made, the new rules provide for an extension of this time limit to nine months after the end of the period. In addition no tax is payable if the loan has been repaid by the time the tax becomes due for payment.

In *Joint* v *Bracken Developments Ltd* [1994] STC 300 the question was whether the provisions of s419 concerning loans to participators referred to a charge to tax which was under a law relating to corporation tax. This was in order to determine the interest charge for late payment under s88 TMA 1970. The findings of the General Commissioners were reversed, and interest was made applicable. Section 109 TMA 1970 imposed the obligation to notify under s10 TMA 1970 in respect of liability arising under transactions within s419 ICTA 1988.

It may happen that the company chooses to release the debtor/participator from his liability. If it does so, s421 applies – and this section *does* impose a liability on the participator. The sum released is grossed up at the basic rate of tax, and the amount so computed is brought into charge as part of the participator's total income. While he is not charged at the basic rate, he will, if his personal circumstances warrant it, be liable to income tax at the excess liability rates. No repayment claim may be made on the Revenue if the participator is not liable to tax at all. Having released the individual from his obligation to repay, by s419(4) the company will not be able to recover the tax it has paid under s419. Even at this stage, however, the tax paid is still not converted into ACT. Sections 419 and 421 are indubitably penal.

18.9 Apportionment of income and chargeable gains

Provisions existed in the Taxes Acts to prevent close companies accumulating income otherwise than for legitimate business purposes. The method adopted was to treat 'relevant income' as having been distributed – to apportion it among the participators (see below) – even though it had actually been accumulated, and then to charge tax accordingly. These provisions were to be found in ss423–430 ICTA 1988 (shortfall apportionment provisions), but were repealed by s103 Finance Act 1989.

As noted in Chapter 19, section 19.4, the chargeable gains made by non-resident 'close' companies may be apportioned, under s13 TCGA 1992, to the participators of the company and charged on them at their appropriate rate of tax. By definition a close company must be UK resident (s414(1)(a)) but the s13 provisions are aimed at companies which, if they were UK resident, would be regarded as 'close' for the purposes of ss414 et seq. Prior to 1996, these provisions applied only to shareholders of the company but were extended by FA 1996 to ensure that they continued to target the true economic beneficiaries of the gains, following the growth of schemes involving, inter alia, the use of companies limited by guarantee – ie without shareholders – to shelter offshore gains from UK tax.

See also section 18.12 below for the effect of transfer of assets by close companies at an undervalue.

18.10 Small companies' rates not available to CICs

Section 13A ICTA 1988 disentitles close investment holding companies from the small companies' tax rates as allowed by s13, the definition of CICs having been altered by FA 1989. It provides that a close company will be classified as a close investment holding company for the purpose of s13(1) unless throughout any given accounting period it exists for one or more of the following purposes:

1. to carry on a trade or trades on a commercial basis;
2. to make investments in land or estates or interests in land in cases where the land is or is intended to be let to persons other than connected persons, or the spouse or a relative, or the spouse of a relative of a connected person;
3. to hold shares in, or securities of, or make loans to, one or more companies each of which is a qualifying company, or a company which controls or is controlled by the relevant company, and itself exists wholly or mainly for the above purposes. The relevant company is the close company under consideration, and a 'qualifying company' is defined by s13A(3);
4. to co-ordinate the administration of two or more qualifying companies;
5. to facilitate the trade or trades carried on on a commercial basis by one or more qualifying companies or by a company which has control of the relevant company;

6. to make investments by one or more qualifying companies or by a company which has control of the relevant company. The investments concerned must be those stated in (2) above.

Section 13A(3) defines a qualifying company as a company which is under the control of the relevant company or a company which controls the relevant company and which exists wholly or mainly for either or both of the purposes at (1) or (2) above. For control see s416 and section 18.6.

Generally speaking, the new system is more benevolent to the close company than the old system. The purpose of the new provisions is to ensure that accumulation companies do not get the benefits of the lower rates of taxation allowed to assist smaller trading companies. Provisions a–f of s13A define the conditions which have to be satisfied for the Inland Revenue to agree that the lower rates are properly applicable.

18.11 Profit distributions by CICs

Section 231(3A–3D) ICTA 1988 is aimed at the situation where profits of a CIC are unevenly distributed to low rate taxpayers. These sub-sections state that if 'arrangements' exist which are designed to achieve this disproportionate distribution of income profits, then the inspector may restrict the extent of tax credit available to the receipients of these profits to what appears to him to be just and reasonable. Subsequent amendments were made by Schedule 12 FA 1989.

18.12 Transfer of assets at an undervalue: s125 TCGA 1992

The provisions of s125 are aimed at ensuring that a company under close control does not distribute assets advantageously to its shareholders. Where assets are transferred out of a close company in a transaction which is not 'at arm's length' then the section provides that the acquisition cost of the shares held by each of the shareholders shall be reduced in proportion to the value taken out of the company's assets as a result of the transaction. In each case therefore the amount is apportioned to each shareholder and deducted from the acquisition cost when the shares are ultimately disposed of.

By concession, however, the rule is not applied where the participator or his associate is treated as receiving an income distribution under s209(2)(b) or (4) ICTA 1988 or a capital distribution under s122 TCGA 1992 or where the transferee is assessed under Schedule E as an employee on the difference between the amount paid and the value of the asset transferred.

19

Capital Gains Tax: General

19.1 Introduction

19.2 The charge

19.3 Persons chargeable

19.4 Non-resident with United Kingdom branch or agency

19.5 Chargeable assets

19.6 'Disposal'

19.7 Timing of a disposal

19.8 Computation

19.9 Calculation of gains and losses

19.10 Valuation of disposal consideration

19.11 Exemptions and reliefs

19.12 Partnership

19.13 Company transactions

19.1 Introduction

Capital gains tax was introduced by the Finance Act 1965 and has most recently been consolidated in the Taxation of Chargeable Gains Act 1992. Its predecessor, the Capital Gains Tax Act 1979, had many changes made to it by each succeeding Finance Act. All references in this and subsequent CGT chapters are to the 1992 Act, save where otherwise indicated.

19.2 The charge

Section 1(1) provides:

'Tax shall be charged in accordance with this Act in respect of capital gains, that is to say chargeable gains computed in accordance with this Act and accruing to a person on the disposal of assets.'

It is the concept of 'disposal' which is central to the operation of the Act. The use of the word 'person' rather than 'individual' indicates that a wide range of legal personalities are rendered liable to CGT. It will be remembered that United Kingdom resident companies are subject to corporation tax, not CGT, on their chargeable gains, but such chargeable gains are, however, still computed in accordance with TCGA 1992.

Formerly, CGT was imposed at a single rate of 30 per cent, but under s4 it is now charged at the individual taxpayer's marginal rate of income tax for chargeable gains arising on or after 6 April 1988. This includes, where appropriate, the new lower rate (s4(1A)).

Capital gains tax is due for payment, under the self-assessment provisions, in one sum on 31 January following the year of assessment in which the gain is made – s59B TMA 1970.

19.3 Persons chargeable

The connecting factor for CGT is residence in the United Kingdom. If a person is resident or ordinarily resident in the United Kingdom for even part of a year of assessment, he is, technically, liable to CGT on the chargeable gains accruing on the disposal of assets, wherever situated, and whenever during the year of assessment he makes the disposal. By extra-statutory concession No D2 the Inland Revenue is willing to treat a taxpayer who becomes resident at sometime during the year of assessment, or who ceases to be resident in the year, as liable to CGT only on gains accruing to him during the part of the year during which he is physically present in the United Kingdom. This concession is not available, though, to a person who tries to make use of it in order to avoid tax: *R v IRC, ex parte Fulford-Dobson* [1987] STC 344.

19.4 Non-resident with United Kingdom branch or agency

There are three other modifications to the usual rule, two of which deal with CGT charges on non-residents and the other which restricts the charge on non-domiciled persons.

Section 10: non-resident with United Kingdom branch or agency

Where a person is neither resident, nor ordinarily resident, in the United Kingdom, yet carries on a trade there through a branch or agency, he will be chargeable to

CGT on gains accruing on the disposal of assets *situated in the United Kingdom* used in or for the purposes of the trade, or used or held for the purposes of the branch or agency. Section 10(5) ensures that the same provision applies to professions and vocations with a branch or agency within the United Kingdom.

Section 172 provides relief from CGT where a non-resident company transfers all or part of a United Kingdom branch or agency to a United Kingdom resident company, provided that the foreign company and the United Kingdom transferee are all members of the same group.

The incorporation of the branch or agency is treated, if an election is made within two years from the end of the relevant accounting period, as giving rise to neither a gain nor a loss in respect of the assets transferred to the company. The effect is to defer the gain on the increase in value until such time as the company is disposed of.

Anti-avoidance

Previously non-residents were able to avoid CGT by either removing the asset concerned from the United Kingdom prior to its disposal or ceasing to trade in the United Kingdom prior to disposal. These loopholes have now been plugged: a deemed disposal arises on the removal from the United Kingdom of any asset which is chargeable within these sections (s25(1)), and a deemed disposal of a chargeable asset arises if the non-resident concerned ceases to trade (s25(3)).

The s10 charge applies only to disposals before cessation of business (s10(2)). On cessation, however, the deemed disposal in s25(3) arises.

Section 12: foreign assets of persons with a foreign domicile

Where an *individual* is resident or ordinarily resident in the United Kingdom but is domiciled abroad, CGT is only chargeable on the disposal of assets situated abroad on a *remittance basis*. The wide definition of 'remittance' provided by s65 of the Income and Corporation Taxes Act 1988 applies to s12.

Section 13 – gains of non-resident 'close' companies

As discussed in Chapter 18, section 18.9 above, under s13 the gains of non-resident companies which would be close companies if they were United Kingdom resident can be attributed to and taxed on their United Kingdom resident participators. Any tax paid is treated as an additional cost of the shares when disposed of: s13(7).

19.5 Chargeable assets

CGT, as provided for in s1(1), is levied on the gain accruing on the disposal of *assets*. 'Asset' is defined by s21(1):

224 Capital Gains Tax: General

'All forms of property shall be assets for the purposes of this Act, whether situated in the United Kingdom or not, including:
a) Options, debts, and incorporeal property generally, and
b) any currency *other than sterling*; and
c) any form of property created by the person disposing of it, or otherwise coming to be owned without being acquired.'

This would clearly seem to indicate that all forms of property are assets for CGT purposes. Nevertheless, if one examines the interpretation of this provision by the courts the scope of its application has not always been certain.

In *Davis* v *Powell* [1977] STC 32 the taxpayer was a tenant farmer who surrendered his tenancy in return for compensation to which he was entitled as a result of the statutory right accorded him by s34(2) of the Agricultural Holdings Act 1948. This Act imposed on the landlord an obligation to compensate the tenant for 'loss or expenses directly attributable to the quitting of the holding'. Templeman J held that the sum was not taxable because one could not obtain a chargeable gain in respect of a sum given to compensate for loss incurred. In *Drummond* v *Austin-Brown* [1984] STC 321 Walton J reached the same conclusion in respect of the right to compensation accorded to the taxpayer business tenant under s25 Landlord and Tenant Act 1954: that the sum received was not a capital gain.

In contrast, in *Davenport* v *Chilver* [1983] STC 426 Nourse J stated that the taxpayer's right to compensation accorded to her under the Foreign Compensation (Union of Soviet Socialist Republics) Order 1969 (SI 1969/735) in respect of her mother's land was an asset for CGT purposes. (The Order was granted to allow British taxpayers whose property in Latvia had been appropriated by the government of the USSR to receive compensation for their losses.) Consequently the compensation sum paid was deemed to be derived from an asset within s22(1) and was therefore liable to CGT.

It becomes difficult to distinguish these cases, especially as the right to compensation in all three cases satisfies the test enacted by the House of Lords in *O'Brien* v *Benson's Hosiery (Holdings) Ltd* [1979] STC 735. In that case the taxpayer company sought to impose a limitation on its application by claiming that a right which it enjoyed did not amount to 'property' as supposedly required by s21. It had been paid £50,000 by one of its employees, who wished to be released from his obligations under a long-term service agreement in order to take a better-paid job. The company argued that the sum received did not accrue on the disposal of an asset since the rights of an employer under a service contract could not be transferred or assigned. The House of Lords held it was sufficient that the employer could 'turn' his rights 'to account', so that the rights did amount to an 'asset'.

The way of distinguishing between *Davis*, *Drummond* and *Davenport* is to state that in *Davis* (and presumably in *Drummond* also) the taxpayers merely had a right to reimbursement for an actual loss suffered, while in *Davenport* the taxpayer had not suffered any actual loss (it was her mother's land that she was compensated for) and so the right to compensation constituted an 'independent proprietary right to share in a designated fund'. Indeed in *Zim Properties Ltd* v *Proctor* [1985] STC 90, Warner J seemed to agree with this distinction and held that:

'... a right to bring an action to seek to enforce a claim that was not frivolous or vexatious, which right could be turned to account by negotiating a compromise yielding a substantial capital sum was an asset for capital gains tax purposes.'

He also stated that as a result of his analysis of the House of Lords' decision in *O'Brien* he understood that in their Lordships' opinion the meanings of the words 'asset' and 'disposal' in the capital gains tax legislation were crucial, whereas the meaning of the word 'property' was largely irrelevant. He concluded that there were two ways in which their Lordships might have reached that result. One was to take the view that s21 was not intended to provide an exhaustive definition of 'assets' but merely to enact that, whatever else might be comprised in that concept, it included 'all forms of property'. On that view, 'assets' was a wider concept than 'property' and included any right that could be turned to account, even though a lawyer might not regard it as 'property'. The other possibility was that their Lordships agreed with Fox J that the word 'property' was not a precise term but one of which the meaning might vary with the context. On this subject see also *Pennine Raceway Ltd* v *Kirklees Metropolitan Council (No 2)* [1989] STC 122 and *Donald Fisher (Ealing) Ltd* v *Spencer* [1989] STC 256.

During the 1990s it has become common for payments to be made to investors (members) of building societies when these are either merged with others or incorporated as banks. The Inland Revenue confirmed in a press release dated 21 March 1996 that it regarded cash payments made to holders of share accounts, as opposed to deposit accounts, when a society is taken over as being chargeable to capital gains tax. The view given was that the sum derived from a chargeable asset of either the investor, borrower or depositor through rights conferred under the contract between the individual and the society. The payment would have no corresponding expenditure (acquisition cost) to set against it and therefore the full amount would be liable for capital gains tax, subject to the usual deduction for annual exempt amount. This position would be applied either on a take-over or on the conversion of the building society to the status of a company, normally on acquiring bank status.

The above view was however successfully challenged before the Special Commissioners in a decision reported early in 1997 (*Foster* v *Williams*; *Horan* v *Williams* [1997] STC (SCD) 112) but applicable only to the facts of that particular take-over. The payments made in that case were made equally to share account holders and deposit account holders alike and without distinction. The Special Commissioner held that the payments could not therefore be held to have been received in exchange for the giving up of any of the equity rights, as contended by the Inland Revenue, in view of the even handed payments to members with or without share account holdings. The Inland Revenue subsequently announced that they did not propose to contest the case, but it does not mean that their normal view of payments to share account members will in most instances be made in return for the release of their rights and will therefore normally give rise to a capital gains tax liability.

In addition, where the conversion gave rise to an issue of shares rather than cash payment to the investor or depositor or borrower, no capital gains tax liability would arise on the receipt of the shares but there would be a capital gains tax liability on the disposal of the shares. As above, it is unlikely that there would be any corresponding acquisition cost to deduct from the value received for the shares and the full amount would therefore be a chargeable gain.

The press release also confirmed, however, that payments made in cash on the mergers of building societies would be chargeable to income tax.

It was also common that various payments or 'cashbacks' would be made to borrowers and the press release confirmed that such incentives did not derive from any chargeable asset from capital gains tax purposes, but as an inducement to enter into a contract. In the circumstances the payment would therefore not be liable for capital gains tax.

19.6 'Disposal'

The asset disposed of

The charge to CGT arises on the disposal of an asset. This concept is not defined by the Act, but it can be said that any form of transfer or alienation of the beneficial title to an asset (whether legal or equitable) by one person to another will involve a disposal by one person and an acquisition by the other.

Thus one must decide which asset the taxpayer disposed of in order to receive the capital sum. With regard to the reliefs afforded to companies on a reconstruction or reorganisation (see section 19.13, 'Company Transactions', and ss126–138) the relief is achieved by s127, which provides that the relevant transaction 'shall not be treated as involving any disposal ... or any acquisition ...'. Therefore if there is no disposal there is no basis for any liability to CGT. In every other case the question to be asked is what is the asset from which the capital sum is derived, and this is not necessarily its immediate source. In *Zim Properties* (above) Warner J decided that when, through the negligence of a solicitor, his client could not make good title on a sale of a building and the sale fell through, the damages subsequently received by the client from the solicitor flowed from the chose in action which arose on the negligent act, namely the right to sue, and not from the building in relation to which the solicitor had been negligent. Accordingly, expenditure on the building, such as its purchase price, could not be deducted in computing the gain realised by the taxpayer on the disposal of the chose in consideration of the payment of the compensation. Thus the taxpayer had an asset for which there was no deductible acquisition cost and the whole amount of the proceeds was chargeable. In *Davenport*

Nourse J held that the compensation the taxpayer received as a result of the appropriation of *her* own property was deemed to derive as a result of disposal of that property, while the compensation that she received as a result of the appropriation of her mother's land was deemed to derive from the disposal of her 'right' under the foreign compensation order.

Statute will also sometimes dictate from which asset the capital sum is derived; for example, s140(2) provides that capital sums received under an insurance policy are deemed to be derived from the asset insured despite the fact that the rights under the insurance policy may be assets in their own right. Following the *Zim Properties* case the Inland Revenue issued a press release of 19 December 1988 stating the assets from which taxpayers would be deemed to derive compensation. Under the terms of that statement, damages and compensation received are treated as derived from any 'underlying assets' unless there is no 'underlying asset', whereupon the damages or compensation will be treated as exempt. Where there is an underlying asset the damages will be exempt if the underlying asset is exempt, but taxable if the underlying asset is taxable.

Part disposals

Section 21(2) provides that:

1. References to a disposal include ... references to a part disposal of an asset; and
2. There is a part disposal of an asset:

    - where an interest or right in or over the asset is created *by* the disposal as well as where it subsists before the disposal; and, generally,
    - where, on a person making a disposal, any description of property derived from the asset remains undisposed of.

Owing to the very wide definition of 'asset', where a person disposes of the whole of his own interest in an asset, he is disposing of an asset, and *not* merely making a part disposal.

Section 22

Section 22 extends the meaning of 'disposal' beyond cases where an asset is transferred from one party to another. It provides:

> 'There is a disposal of assets by their owner where any capital sum is derived from assets notwithstanding that no asset is acquired by the person paying the capital sum.'

In particular this covers:

1. capital sums received by way of compensation for any kind of damage or injury to assets or for the loss, destruction or dissipation of assets or for any depreciation or risk of depreciation of an asset;

2. capital sums received under a policy of insurance of the risk of any kind of damage or injury to, or the loss or depreciation of, assets;
3. capital sums received in return for forfeiture or surrender of rights, or for refraining from exercising rights;
4. capital sums received as consideration for use or exploitation of assets.

In all these cases, the disposal takes place at the time that the capital sum is received.

Marren v *Ingles* [1980] STC 500 shows that s22 applies whether or not the payer acquired an asset. In this case the right to receive the further consideration was held to be an asset in itself, giving rise to a capital sum for s22 purposes. In *Kirby* v *Thorn EMI* [1987] STC 621, the Court of Appeal considered whether there could be a disposal of an asset when the asset was created by the transaction in question. There, a company covenanted to refrain from competing with a purchaser of the shares in certain of its subsidiaries but which operated in a market in which it personally had never engaged. Nicholls J held that while the agreement conferred rights on the purchaser which constituted an asset in its hands, that asset had never existed in the hands of the covenantor, so that there could not be a disposal for CGT purposes:

> 'Thus the basic structure of the tax is a charge on gains accruing to a person on the disposal of an asset by him. There is no statutory definition of disposal but, having regard to the context, what is envisaged by that expression is a transfer of an asset (ie of ownership of an asset), as widely defined, by one person to another. The Act presupposes that, immediately prior to the disposal, there was an asset and that the disponor owned it. Section [21(2)(a)] then deals with the case where only part of an asset is disposed of, and section [21(2)(b)] covers the case where, although the disponor owned an asset before the disposal, what he did by the disposal was not to transfer that asset but to carve or create out of it a right in favour of another. The grant of an easement over land is an obvious example. That is also stated to be a part disposal ... the present type of case, where rights were conferred by the taxpayer accepting restriction on his future freedom of action, is not the only type of case where a transaction may result in the acquisition of an asset by a person without a disposal of that asset to him. Another example would be subscribing for shares in a company.'

The court held that the covenant in the particular case was a part disposal by the company of its corporate goodwill, and thus it was rendered liable to CGT on the capital sum received.

Section 26

Section 26 provides for the case of mortgages or charges taken over property by way of security. Any conveyance or transfer made in connection with such a case is not treated as a disposal. Furthermore, if the mortgagee or chargee enforces his security, his dealings with the asset are treated as nominee dealings on behalf of the mortgagor or chargor, and it is the latter who will be liable for any chargeable gain accruing as a result.

If a person buys an asset subject to a mortgage, he is deemed to give, as part of the consideration for the asset, a sum equal to the full amount of that outstanding liability. Thus if A buys a house from B for £40,000, agreeing to take over the outstanding mortgage of £15,000, he gives total consideration of £55,000.

In the same way (although this is not often realised), if A gives B his farm, subject only to the mortgage on the property, it is not a gift but a sale, the consideration for which is the undertaking of the mortgage. Provided that the mortgage does not exceed the consideration originally given for the property by A, the transaction will not be subject to CGT.

Value shifting

Section 29 provides that three types of transaction are to be treated as disposals of assets, notwithstanding that no consideration passes, and that they are to be treated as made for a consideration equal to market value if, had the parties been at arm's length, consideration or additional consideration would have been given. The transactions are:

1. Where a person having control of a company exercises his control so that value passes out of shares in the company owned by him or by a person with whom he is connected and passes into other shares in or rights over the company. For an example of this, and a discussion of the meaning of 'person exercising control', see *Floor* v *Davis* [1979] STC 379.
2. Where, after a transaction which involves the owner of land or of property becoming the lessee of the property, there is any adjustment of the rights and liabilities under the lease, whether or not involving the granting of a new lease, which as a whole is favourable to the *lessor*. In such a case, there is a disposal by the lessee of an interest in the property.
3. Where a person extinguishes or abrogates, in whole or in part, any description of right or restriction which he holds over an asset.

Section 30 goes even further and provides that where there has been an actual disposal of an asset, and it has been either preceded or followed by a scheme which has been effected, or arrangements which have been made, whereby:

1. the value of the asset has been materially reduced; *and*
2. a tax-free benefit has been or will be conferred either on the disponor or a person connected with him, or on any other person,

then any allowable loss or chargeable gain accruing on the disposal of the asset is to be calculated as if the consideration for the disposal were increased by such amount as appears just and reasonable to the inspector, having regard to the scheme and the tax-free benefit.

Section 30 will not apply where a tax-free benefit is conferred only on a person not connected with the disponor if it can be shown that the avoidance of tax was not the main purpose of the scheme.

Assets lost, destroyed, or whose value becomes negligible: s24

The occasion of the entire loss, destruction, dissipation or extinction of an asset is deemed to be a disposal for the purposes of CGT whether or not any capital sum is received by way of compensation or otherwise. The effect of this relieving section can be seen in the following example:

Example
1. A buys a yacht for £100,000. Two days later, before he has had a chance to insure it, he strikes a rock and the yacht sinks irretrievably to the bottom of the ocean. A is deemed to have disposed of the yacht for nil consideration and has thus made an allowable loss of £100,000.
2. A then buys another yacht, and this time insures it immediately for its replacement value. Shortly afterwards the yacht rises in value to £125,000. A takes the yacht out, strikes the same rock and, three years later, after much litigation, recovers £125,000 from his insurers.

He is deemed to have made an allowable loss of £100,000 in the year of assessment in which it sank, which he may use to set against any chargeable gains of that or any subsequent year: s24(1). He is also considered to have made a chargeable gain of £125,000 in the year of assessment in which he recovers the insurance monies under s23(1). If he has not already made use of his allowable loss he will be able to use it now to reduce his chargeable gain to £25,000: *Golding* v *Kaufman* [1985] STC 152, 162–3.

Section 24 is thus a relieving section, and an extension of this relief is given by s24(2): if an owner claims that the value of an asset has become negligible and the inspector agrees that this is so, then the owner is deemed to have sold and to have reacquired the asset for that negligible amount *on the date on which the inspector signified his agreement.* The owner is thus enabled to crystallise the loss inherent in his unsaleable asset. It must be stressed, though, that it is the date of agreement which is all-important, and if, therefore, the year of assessment has ended, the owner will lose the opportunity to set the loss thus created against gains realised in the previous year: *Williams* v *Bullivant* [1983] STC 107.

19.7 Timing of a disposal

In most cases it will be easy to say when the disposal took place because the parties will agree, and the asset will immediately thereafter be disposed of in return for the consideration. What if, however, the contract precedes the conveyance – as will almost always be the case with real property – or if the contract is made but completion never takes place?

Section 28 sets out the rules:

'(1) Where an asset is disposed of and acquired under a contract, the time at which the disposal and acquisition is made is the time the contract is made (and not, if different, the time at which the asset is conveyed or transferred).
(2) If the contract is conditional (and, in particular, if it is conditional on the exercise of an option) the time at which the disposal and acquisition is made is the time when the condition is satisfied.'

A conditional contract is one whose existence depends on the satisfaction of a condition, *not* a contract containing conditions. Moreover, for the purposes of TCGA 1992 the condition in question must be a condition precedent and not merely a condition subsequent: *Eastham* v *Leigh London and Provincial Properties Ltd* [1971] Ch 871; *Parway Estates Limited* v *IRC* 45 TC 135; and *IRC* v *Ufitec Group Ltd* [1977] STC 363.

Far more difficult is the question of the proper analysis of a case where completion never takes place. The better view is that no disposal and acquisition take place at all. Section 28 provides: 'where an asset *is* [author's italics] disposed of and acquired under a contract'; one can accept this as referring to *actual* disposal, so that if no actual disposal occurs the section cannot apply. Once completion has occurred, a reference back takes place. If an exceedingly long time is to elapse between contract and completion, no doubt the Revenue will insist on its money, as usual, under s59B TMA 1970, on 31 January following the end of the year of assessment in which the contract is made (s7), and will repay, with supplement, if completion is cancelled.

Where the disposal is one falling under s22(1), s28 does not apply; instead, s22(2) provides that disposal occurs on receipt of the money.

Section 27 deals with the time of disposal in hire-purchase. Contrary to the legal niceties, but in line with s28, the disposal occurs not when property passes but when the hire-purchaser first enters upon the use and enjoyment of the asset, with adjustments if no property finally passes.

19.8 Computation

Liability

CGT is charged on the total amount of chargeable gains accruing to a person in the year of assessment, after deducting any allowable losses accruing in the year and losses carried forward unused from previous years (s4).

Married couples are taxed separately on their capital gains. The rate of tax that each spouse pays on his or her gains is equivalent to his or her respective marginal rate of income tax. Each spouse is entitled to a separate annual exemption, and neither is able to surrender any unused exemption and/or unused losses to the other partner: s58.

Section 3 provides that an *individual* is not chargeable to CGT in respect of so much of his taxable amount for any year of assessment as does not exceed the exempt amount for the year. A person's taxable amount is defined to ensure that unused losses carried forward from a previous year (the only time that losses can be rolled back is on death) are set against his net gains for the year. In effect there are three stages to the calculation:

1. Calculate the taxpayer's chargeable gains and allowable losses for the current year of assessment. Deduct the one from the other. If losses exceed gains, the surplus may be carried forward to the next year of assessment. If gains exceed losses, go on to stage (2).
2. Deduct the 'exempt amount for the year' from the excess of gains calculated under stage (1). The 'exempt amount' is index-linked by reference to the retail prices index, and will increase once a year (s80 FA 1982) unless Parliament otherwise determines (for 1997–98 it stands at £6,500). If it exceeds the gains, no CGT is payable. Any surplus exempt amount *cannot* be carried forward. As illustrated below, the annual exemption is deducted before any brought-forward losses.
3. If the taxpayer has unused allowable losses brought forward from previous years, they may be deducted at this stage. If gains exceed losses brought forward, CGT is charged in accordance with s4.

Examples

1. Fred has allowable losses which have accumulated over the years, amounting to £10,000. In 1997–98 he makes chargeable gains of £6,000 and incurs allowable losses of £2,000. His net gains are £4,000. Since this is less than the exempt amount for the year, he pays no CGT and carries forward £10,000 of losses.

   Only if a person's allowable losses exceed his chargeable gains for a year of assessment can any loss be carried forward – and then only the excess.

2. James earns £50,000 pa and therefore his marginal rate of income tax is 40 per cent. He bought an asset in 1983 for £20,000. In 1997–98 he sells it for £37,000. This is the only disposal he makes during the year.

	£	£
Sale price	37,000	
Purchase price	20,000	
Chargeable gain (and taxable amount)		17,000
Exempt amount		6,500
		£10,500
Tax payable: £10,500 x 40%		= £4,200

Note: indexation allowance would be deductible from the above chargeable gain before tax is charged – see section 19.9.

Exemptions

Schedule 1 to the Act provides some exemptions for persons other than individuals:

Trustees

Trustees, at best, get only one £3,250 exemption in relation to gains accruing to them on the disposal of trust assets. If a settlor has created more than one settlement since 6 June 1978, the amount of £3,250 is divided by the number of settlements, save that the minimum exempt amount is £¹/₁₀ – thus if a settlor created 12 settlements after 1978, each set of trustees would receive an exemption of £325.

Personal representatives

For the year of death and the next two following years of assessment, personal representatives get a £6,500 exemption. Thereafter, they get nothing. If the PRs are, as often happens, also the trustees of trusts created by the testator in his will, they will obtain a trustees' exemption for the trust assets only from the year of assessment in which they assent to the property vesting in themselves as such trustees.

19.9 Calculation of gains and losses

This matter, which used to be relatively straightforward, has been much complicated by the introduction of rebasing and of index-linking for CGT. The problem was that most CGT was imposed on the increases in the value of assets through the workings of inflation. With respect to assets acquired since 31 March 1982, index-linking addresses the problem completely. Rebasing, together with index-linking, has completely addressed the problem with respect to assets held before 31 March 1982 and disposed of on or after 6 April 1988. It is necessary to explain, first, the old rules (which still apply) and, secondly, the modifications to them by the FAs 1982, 1985 and 1988.

Section 38

Since CGT is, primarily, a tax on the *gain* which accrues to a person on the disposal of an asset, some deduction must be allowable from the consideration actually received by the disponor in order to calculate that gain. Section 38 sets out the rules determining what is such allowable expenditure. It *restricts* the sums allowable as a deduction in the computation of the gain to:

1. '(a) the amount or value of the consideration, in money or money's worth, given by the (disponor) or on his behalf *wholly and exclusively* for the acquisition of the asset', together with 'the incidental costs to him of the acquisition'; or, if he made the asset, rather than acquired it, 'any expenditure wholly and exclusively incurred by him in providing the asset'.

2. '(b) the amount of any expenditure wholly and exclusively incurred on the asset by him or on his behalf for the purpose of enhancing the value of the asset, being expenditure reflected in the state or nature of the asset at the time of disposal, [and] any expenditure wholly and exclusively incurred by him in establishing, preserving or defending his title to, or to a right over, the asset'.

From this it can be seen that *abortive* expenditure is not deductible, simply because it cannot be said that part of the consideration received on the disposal is either attributable to that expenditure or that the expenditure is 'reflected in the state or nature of the asset at the time of disposal'.

3. '(c) the incidental costs to him of making the disposal.'

'Incidental costs' fall into two categories:
- costs of *professional* services in connection with the transfer; and
- the costs of the transfer or conveyance, including stamp duty.

Section 42

Section 42 provides special rules which must be applied to part disposals. Since part of the asset, ex hypothesi, remains undisposed of, allowable expenditure incurred on the asset must be attributable both to the part disposed of and the part retained. The rules are:

1. The incidental costs of the part disposal are attributable to the part disposed of and not to the part retained, and may thus be completely deducted from the consideration for the part disposed of. All other allowable expenditure must be apportioned, and where A is the amount or value of the consideration for the disposal; and B is the market value of the part undisposed of, only the fraction $A/_{A+B}$ of such expenditure may be deducted from the consideration for the part disposal, *unless* the expenditure was incurred entirely on the part disposed of or on the part retained. In the former case, the whole of that sum may be deducted, while in the latter, none of it may be.

Example

X buys a freehold investment for £60,000, incurring £5,000 legal fees. He spends £35,000 converting it into five flats, and sells the first for £30,000, within a year of purchase, incurring £2,000 legal and estate agent's fees. The remaining flats are worth £120,000.

	£	£
Sale proceeds		30,000
Incidental costs of disposal		2,000
		£28,000
Other allowable expenditure:	60,000	
	5,000	
	35,000	
	£100,000	
(A: 30,000; B: 120,000)		
Brought-forward receipts		28,000

$$\frac{A}{A+B} = \frac{30,000}{150,000} = \frac{1}{5}$$

So $\frac{1}{5} \times 100,000$ can be deducted = 20,000

GAIN £8,000

The rest of the allowable expenditure (£80,000) will be carried forward to be apportioned again on the sale of the next flat, and so on.

The indexation allowance

FA 1982 introduced the indexation allowance to mitigate (albeit to a limited extent) the effects of inflation. It applied to disposals of chargeable assets which took place on or after 6 April 1982 (or 1 April 1982 for companies) and before 6 April 1985. The allowance was originally calculated by multiplying the allowable expenditure described in s38(1)(a) and (b) (ie acquisition costs and enhancement expenditure) by the increase in the retail prices index between March 1982 (where assets were acquired prior to April 1981) or 12 months after the expenditure was incurred, whichever was the later, and the month of the disposal of the assets. It did not mitigate the effects of inflation prior to March 1982, or apply to disposals within 12 months of acquisition, and could not be used to create or increase a loss – it could merely reduce or negate a gain.

The rules governing the indexation allowance in relation to disposals on or after 6 April 1985 (or 1 April 1985 for companies) were substantially modified by FA 1985, and these provisions were consolidated in TCGA 1992. In particular:

1. In the case of an asset acquired before 31 March 1982, an election may be made to calculate the indexation allowance by reference to its market value at 31 March 1982 if more advantageous (s55(1) TCGA).
2. A 12-months qualifying period is no longer necessary, and the indexation allowance is to be calculated from the month in which the asset is acquired, or March 1982, whichever is the later time.
3. The indexation allowance could be used to turn a gain into an allowable loss (s53(1)), but this is no longer allowed for disposals after 30 November 1993.

Indexation may not increase a capital loss nor turn a gain into a loss. When the allowance is applied to a gain, it is therefore restricted to an amount required to reduce the gain to nil and for an existing loss is ignored.

Note: shares are subject to a special regime within the indexation allowance rules.

Rebasing

FA 1988 introduced rebasing to mitigate the effects of inflation further. Broadly speaking, s35(2) TCGA 1992 will entitle the taxpayer to rebase an asset which he held on 31 March 1982 and which he disposed of on or after 6 April 1988. If under s35(2) the taxpayer is entitled to rebase, he will be deemed to have disposed of the asset on 31 March 1982 and immediately re-acquired it at its then market value with no charge to CGT. Thus the taxpayer's allowable expenditure on disposal of his asset after 6 April 1988 will be deemed to be equivalent to the market value of the asset on 31 March 1982. All the taxpayer's capital gains before 31 March 1982 will be wiped out. In addition, the application of s55 ensures that all the taxpayer's post April 1982 inflationary gains will also escape tax. He will thus only be taxed on the real gains that have accrued from 31 March 1982 until the date of disposal.

However, s35(2) is subject to s35(3) and (5). Section 35(3) will prevent a taxpayer from rebasing in three main circumstances:

1. Section 35(3)(a) – if rebasing would result in the taxpayer making a gain and not rebasing would result in the taxpayer making a smaller gain or a loss, then he will not be able to rebase. (Moreover, s35(4) states that where rebasing would substitute a gain for a loss then the taxpayer shall be deemed to make a no-gain/no-loss disposal.)
2. Section 35(3)(b) – if rebasing would result in the taxpayer making a loss and not rebasing would result in the taxpayer making a gain or a smaller loss, then he will not be entitled to rebase. (Section 35(4) states that where rebasing would substitute a loss for a gain then the taxpayer shall be deemed to make a no-gain/no-loss disposal.)
3. Section 35(3)(c) and (d) – if not rebasing would result in the taxpayer having a no-gain/no-loss disposal, either because the figures produce that result or because the particular transaction is specified to be a no-gain/no-loss disposal by the CGT legislation, then the taxpayer is not entitled to rebase.

Notes:
1. If the taxpayer elects for all disposals to be rebased (irrespective of whether or not it is tax efficient to rebase) then s35(5) overrides s35(3) and he is entitled to rebase on *every* transaction irrespective of the outcome.
2. If there is a disposal after 6 April 1988 of an asset acquired before 31 March 1982 but there has been a part disposal of the asset between those dates, the sums to be apportioned under s42 are ascertained on the assumption that the

asset was disposed of and immediately reacquired on 31 March 1982 by the person making the disposal.

Thus, assuming that the taxpayer has not elected for s35(5) to apply, in order to see whether he can rebase one must apply the CGT rules, using both the original allowable expenditure figure and the rebased allowable expenditure figure for the asset. After the CGT consequences of calculations have been compared, s35(3) is examined to see whether the taxpayer can or cannot rebase.

Examples
1. X buys a chargeable asset in 1980 for £20,000. (Its market value on 31 March 1982 was £24,000.) X later disposed of the asset for £36,000.

    CGT consequences if X does not rebase

	£
Sale proceeds	36,000
Allowable expenditure	20,000
Chargeable gain	£16,000

    CGT consequences if X does rebase

	£
Sale proceeds	36,000
Deemed purchase price as a consequence of rebasing	24,000
Chargeable gain	£12,000

    Thus rebasing results in X making a gain of £12,000, while not rebasing results in his making a larger gain of £16,000; as a result, X can rebase, and his chargeable gain will be £12,000. (The consequences of indexation allowance have been ignored for the purposes of this example.)

2. A buys a chargeable asset in 1978 for £300,000. (Its market value on 31 March 1982 was £150,000.) A later disposed of the asset for £320,000.

    CGT consequences if A does not rebase

	£
Sale proceeds	320,000
Allowable expenditure	300,000
Chargeable gain	£20,000

    CGT consequences if A does rebase

	£
Sale proceeds	320,000
Deemed purchase price as a consequence of rebasing	150,000
Chargeable gain	£170,000

    Rebasing therefore produces a gain but not rebasing produces a smaller gain, and so s35(3) denies A the right to rebase. His chargeable gains will be £20,000. (The consequences of indexation allowance have been ignored for the purposes of this example.)

3. S buys a chargeable asset in 1980 for £50,000. (Its market value on 31 March 1982 was £48,000.) S later disposed of the asset for £50,000.

CGT consequences if S does not rebase

	£
Sale proceeds	50,000
Allowable expenditure	50,000
Chargeable gain	0

CGT consequences if S does rebase

	£
Sale proceeds	50,000
Deemed purchase price as a consequence of rebasing	48,000
Chargeable gain	£2,000

Rebasing therefore produces an allowable loss, but not rebasing produces a no-gain/no-loss transaction, so s35(3) denies S the right to rebase. His chargeable gains will be £0. (The consequences of indexation allowance have been ignored for the purposes of this example.)

Note should also be taken of the effects of applying Schedule 3 and 4.

Schedule 3
According to Schedule 3 para 1, even though the asset was not held by the taxpayer on 31 March 1982 he may still be deemed to hold it for the purposes of rebasing. Schedule 3 para 1 states that if the taxpayer acquired the asset by means of a no-gain/no-loss transaction, and either the transferor held the asset on 31 March 1982 or the taxpayer has acquired it as a result of a series of no-gain/no loss disposals all taking place after 31 March 1982, then he shall be deemed to have held the asset on 31 March 1982.

The no-gain/no-loss disposals to which Schedule 3 para 1 refers are listed in Schedule 3 para 3 and include among others ss58 and 73 TGCA.

Schedule 4
Schedule 4 applies, in a number of circumstances, to wipe out half of any gains which were realised before 1 April 1982 but were rolled over or held over against allowable expenditure in a transaction taking place after April 1982. For this gain to be partially wiped out it must be wholly or partially attributable to gains accruing on the disposal before 6 April 1988 of assets acquired before 31 March 1982. The transactions which attract this relief are listed in Schedule 9 para 4 and include, amongst others, personal gifts (s67), gifts of business assets (s165), and purchase of replacement land following compulsory acquisition (s247).

Further very technical provisions are contained in Schedule 4 para 5.

Losses

Losses are generally computed in the same way as gains: s16. Allowable losses accruing in a particular year of assessment may be deducted from the chargeable gains of that year. Any surplus may only be carried forward to set off against chargeable gains of the future. Only on death (see below) may losses ever be rolled back.

Wasting assets

An asset with a predictable life of less than 50 years is a 'wasting asset'. Plant and machinery are always wasting assets. Section 46 requires that expenditure on a wasting asset be written off at a uniform rate over the predictable life of the asset, thus increasing the amount of any chargeable gain on its disposal.

Example
A wasting asset with a predictable life of 40 years was purchased for £10,000. Ten years later it was sold for £20,000.

	£
Sale proceeds	20,000
Deduct allowable cost: £10,000 x $\frac{30 \text{ years}}{40 \text{ years}}$	7,500
Chargeable gain	£12,500

Where leasehold property is concerned, the 'line of wastage' is curved and wastage accelerates as the end of the lease approaches; see Schedule 8 for a table showing the percentage of cost deductible on disposal, etc, of a lease, by reference to the remaining life of the lease.

Consideration by instalments

When payments for an asset are to be made by instalments, the consideration for the disposal is the capitalised value of the payments. If the period during which payments will be made exceeds 18 months, s48 permits the tax on the chargeable gain to be paid by instalments over a period not exceeding eight years if the Revenue is satisfied that a lump sum payment would involve undue hardship. In no case, though, may the last payment of tax be made after the last instalment of consideration has been received. 'Hardship' is interpreted by the Revenue as meaning that the tax payable exceeds the sums which have been received by the vendor.

Assets held on 6 April 1965: Schedule 2

Other than quoted shares and securities

CGT came into force in respect of disposals of assets after 6 April 1965, so gains accruing before 6 April 1965 were not assessed to tax. Therefore, where an asset other than quoted shares or securities was purchased prior to 6 April 1965 and was disposed of after that date but before 6 April 1988, an apportionment of the gain was made in order to determine the chargeable gain which could be deemed to have accrued after the introduction of the tax. The gain (or loss) was deemed to accrue at a uniform rate over the period of ownership. Such rules continue to apply even if assets are disposed of after April 1988 if s35(3) does not permit the taxpayer to rebase. Thus:

$$\frac{\text{Total gain} \times \text{period of ownership after 6.4.65}}{\text{Total period of ownership}} = \text{the chargeable gain}$$

Example

X makes a gain of £28,000 on an asset which he purchased on 6 April 1961 and sold on 6 April 1996.

Computation of chargeable gain:

$$£28,000 \times \frac{31}{35} = £24,800$$

In using the time-apportionment formula, no period prior to 6 April 1965 can be considered.

Moreover, it should be noted that the taxpayer can make an election under Schedule 2 para 17 to have the gain computed by reference to the market value of the asset at 6 April 1965. The election, which is irrevocable, must be made within two years of the end of the year of assessment in which the gain arises. Such an election cannot increase a loss, or replace a gain by a loss, but may merely cancel the gain. If, however, the taxpayer disposes on or after 6 April 1988 of an asset which he held on 6 April 1965, then the previous rules are inapplicable if he can rebase under s35. This is because, as a consequence of rebasing his allowable expenditure will be deemed to be equivalent to the market value of the asset as of 31 March 1982.

Interaction of indexation and time-apportionment

The case of *Smith* v *Schofield* [1993] STC 268 HL held that the correct method of dealing with the indexation allowance where time-apportionment also applied was to deduct the allowance first before the apportionment was made of the gain to be taxed for the period after 6 April 1965.

Quoted shares or securities held on 6 April 1965

The general rule is that where quoted shares were held on 6 April 1965, the date on which CGT was introduced, the mid-market price on that day is taken as the allowable expenditure in determining the chargeable gain. If, however, either this computation would result in a gain, but a smaller gain or a loss would be created if the original cost price was taken as allowable expenditure, or it would result in a loss, but a smaller loss or a gain would accrue if the original cost price were taken as allowable expenditure, then:

1. If the gain or loss would thus be reduced, the original cost price is substituted as allowable expenditure.
2. If a loss would be converted into a gain, or a gain into a loss, by the substitution of cost price for 6 April 1965 market value, the sale of the shares is treated as an occasion of disposal for no gain and no losses.

The time apportionment basis is *never* used.

Example

Original acquisition cost prior to 6.4.65 £	Market value at 6.4.65 £	Sale proceeds £	Chargeable gains £	Allowable loss £
85	95	105	10	
80	75	90	10	
75	80	70		5
100	90	85		5
100	80	90	no gain – no loss	
80	100	90	no gain – no loss	

'Market value' for this purpose means the mid-market quotation on 6 April 1965. Again, if the quoted shares and securities are disposed of on or after 6 April 1988 and the taxpayer is entitled to rebase under s35, the previous provisions will be inapplicable. The taxpayer's deemed allowable expenditure for a subsequent disposal of the asset will be equivalent to the market value of the asset on 31 March 1982.

19.10 Valuation of disposal consideration

Cash as consideration

The usual rule is very straightforward: where the disponor pays cash for the acquisition of the asset, following a bargain at arm's length, the consideration is the cash, and it is from this that the allowable expenditure is deducted to arrive at the chargeable gain.

Agreed consideration

Where, however, the parties exchange one asset for another, it is the 'agreed consideration' which is the value of the disposal consideration. What the parties agreed was the monetary equivalent: see *Stanton* v *Drayton Investment Ltd* [1982] STC 585. If the parties fail to come to any such agreement, or put an unrealistic valuation out as the 'agreed consideration', presumably market value will be substituted.

See also the decision of the High Court in *Goodbrand* v *Loffland Brothers North Sea Inc* [1997] STC 102, in which it was held that consideration paid in instalments in foreign currency was to be valued as at the date of contract since a subsequent 'loss' in sterling terms due to exchange rate variations did not amount to 'irrecoverable consideration' for the purpose of reduction under what is now s48 TCGA 1992.

Market value

In some cases, however, the actual consideration is disregarded and market value is substituted. In others, market value is taken as the notional consideration, because no consideration was actually charged. And in other cases, the disposal is treated as if it took place for such a consideration that neither a gain nor a loss was incurred. It is these latter cases which are discussed below.

Section 17 provides:

'(1) ... a person's acquisition or disposal of an asset shall be deemed to be for a consideration equal to the market value of the asset ...
a) where he acquires or, as the case may be, disposes of the asset, otherwise than by way of a bargain made at arm's length, and in *particular*:
where he acquires or disposes of it by way of gift or on a transfer into settlement by a settlor or by way of distribution from a company in respect of shares in the company; or
b) where he acquires, or, as the case may be, disposes of the asset:
i) wholly or partly for a consideration that cannot be valued;
ii) in connection with his own or another's loss of office or employment or diminution of emoluments;
iii) or otherwise in consideration for or recognition of his or another's services or past services in any office or employment or of any other service rendered or to be rendered by him or another.'

Really, (a) and (b)(i) are the important cases.

Section 18 provides that where the transferor is *connected with* the transferee there is an irrebuttable presumption that the transaction is otherwise than by way of a bargain at arm's length. Accordingly, market value is inevitably substituted for the actual consideration given in disposals between connected persons.

Connected persons

Section 286 defines who are connected persons:

1. An individual is connected with:
   - husband or wife;

- brother, sister, parents, grandparents, children and grandchildren;
- husband or wife of any relative mentioned above;
- husband's or wife's relatives.

2. A trustee is connected (in that capacity, not as an individual) with the settlor, with any person connected with the settlor and with any company deemed by s286(3A) of the Income and Corporation Taxes Act 1988 to be connected with the settlement.
3. A person is connected with his partner and the partner's spouse, save in commercial deals relating to the partnership assets.
4. A company is connected with another company if one has control of the other or both are controlled by the same person.

If a loss which would otherwise be allowable is incurred on a disposal between two connected persons, it can only be set off against a chargeable gain accruing on another disposal between the same connected persons.

Although husbands and wives are connected persons, the disposal at market value rules of ss17 and 18 do not apply to disposals between them while they are living together. Instead, s58 provides what is known as 'roll-over relief' on the disposal. The transferor is considered to dispose of the asset for a consideration such that neither a gain nor a loss accrues.

Example
H buys an asset for £10,000, and six months later, when it is worth £12,000, he sells it to his wife for £8,000. They are living together at the time. Section 17 does not apply, so the consideration cannot be £12,000; nor is it £8,000, since s44 provides that neither shall any loss be deemed to accrue. Therefore the husband is deemed to dispose of it, and the wife to acquire it for £10,000.

The indexation provisions enable a person who disposes of an asset which was previously acquired from his spouse to elect that the indexation allowance be calculated by reference to the asset's market value at 31 March 1982 if the first spouse owned it at that date. So if the wife chose to dispose of the asset on or after 6 April 1988 then she would still have been entitled to rebase under s35 if the husband had held the asset on 31 March 1982 and she had subsequently acquired it as a consequence of a no-gain/no-loss disposal: see Schedule 3.

When, however, a couple have separated, while they are no longer treated as living together they will nevertheless remain connected persons for CGT purposes until they obtain a decree absolute. The consequences of this can be seen most clearly in *Aspden* v *Hildesley* [1982] STC 206. See Chapter 15, sections 15.6 and 15.7.

Hold over relief – gifts of business assets

The law on hold over relief was substantially altered by s124 FA 1989 (now s67 TCGA). The scheme of the new legislation is to restrict hold over relief to business assets (s165 and Schedule 7 TCGA 1992). General hold over relief for gifts, as introduced by s79 FA 1980, and hold over relief for transfers into and out of settlements, as introduced by s82 FA 1982, are no longer available other than for business assets. Roll-over relief is also available under s260 for gifts of assets on which a liability to inheritance tax is incurred but is not available where the transferee is non-UK resident.

The current legislation

Section 79 FA 1980 (the general hold over provision for gifts between individuals) was repealed with effect from 14 March 1989. However a number of non-business gifts will continue to attract hold over relief in certain circumstances:

1. Section 260(2)(a) TCGA 1992: disposals which are immediately chargeable transfers for Inheritance Tax purposes, but not those which are potentially exempt transfers;
2. Section 260(2)(b) TCGA 1992: transfers exempt under ss24, 26, 27 and 30 of the Inheritance Tax Act 1984, namely those to political parties, for public benefit, to maintenance funds for historic buildings etc, and of designated property;
3. Section 260(2)(c)–(e) TCGA 1992: certain other transfers including transfers by trustees;
4. Conditionally exempt transfers under s30 IHTA 1984, although these already attract a hold over type relief under s258(3) CGTA 1979.

The provisions of s165 TCGA 1992

Section 165 TCGA 1992 continues to permit hold over relief for the transfer of business assets in certain circumstances. It applies to transfers by individuals to persons (individuals or trustees or companies) of:

1. an asset or an interest in an asset used for the purposes of the individual's or his family company's trade; or
2. unquoted shares or securities of a trading company (or the holding company of a trading company) which is the individual's family company.

Section 165 applies if the transfer is otherwise than under a bargain at arm's length, and the relief is available only if the transferee is a person who is resident or ordinarily resident in the United Kingdom. If the donee ceases to be resident, hold over relief is clawed back.

The claim for relief must be made jointly by transferor and transferee unless the transferee is a trustee, in which case only the transferor must elect for hold over relief. The relief may be also apportioned if only part of the asset is used for the relevant purposes or if it has been so used for part only of the period in which it has belonged to the transferor (and therefore the period during which the chargeable gain will have accrued).

Other provisions

There is no relief in respect of gifts to non-resident donees (s166) or to companies controlled by non-resident persons connected with the donor (s167). A charge to CGT arises if the donee is a resident company owned by resident trustees connected with the donor if the donor becomes non-resident (s168). In respect of the disposal of certain assets, the person paying the CGT may elect to pay it by ten equal yearly instalments. Interest is payable if such an election is made.

Appropriations to and from stock in trade

As a general rule, stock in trade will not be susceptible to CGT since income tax will be levied on the profit made on its sale. Section 161 has made provision for two exceptions to this rule:

Appropriations to stock in trade

When a trader appropriates a capital asset to trading stock this is treated as a disposal at market value. The trader can either pay tax on the chargeable gain accruing on the disposal, restricting his potential income tax liability to that on the profit realised on a sale in excess of that figure, or he can avoid paying CGT by bringing the asset into stock at market value *reduced* by the chargeable gain – that is to say, at his CGT base value. Subsequently, of course, he will have to pay income tax on the inherent profit.

Equally, if, on the appropriation, market value is so low that an allowable loss would be created, he can either treat that loss as having been realised on the appropriation and as reducing chargeable gains for that year of assessment in the normal CGT manner, or he can increase the sum at which he would bring it into stock by an amount equal to the loss – again, at his base value for CGT purposes.

Appropriations from stock in trade

In this case, the problem is to determine the asset's base value for CGT purposes. The rule is that the base value is the sum at which the asset will have been brought into the accounts of the trade – market value, under *Sharkey* v *Wernher* (1955) 36 TC 271.

Trust transactions

It will be seen in Chapter 20 that certain transactions involving trustees are treated as disposals (whether or not they would fall under that heading otherwise). Being notional transactions, they must be made for a notional consideration.

19.11 Exemptions and reliefs

Miscellaneous exemptions from CGT

Private motor vehicles: s263
The vehicle must be either commonly used as a private vehicle or suitable to be so used. A road-roller or an omnibus would not be exempt from tax. Since most cars depreciate in value, it should be remembered that, by exempting them, s263 prevents losses from being allowable.

Decorations for valour or gallantry: s268
The gain accruing on the disposal of a medal is not chargeable unless the medal was purchased (eg by a collector).

Foreign currency for personal expenditure: s269
Foreign currency, it will be remembered, unlike sterling, is expressly included in the list of 'assets' in s19(1). A gain made on the reconversion into sterling of left-over currency intended to be used for personal expenditure outside the United Kingdom by the taxpayer or his family is not, however, a chargeable gain. 'Personal expenditure' includes expenditure on the provision or maintenance of a residence outside the United Kingdom.

A foreign currency account with a bank is a chargeable asset, except where it is for the account holder or his family's personal expenditure outside the United Kingdom.

Gambling winnings: s51
Winnings from betting, including winnings on the pools or lotteries, are not chargeable gains. Equally, of course, the taxpayer cannot claim to set his gaming losses against chargeable gains.

Personal injury compensation: s51
Sums paid by way of compensation or damages for any wrong or injury suffered by an individual 'in his person', or 'in his profession or vocation' (eg slander of title) are not chargeable gains. It would not appear that compensation for loss of office falls into this category. Nevertheless, s37(1) provides that one excludes any money or money's worth charged to income tax, or taken into account as a receipt in computing income or profit or gains or losses of the person making the disposal for the purposes of the Income Tax Acts, is excluded from the consideration for the disposal of assets in the computation of the gain.

Section 52(2) further provides:

> 'References ... to sums taken into account for the purposes of income tax shall include references to sums which would be so taken into account but for the fact that any profits or gains of a trade, profession, employment or vocation are not chargeable to income tax or that losses are not allowable for those purposes.'

The effect of this latter provision is to remove from the charge to CGT not only the amount of compensation actually charged on an employee under s148 ICTA 1988 but also the first £30,000 (and any other amount) which is excluded from charge by s188 ICTA 1988.

Debts: s251

As far as the original creditor is concerned, debts, other than 'debts on a security', do not give rise to chargeable gains – or, more likely, allowable losses. Secondhand debts are, however, chargeable assets. Thus when a person purchases a debt at a discount and either sells it on at a profit, or obtains satisfaction of it, he will make a chargeable gain on his 'turn'.

No definition of 'debt on a security' is given. 'Security' itself is defined by s132 as:

> 'includ[ing] any loan stock or similar security whether of the Government of the UK or of any other government, or any public or local authority in the UK or elsewhere, or of any company, and whether secured or unsecured.'

The full phrase has been discussed in *IRC v Cleveley's Investment Trust Co* (1971) 47 TC 300, *Aberdeen Construction Group Ltd v IRC* [1978] STC 127, and *WT Ramsay Ltd v IRC* [1981] STC 174; [1982] AC 300 (HL), and the following conditions would seem to be necessary for a debt to be a debt on a security:

1. It must be marketable, that is capable of being dealt in and therefore assignable.
2. There must be some document or certificate relating to it which must either be, or be similar to, the loan stock of a government, local authority or company, having ordinary terms of repayment, with or without provision for interest.

Although 'security' for s251 purposes is as defined in s132, which deals with conversion of securities, there is nothing in the decided cases to indicate a requirement that the debt has to be a convertible security.

Loans to traders (s253) and qualifying corporate bonds (s254)

Section 253 used to allow qualifying loans to traders to constitute an allowable loss for CGT purposes when they were written off. A qualifying loan existed where the loan was a simple debt rather than a debt on a security, and the borrower was a United Kingdom resident who used the loan for the purposes of his trade.

Section 84 FA 1990, with retrospective effect, inserted s254 into the CGT legislation, which had the effect of widening the definition of 'qualifying loan' to include a debt on a security. Thus, broadly speaking, the lender or security holder can now claim an allowable loss on a debt on a security if the value of the security has become negligible, and if the latest date for redemption of the security has passed and the whole or part of the outstanding amount of the principal of the loan is irrecoverable or has proved to be so. In addition, according to s253(4) a guarantor is accorded such relief in respect of a qualifying loan irrespective of whether it constitutes a simple debt, a debt, or a security.

Section 254 became necessary when debts on a security issued by a company (ie the company was the borrower) came within the definition of 'qualifying corporate bonds' for which no capital gains tax loss relief was available under the normal 'debt on a security' provisions. If the value of that security becomes negligible or irrecoverable then relief for the loss is allowed under s254. For the definition of 'qualifying corporate bonds' see s117 TCGA 1992, as amended following the introduction of the 'loan relationships' provisions of the Finance Act 1996.

A loss is not allowable if the borrower and lender are a married couple or a company within the same group. In addition the lender must not have assigned his rights in respect of the loan. For this purpose companies have therefore had to structure loans on the basis of their being a debt on the security in order to qualify for loss relief.

Section 83 FA 1990 inserted s253(6)–(8) into the CGT legislation; this provides that if the guarantor (or if the guarantor is a member of a group, a fellow member of the group) wholly or partially recovers the debt on which relief has been claimed, then this will constitute a chargeable gain on which CGT is payable up to the amount of the loss.

Private residences

Section 223 provides that no part of a gain accruing to an individual which is attributable to the disposal of, or of an interest in, either:

1. a dwelling house which is, or has at any time in his period of ownership been, his only or main residence, or
2. land (up to 0.5 hectare in extent) which he has for his own occupation and enjoyment with that residence as its garden or grounds (where the house is substantial, a greater amount of ground will be permitted)

is to be a chargeable gain if the property has been his only or main residence for all but the last three years of his period of ownership.

'Dwelling house'

There have been a number of cases taken before the courts to determine what amounts to a 'dwelling house'. In *Batey* v *Wakefield* 55 TC 550, the Court of Appeal held that the phrase could include not only the principal house but also buildings which were separate from it but appurtenant to it and occupied for its purposes. In *Markey* v *Sanders* [1987] STC 256, Walton J relied on the earlier case as authority that there were two conditions which had to be satisfied before an outbuilding qualified for relief. The first was that the occupation of the building in question increased the enjoyment by the taxpayer of the main building. This, he said was necessary but not sufficient. The second was that the other building had to be 'very closely adjacent' to the main house. Again, this was necessary but not sufficient. In *Williams* v *Merrylees* [1987] STC 445, on the other hand, Vinelott J said that he found it very difficult to spell two separate tests out of the decision of the Court of Appeal in *Batey*. He thought that the Court only intended to lay down a single test:

> 'What one is looking for is the entity which in fact constitutes the residence of the taxpayer.' (per Fox LJ in *Batey*),

but that in coming to a decision on this matter, the propinquity of the various outbuildings was an important factor to be weighed.

However, in *Lewis v Rook* [1992] STC 171 Balcombe LJ in the Court of Appeal cast doubt on the test laid down in *Batey v Wakefield*:

> 'To seek to identify the taxpayer's residence may lead to confusion because where, as here, the dwelling house forms part of a small estate, it is all too easy to consider the estate as his residence and from that to conclude that all the buildings on the estate are part of his residence. In so far as some of the statements made in *Batey v Wakefield* suggest that one must first identify the residence, they must, in my judgment, be considered to have been made per incuriam.' (at p177).

He preferred a test similar to that laid down by Buckley LJ in *Methuen-Cambell v Walters* [1979] QB 525 at 543. This test is much stricter and requires the ancillary building to be appurtenant to, and within the curtilage of, the main house. This, according to Balcombe LJ, '... coincides with the close proximity test to which the other cases refer'.

It also, in his view, avoids the problem that the 'permitted area' of grounds exempt within s222(2) is limited to 0.5 hectare:

> '... it does seem to me remarkable that a separate lodge or cottage which by any reasonable measurement must be outside the permitted area can nevertheless be part of the entity of the dwelling house.'

It must be stressed, however, that each case is to be decided on its own particular facts. In that of *Honour v Norris* [1992] STC 304 the taxpayer unsuccessfully attempted to include flats in the same square, which had been occasionally used as accommodation for family members, as a composite part of his main residence. There seems little logic in some of the cases being able to include separated buildings of an estate with employee accommodation as part of the main residence without laying down sufficient guidelines to follow in later cases such as *Honour v Norris*.

Main residence

If the house was not the taxpayer's only or main residence for *all* his period of ownership, then time-apportionment takes place, and the fraction of the gain which is not chargeable is the fraction:

$$\frac{\text{period of only or main residence (including in any event the last 36 months)}}{\text{total length of ownership}}$$

Certain periods of absence are treated as periods when the property was the individual's only or main residence, as long as there is a period in which it was actually such both before and after each period. These are:

1. any period of up to three years (or aggregate of periods); and,
2. any length when he worked in an office or employment all the duties of which were performed outside the United Kingdom; and,
3. periods in aggregate of up to four years throughout which he was prevented from living in the house because of the situation of his work or because his employer reasonably imposed a condition that he reside elsewhere in order to secure the effective performance of his duties.

If any such period is claimed, the individual cannot also claim in respect of the same period that his actual only or main residence was elsewhere, and that he is not chargeable on the gain accruing on that residence either. It was previously feared that the Inland Revenue might claim that if a period specified above is exceeded (for example, the taxpayer is absent for reasons not falling within (2) or (3) for three years and two months) then he loses the entire relief and is not merely restricted to claiming the maximum. However, the Revenue's position is set out in paragraph 13 of an agreed press release issued on 10 March 1983 by the Institute of Chartered Accountants of England and Wales, relaying the outcome of a meeting with the Inland Revenue. It is confirmed that if any of these periods is exceeded then exemption still applies up to the relevant proportions, and only the excess period does not qualify for exemption.

If a person has two residences (eg a flat in town and a country mansion), both of which could qualify, he may nominate one or other for exemption as being his main residence even though he spends relatively little time there. The only restrictions are that both must actually be residences of his, and that, unless the election is made within two years of the period for which exemption is claimed, the inspector is given power to decide which *in fact* was his main residence for the period. If the taxpayer disagrees with the Revenue's assessment, he may appeal to the General Commissioners: see *Griffin* v *Craig-Harvey* [1994] STC 54.

A married couple living together enjoy only one private residence relief.

See also *Goodwin* v *Curtis* [1996] STC 1146, where short occupancy of a house before sale indicated a primary intention to realise profit from the ownership of the property and private residence relief was denied.

Business use

If part of the property is exclusively used for business purposes, the gain has to be apportioned between the private and business parts. The Inland Revenue has addressed the matter in the *Tax Bulletin* Issue 12 at page 148, indicating that s224(1) only applies to cases where the business use has continued throughout the entire period of ownership so that no relief is due on the business portion. In other cases a just and reasonable basis is all that can be applied. It is apparently the view of the

Revenue that such apportionment must be made according to the respective values of the two parts; it could be argued, though, that any apportionment should be made on an area basis. If, however, a room is used for multiple purposes, no apportionment will have to be made. Correspondingly, in cases where the taxpayer has set aside particular rooms for his business, any gain attributable to those rooms may be postponed by a claim for roll-over relief under s152 CGTA 1979. The interaction of the relief for the replacement of business assets and private residence exemption can sometimes give rise to difficulties, though: see *Todd* v *Mudd* [1987] STC 141, discussed in 'Replacement of business assets', below.

Private residence occupied under the terms of a settlement

This is a special relief which should be noted. Section 225 provides that where trustees sell settled property which during their ownership has been used as the only or main residence of a person entitled to occupy it under the terms of the settlement, they and the beneficiary may together give a joint notice that ss222 and 223 should apply to exempt the gain or part of the gain. *Sansom* v *Peay* [1976] STC 494 gave a wide meaning to 'entitled to occupy under the terms of the settlement', Brightman J holding that one determines entitlement retrospectively; if trustees exercise a *power* to permit a beneficiary to reside in the property, that is sufficient for the exemption to apply. What the case settled was the question of whether it was sufficient for a beneficiary to be in occupation with the trustees' permission rather than by reason of a specific right to occupy under the terms of the trust.

Tangible movable property: s262

A gain accruing on the disposal of an asset which is tangible movable property is not a chargeable gain if the amount or value of the consideration for the disposal does not exceed £6,000. If a person sells such an asset at a loss for a consideration of less than £6,000, that loss is restricted by deeming the asset to have been sold for £6,000.

Example
Thomas buys an asset for £10,000. He sells it for £5,000. His actual loss is £5,000, but s262(3) deems it to have been sold for £6,000 and restricts the allowable loss to £4,000.

If a person sells an asset which is tangible movable property for more than £6,000, tapering relief may be available. The section provides that one may exclude from any chargeable gain so much of it as exceeds five-thirds of the difference between the amount or value of the consideration and £6,000.

Examples
1. Thomas buys an asset for £1,000 and sells it for £8,000. It is tangible movable property.

	£
Sale proceeds	8,000
Purchase price	1,000
Actual gain	£7,000

Excess of consideration over £6,000 = £2,000 × ⁵⁄₃ = £3,333

Only the £3,333 is brought into charge as a chargeable gain. The actual gain of £7,000 is ignored.

2. Thomas buys an asset for £6,500 and sells it for £6,600. The asset is tangible movable property.

	£
Sale proceeds	6,600
Purchase price	6,500
Actual gain	£100

Excess of consideration over £6,000 = £600 × ⁵⁄₃ = £1,000

Clearly, in this case excluding so much of the gain as exceeds five-thirds of this excess of the consideration over £6,000 accomplishes nothing, so the gain remains £100.

Works of art: s258
Gains which would accrue when works of art are given to an organisation falling within s26(2) IHTA 1984 are not chargeable gains if the Treasury gives a direction in relation to the asset under s26(1). The Treasury may, in this sort of case, require an undertaking to be given that the asset will be properly maintained and preserved, and that reasonable access will be given to the public.

Gifts to charities: s257
Where a disposal to a charity is made otherwise than by way of a bargain at arm's length, roll-over relief is afforded.

Disposals by charities: s256
Gains accruing to charities applicable and applied for charitable purposes only are not chargeable gains. If, however, assets held on charitable trusts cease to be so held, the trustees are deemed to dispose of and reacquire the assets at their market value, realising any inherent gains and bringing them into charge.

Miscellaneous CGT reliefs

Replacement of business assets: ss152–158
Where a person carrying on a trade or business sells a qualifying asset which has been used throughout its period of ownership for the purposes of the trade, and

buys new qualifying assets with the consideration, roll-over relief is afforded as follows:

1. He is treated as disposing of the old asset for a sum equal to its allowable expenditure; and
2. The consideration given for the new asset is treated as reduced by the rolled-over gain. The new assets must be purchased within three years after or one year before the disposal of the old one if s152 relief to be given.

As found in *Campbell Connelly & Co Ltd v Barnett* [1994] STC 50, the new asset must be taken into use 'on acquisition': that means without unavoidable delay and without the asset having been let at any time since acquisition.

The assets have to fall within one of the following classes:

1. land and buildings;
2. plant and fixed machinery (see *Williams v Evans* [1982] STC 498);
3. ships;
4. aircraft, spacecraft, satellites and space stations;
5. goodwill;
6. hovercraft;
7. EU milk quota premium rights.

There is no restriction on the relief for disposing of assets of one category and replacing them with assets of another category.

Relief is also available for assets used by a person's 'personal company' (formerly called a family company) as provided by s157, as amended by Schedule 7 FA 1993.

Example
James bought freehold premises for the purposes of trading for £110,000. Later he moved into new premises, for which he paid £450,000, and sold the old premises for £380,000. He can elect to roll-over the gain of £270,000 into the new premises or other assets, whose acquisition cost for the purposes of s32 will then be reduced to £180,000.

If he were to sell the new premises for £600,000 and move into new premises costing £750,000, he could do the same again, rolling over the gain of £420,000 into the new premises, whose acquisition cost would be reduced to £330,000.

Where a person carries on more than one trade, the gain on the sale of a qualifying asset used for the purposes of one trade can be rolled over into a new qualifying asset purchased for the other. If the trader only uses part of the consideration received in purchasing new assets, the relief is curtailed, and he is treated as using the non-gain part first (s153). The effect of this is to charge tax on the gain up to the amount not reinvested in qualifying assets.

Example
John buys premises from which to trade for £350,000. Some years later he sells

them for £600,000, buying new premises for £500,000. He can only roll over £500,000 - £350,000 = £150,000 of the gain into the new premises and must pay CGT on the other £100,000. His new premises then have a base value of £500,000 - £150,000 = £350,000 – his original asset's purchase price.

See *Todd v Mudd* [1987] STC 141 where although reinvestment of the required full amount took place, the taxpayer did not, as a matter of property law, have the full 100 per cent interest in the qualifying business proportion of the premises into which the reinvestment was made.

In the case of *Watton* v *Tippett* [1996] STC 101 the taxpayer claimed, following a disposal of part of an asset, that there was an entitlement to roll-over relief under s252 against the purchase price of the original complete asset. It was held that there was no 'new asset' distinct from the part disposed of, to qualify for relief under the section.

Under the requirements of self assessment s141 Finance Act 1996 introduced a new s153A into the provisions. The taxpayer making a chargeable gain is able to make a declaration, when submitting a tax return for self assessment, to the effect that the proceeds from the sale of the chargeable asset are to be reinvested in a qualifying asset within the three-year time limit. Such a declaration remains in force until it is withdrawn, superseded by an actual claim to roll-over relief or (for companies) on the fourth anniversary of the accounting period in which the disposal occurred or (for individuals, partnerships and others) on the third 31 January following the year of assessment in which the disposal occurred.

Transfer of business on retirement: ss163, 164 and Schedule 6
The provisions are contained in ss163 and 164 and Schedule 6, and give the taxpayer full relief on gains up to a maximum of £250,000, and 50 per cent relief on gains between £250,000 and £1,000,000. To obtain retirement relief the taxpayer must attain the age of 50 (or retire under that age on the grounds of ill health (s163(1)), and make a material disposal of business assets. The minimum qualifying age was reduced from 55 to 50 for disposals after 28 November 1995.

The definition of 'business assets' is further set out in s163(2). There is a disposal of business assets whenever a taxpayer disposes of:

1. the whole or part of a business (s163(2)(a));
2. one or more assets which were in use in the business at the time the business ceased to be carried on (s163(2)(b));
3. shares or securities in the company (s163(2)(c)).

For each of the above possible scenarios in which a disposal may qualify for retirement relief, s163 sets out the conditions which must be satisfied in each case, depending on whether it amounts to a disposal of the whole or part of the business, the disposal of assets in conjunction with the cessation of business or the disposal of shares or securities. In addition to these, s164 provides relief where an employee disposes of assets (directors of personal trading companies qualify under s163). Disposals by trustees of a family trust will qualify where the relevant beneficiary would qualify if disposing as an individual. Assets owned by an individual and in use by a partnership may qualify for retirement relief when disposed of.

The definition of 'material disposal' is further set out in s163(3), (4), (5). There is a material disposal of:

1. the whole or part of the business if the individual making the disposal has owned it throughout a period of at least one year ending with the date of the disposal (s163(3));
2. assets on the cessation of a business if the individual making the disposal owns the business and, on or before the date on which the business ceased, he has owned the business for at least a year (s163(4));

    Note: if claiming relief under s163(2)(a), it is not adequate merely to dispose of business assets – there must be a disposal of the *business*: *McGregor* v *Adcock* [1977] STC 206. Even in a case where retirement relief is being claimed for the gain realised on the disposal of assets under s164(6) and (7), there must also have been a prior disposal of the business: see *Clarke* v *Mayo* [1994] STC 570. In this case the taxpayer was making a disposal of his 25% interest in an asset – s164(6) – and linking that to 'an associated disposal of assets' – s164(6)(b), as defined in s164(7) on his disposal of the shares in the family company. The Inland Revenue's argument was that a gap of one month between the disposal of the property and the company ceasing to trade, made the relief ineffective. However, the court ruled that the disposal of the property did qualify, after considering the implications of 'immediately before' in s164(7).
3. shares and securities in a company owning a business, when the individual disposing of the shares has owned them for a period of at least one year; or shares and securities in the individual's 'personal company' (which replaces the existing 'family company' concept – Schedule 7 FA 1993 – and is a company in which an individual can exercise at least 5 per cent of the voting rights) (s163(5)). The individual must also be a 'full-time working officer or employee' of the personal company (Schedule 7 para 1(4) FA 1993). However, in *Plumbly* v *Spencer* [1996] STC (SCD) 295 (a reported decision of the Special Commissioners), it was held that the disposal of land used by the 'personal company' of the taxpayer could not attract retirement relief on the grounds that s163(2)(b) does not extend to assets not owned by the company.

Amount of retirement relief available to the taxpayer

The amount of relief that is available to the taxpayer is dependent on his period of ownership of the business. The maximum relief of £250,000 plus 50 per cent of (£1,000,000 - £250,000) is available if the taxpayer has owned the business (and not the asset) for ten or more years: Schedule 6 para 13 FA 1993. The maximum amount of retirement relief is therefore £625,000.

If the taxpayer has owned the business for less than ten years he gets a percentage of the maximum relief available on retirement. The length of time that the taxpayer held the business before the material disposal of the business asset has to be determined, and then the percentage of the ten-year period which that time would constitute. The percentage of maximum relief which the taxpayer can claim is then clear.

Examples
1. If a taxpayer held a business for three years before the material disposal he would obtain

    $^{3}/_{10} \times 100 = 30\%$

    of the maximum retirement relief that was available.

2. X, the taxpayer, retires on his 65th birthday, having owned his business for four years at the date of disposal. His gains attributable to the disposal of his business constitute £370,000. To calculate the gains for which he can claim retirement relief one needs to determine the percentage of relief to which he is entitled. This is four-tenths, ie 40 per cent. Thus the maximum bands of relief which he can claim are:

    £0 – ($^{4}/_{10}$ × £250,000) at full relief, and
    ($^{4}/_{10}$ × £250,000) – ($^{4}/_{10}$ × £1,000,000) at half relief,

    with the result that his bands of relief are:

    £0 – £100,000 at full relief, and
    £100,000 – £400,000 at half relief.

    So the taxpayer receives retirement relief for:

	£
$^{4}/_{10}$ × £250,000	100,000
½ × £(370,000 – 100,000)	135,000

    His total retirement relief is £235,000, and the gains charged to tax (£370,000 – £235,000) is £135,000.

Roll-over relief on re-investment of gains on shares
Schedule 7 FA 1993 introduced a new form of roll-over relief under ss164A–M TCGA 1992 for disposals of 'qualifying investments' after 16 March 1993. A qualifying investment is a holding of 5 per cent of the eligible shares. The relief is akin to the replacement of business assets relief (s152 TCGA 1992 – see 'Replacement of business assets', above) and allows the charge on gains on the sale of shares in unquoted trading companies to be deferred and rolled-over into similar 'qualifying investments'. The same time limits apply as for s152 relief. The

exclusion of property development companies as qualifying investments was removed from 29 November 1994.

Finance Act 1996 provisions extended the re-investment relief to include gains arising when a disposal of a 'qualifying corporate bond (QCB)' crystallises a capital gains tax charge on an asset rolled over into a QCB, for example on a reorganisation where the QCB was given in exchange for the shares disposed of. Under s115 TCGA 1992, gains made on the disposal of a 'qualifying corporate bond' are exempt from capital gains tax.

Relief for trading losses
Under s72 FA 1991, relief under s380 ICTA 1988 for trading losses is extended to include not only general income but also the trader's capital gains whether derived from his business activities or not. The loss may be set off against gains of the year and following year insofar as it is not capable of being relieved against income. A claim under this section should not be made where the gains are covered by the CGT annual exempt amount, as the loss is taken before the exemption is applied. The business must still be carried on in the year of claim.

19.12 Partnership

Section 60 provides that where two or more persons carry on a trade or business in partnership, tax in respect of chargeable gains accruing to them on the disposal of any partnership assets shall be assessed and charged on them separately, and any partnership dealings shall be treated as dealings by the partners and not by the firm as such. Each partner has a fractional share in each partnership asset and it is this which he disposes of when a partnership asset is sold; accordingly, the appropriate fraction of the gain or loss will be attributed to him.

In dealings between the partners themselves two points arise:

1. Does a change in partnership relationship involve acquisitions and disposals by partners of part of their interests in the underlying assets of the partnership? The answer is that this depends on the construction of the new agreement. Unless otherwise specified, a partner takes an interest in the capital assets of the partnership in accordance with the profit-sharing ratios.
2. What is the consideration for the disposal? The answer is that this may be either the actual consideration paid (which may be nil) or market value. It is to be remembered that partners are connected persons within s286(4), but that subsection does not treat partners as connected 'in relation to acquisitions or disposals of partnership assets pursuant to bona fide commercial arrangements'.

The Revenue practice set out in a statement of practice dated 17 January 1975 (which is most important in this area) is that where there is a change in profit-sharing ratios (including that occurring on the admission of a new partner) the disposal will be treated as taking place for a consideration giving rise to neither a gain nor a loss. A partner who takes a smaller percentage of the profits will carry forward a smaller proportion of allowable expenditure; a partner whose share increases will carry forward a greater amount.

19.13 Company transactions

Disposals and acquisitions between a company and its shareholders

The allotment and issue of shares

A company never owns the shares which it issues, and for that reason it does not 'dispose' of them when it allots them to shareholders: *Kirby* v *Thorn EMI* [1987] STC 621. Nevertheless, that will be an acquisition by the shareholder, and the question of whether he brings in as allowable expenditure the market value of the shares or the actual consideration given depends on whether the shares were issued by way of a bargain at arm's length: see *Harrison* v *Nairn Williamson Ltd* [1976] STC 67 (CA).

For some years this rule was taken advantage of by companies involving themselves in 'reverse *Harrison* v *Nairn Williamson*' schemes. The company would issue shares at a nominal price, far below market value, and by reason of the predecessor of s17 the shareholder would be deemed to acquire the shares at market value; since, however, there was no disposal, no CGT could be charged on the company. This scheme was ousted by s17(2), which provided that s17(1) was only to apply where there was a corresponding disposal *or* consideration in money, or money's worth, at least equal to the market value of the shares.

Alteration of share rights

Rights attaching to shares may be altered without the consent of the owner. A common practice is to use a special resolution altering such rights as a means of transferring value from one set of shares, and thus from one shareholder, to another. This sort of transaction is caught by the value-shifting provisions of s29(2) (see section 19.5, Chargeable assets'). *Floor* v *Davis* [1978] STC 436 shows that:

1. A person can exercise control for the purposes of s29(2) by refraining from voting, as well as by voting.
2. Section 29(2) can apply where several persons together have, and exercise, control.

Capital distributions by the company

If a chargeable asset is distributed by the company in respect of its shares, the shareholder acquires the asset, and the company disposes of it, for CGT purposes, at market value.

Section 122(1) sets out the basic rule for capital distributions:

'Where a person receives ... any capital distribution from the company, he is treated as if he had, in consideration of that capital distribution, disposed of an interest in the shares.'

So, each time, the individual makes a part disposal of his shares. 'Capital distribution' is defined by s122(5)(b) as:

'any distribution from a company, including a distribution in the course of dissolving or winding up the company, in money or money's worth except a distribution which, in the hands of the recipient, constitutes income for the purposes of income tax'.

In most cases such a distribution will be liable to income tax in the recipient's hands. The exception is where the company is in liquidation and the liquidator makes an in specie distribution to the members.

If the amount distributed is small compared with the value of the shares in respect of which it is distributed, s122(2) permits the inspector to postpone the charge to CGT by deducting the distribution from the recipient's allowable expenditure on the shares.

Where there is a bonus issue or a rights issue, any new shares allotted to the shareholders are treated as being acquired when the original shares were acquired at a price equal to the cost of the original shares plus (if any) the sum paid for the new holding: s127.

Where *no* new consideration is given, this rule would appear to continue to apply after the introduction of the indexation allowance in FA 1982. Where consideration is given for the acquisition of the new holding, however, that consideration is treated as expenditure incurred when it was paid, for the purposes of the indexation allowance.

Reorganisation of share capital

Where shares of an existing company are acquired by another company in exchange for shares in the company that is taking over, there is no acquisition or disposal by the shareholders of the existing company: s135. Instead, s127 applies to treat the new shareholding to have been acquired at the date when the original holding was acquired, and for the consideration paid for that holding. Accordingly, the tax is postponed until the new holding is disposed of for cash.

Sale of shares by shareholder

Prior to 1982 shares of the same class held by the same person were treated as one asset, the allowable expenditure in respect of which was the aggregate of the expenditure on all the shares. Accordingly, each time some of the shares were sold there was a part disposal.

This arrangement clearly could not survive the introduction of the indexation allowance, which originally computed the allowable expenditure on each asset by reference to the rise in the Retail Prices Index over all but the first year of the period of ownership, and elaborate provisions were enacted, particularly in relation to the identification of securities. The FA 1985 made a number of detailed amendments to these provisions to take account of the fact that the 12-month qualifying period no longer applies. They are complex, and are outside the scope of this work, except to say that pooling arrangements were reintroduced for shares acquired after 6 April 1982 (or 1 April 1982 for companies): Schedule 2 para 4 TGCA 1992.

Capital gains of companies

This has already been dealt with in Chapter 16, section 16.3. The rule is that corporation tax is imposed at 33 per cent on a company's chargeable gains or at the small companies rate if appropriate. It will be noticed that there will be a double charge on the capital gains of a company:

1. Gains in the hands of a company are charged to corporation tax.
2. Those gains will increase the value of a shareholder's shares. When he sells them, he will be charged to CGT on the rise in value as well.

Correspondingly, if the company makes a capital distribution, that will give rise to a charge to corporation tax on the capital gain accruing or deemed to accrue to the company. The individual shareholder will be liable to income tax under Schedule F on the value of that distribution, while the company will pay ACT: s209 ICTA 1988.

20

Death and Settled Property in CGT

20.1 Death

20.2 Variations of dispositions made on death

20.3 Losses unused at the date of death

20.4 Settled property: introduction

20.5 'Settled property'

20.6 'Trustees'

20.7 Gifts in settlement

20.8 Sales of trust assets

20.9 Persons becoming absolutely entitled to settled property and the settlement comes to an end

20.10 Termination of a life interest where the settlement continues

20.11 Disposal by a beneficiary of his interest

20.12 The foreign element of trusts in CGT

20.1 Death

When a person dies there will obviously be many assets in his estate which have increased in value during his lifetime. Those assets will be transferred to the personal representatives and thence to the beneficiaries under his will, or the trustees of trusts created by the will, or in accordance with the law of intestacy.

Originally, the legislation was designed to bring into charge all that inherent gain. The personal representatives then took at the market value at the date of death, and roll-over relief was afforded when they distributed the estate. All this changed in 1971, when the charge to tax on death was abolished, but the personal representatives still take at the market value at the date of death and roll-over relief is given to the beneficiaries.

Section 62 of the Taxation of Chargeable Gains Act 1992, which consolidates those provisions, states:

> '1) For the purposes of this Act, the assets of which a deceased person was competent to dispose:
> a) are deemed to be acquired on his death by the personal representatives or other person on whom they devolve for a consideration equal to their market value at the date of the death; but
> b) shall not be deemed to be disposed of by him on his death (whether or not they were the subject of a testamentary disposition).'

Since capital gains tax (CGT) is a tax on disposals (even if they be notional), when there is no disposal there is no charge. Accordingly, all the gains and losses which are inherent in the testator's assets are wiped out on his death.

Section 62(10) further elaborates on the assets of which the deceased was competent to dispose: in short, they include all assets of which he could have disposed by will, together with the severable share in any assets to which he was beneficially entitled as a joint tenant – and thus of which he could not, without prior severance, have so disposed.

If the personal representatives sell assets (in order to pay off the testator's debts, for example), CGT is charged only on the increase in the value of the assets since the date of death or, more accurately, on the excess of the consideration received on the disposal of the asset over its value at that time.

If the composition of the personal representatives changes – for instance, because one dies – no charge to tax occurs when the new ones vest the assets in themselves, since s62(3) provides that personal representatives shall be treated as a single and continuing body of persons, having the deceased's residence, ordinary residence and domicile at the date of death. The individual constituents of that body are thus ignored, and their replacement becomes irrelevant for the purposes of CGT.

When a person acquires an asset 'as a legatee', roll-over relief is afforded (s62(4)); the personal representatives make no chargeable gain, and their acquisition of the asset is treated as that of the legatee. Section 62(7) defines 'legatee', which:

> 'includes any person taking under a testamentary disposition or on an intestacy or partial intestacy, whether he takes beneficially or as trustee'.

It also includes a person taking under a donatio mortis causa, and thus a person making a disposal by donatio mortis causa is also not deemed to make a gain under s16(1)(a): s62(5).

Example
A dies in May 1993, leaving his house which he bought for £50,000 in 1984 to his brother, B. At A's death the house is worth £70,000. His executors are D and E, two of the partners of a firm of solicitors. After six months, E retires and F takes his place. At this time, the house is worth £75,000. On 6 June 1996, when it is worth £85,000, D and F assent to the property vesting in B, who sells it shortly after for £92,000.

When A died, D and E, the personal representatives, were deemed to acquire the house for £70,000, but A was not deemed to dispose of it, so no chargeable gain could accrue (whether or not the house was A's only or main residence). When E retired and the property was transferred by the personal representatives to D and F, the person transferring and the person acquiring were deemed to be the same person, so no disposal could occur for CGT and no charge to tax could arise. When D and F assented to the house vesting in B, s62(4) treated that as a disposal on which no chargeable gain accrued, and no tax was payable. The original personal representatives' acquisition was assumed to be B's, so he was treated as having acquired the asset on A's death for £70,000 and having owned it ever since. When he sells it for £92,000, he thus is deemed to realise a chargeable gain of £22,000 – subject always to the indexation allowance which has accrued since A's death in May 1993.

20.2 Variations of dispositions made on death

Section 62(6) TCGA 1992 provides that, within two years of the date of death, a legatee who would take beneficially can, by an instrument in writing, disclaim or redirect the benefit he would take under the will or on intestacy (or even by survivorship) without there being a charge to CGT.

A 'variation' occurs where the legatee chooses who should take in his place, and a 'disclaimer' is a refusal by a person to take a benefit under the will. This will then fall into residue. The only consideration a person can receive for making a variation or disclaimer is the making of a variation or disclaimer by another beneficiary.

The variation or disclaimer is treated not as a disposal but as a testamentary disposition effected by the deceased, although this is only for the purposes of s62. If, therefore, a beneficiary uses s62(6) to settle an asset on trust for A for life, remainder to himself absolutely, while CGT will be avoided on the creation of the settlement, the original beneficiary will, on A's death, be treated as the disponor to whom the property reverts, with the result that s73(1)(b) will apply, limiting the relief then available to roll-over relief; there will be no 'free uplift' under s73(1)(a). For s62(6) to apply, an election in writing must be sent to the Revenue within six months of the execution of the instrument.

A similar relief exists for Inheritance Tax in ss17 and 142 of the Inheritance Tax Act 1984, but no such provision exists for income tax; any deed of variation will be deemed to have been made by the beneficiary, not the deceased. Thus, where the beneficiary wishes to benefit his infant children by a variation, s660A of the Income and Corporation Taxes Act 1988 must be considered. This may not be the case on a disclaimer where the reallocation of the benefit occurs by operation of law: see the House of Lords decision in *Marshall* v *Kerr* [1994] 3 WLR 299, where property settled by a legatee following a variation of the deceased's intentions was held to be a settlement created by the legatee and not a settlement made by the deceased, who had been non-United Kingdom domiciled.

20.3 Losses unused at the date of death

One of the duties of the personal representatives will be to pay any outstanding liability of the testator to CGT in respect of gains accruing on disposals during his lifetime. Section 62(2) permits them to deduct from those gains any allowable losses sustained by the deceased during the year of assessment of death, and other losses carried forward may also be so set off. The subsection also permits allowable losses to be rolled back and deducted from chargeable gains accruing in the three years of assessment preceding that of death. Losses which have been carried forward cannot, however, then be rolled back under s62(2).

20.4 Settled property: introduction

Sections 68–79 provide a special regime for the capital gains taxation of settled property and settlements. Broadly, there are three potential occasions of charge in respect of settled property:

1. when a settlor makes a transfer into settlement;
2. when the trustees dispose of an asset to an unconnected person; and
3. when a person becomes absolutely entitled as against the trustees to settled property.

Two events do not, however, give rise to a charge to CGT: where a beneficiary disposes of his interest in settled property *even* for full consideration, and when (1) or (3) above occur on death.

It should be noted that when trustees are liable to pay GCT they will ordinarily pay tax at their marginal rate of income tax. However, under s5 the trustees of both an accumulation and maintenance trust and a discretionary trust are required to pay CGT at the rate applicable to trusts under s686 ICTA 1988, which for 1997–98 totals 34 per cent (see Chapter 13, Trust Income, above.)

However, according to s77, if the settlor retains an interest in the settlement then the chargeable gains of the trust are treated as accruing to him. Consequently he has to pay tax on those chargeable gains at his marginal rate of income tax. Section 77(3) states that a settlor retains an interest in the property if any property and/or income of the settlement may become applicable for the benefit of himself or his spouse, or, if the settlor or his spouse may directly or indirectly enjoy the benefit of any property in the settlement.

Note: these provisions apply to all settlements unless the settlor and his spouse are both deceased.

20.5 'Settled property'

Section 68 provides:

> 'Settled property' means any property held in trust, other than property to which s60 above [nominees and bare trustees] applies.'

Section 60 defines nominee property (which is not settled property for the purposes of the Act) thus:

> '(1) In relation to assets held by a person as nominee for another person, or as trustee for another person absolutely entitled as against the trustee, or for any person who would be so entitled but for being an infant or other person under disability (or for two or more persons who are or would be jointly so entitled), this Act shall apply as if the property were vested in, and the acts of the nominee or trustee in relation to the assets were the acts of, the person or persons for whom he is the nominee or trustee (acquisitions from or disposals to that person or persons being disregarded accordingly).
> (2) It is hereby declared that references in this Act to any asset held by a person as trustee for another person absolutely entitled as against the trustee are references to a case where that other person has the exclusive right, subject only to satisfying any outstanding charge, lien or other right of the trustees to resort to the asset for payment of duty, taxes, costs or other outgoings to direct how that asset shall be dealt with.'

It will be noticed that, throughout the Act, the emphasis is on the assets being 'settled property' rather than being assets held in a settlement. It will be shown below that it is possible, in the same settlement, for some assets to be settled property and some assets to be, for want of a better phrase, nominee property.

The effect of s60(1) is that nominee property is *not* settled property, so:

1. One treats all disposals by the trustees as disposals by the beneficiary, and the beneficiary is charged to CGT under the usual rules set out in Chapter 19 above, including the rule giving him exemption from tax on his first £6,500 of chargeable gains.
2. Any disposal by the trustee to the beneficiary is ignored, because the beneficiary is already notionally in possession of the asset.

Difficulties remain however, as to:

1. when one person is absolutely entitled as against the trustees;
2. when one person would be absolutely entitled 'but for being an infant';
3. when persons are 'jointly' so entitled.

Looking at each in turn:

'... absolutely entitled as against the trustees'

Clearly, infants and persons of unsound mind are *not* absolutely entitled, because they cannot give a good receipt for the assets, and so cannot direct the trustees how to deal with the assets. This, in fact, is expressly acknowledged by s60(1): 'or would be but for being an infant or other person under disability'. The section avoids the problem by providing that the same consequences shall follow in such a case as would apply if they were absolutely entitled. There are further problems, though, in deciding when a person is someone who would be absolutely entitled but for being an infant etc – see below.

Section 60(2) describes absolute entitlement, saying, inter alia, that a person can be absolutely entitled even though the trustees have a right to resort to the asset for the payment of 'other outgoings'. The Court of Session in *IRC* v *Cochrane's Executors* [1974] STC 335 held that 'other outgoings' must be construed eiusdem generis with 'duty, taxes [and] costs', and therefore did not extend to payments of a beneficial nature, such as annuities.

Section 60(1) only says 'absolutely entitled as against the trustees'. It does not say 'absolutely *and beneficially* entitled as against the trustees'. Accordingly, a separate set of trustees (who may even be the same individuals) can be so entitled: *Hoare Trustees* v *Gardner, Hart* v *Briscoe* [1979] Ch 110. But when is it that this happens? The rule is that the trustees become so entitled when other trustees make a disposal to, or create, a separate settlement. Nevertheless, distinguishing between a sub-trust and a new settlement has much perplexed the courts, for example in *Roome* v *Edwards* [1981] STC 96 and *Bond* v *Pickford* [1983] STC 517. In the former case, Lord Wilberforce said:

> 'There are a number of obvious indicia which may help to show whether a settlement, or a settlement separate from another settlement, exists. One might expect to find separate and defined property, separate trusts, and separate trustees. One might also expect to find a separate disposition bringing the separate settlement into existence. These indicia may be helpful, but they are not decisive. For example, a single disposition, eg a will with a single set of trustees, may create what are clearly separate settlements, relating to different properties, in favour of different beneficiaries, and conversely, separate trusts may arise in what is clearly a single settlement, eg where the settled property is divided into shares.
>
> I think the question whether a particular set of facts amounts to a settlement should be approached by asking what a person, with knowledge of the legal context of the word under established doctrine and applying this knowledge in a practical and common-sense manner to the facts under examination would conclude ... It is established doctrine that the trusts declared by a document exercising a special power of appointment are to be read into the existing settlement (*Muir* v *Muir* [1943] AC 468). If such a power is exercised, whether or not separate trustees are appointed, I do not think it would be natural for such a person as I have presupposed to say that a separate settlement had been created, still less if it were found that the provisions of the original settlement continued to apply to the appointed fund, or that the appointed fund were liable, in certain events, to fall back into the rest of the settled property. On the other hand there may be a power to appoint and appropriate a part or portion of the trust property to beneficiaries and to settle it for their benefit. If such a power is exercised, the natural conclusion might be that a separate settlement was created, all the more so if a complete new set of trusts were declared as to the appropriated property, and if it could be said that the trusts of the original settlement ceased to apply to it.'

In the latter case the Court of Appeal drew a distinction between powers to alter the current trusts of a settlement which expressly or by necessary implication authorise the trustees to remove assets altogether from the original settlement (without rendering anyone absolutely beneficially entitled to them), and powers of this nature which do not confer on the trustees such an authority. Slade LJ called these powers, respectively, powers in the wider and the narrower form and stated that the latter could never create a new settlement (so there would never be an exercise under which one set of trustees became absolutely entitled against the other) while the former could be, but need not necessarily be, exercised to create a new settlement. The distinction was close to but not precisely the same as that between special powers of appointment (in their nature, in the narrower form) and powers of advancement (in the wider).

' ... absolutely entitled but for being an infant or other person under disability'

The rule is that unless infancy (or disability) is the *only* reason for a person not being absolutely entitled, s60(1) does not apply. Clearly, s60(1) cannot apply to a trust 'to A if he attains the age of 25', for in order to be able to give a good receipt he must not only attain the age of 18, but he must also reach the age of 25. But what of the case 'to A if he attains the age of 18'? *Tomlinson* v *Glynn's Executor and Trustee Co Ltd* [1970] Ch 112 (Court of Appeal) held that in such a case the property was *not* nominee property. There were *two* contingencies which had to be satisfied – one of ceasing to be an infant, the other of reaching 18. Until both were satisfied, it could not be said that the beneficiary was absolutely entitled, for if the age of majority was lowered below his present age, he would still have to satisfy the contingency of reaching 18. Accordingly, only if the infant has a vested interest (subject to s31 of the Trustee Act 1925) does s60(1) apply to the property held in trust for him.

'... or are or would be jointly so entitled'

'Jointly' in this context does not bear its technical meaning in English real property law. The CGT legislation has to apply to all parts of the United Kingdom: *Kidson* v *MacDonald* [1974] Ch 339. Accordingly, 'jointly' applies to both joint tenants and tenants in common. The matter has been greatly clarified by the judgment of Goulding J in *Booth* v *Ellard* which was later approved by the Court of Appeal ([1980] STC 555):

> 'Looking at the judgments by which I have to be guided, of Foster J and Walton J, I find they appear to lay down at most two requirements for the application of s60(1) where there is a plurality of beneficial owners.
>
> The first requirement is that the interests of the beneficial owners must be *concurrent and not successive*, like the interests of a life tenant on the one hand and a remainderman

or reversioner on the other. See *Kidson* v *MacDonald*. If one has a trust for A for life with remainder to B absolutely, A and B together are able to direct the trustees how to deal with the settled property, but such a limitation is clearly settled property and is not excluded by s60(1).

The second requirement for the application of s60(1) ... is that the interests of the co-owners should be the same: see Walton J in *Stephenson* v *Barclays Bank* [1975] 1 All ER 625.

The definition says "jointly", it does not say "together". I think this is because it is intended to comprise persons who are, as it were, in the same interest.

The reference, I think, is certainly to a similarity of interests in quality, not equality in quantity, because I do not think there is any hint in the decision that tenants in common in unequal shares could be treated differently from tenants in common in equal shares.'

In other words, there has to be qualitative, not quantitative, similarity. No difficulty is encountered, therefore, if all the tenants in common are of full age, or all the tenants in common have vested interests, whether or not they are of full age, for in the latter case the beneficiaries *would* jointly be absolutely entitled as against the trustees if they were all of full age – which is sufficient if s60(1) is to apply. See also *Anders Utkilens Rederi A/S* v *O/Y Lovisa Stevedoring Co A/B* [1985] STC 301, where under the terms of a compromise (*Tomlin*) order the defendant to a negligence action agreed to sell his premises and to divide the proceeds with the plaintiff. Goulding J held that the order was capable of specific performance, being for the sale of landed property for the benefit of more than one party. This thus imposed an immediate trust for sale and division of the proceeds of sale under which the plaintiff's and defendant's interests were qualitatively similar, so that there had been a disposal by the defendant of part of his interest in the property on reaching the compromise agreement.

Difficulties with both requirements *are* encountered in trusts such as 'To such of A, B and C as attain the age of 18, if more than one, in equal shares', where A and B have satisfied that contingency, but C is still an infant. In a case like this, under *Tomlinson*, C is not a person who would be absolutely entitled but for being an infant, since his interest is contingent. So A, B and C together do *not* fall within the class in (b) above. Can A and B be *individually* absolutely entitled? The answer lies in whether they can call for their share of the trust fund to be given to them. In general trust law this depends on the nature of the asset. It is for this reason that in the same settlement some assets may be settled property whereas others are not. The cases on this matter are *Crowe* v *Appleby* 51 TC 374 and *Stephenson* v *Barclays Bank* [1975] 1 All ER 625.

These cases decide that if the trust asset is land, in all cases, or mortgage debts (ie the trustees are mortgagees), or, in very special cases, shares in private companies, then, until all beneficiaries have vested interests and can together tell the trustees how to deal with the assets, those assets remain settled property, not subject to s46.

20.6 'Trustees'

Section 69 provides for trustees in the same way as for personal representatives:

> 'In relation to settled property, the trustees of a settlement shall be treated as a single and continuing body of persons (distinct from the persons who may from time to time be the trustees).'

Consequently, no disposals occur for CGT purposes when the composition of that body is altered. It also provides that, unless the general administration of the trust is carried on outside the United Kingdom *and* a majority of the trustees are not resident or ordinarily resident in the United Kingdom, the body of trustees shall be considered to be resident and ordinarily resident in the United Kingdom.

Professional trustees are treated, however, as not resident in the United Kingdom if the settlor was not, when the settlement was created, resident, ordinarily resident or domiciled in the United Kingdom. If, on this basis, the majority of the trustees are non-resident, the general administration requirement is overridden and the body of trustees will be non-resident.

20.7 Gifts in settlement

Section 70, the first of the trust charging provisions, states:

> 'A transfer into settlement, whether revocable or irrevocable, is a disposal of the entire property thereby becoming settled property, notwithstanding that the transferor has some interest as a beneficiary under the settlement and notwithstanding that he is a trustee, or the sole trustee, of the settlement.'

Section 17(1)(a), it will be recalled, provides that a transfer into settlement is a particular example of a transaction otherwise than by way of a bargain at arm's length. Accordingly, where a taxpayer creates a settlement he makes a full disposal of any asset settled, whether he declares himself trustee or even retains for himself some form of beneficial interest under the trust. With s17 applying, the disposal to the trustees is deemed to take place for a consideration equal to the market value of the assets settled, and CGT is payable on the notional gain. Before 14 March 1989 the settlor used to be able to elect to hold over any gains chargeable on transfer into settlement, and the trustees would accordingly acquire the transferred property at the settlor's acquisition cost: s79 of the Finance Act 1980 and s82 FA 1982. Since 15 March 1989 the settlor must pay CGT on transfers into settlement unless he can claim the benefits of ss165 and 260 of the Taxation of Chargeable Gains Act 1992.

20.8 Sales of trust assets

If trustees sell trust assets to unconnected persons, they will be liable to CGT under s1, the general charging provision, on the gain which is deemed to accrue to them – being, in essence, the difference between the market value on acquisition (less the held over gain, if any) and the sale proceeds.

20.9 Persons becoming absolutely entitled to settled property and the settlement comes to an end

Section 71 provides that on the occasion when a person becomes absolutely entitled to any settled property as against the trustee:

> 'all the assets forming part of the settled property to which he becomes so entitled shall be deemed:
> a) to have been disposed of by the trustee; and
> b) immediately to have been reacquired by him in his capacity as a bare nominee under s46(1) for a consideration equal to their market value.'

Consequently, there is a charge to CGT imposed on the trustees on the gain in the value of the assets during their period of ownership.

If, however, the beneficiary becomes absolutely entitled on the termination of a life interest by the death of the person entitled to it, s73(1) provides that no chargeable gain shall accrue on the disposal. This, of course, corresponds to the 'free uplift' under s62 in respect of free estate, and it applies where the trust is, for example, 'A for life and then to B'. On A's death, B becomes absolutely entitled to the settled property. He takes the assets with a base value equal to their market value at A's death, but no CGT is payable.

Section 73(1)(b) provides an exception. If the person becoming absolutely entitled is the settlor or his wife, only roll-over relief is given and not a free uplift.

The application of s74 is now limited; it still operates in the same manner but only applies when the settlor is entitled to claim hold over relief on transfer into settlement. Since the abolition of s79 FA 1980 the settlor can only claim hold over relief under ss165 and 260, and consequently s74 only operates when the settlor made a claim for relief under s165 or s260 in respect of the disposal of an asset to a trustee, and the trustee is deemed to have disposed of all or part of the asset under s71(1) or s72(1)(a) – see section 20.10.

20.10 Termination of a life interest where the settlement continues

Section 72 provides:

> 'On the termination, on the death of the person entitled to it, of a life interest in possession in all or any part of the settled property,

a) the whole or a corresponding part of each of the assets forming part of the settled property and not ceasing at that time to be settled property shall be deemed to be disposed of and immediately reacquired by the trustees for a consideration equal to the whole or a corresponding part of the market value of the asset; but
b) no chargeable gain shall accrue on that disposal.'

Contrast this with the charge made when the settlement comes to an end as a result – see section 20.9.

Example
S created a settlement, with assets then worth £10,000, in the following terms:

'To A for life or until she remarries, then to B for life, then to C absolutely'.

Later, first, A remarries, and, secondly, B dies. The assets on each occasion are worth £70,000.

On A's remarriage no charge to CGT arises, but neither does s55 apply, so the trustees now hold the assets on the following trusts 'To B for life, then to C', at a base value of £10,000. Any sale of trust assets will give rise to a charge to CGT.

On B's death s55 applies: there is no charge to CGT, but rather a 'free uplift'. The trustees' base value increases to £70,000. Any sale of trust assets will not give rise to a charge to CGT unless they are sold for a sum in excess of £70,000.

20.11 Disposal by a beneficiary of his interest

Section 76 provides that no chargeable gain shall accrue on the disposal of an interest created by, or arising under, a settlement, by the person for whose benefit the interest was created, or by any other person, except one who acquired, or derives his title from one who acquired, the interest for a consideration in money or money's worth, other than consideration consisting of another interest under the settlement. Thus if A sells his life interest to B for £30,000, A does not incur a charge to CGT. If B sells it to C for £40,000, B will pay CGT on the gain he makes of £10,000.

Furthermore, if a person purchases a reversionary interest which subsequently falls into possession, so that he thereby becomes absolutely entitled as against the trustees, he is deemed to dispose of that interest in return for the trust assets, even though there may be no charge on the trustees – for example because the interest falls into possession on the death of the life tenant.

Example
Settled property worth £100,000 is held on trusts 'To A for life, then to B'. B sells his interest to C for £60,000. Shortly thereafter A dies and C becomes absolutely entitled to the trust assets, now worth £130,000. C is deemed to dispose of his interest (with allowable expenditure of £60,000) for £130,000 of assets, and realises a chargeable gain of £70,000.

20.12 The foreign element of trusts in CGT

Migrant settlements: ss80–85

The new regime for trusts, introduced in 1991 and now consolidated in TCGA 1992, contained provisions to counter the use of non-resident trusts to defer tax on gains which would otherwise be subject to a CGT charge until the gains were distributed by 'capital payments' to United Kingdom resident beneficiaries. Notwithstanding the s87 matching provisions above, CGT could be avoided entirely if the distributions were eventually made to beneficiaries who were non-resident or not ordinarily resident, or it could be deferred until capital payments were actually made.

The provisions introduced three new charges to CGT in certain circumstances:

1. Where the trustees of the settlement cease to be resident in the United Kingdom on or after 19 March 1991 within s80 (or where they become dual resident trustees and, because of a double taxation agreement, gains on disposals of settled property cease to fall within the United Kingdom charge): the trustees are treated as having disposed of the assets immediately before they became non-resident ('the relevant time') and having immediately reacquired them at that time at market value.

   The charge does not apply to assets used for a trade in the United Kingdom carried on by the trustees through a branch or agency: s80(4). Section 81 contains provisions to limit the charge where the non-residence results from the death of a trustee, and United Kingdom residence is resumed within six months.
2. On settlors of certain non-resident settlements: where the settlor has an interest in the settlement and is domiciled and resident or ordinarily resident in the United Kingdom, any gains on the settlement computed as if the trustees were resident will be treated as accruing to the settlor. The definition of 'interest' is broadly similar to that in income tax provisions.
3. On beneficiaries of non-resident settlements: a supplementary charge is made on the tax payable when past undistributed deferred gains realised by the non-resident trust are distributed. The charge is 10 per cent of the tax payable on final distribution for each year which tax has been deferred to a maximum of six years. The charge will apply only to trust gains distributed after 6 April 1992.

Disposals by beneficiaries of interests under foreign trusts

Section 85(1) provides that if at the time of a disposal under s76 the trustees are neither resident nor ordinarily resident in the United Kingdom, s76(1) shall not apply and the disposal will be a chargeable disposal, giving rise to chargeable gains. It also prevents a double charge arising by reason of the application of new provisions with regard to migrating trusts (see below) where a beneficiary has disposed of an interest in a trust which has become non-resident according to s80.

Section 85(3) provides that:

'For the purpose of calculating any chargeable gain accruing on the disposal of the interest, the person disposing of it should be treated as having –
(a) disposed of it immediately before the relevant time, and
(b) immediately reacquired it, at its market value at that time.'

Thus the gain on disposal under s85(1) is restricted by s88(3) to any gain accruing *after* the trust has become non-resident under s80. (This is because under s80 there is an exit charge on the trustees on migration: see, again, below.)

Gains of non-resident settlements

If the settlor was when he created a settlement, or is in the year of assessment in question, domiciled and either resident or ordinarily resident in the United Kingdom, s87 provides special rules where the trustees of the settlement are neither resident nor ordinarily resident. Section 97 provides a definition of 'settlor' and 'settlement' for the purposes of ss87 to 90: 'gains on a non-resident settlement'. The definition is that provided in s660G ICTA 1988:

'In this Chapter –
"settlement" includes any disposition, trust, covenant, agreement, arrangement or transfer of assets, and
"settlor", in relation to a settlement, means any person by whom the settlement was made.'

The trustees are required to compute the amount of the gains on which they would have been chargeable had they been resident in the United Kingdom. This amount is known as the 'trust gains' for the relevant year of assessment. These trust gains may be attributed to beneficiaries who in that year or in previous years of assessment have received 'capital payment' from the trustees. If a beneficiary to whom such a gain is attributed is resident or ordinarily resident in the year of assessment in question, he is liable to CGT on that gain as if it were a chargeable gain which had accrued to him on the disposal of an asset. A capital payment is defined by s97(1) as:

'any payment which is not chargeable to income tax on the beneficiary or, in the case of a beneficiary who is neither resident nor ordinarily resident in the UK, any payment received otherwise than as income'.

'Payment' is to include the transfer of an asset and the conferring of any other benefit, and s97(4) explains that this can include the making of a payment by way of loan, when the amount of the payment is to be taken as being equal to the value of the benefit conferred. Oddly, the section contains no provision enabling the amount of such a benefit to be computed, and Schedule 7 para 3 ICTA 1988, in relation to beneficial loan arrangements for employees, should be compared.

In *De Rothschild* v *Lawrenson* [1995] STC 623, the Court of Appeal upheld the earlier decision of Vinelott J, where it had been held that gains realised in 1988–89 by the non-resident trustees of a settlement under which the United Kingdom resident settlor enjoyed a life interest were to be treated as trust gains for the purposes of s80 FA 1981 (currently s87 TCGA 1992). The Court of Appeal held that in making the computation required by s80(2) FA 1981 (currently s87(2) TCGA 1992), the deeming provisions in Schedule 10 para 1(2) FA 1988 (currently s77(2) TCGA 1992) – which state that chargeable gains accruing to trustees in these circumstances are to be treated as accruing to the settlor – were to be ignored.

Once a gain has been set off against a capital payment, both are exhausted. If, in any year, insufficient capital payments have been made to which the trust gains can be attributed, the surplus gains are carried forward and can be set against future capital payments.

Migrant settlements: s89

When a United Kingdom resident body of trustees goes non-resident, capital payments made to beneficiaries in the years of residence are ignored for the purposes of s87 above, unless made in anticipation of a disposal by the trustees during their period of non-residence: s89(1).

When a non-resident body of trustees become resident in the United Kingdom, and there are surplus capital gains left in the trust which have not been attributed to beneficiaries, these gains are nevertheless attributed to beneficiaries who subsequently receive capital payments until the gains are exhausted: s89(2).

Transfers between settlements

It would be possible to avoid ss87 and 89(2) by transferring the settled property of the overseas settlement (which will include the amount of any undistributed trust gain) to another settlement, whose trustees would not have realised the gain in question. Section 90 prevents this by treating the gains of the transferee settlement as increased by the outstanding trust gains of the transferor settlement in a case where s87 applies to the transferee settlement too, whereupon the beneficiaries of the transferee will be deemed to have made chargeable gains to the extent that they receive capital payments from their trustees. If the transferee settlement is not one to which s87 applies, it is instead treated as one which has just become resident after having received trust gains in its non-resident period, in which case s89(2) is applied.

21

Inheritance Tax: General

21.1 Introduction

21.2 The basic charging provisions

21.3 Transfer of value

21.4 The value transferred

21.5 The rate of tax

21.6 Liability for IHT and 'grossing-up' and calculation of IHT

21.7 Death

21.8 Gifts with reservation of benefit – Schedule 20 and s102 FA 1986

21.9 Associated operations

21.10 Excluded property

21.1 Introduction

On 26 March 1974 the Labour Government announced its intention to abolish estate duty and to replace it by a tax which would operate in relation not only to transfers on death but also lifetime gifts. This was to be Capital Transfer Tax (CTT). This tax lasted for some twelve years, eventually being replaced by a modified form which has strong affinities with estate duty: Inheritance Tax (IHT). This applied with effect from 18 March 1986, but the tax payable on chargeable transfers (see section 21.2) may well be calculated by reference to earlier transfers made during the existence of CTT. In essence, IHT is payable on the value of property held on death and on gifts made by a transferor to other individuals or into favoured settlements on, or within the seven years prior to, his death. It is also payable at any time in relation to transfers into or in connection with discretionary settlements and to transfers of value by close companies. Tax is not, however, chargeable on what is termed 'excluded property', nor on transfers which are exempt due to the nature of the recipient, as for example transfers to a spouse: see section 21.10 and Chapter 22, sections 22.3 and 22.4.

Unless expressly stated otherwise, all references in this chapter are to the Inheritance Tax Act (IHTA) 1984.

21.2 The basic charging provisions

Although IHT was not introduced until 1986, the manner of implementation was to take the Capital Transfer Tax Act 1984, change its name, and tack on various provisions amending or limiting its scope.

Section 1 provides that IHT is to be charged on the value transferred by a chargeable transfer, and s2(1) provides that:

> 'A chargeable transfer is any transfer of value which is made by an individual but is not an exempt transfer.'

Accordingly, for IHT to be imposed the following must apply:

1. There has to be a transfer of value.
2. That transfer is not exempt from IHT.
3. The value has to be transferred out of the individual's estate.

Thus IHT is imposed only on individuals. Special rules exist, however, to charge individuals in respect of dispositions made by close companies and to bring trustees within the scope of the tax.

Section 3(1) defines a 'transfer of value' as:

> 'a *disposition* made by a person ("the transferor") as a result of which the value of his *estate* immediately after the disposition is less than it would be but for the disposition; and the amount by which it is less is the "value transferred" by the transfer.'

'Disposition' is not defined by the Act. The draftsman has been careful to avoid using the CGT word 'disposal', although it must have very much the same width and include any transaction by which a person disposes of an interest in an asset or creates a new interest in another person in an asset. The Act does, however, extend the meaning of 'disposition' by s3(3):

> 'Where the value of a person's estate is diminished and that of another person's estate, or of settled property in which no interest in possession subsists, is increased by the first-mentioned person's omission to exercise a right, he shall be treated for the purposes of this section' [ie for the purposes of determining whether or not there has been a transfer of value] 'as having made a disposition at the time, or the latest time, when he could have exercised the right, unless it is shown that the omission was not deliberate.'

It must be shown that by one person omitting to exercise a right, another person was benefited. Even so, the value transferred is not the amount by which the latter person's estate was increased but the amount by which the transferor's estate was diminished.

Example

Jean, John's daughter, has been squatting in a house owned by John, denying John's title to the property, since 1 January 1985. On 1 January 1997, twelve years' adverse possession has run and Jean acquires title to the property. If John has deliberately failed to seek a court order to have Jean evicted, he will be deemed to have made a disposition. As a result, the value of his estate will be less than it would be but for the omission and he will be deemed to have made a transfer of value, for the purposes of IHT.

21.3 Transfer of value

The essence of IHT is the reduction in the transferor's estate. A sale of an asset is a disposition because it transfers an interest in an asset to another person, but since it is to be anticipated that the transferor will in return have received the market price for the asset, there will have been no reduction in the transferor's estate, and there can have been no 'transfer of value': see s3(1). In other words, IHT is fundamentally a tax on gifts, and in particular on gifts made within seven years of a person's death and on chargeable transfers made on death.

Section 10 dispositions

A reduction in the value of a person's estate can occur, however, without there being any element of gift; where, for example, a trader (or a purchaser) makes a bad bargain, then prima facie this would be a transfer of value, and chargeable to IHT. This anomaly is catered for by s10:

> '(1) A disposition is not a transfer of value if it is shown that it was not intended to confer any gratuitous benefit on any person and either:
> a) that it was made in a transaction at arm's length between persons not connected with each other; or
> b) that it was such as might be expected to be made in a transaction at arm's length between persons not connected with each other ... '

The meaning of 'connected persons' is explained by s270: reference must be made to s286 of the Taxation of Chargeable Gains Act 1992, adopting the definition there used, save that 'relative' as used in the CGT context is extended to include uncles, aunts, nephews and nieces for IHT purposes.

Section 10 thus imposes two conditions if a reduction in a person's estate is not to be chargeable to IHT:

1. There must be no intent to confer any gratuitous benefit on any person. Stress must be laid on 'any': a transaction can be a perfectly commercial one as between the parties privy to the contract and yet confer a gratuitous benefit on a third party. The classic example is that of the grandfather who pays for his

grandchild's education; as between the grandfather and the school, there is a bargain at arm's length made between persons not connected with each other, and yet a gratuitous benefit, free education, is conferred on the grandchild. Accordingly, a transfer of value has occurred.
2. There must be, or it must be as if there were, a bargain at arm's length between persons not connected with each other. The reason for this as a separate requirement is the possibility of a transaction being effected to reduce the value of a person's estate without conferring any gratuitous benefit on anyone.

Example
John owns a 51 per cent shareholding in Miko Ltd. This majority shareholding is worth £100,000. He sells half of it to his son, Peter, at its market price of £35,000, and correspondingly his remaining holding is also now worth only £35,000. No gratuitous benefit can be shown – Peter has paid full value for what he got. But no one would sell his majority shareholding in a company in small parcels. So it is not a transaction such as might be expected to be made (at arm's length) between persons not connected with each other. There is, therefore, a transfer of value of £30,000. The idea behind the sale is, of course, that on John's death Peter will receive the rest of the shares with less IHT being payable.

Where the property disposed of is unquoted shares, a third condition must be satisfied before the disposition is deemed not to be a transfer of value: the price must be freely negotiated at the time of sale, or must be the one which would have been expected had it been freely negotiated then. The latter rule is necessary because it would otherwise be possible to avoid IHT by imposing a fetter on disposition in the Articles of Association of the company.

Other dispositions

Certain other dispositions are also deemed not to be transfers of value:

Dispositions for the maintenance of one's family: s11
Section 11 provides that a disposition is not a transfer of value if it is made by one party to a marriage in favour of the other party or of a child of either party and is:

1. for the maintenance of the other party; or
2. for the maintenance, education or training of the child to the year in which he attains the age of 18, or, when he ceases to undergo full-time education or training if later.

The primary purpose of (1), in fact, is to cater for maintenance payments made on a divorce. Section 11(6) applies also to dispositions made on the dissolution or annulment of a marriage, and to a disposition varying such a disposition. However, it should be noted that a transfer on death is not capable of coming within s11, and in addition that the spouse must always ensure that the transfer is *in favour* of the other spouse in order to benefit from s11.

Payment (2) is self-explanatory. It is possible, however, for a person other than a parent to make payments falling within s11 (and thus not a transfer of value) if the child who benefits is not in the care of a parent. If such payments will benefit the child after he attains 18 it must also be shown that the child was, before attaining that age, in the care of the transferor for substantial periods.

Section 11(3) also provides that dispositions made in favour of a dependent relative of the transferor are not transfers of value if they are no more than reasonable provisions for the dependent relative's maintenance. 'Dependent relative' has its usual fiscal meaning.

Dispositions under ss12–15

Sections 12–15 provide other sorts of dispositions which are not transfers of value:

1. Section 12: dispositions which are allowable in computing the transferor's profits or gains for income tax purposes, for example a bonus to an employee, which, although something to which the employee is not contractually entitled, has been paid by the employer in order to foster good relations with his work force – the classic example being the ex gratia payment made on retirement to a loyal employee. Section 12 further provides that contributions to retirement benefits schemes shall not be transfers of value.
2. Section 13: transfers of property by a close company to trustees to hold on trusts for the benefit of employees.
3. Section 14: waiver of remuneration which would have been assessable under Schedule E if, but for the waiver, it would have been deductible in computing profits and, as a result of the waiver, will no longer be so.
4. Section 15: waiver of dividends within 12 months before the right to the dividend accrues.

Agricultural tenancies

Finally, s16 provides that a grant of an agricultural tenancy is not to be a transfer of value if made for full consideration in money or money's worth. It may not be sufficient for the parties to agree that a full rack rent be paid; if the market will also bear a premium on the grant of such a tenancy (as it very often will), such a premium must be taken if the transfer is to fall within s16. Such a grant inevitably depresses the value of a person's estate because of the extensive rights given to agricultural tenants. Section 10 might not apply to the lease, on the basis that a grantor of such a tenancy must have intended to confer gratuitous benefit on the grantee since otherwise he would have given the grantee nothing more than a 364-day grazing licence or a tenancy for one year and 364 days (neither of which confers on the grantee rights under the Agricultural Holdings Act 1986).

Agricultural tenancies beginning on or after 1 September 1995 qualify for agricultural property relief, as do those transferred to a successor under the relevant statutory provisions on or after that date – see under 'agricultural property' Chapter 22, section 22.4.

21.4 The value transferred

Section 3(1), it will be recalled, provides that the value transferred by a transfer of value is the amount by which the transferor's estate is less than it would be but for the disposition. The meaning of 'estate' is given by s5(1) as 'the aggregate of all the property to which he is beneficially entitled ...' and includes any property over which the transferor has a general power – that is to say a power enabling him to dispose of property as he thinks fit – other than a general power over settled property.

As a result of the terms of s3(1) the value transferred by a person is not necessarily the same as the value received by the transferee. Some simple examples will explain this.

Examples
1. X has a pair of Ming vases. Individually, each is worth £5,000; as a pair, they are worth £15,000. X gives one to Y. What Y receives is worth £5,000. What X has left is worth, however, £5,000, not £10,000. Since X's estate has thus been diminished by £10,000, that is the value transferred.
2. A has a 51 per cent shareholding, worth £1,000,000, in B Ltd, a company with an issued share capital of 100 £1 shares. As part of a minority shareholding, each share would be worth £10,000. A gives two shares to C. C thus receives shares worth £20,000. A has, however, thus converted his majority shareholding into a minority shareholding worth £490,000. A has, therefore, made a transfer of value of £510,000.

21.5 The rate of tax

IHT is levied by reference to the values previously transferred by the transferor as well as by reference to value of the present transfer. The rates at which inheritance tax is charged are set out in Schedule 1 IHTA 1984. As from 6 April 1997, £215,000 (Schedule 1) of chargeable transfers attract no tax, the rate being 'nil'. Transfers in excess of that sum attract tax at 40 per cent. As will subsequently be explained, most lifetime transfers are not chargeable transfers; instead they are termed 'potentially exempt', and no IHT will be paid in respect of such a transfer unless the transferor dies within the following seven years. In such a case, the transfer is said to have 'proved chargeable' and tax is then levied. Finally, there is this distinction between lifetime transfers and those made on death: any transfer made on, or within three years before, a transferor's death is taxed at the full rate of 40 per cent found in the table in Schedule 1. Transfers made at other times are subjected only to tax at half the death rate: s7(2).

Section 7 provides that:

1. Lifetime chargeable transfers, other than potentially exempt transfers (PETs) (see Chapter 22, section 22.2) which have proved chargeable, are taxed at *half* the death rate unless made within five years of the death of the transferor, when the higher rate imposed by s7(4) applies: s7(2),(5).
2. Subject to (1), transfers made within the seven years prior to the transferor's death are taxed at the following proportion of the death rate:

Number of years before death	*Percentage of the applicable death rate*
Fewer than three	100%
More than 3 but fewer than 4	80%
More than 4 but fewer than 5	60%
More than 5 but fewer than 6	40%
More than 6 but fewer than 7	20%

When tax (or more tax) becomes payable by reason of the death of the transferor, the tax payable is calculated by reference not to the table applicable at the time of the transfer but to that applicable at the date of death, and by using the chargeable amount as valued at the time of the transfer. Given inflation, this may well benefit the taxpayer. Nevertheless, the rates will still be calculated by reference to the chargeable transfers made by the deceased in the seven years prior to the transfer in question. Thus, if A makes three PETs each of £100,000, on 1 June, 1 July and 1 August 1989, and dies on 30 June 1996, the one made on 1 June 1989 will be exempt (being made more than seven years before his death) whereas the latter two will prove chargeable. That of 1 July will be his first chargeable transfer and be calculated as if the transferor had no cumulative total, and that of 1 August will be taxable as made by a transferor making a chargeable transfer of £100,000, who has a cumulative total of £100,000.

21.6 Liability for IHT and 'grossing-up' and calculation of IHT

Liability for tax

Sections 199–201 provide the rules as to who is liable for IHT. In the case of a lifetime transfer by an individual, s199 charges:

1. the transferor;
2. any person the value of whose estate is increased by the transfer;
3. so far as the tax is attributable to particular property, any person in whom the property is vested at any time after the transfer, whether beneficially or otherwise, or who has an interest in possession in the property;

4. where by the transfer the property becomes settled property, any person for whose benefit the property or income from it is applied.

Primary responsibility for the tax remains with the transferor or settlement trustees, with the donee or beneficiary of a trust only liable in the event that the tax remains unpaid. However, for PETS which become chargeable on death the donee becomes primarily responsible, because s204(7) and (8) limit the personal representatives' liability to assets within their control. The value of the property attributed to a PET which becomes chargeable is the value *at the time the gift was made* and not of the property at the date of death.

Section 204(6) imposes a limitation on liability: where a person is liable otherwise than as transferor, he is only liable if the tax remains unpaid after it ought to have been paid. Thus the transferor is primarily liable. However, this rule does not apply where the tax exceeds what it would have been had the transferor died more than seven years after the transfer; in other words, it does not apply in relation to PETs, when the transferee is equally liable to the tax which arises on the transferor's death.

Similar rules apply for settlements: see ss201 and 204(6)(b). Primarily the trustees are liable for the tax payable on the value transferred by a chargeable transfer of settled property under ss43–93. The exception is the tax payable on the death of a person with an interest in possession: here s200 applies. On this occasion, the tax is principally divisible between the personal representatives of the deceased and the trustees of the settlement, in proportion to the parts of the value transferred attributable to free and settled property. For example, if A dies with a free estate of £100,000 and a life interest in a settled fund of £200,000, one-third of the IHT will be payable by his PRs and two-thirds by the trustees.

Valuation – s5 IHTA 1984

As has been explained above, the amount on which tax is payable is not necessarily the value which has been received by the donee. In many cases, the asset transferred will have had additional value as part of a set in the transferor's estate, and in some cases – in particular, on the transfer of property into a discretionary trust – it may well be that the value transferred will have to take account of the IHT payable on the transfer.

Section 5 deals with valuation:

> '(3) In determining the value of a person's estate at any time his liabilities at that time shall be taken into account, except as otherwise provided by this Act.
> (4) The liabilities to be taken into account in determining the value of a transferor's estate immediately after a transfer of value include his liability for tax on the value transferred but not his liability (if any) for any other tax or duty resulting from the transfer ... '

That is to say, if a transferor is liable to pay IHT on a chargeable transfer (which he will be under s199, unless there has been specific agreement to the contrary), his estate is to be considered as diminished not merely by the loss of the property transferred but also by the amount of IHT (and IHT alone) payable on the transfer of value. Accordingly the value transferred includes the IHT payable on the gross sum, and the net sum by which the transferor's estate is prima facie diminished must be considered as a net sum corresponding to a gross sum from which the IHT has been deducted.

Grossing up

In order, therefore, to determine the IHT payable by a *transferor* on a transfer of value, the transfer of value must be 'grossed up'. No grossing-up is necessary, of course, where the transferee pays the IHT – as will usually be the case where a PET proves chargeable – since the transferor's estate is not then diminished by the tax payable. Even in cases where the transferee pays the tax, the rate of tax is determined by reference to the transferor's cumulative total. The process which must be followed in such cases is the same as that used for paying net annual amounts such as to a charity under a deed of covenant – s347A ICTA 1988. Thus in those cases a payment of £770 was a net sum corresponding to a gross sum of £1,000 after tax at the basic rate of 23 per cent had been deducted.

The calculations are, however, more complicated where IHT is concerned, since grossing-up must be applied over the whole range of rates applicable. To this end, in practice, grossing-up tables are used which will inform the user, on consideration of the net amount transferred and the aggregate of chargeable transfers made by the transferor in the previous seven years, what are the gross transfer of value and the amount of IHT payable.

If no such tables are available, however, the result can be arrived at by using the grossing-up formulae, where r = the rate of tax:

$$\frac{r}{100-r} \text{ to give the tax payable}$$

and

$$\frac{100}{100-r} \text{ to give the gross amount transferred.}$$

In fact, these formulae only have to be used at the last stage, since the amount of tax payable on each band of income transferred remains constant and is easily calculated.

Cumulation

To determine the amount on which tax is chargeable at any given time, whether for lifetime transfers or on death, the period to be examined is the previous seven years. However, all transfers which are not chargeable at that point are excluded: that is, PETs which are still then PETs and excluded property (see section 21.10) or exempt transfers. Some previously charged transfers will fall out of the reckoning if more than seven years have elapsed since they were made. The nil rate band is applied on each occasion of charge – in other words it is repeated, since any cumulative total includes only the chargeable transfers of the previous seven years.

Example

In year 1 X settles property on trust amounting to £250,000 on which tax is paid by the trustees.

In year 5 X gifts £150,000 to charity (exempt) and £150,000 to a relative (PET), and settles a further £200,000 on the above trust (chargeable transfer).

In year 7 X settles a further £350,000 on discretionary trust (chargeable transfer).

In year 9 X dies, leaving free estate of £500,000.

In year 5 X's cumulative total of chargeable transfers was £250,000 + £200,000 = £450,000. Tax was charged on £450,000 at year 5 rates, and the actual amount of tax paid in year 1 was deducted, leaving a balance to be paid now.

In year 7 X's cumulative total became £350,000 + £250,000 + £200,000 = £800,000, on which tax was calculated at year 5 rates less tax on the previous two transfers.

On X's death, his cumulative total is £500,000 + £350,000 + £200,000 + £150,000 = £1,200,000, on which tax at the death rate, less tapering relief on the PET (see section 21.5), will be calculated.

In addition to the charge on death, the year 7 calculation is reworked to take account of the fact that the cumulative total for charge in that year initially excluded the year 5 PET, which is now no longer exempt.

21.7 Death

IHT is primarily a tax on the property belonging to a taxpayer on death. The reason for charges being imposed in respect of lifetime transfers is to prevent taxpayers from enjoying the benefit of property until the moment before death, and then making death-bed transfers free from IHT. The death charge is effected by treating the deceased as making a transfer of value on death but at a value equal to the value of his estate immediately before the event.

Section 4(1) provides:

> '(1) On the death of any person after the passing of this Act, tax shall be charged as if, immediately before his death, he had made a transfer of value, and the value transferred by it had been equal to the value of his estate immediately before his death ...'

IHT is thus payable on the value of the whole of the deceased's estate. Some relief is given by the general rule of valuation laid down by s171, namely that in determining the value of a person's estate immediately before his death, changes in the value of his estate, whether by addition (eg a life policy maturing) or by increase or decrease in the value of property comprised in the estate, are to be taken into account. There are some exceptions to this rule:

1. the termination on the death of any life interest, and
2. the passing of any interest by survivorship.

The importance of (1) can only be understood by reference to the settled property provisions and, in particular, s49(1). This subsection provides that a person who is beneficially entitled to an interest in possession in settled property is to be deemed to be beneficially entitled to the property in which the interest subsists. Although this vital provision will be discussed in greater detail in Chapter 23, its significance can be understood in the following example.

Example
X, who is 95 and close to death, has a life interest in settled property worth £2,000,000. Because of his advanced age and precarious state of health, his life interest is worth only £10,000. When he dies he will not be considered to have made a transfer of value of the value of his free estate together with £10,000, the value of the life interest, but of that estate plus £2,000,000, the value of the settled property itself.

There are two exceptions to the rule that the settled property in which a person has an interest in possession is to be brought into account on his death:

1. Reverter to settlor (s4): Where the settled property reverts to the settlor in the settlor's lifetime and the reversionary interest was not purchased by the settlor or his wife, the value of the settled property is left out of account in determining the value transferred under s4(1).

Example
A transfers property to trustees to pay the income therefrom to X during his life. On X's death, a resulting trust effects a reverter of the settled property to A. The property does not form part of X's estate if A is still alive.

2. Reverter to the settlor's spouse: The same consequences and rules apply with the following additions:

    – The settlor's spouse must be domiciled in the United Kingdom at the date of the death.
    – If the settlor has predeceased the life tenant, the settlor's widow must acquire the settled property on the life tenant's death within two years of the death of the settlor.

Liability to pay tax on death

Section 200(1) provides that where a chargeable transfer is deemed to be made on death, the persons liable to pay the tax are, generally speaking, the deceased's personal representatives, but in respect of property comprised in a settlement (ie property in which the deceased had an interest in possession), the trustees of the settlement. If, however, the settled property is settled land situate in the United Kingdom which devolves on the deceased's personal representatives, then, once again, it is they who are liable to pay the tax attributable to the value of the land.

It will be recalled (see section 21.5) that tax or more tax may prove chargeable on the death of the transferor within seven years of a lifetime disposition. Where this is so, clearly there will have to be an adjustment of the amounts of tax (if any) originally found to be payable. Any excess IHT thus found to be due is payable by the transferee alone: s199(2), s204(6),(7).

Deeds of family arrangement

This matter is now governed by ss17(a) and 142. When a person has been left property by will, or under the intestacy rules, any transfer of that property to a third party would, without more, be a transfer of value, potentially liable to IHT. In order to mitigate this in cases where the original donee is doing no more than redirecting the dispositions of the deceased, ss17(a) and 142 provide that:

1. In certain circumstances, the variation of dispositions of the property comprised in a person's estate immediately before his death shall not be a transfer of value, so that no IHT will be exigible; and
2. The IHT rules contained in IHTA 1984 are to apply as if the variation had been effected by the deceased.

Sections 17(a) and 142 apply both to variations and to disclaimers. A variation occurs when the beneficiary redirects property to some third party of his own choosing, and a disclaimer when the benefit is merely refused and falls instead into residue or to be redirected by operation of law. One important difference is that the deeming provisions of ss142(1) and 62(6) TCGA 1992 have no counterpart for income tax. The Revenue's view is that if a parent redirects property left to him by will in favour of his infant unmarried children, the redirection will be a settlement for the purposes of ss663 and 664 ICTA 1988 if effected by means of a variation but not if by a disclaimer (since the latter is an operation of law, rather than of the parent).

The following conditions had to be satisfied in order for a variation or disclaimer to be within s62 TCGA 1992:

1. The variation must be made within two years after the death of the testator or intestate.

2. The variation must be made by an instrument in writing made by the person or persons who would benefit under the dispositions so varied.
3. An election in writing must be submitted to the Board of Inland Revenue, that the provisions of s142 should apply. The election must be made by the persons making the instrument and also by the personal representatives, if the variation has the effect that more IHT will be payable by them.
4. The variation must not be made for a consideration in money or money's worth other than consideration consisting of the making of another variation to which s142 applies.

Section 142 cannot apply to every type of property to which the deceased may be deemed to have been beneficially entitled at the time of his death; s142(5) excludes settled property in which he had an interest in possession under s49(1) from the operation of s142(1). Furthermore, one should note that if one beneficiary varies his legacy in favour of another, and by a separate instrument that other varies his legacy in favour of yet another, then the latter variation is regarded as a gift.

Example
D leaves property to X who then re-directs the property to Y, and Y subsequently re-directs the property to Z. This second variation constitutes a gift from Y to Z, and IHT is payable: *Russell* v *IRC* [1988] STC 195.

Section 142 is, of course, complementary to s62(6) TCGA 1992.

Sections 143, 144, 145, 146

There are certain other provisions which are designed to have a similar effect:

Precatory transfers: s143
If the deceased expressed a wish that property bequeathed by his will should be transferred by the legatee to others, then any transfer in compliance with that wish within two years of the deceased's death is treated as made by the deceased.

Testamentary discretionary trusts: s144
If the will creates a discretionary trust, distributions out of that trust within two years of the death are treated as made by the deceased. See *Frankland* v *IRC* [1996] STC 735, where the exemption provided for by s144(2) for transfers which would be chargeable but for rewriting the provisions of a will, was held not be available for a transfer from a discretionary trust to one in which the deceased's husband had an interest in possession. The transfer was intended to achieve s18(1) inter-spouse exemption if successfully avoiding a charge under s65 (by using s144) on the transfer out of the discretionary trust into an interest in possession trust in which the deceased's husband had an interest. This failed because the husband's interest did not arise under the will as the rewriting had occurred within the first three months,

forbidden by s65(4). In effect the two-year period is reduced at the start by three months for such transfers.

Redemption of surviving spouse's life interest: s145

If the deceased died intestate leaving a spouse and children, the spouse will take the personal effects of the deceased, a capital sum and a life interest in half the residue of the estate. That life interest he or she can claim to redeem for an actuarially calculated capital sum under s47A of the Administration of Estates Act 1925. If that election is made, the sum received is treated as left to the spouse on death, and the remainder of the property, which passes to the children, as having been left to them by their deceased parent. The effect is that tax is paid on the part thus passing to the children at the deceased's death rates.

Claims under the Inheritance (Provision for Family and Dependants) Act 1975: s146

Section 146 ensures that where any type of order is made under the 1975 Act requiring the transfer of property from one person to another, tax shall be charged as if the earlier disposition which the order reverses had not occurred.

21.8 Gifts with reservation of benefit – Schedule 20 and s102 FA 1986

It would be all too easy for a taxpayer to avoid IHT by making a lifetime gift of property to the person whom he would ultimately wish to benefit on his death and then to 'borrow' the assets for the remainder of his life. Provided that the original gift were made more than seven years before his death, this would, without more, be a successful PET. In order to preclude wholesale avoidance of this sort, s102 of the Finance Act 1986 provides that, subject to certain acceptable transfers of this sort, property subject to a reservation is to be treated as continuing to form part of the estate of the deceased donor at his death, even though it would also be taken into account in determining the estate of the donee were he to die at or about the same time.

A gift with reservation occurs where:

'(1) an individual disposes of any property by way of gift and either –
(a) possession and enjoyment of the property is not bona fide assumed by the donor at or before the beginning of the relevant period; or
(b) at any time in the relevant period the property is not enjoyed to the entire exclusion, or virtually to the entire exclusion, of the donor and of any benefit to him by contract or otherwise.'

The 'relevant period' is the period of seven years ending with the death of the donor – the test is thus applied ex post facto. If, therefore, a donor gives an asset to his son ten years before he dies, but borrows it and continues to use it for two years after the original gift, the property will not be subject to a reservation on the donor's death, since eight years will have elapsed since it was last enjoyed by him.

A similar test applied for estate duty, and considerable case law was established on the ambit of those rules. It is not certain that the courts will have much regard to such authorities in interpreting the current law: compare the complete refusal of the House of Lords in *Pearson v IRC* [1980] 2 WLR 872 to consider estate duty authorities in interpreting the meaning of 'interest in possession'. Nevertheless, those decisions must be treated as shedding some light on the likely meaning of the test for IHT, subject always to the proviso that the climate for tax avoidance has changed dramatically since most of the cases were heard.

'Gift' is not defined by FA 1986. It has been taken to include any transaction which involves *some* element of bounty, eg a sale at an undervalue: *Re Earl Fitzwilliam's Agreement* [1950] Ch 448. The Revenue has announced that it will treat such a sale not as a gift with reservation (as is possible on one interpretation of 'any benefit to him by contract or otherwise') but as a sale for full consideration of part and a PET to the extent of the undervalue.

Bona fide possession and enjoyment is assumed by the donee

There is no need for the donee to be given the legal title to the property, or to go into *actual physical possession*. So, for example, if the donor declares himself trustee of a freehold subject to a tenancy of a third person, the donee is in actual enjoyment if he obtains the benefit of the rent. Similarly, the donee is in bona fide possession and enjoyment if the asset given is transferred to trustees: *Oakes v Commissioner of Stamp Duties* [1954] AC 57; *Commissioner of Stamp Duties v Perpetual Trustee Co Ltd* [1943] AC 435.

The property is enjoyed virtually to the entire exclusion of the donor

In most cases it will be relatively easy to determine whether the donor is so excluded – is he making use of the property which has been given away? It was of the essence of the estate duty cases, though, that one had carefully to identify precisely what was the subject-matter of the gift. If it was only a limited interest in a larger asset owned by the donor, then provided that the donor restricted his enjoyment of the larger asset to that to which his own interest entitled him, there was no infringement of the rights of the donee. For example, if the donor transferred property to trustees to hold upon trust to pay the income thereof to the donee for life and after his death upon trust as to both capital and income for the settlor absolutely, the reversionary interest of the donor was not a reservation of benefit, since all that he had given was the beneficial life interest in income: *St Aubyn v Attorney-General* [1952] AC 15; *Commissioner of Stamp Duties v Perpetual Trustee Co Ltd*. Again, if the donor declares that he holds land of his on trust for himself and his children in equal undivided shares, all the children are given is their undivided share. Joint occupation of that land will not be a reservation of benefit: *Oakes*. The Capital Taxes Office of the Inland Revenue has tried to impose some limitation on this, arguing that if the donor alone is in occupation, this is an infringement of the rights of the others. It is difficult to see how this may be so, unless the argument is that there has been no acquisition of possession and enjoyment, as required by s102(1)(a). Difficulties abound, though, where that which is given to the donee is the freehold reversion of land belonging to the donor and occupied by the donor under a pre-existing tenancy. Is it right to say in this sort of case that the retention of the lease does not infringe the enjoyment by the donee of what, in reality, is a freehold interest subject to, but with the benefit of, a lease? In *Nicholls* v *IRC* [1975] STC 278, the Court of Appeal was willing to find (although the question was, in the circumstances of that case, obiter) that:

> 'A grant of the fee simple subject to and with the benefit of a lease back, where such a grant is made by a person who owns the whole freehold free from any lease, is a grant of the whole fee simple with something reserved out of it, and not a gift of a partial interest leaving something in the hands of the grantor which he has not given. It is not like a reversion or remainder expectant on a prior interest.
>
> It gives an immediate right to the rent, together with a right to distrain for it, and, if there be a proviso for re-entry, a right to forfeit the lease.'

That case was one where the owner of the freehold had transferred the property to his son subject to a supposed obligation on the latter to grant his father a lease. It was thus not the case where the gift was of an asset from which something had previously been removed:

> 'Where it is a condition of the gift that a lease back shall be created, we think that must, on a true analysis, be a reservation of benefit out of the gift and not something not given at all.'

It was not clear (although it has since been addressed in *Ingram* v *IRC* (see below)) that this should extend to cases where, immediately before the gift is made, the donor takes steps to grant a lease to a nominee and gives away the fee simple subject to that lease, which he retains for his own purposes. It is certainly true that not all pre-existing leases are taboo – in *Munro* v *Commissioner for Stamp Duties* [1934] AC 61, the owner of grazing land formed a partnership with his six children in 1909 and conferred a contractual licence on the partnership to graze the land. In 1913 he gave the land to his three sons, but the partnership continued grazing the land until his death. The Privy Council held that that was not a gift with reservation, since what was given was:

> 'the property shorn of the right which belonged to the partnership ... and the benefit which the donor had as a member of the partnership in the right to which the gift was subject was not a benefit referable to the gift. It was referable to the agreement of 1909 and nothing else.'

In *Nicholls* the court distinguished *Munro*:

'Of course, where as in the *Munro* case, the lease, or, as it then may have been, the licence coupled with an interest, *arises under a prior independent transaction*, no question can arise because the donor then gives all that he has ... '

The Revenue claims to rely on the dictum of the Court of Appeal as authority that an 'asset-shearing operation', under which the donor creates the lease shortly before giving the fee simple away, is a gift of property subject to a reservation, since there is no prior independent transaction. The response to this may be that the transaction creating the lease is *prior* to the gift and is also *independent* of the donee, though not of the donor, and that this was all that the court was considering there. See, however, the case of *Kildrummy (Jersey) Ltd v IRC* [1990] STC 657, where it was held that a lease in favour of a nominee did not create a beneficial interest.

In *Lady Ingram's Executors* v *IRC* [1995] STC 564 the Inland Revenue did not contend the obiter statement in *Nicholls* and therefore appeared tacitly to have accepted the principle that an interest carved out before the transfer takes place is not a reservation of benefit. The central point argued in *Lady Ingram's Executors* was at what point the leasehold or other interest in favour of Lady Ingram arose. Ferris J had already dispensed with the land law aspect, following *Kildrummy* to hold that the nominee could not create a legal lease in her favour in terms of the Law of Property Act, so her interest could only be one in equity. That interest was one which the trustees to whom the properties were transferred would be required to recognise, in that they were holding the properties for the beneficiaries subject to her interest. The outcome was that Ferris J concluded that the trustees had never held the properties without their being subject to Lady Ingram's interest, that there had been no other intention on her part when the transfers were made, and that there was therefore no benefit returned to the donor which could be held to be a benefit reserved out of the gift once made. Unless the case goes forward to the Court of Appeal or House of Lords, the issues arising but not ultimately ruled on in the earlier cases may now have progressed.

It is not necessary that the reservation be immediate. If, for example, A gives B a house in which B lives for five years, at which time A takes up residence in it again, that is within s102 if A dies within seven years of such enjoyment. Nor is it necessary for the benefit reserved to flow directly from the asset given. In *Attorney-General* v *Worrall* [1895] 1 QB 99, a father gave his son £24,000 and in return the son covenanted to pay his father an annuity of £735. The gifts were thus conditional one on the other, and the benefit received by the father (in reality, equivalent to the income the son would obtain from the £24,000) was sufficiently associated with the gift to bring it with the predecessor to s102.

Benefits reserved for consideration

In *Chick* v *Commissioner of Stamp Duties* [1958] AC 435, a father gave land to his son and subsequently entered into partnership with him to farm the gifted land. Although the partnership paid a full rent for the land, it was held that it was enough that the father had not been excluded from the asset, which thus was subject to a reservation. In order to temper the severity of this decision, Schedule 20 para 6(1)(a) FA 1986 provides that:

> 'In determining whether any property which is disposed of by way of gift is enjoyed to the entire exclusion or virtually to the entire exclusion of the donor and of any benefit to him by contract or otherwise –
> (a) In the case of property which is an interest in land or a chattel, retention or assumption by the donor of actual occupation of the land or actual enjoyment of an incorporeal right over the land, or actual possession of the chattel shall be disregarded if it is for full consideration in money or money's worth.'

The exemption is only given if *full consideration* is paid, no reduction being afforded if the consideration is not (or, within the seven years prior to the donor's death, ceases to be) full. Nor is any exemption available if the donor goes out of actual possession, for whatever reason.

Section 102 makes provision for 'virtual exclusion' of the donor; if the donor's enjoyment is of little significance, there will be no reservation of benefit. If, for example, the donor gives the donee a dwelling house, visits by the donor will not be taken to be enjoyment. It may well be different if the donor resumes long-term occupation, albeit that such occupation be wholly precarious: cf *Attorney-General* v *Seccombe* [1911] 2 KB 688.

Other exceptions

No reservation of benefit exists if a donor gives an interest in land to a donee who is a relative of his and subsequently, in circumstances which were unforeseen at the time of the gift, the donor is permitted to occupy the land, provided that the donor is no longer able to maintain himself through old age or infirmity, and that the occupation represents reasonable provision for the donor by the donee: Schedule 20 para 6(1)(b) FA 1986.

Section 102 does not apply if the disposal is an exempt transfer within any of the following sections of IHTA 1984:

1. section 18 (transfers between spouse);
2. section 20 (small gifts);
3. section 22 (gifts in consideration of marriage);
4. section 23 (gifts to charities);
5. section 24 (gifts to political parties);
6. section 25 (gifts for national purposes);
7. section 26 (gifts for public benefit);
8. section 27 (historic buildings: maintenance funds);
9. section 28 (employee trusts).

It continues to apply to transfers covered by, for example, the annual exemption under s19 and normal expenditure out of income (s21), but it does not apply if the gift was made prior to 18 March 1986.

The effect of property being subject to a reservation is explained by s102(3):

'If, immediately before the death of the donor, there is any property which, in relation to him, is property subject to a reservation then, to the extent that the property would not, apart from this section, form part of the donor's estate immediately before his death, that property shall be treated for the purposes of the 1984 Act as property to which he was beneficially entitled immediately before his death.'

It thus increases the value of his estate at that time for the purposes of s5 IHTA 1984 and will be taken into account in determining the value transferred by the transfer of value he is then deemed to make.

If the donor abandons enjoyment before his death, s102(4) applies:

'If, at a time before the end of the relevant period, any property ceases to be property subject to a reservation, the donor shall be treated for the purposes of the 1984 Act as having at that time made a disposition of the property by a disposition which is a potentially exempt transfer.'

That transfer, being made in the 'relevant period', inevitably will prove chargeable. The advantage of being a PET, though, is that the tax charged on the transfer is calculated in accordance with the reduced rates provided by s7(4) IHTA 1984.

21.9 Associated operations

Where a transfer of value is made by associated operations, s268 provides that it shall be treated as made at the time of the last of them. This can be of significance in three different cases:

1. When the earlier transfer or transfers are exempt: for example, A gives £6,000 to his wife, W, and £6,000 to his daughter, D, having arranged with W that she should transfer the £6,000 on to D, which she duly does. Both A and W have available to them the previous year's s19 exemption.

    If the transfers were not associated operations, A's transfer to W would be exempt under s18 and those to D would be exempt under s19. If they are, however, associated operations, A will be treated as making a transfer of value of £12,000 when W makes the transfer to D, of which £6,000 will be a chargeable transfer.
2. Where the last of the associated operations is made within seven years of the transferor's death.
3. In determining the aggregate of transfers of value made by a transferor within the seven years preceding a chargeable transfer, or in determining into which year of assessment a transfer of value falls for the purpose of the exemption under s19. 'Associated operations' are defined by s268(1) as:

    'any two or more operations of any kind, being –
    (a) operations which affect the same property, or one of which affects some property

and the other or others of which affect property which represents, whether directly or indirectly, that property, or income arising from that property representing accumulations of any such income; or

(b) any two operations of which one is effected with reference to the other, or with a view to enabling the other to be effected or facilitating its being effected, and any further operation having a like relation to any of those two, and so on;

whether those operations are effected by the same person or different persons and whether or not they are simultaneous: and "operation" includes an omission.'

Two restrictions only are imposed on this definition: the granting of a lease for full consideration in money or money's worth is not to be associated with any operation effected more than three years later, and transfers prior to 27 March 1974 are left out of account. Thus a grant of a lease, being likely to reduce the value of the freehold, even once the rents have been capitalised, will be a transfer of value unless it falls within s10(1). If it does not fall within s10(1) the Revenue will not need to rely on s268 on any sale of the reversion to the tenant; the disposition will already have been brought into charge to tax. If, however, it does fall within s10(1), any later sale to the tenant would undoubtedly have been claimed by the Revenue to have fallen within s268. The effect of this would be to render the earlier operation (the grant) a transfer of value and to charge tax at the time of the sale. For s10(1) provides:

'A disposition is not a transfer of value if it is shown that it was not intended and was not made in a transaction intended, to confer any gratuitous benefit on any person ...

In this subsection "transaction" includes a series of transactions and *any associated operations*.'

Section 268(2) allows the Revenue to do this, however, only where the sale takes place within three years of the granting of the lease – in particularly blatant cases. See *Simons Tax Intelligence*, 1985, p571 for the Revenue's view on the application of *Furniss* v *Dawson* [1984] AC 474.

Example
John owns Blackacre, worth £100,000. He grants Michael a lease for 21 years, at a premium of £25,000, with a nominal ground rent. John's freehold reversion is worth £60,000. Although there has been a diminution in the value of his estate of some £15,000, prima facie this is a transaction at arm's length falling within s10(1) with no gratuitous intent.

Two years later John sells the freehold reversion to Michael for £60,000. The operations are associated operations: their close proximity is, in itself, evidence of gratuitous intent, and John will be deemed to have made a transfer of value of £15,000 on the sale of the freehold reversion.

Associated operations are also of significance in relation to gifts with reservation of benefit: see section 21.8.

21.10 Excluded property

Section 3(2) provides that, when determining whether a disposition is a transfer of value, or when calculating the value transferred by a transfer of value, no account is to be taken of the value of excluded property which ceases to form part of a person's estate as a result of the disposition. Essentially, this means that dispositions of 'excluded property' are not transfers of value, and thus are not chargeable to IHT.

'Excluded property' is defined in part by s6:

Property outside the United Kingdom

Property situated outside the United Kingdom is excluded property if the person beneficially entitled to it is an individual domiciled outside the United Kingdom. Thus the territorial limitations of IHT are determined by the concept of excluded property. The rules are:

1. If property is situated in the United Kingdom it does not matter where the beneficial owner is domiciled – it will be subject to IHT if it is transferred by a chargeable transfer. The situs of property is determined by the general rules of Private International Law. There are certain exceptions to this rule contained in ss48, 153 and 158 which exist either for diplomatic reasons or to encourage foreign investment in government stock and other governmental borrowing. IHT is not applicable on the disposition of:

   – specified gilts in foreign ownership: s48(4)–(7);
   – overseas pensions: s153;
   – savings certificates, premium bonds and similar investments owned by persons domiciled in the Channel Islands: ss6(3) and 267(2);
   – emoluments and tangible movable property belonging to members of visiting armed forces: ss6(4) and 155;

   or where double taxation relief is available: ss158 and 267(2).

2. If property is situated outside the United Kingdom it is only chargeable to IHT if it belongs to a person domiciled in the United Kingdom. Section 267 provides a wider than usual meaning of 'domiciled in the United Kingdom':

   – A person is domiciled in the United Kingdom, if he is domiciled in one of the countries of the United Kingdom according to the general rules of Private International Law.
   – A person is also treated as domiciled in the United Kingdom if:

     • he has been domiciled there at any time within the three years immediately preceding the date of the disposition in question; or
     • he has been resident there in 17 of the 20 years preceding the date of the disposition in question.

Reversionary interests

A reversionary interest is 'excluded property' unless:

1. it has at any time been acquired by a person for a consideration in money or money's worth; or
2. it is one to which the settlor or his wife is or has been beneficially entitled; or
3. it is conditional on the determination of a lease for life treated as a settlement by s43(3).

As will be seen, a person who is beneficially entitled to an interest in possession in settled property is treated as if he were beneficially entitled to the whole of the settled property and not merely to that interest: s49(1). Thus a 90-year-old person, with a life interest worth £30,000 in settled property worth £250,000 is treated as if he were entitled to the property worth £250,000 and not to his interest. That being the case, to tax the reversionary interest as well would be to introduce an element of double taxation. The exceptions (1), (2) and (3) exist to prevent tax avoidance schemes.

22

IHT Reliefs and Related Provisions

22.1 Introduction

22.2 Potentially exempt transfers

22.3 Exemptions and reliefs applying to lifetime transfers only

22.4 Exemptions and reliefs available both during the transferor's lifetime and on death

22.5 Reliefs available only on death

22.1 Introduction

Section 2(1) of the Inheritance Tax Act 1984 provides that a chargeable transfer is any transfer of value made by an individual which is not an exempt transfer. Part II IHTA 1984 contains the majority of provisions relating to fully exempt transfers, and s3A, introduced by the Finance Act 1986, provides for some transfers to be 'potentially exempt'. Unless expressly stated otherwise, all references in this chapter are to the 1984 Act.

22.2 Potentially exempt transfers

Certain transfers of value are treated by s3A as potentially exempt. If so characterised, the transfer is deemed to be an exempt transfer (and thus not a chargeable transfer) unless the transferor dies within seven years of the transfer. If he does so, the transfer 'proves chargeable' and inheritance tax (IHT) is payable in respect of it. There is thus no tax payable on a potentially exempt transfer (PET) unless and until the transferor dies within the specified period.

Originally the only transfers which could be PETs were the following dispositions (which would be chargeable transfers but for being PETs) made by individuals on or after 18 March 1986:

1. a gift to another individual, in other words a disposition whereby either property became comprised in the donee's estate for his absolute benefit, or, while

property did not become so comprised in the donee's estate, his estate was increased in value.
2. a disposition whereby property became held on either accumulation and maintenance trusts satisfying s71, or disabled trusts under s89.

No exception exists for dispositions which increase the value of property held on A&M trusts or disabled trusts without property becoming comprised in the trust in question. For example, if A pays a premium on an insurance policy held by trustees on A&M trusts, that would not constitute a PET, since, although the value of the trust fund would be increased, nothing would become comprised in it. On the other hand, if A paid the same premium on a policy written on his life, held on trust under the Married Women's Property Act 1882 for his child B, that would be a PET by reason of satisfying the second condition in (1) above.

Section 3A was extended by s96 FA (No 2) 1987 with effect from 17 March 1987. Dispositions are now also PETs if their effect is to transfer property into (or to increase the value of property comprised in) interest in possession trusts, or if there is a termination of or transfer of an interest in possession, in consequence of which the property in which the interest subsisted is held on other such trusts (for another person) or becomes the absolute property of another, or is held on A&M trusts under s71 or on disabled trusts under s89.

Rules have also been introduced in ss54A and B to ensure that this extension of relief is not used for avoidance purposes, for example by transferring the property temporarily to an interest in possession trust and out to a discretionary trust when that interest in possession is terminated: see Chapter 23, section 23.5.

If a PET proves chargeable, tax is payable as if the deceased had made a chargeable transfer at the time of the original disposition. Tax is then calculated by reference to the cumulative total of chargeable transfers made by the transferor in the seven years prior to the transfer. See Chapter 21, sections 21.5 and 21.6, for the computational principles involved.

As was explained above, a PET is a transfer of value which without s3A would be a chargeable transfer. With the exception of the annual exemption under s19, it is obviously to the advantage of the taxpayer that full exemptions should be given in priority to potential exemptions. Thus if a transfer would, in any event, be fully exempt (otherwise than under s19), it is unnecessary (indeed incorrect) to apply s3A to it.

22.3 Exemptions and reliefs applying to lifetime transfers only

Transfers of value not exceeding £3,000: s19

Section 19 provides that transfers of value made by a transferor in any year of assessment are exempt to the extent that the value transferred by them does not exceed £3,000. If part of the exemption is not utilised in the year to which it relates, it may be carried forward to the next following year but not beyond and used to relieve transfers of value in excess of £3,000.

If a transfer is potentially exempt, that transfer is ignored in the original allocation of s19 relief – it is assumed that it will not require such relief – and the £3,000 exemption is conferred on other transfers which are immediately chargeable, eg transfers into discretionary trusts. The rule in such a case is that PETs which prove chargeable are treated for the purposes of s19 as being made after chargeable transfers which never were potentially exempt, so a PET proving chargeable only obtains s19 relief to the extent that the relief has not already been exhausted in that year. Nevertheless, it does seem that the PET will take precedence over a chargeable transfer of the following year to which part of the relief was attributed under s19(2). In this case evidently there will have to be a recalculation of tax payable.

Example
In 1993–94 Alan makes a gift of £2,000 to his nephew John and settles £5,000 on discretionary trusts in favour of his family. His £3,000 s19 exemption is not applied against the outright gift (which is a PET) but goes to reduce the chargeable transfer for that year to £2,000. Alan has never before made any chargeable transfers. Accordingly, the value transferred of £2,000 is charged at the nil rate.

In 1994–95 Alan makes a further transfer into the settlement of £1,000. This utilises only part of his s19 exemption, leaving £2,000 to be carried forward to 1995–96.

In 1995–96 Alan makes yet another transfer into the settlement of £4,500. This utilises:

1. his s19 exemption for 1995–96 of £3,000; and,
2. only after that has been exhausted, £1,500 of the unused £2,000 s19 exemption of 1994–95. £500 of his 1994–95 exemption thus remains unused. This can no longer be carried forward, and if he makes chargeable transfers in 1996–97 he will only be able to rely on his s19 exemption for that year.

Small gifts not exceeding £250: s20

Section 20 provides that transfers of value made by a transferor in any year of assessment by outright gift to any one person are exempt if the values transferred by them do not exceed £250. Thus a transferor can make transfers of value, without limit, so long as each recipient does not receive more than £250 (more correctly, the transferor's estate is not diminished by an amount in excess of £250 in respect of each person).

There are, however, certain restrictions:

1. The gifts must be outright gifts; if the transferor *settled* the property, the transfer would not fall within the scope of the exemption.

2. The transferor cannot, in relation to one transferee, make a gift of £250 falling within s20 followed by further gifts in the same year of assessment falling within s19. He can, however, make gifts not exceeding £250 to some people – which gifts would fall within s20 – and larger gifts in excess of £250 to others. These latter gifts would be PETs and any unused s19 exemption could subsequently be set against them if the transferor dies within seven years.

Normal expenditure out of income: s21

Section 21 provides that a transfer of value is an exempt transfer if it is, or to the extent that it is shown to be:

1. made as part of the normal expenditure of the transferor; and
2. (taking one year with another) made out of his income; and
3. such that after allowing for all transfers of value forming part of his normal expenditure the transferor was left with sufficient income to maintain his usual standard of living.

The requirement that it be part of the transferor's normal expenditure means that the transfer must be one which is recurrent. Section 21 is useful to covenantors making dispositions not falling within s11; a deed of covenant to be effective for income tax will have to provide for recurring payments, and such payments will be treated by the Revenue as part of the transferor's 'normal' expenditure from the first year, as long as requirements (1) and (2) are also satisfied.

This is not to say, however, that s21 only applies to deeds of covenant satisfying s347A of the Income and Corporation Taxes Act 1988; any recurring payment out of the transferor's income leaving him enough to maintain his usual standard of living will be exempt. In *Bennett v IRC* [1995] STC 54 an 87-year-old lady directed the trustees of a life interest trust from which she benefited to pay any income which was surplus to her requirements to her three sons. They made payments in February 1989 and February 1990 before she died later that month. It was held that, despite the actual short period over which the payments were made, the pattern of normal expenditure had been sufficiently established, and that it had been intended, barring unforeseen circumstances, to continue for a period sufficient for it to have become regarded as the transferor's normal expenditure out of income.

There is one major exception to s21: a payment of a premium on a policy on the transferor's life is not exempt if the transferor has, at some time, purchased an annuity, unless it can be shown that the purchase of the annuity and the making of the insurance were not 'associated operations': that is to say, one of which is effected with reference to the other, or with a view to ending or facilitating the effecting of the other. The significance of this rule is that it prevents the following scheme:

1. A purchases an annuity for a large sum of money.
2. He is then allowed to buy a life policy at favourable rates.
3. He assigns the benefit of the policy to trustees on trust for his children.

The payments of premiums would be normal expenditure out of income, and, on A's death, no IHT would be payable on the proceeds of the policy (which would not form part of A's estate).

The scheme still works, but undue advantage cannot be taken of it by paying more than the market rate for an annuity in return for a larger sum on the maturity of a life policy. For the premiums to be deductible the taxpayer will have to show that both annuity and policy were written on terms that could have been obtained if one or other were purchased separately (see also ss263 and 268).

Gifts in consideration of marriage: s22

According to *Re Park deceased (No 2)* [1972] Ch 385, a gift is in consideration of marriage only if three conditions are satisfied:

1. It must be made on the occasion of a marriage; and
2. It must be conditional on the marriage taking place; and
3. It must be made for the purpose of, or with a view to encouraging or facilitating, the marriage taking place.

If a gift satisfies the conditions then it will, up to a limit, be an exempt transfer. What that limit is depends on the relationship of the transferor and the parties to the marriage. Those limits are:

- £5,000 given by each parent of a party to the marriage; and
- £2,500 given by a grandparent or remoter ancestor or by one party to the marriage to the other; and
- £1,000 given in any other case.

Any gift falling into category (3) must be made by way of outright gift to either party to the marriage. Gifts within categories (1) and (2) can also, however, be made by way of settlement. In this case, however, the class of beneficiaries must be restricted to persons mentioned in s22(4), and it must be clear that the most important members of the class are husband and wife.

Section 57

The above four exemptions apply only to lifetime transfers. The exemptions under ss19 and 22 can, however, be extended to an occasion of charge caused by the termination of a life interest under s51(1), as s57 provides that the life tenant may within six months of the transfer notify the trustees in the form prescribed by the Board of Inland Revenue that all or part of his appropriate exemption is made available to them. The trustees then use the exemption to reduce the tax payable. On many occasions such a termination will be a PET, so the section is now of limited utility.

22.4 Exemptions and reliefs available both during the transferor's lifetime and on death

Transfers between spouses: s18

Section 18 provides that a transfer of value is an exempt transfer to the extent that the value transferred is attributable to property which becomes comprised in the estate of the transferor's spouse, and so far as the value transferred is not so attributable, the transfer is still exempt to the extent that the spouse's estate is increased in value. The exemption applies:

1. both during life and on death (whether the transfer is by will, through intestacy or under the rules relating to survivorship); and
2. whether or not the spouses are living together at the time.

Thus transfers between spouses which are part of the arrangements leading up to a decree absolute of divorce or nullity are within the exemption, although transfers after the decree are not. In this latter case, however, it may be possible to rely on s10 or s11.

The exemption is without limit, as long as both spouses are domiciled in the United Kingdom. If, though, the transferee is domiciled outside the United Kingdom, the maximum aggregate of transfers of value which can be made under s18 is £55,000.

See *Frankland* v *IRC* [1996] STC 735, discussed under 'testamentary discretionary trusts: s144' in Chapter 21, section 21.7, which was intended to secure the benefit of inter-spouse exemption.

Gifts to charities: s23

Section 23 provides that transfers of value are exempt without limit, to the extent that the value transferred is attributable to property which is given to charities.

Gifts for national purposes: s25

Transfers of value, whenever made, are exempt without limit so far as they are attributable to property which becomes the property of certain national institutions such as:

1. the National Gallery and the British Museum;
2. local authorities, and local authority museums and art galleries;
3. universities, and university libraries, museums and art galleries;
4. the National Trust and the Nature Conservancy Council;
5. government departments.

Gifts to political parties: s24

Transfers of value are, as a general rule, exempt without limit to the extent that the value transferred is attributable to property which becomes the property of a qualifying political party. A qualifying political party is one which at the last general election had either two members elected to the House of Commons, or one member elected and not less than 150,000 votes given to its members.

Gifts to registered housing associations: s24A

Gifts of land (including interests in land but not interests by way of mortgage or other security) to registered housing associations are exempt. The exemption will not apply if the gift is subject to an interest reserved or created by the donor entitling himself, his spouse or a connected person to possess or occupy the whole or any part of the land rent free or at a rent below what would have been negotiated in a transaction at arm's length between unconnected persons.

Gifts for public benefit: s26

Because of the strict rules relating to whether a gift is for charitable purposes only, certain gifts may fall outside the scope of s23. They may, however, yet be exempt transfers under s26, which provides that, if Treasury approval is obtained, a transfer of value is an exempt transfer so far as it is attributable to certain sorts of property (specified in s26(2)) transferred to a non-profit-making body. The non-profit-making body itself must also meet with the approval of the Treasury.

The conditions which must be met in relation to the various sorts of property which can fall within the scope s26 are:

1. in the case of land, that the Treasury must be of the opinion that it is of outstanding scenic or historic or scientific interest;
2. in the case of a building, that the Treasury is of the opinion that special steps should be taken for its preservation by reason of its outstanding historic or architectural or aesthetic interest and by reason of the cost of preserving it. If a building qualifies, land used as the grounds of that building and objects ordinarily kept in, and given with, that building qualify too. Such land and such objects need not qualify under (1) above or (3) below.
3. in the case of prints, pictures, books, manuscripts, works of art or scientific collections, that the Treasury is of the opinion that the article or collection is of national, scientific, historic or artistic interest.

Property given to provide for the upkeep of any property within (1) to (3) above is also exempted if the Treasury is of the opinion that it will not produce much more than is needed for the asset's upkeep. If it will, only a portion of the transfer of value will be an exempt transfer.

The Treasury can require certain undertakings before directing that the transfer be exempt, including undertakings allowing the public reasonable access, or restricting its use or disposal and to secure its preservation. Any disposition in contravention of such an undertaking will be void.

Business property

Sections 103–114 afford relief from IHT by reducing the value transferred by a transfer of business property. Relief is also afforded in a similar way to transfers of settled business property.

Section 104(1) provides that where the whole or part of the value transferred by a transfer of value is attributable to the value of 'any relevant business property', the whole or part of the value transferred is to be treated as reduced by 'the appropriate percentage'. The reduction is made before grossing-up takes place (if necessary). The relief was increased by FA (No 2) 1992, again by s184 FA 1996 and Schedule 41 and is restricted to particular types of business property – 'relevant business property' – and the amount of the relief varies according to the type of asset. Whatever the category of business property, the relief is conditional upon the property being owned by the transferor for a minimum period of two years immediately preceding the transfer: s106. However there are provisions which allow relief where relevant property has been replaced by 'replacement property', such as when a transferee disposes of property received and reinvests the proceeds in other property: s113A and B.

The changes made by s184 FA 1996 and Schedule 41 have substantially simplified the range of relief which previously existed according to the type of property and in particular in relation to the level of shareholding in unquoted trading companies. Prior to 6 April 1996, shareholdings (ie not other securities) of 25 per cent or more in such companies, qualified for 100 per cent relief. From that date, all shares in unquoted companies qualify for 100 per cent relief.

Following the FA 1996 changes, 'relevant business property' means:

For 100 per cent business property relief:
1. Property consisting of a business or interest in a business: this attracts a 100 per cent reduction in the value transferred.
2. Unquoted securities which taken either on their own or combined with any other unquoted securities or unquoted shares gave the transferor control of the company immediately before the transfer. All must be owned by the transferor.
3. Any unquoted shares in a company – providing the company does not carry on a business of dealing in securities, stocks or shares, land or buildings or making or holding investments: s105(3).

For 50 per cent business property relief
4. Shares or securities in a company which are listed on a recognised stock

exchange and which either on their own or when taken together with other shares or securities owned by the transferor, gave the transferor control of the company immediately before the transfer.
5. Land or buildings, machinery or plant which immediately before the transfer was or were used for the purposes of a business carried on by a company which the transferor controlled or by a partnership of which he was a partner: no relief is available where the transferor only has a minority shareholding in a company which uses assets of this kind belonging to the transferor. Thus where a partnership of three uses a factory owned by one of the partners, the building will attract relief if it is transferred before, but not after, the partnership incorporates.
6. Any land or buildings, machinery or plant which immediately before the transfer was or were used wholly or mainly for the purposes of a business carried on by the transferor and was or were settled property in which he was beneficially entitled to an interest in possession: this category is generally redundant since such property will usually attract relief at 100 per cent under s105(1)(a), as forming part of the business assets 'belonging' to the life tenant. In *Fetherstonaugh* v *IRC* [1984] STC 261 the Court held that trust property which was farmed by the tenant for life as part of a business which he carried on as sole trader was (since he was beneficially entitled to an interest in possession in the property) property which, for all the purposes of IHT, was to be considered to be his and thus to form part of his business property. On his death, therefore, the tenant for life was deemed to have made a transfer of value of all his business (including the farmland), attracting business property relief under s105(1)(a) at what would now be 100 per cent.

In considering whether 'control' exists for the purposes of the relief in paragraphs 2 and 4 above, all shares and securities giving rise to voting rights must be considered, irrespective of whether they are exercisable or exercised in practice. In *Walding* v *IRC* [1996] STC 13 it was claimed that a holding of 45 per cent gave control because 24 per cent of the shares in the company were in the name of an infant. It was held that personal capacity did not detract from the requirements of s269 which for this purpose looks at the total shares in which voting rights are 'capable of being exercised'.

Business property relief is never available in cases where the business consists wholly or mainly of dealing in shares or securities or land or buildings, or is an investment business: s105(3). There are a considerable number of other restrictions on and qualifications to the availability of the relief, of which the most important is that either the transferor must have owned the business property transferred for at least two years, or the property must have replaced other property which would have qualified because the transferor had beneficially owned it for at least two of the preceding five years: s106. Relief is also not available if, at the time of transfer, the property is under a binding contract of sale: s113. The relief is for the transfer of business assets, and what is transferred in reality in this latter case is an interest in a fund of money: the sale proceeds.

The relief determines the value transferred, rather than the chargeable transfer, so it takes precedence over the provisions relating to exempt transfers (which operate on the value transferred), in particular over those such as the annual exemption and gifts in consideration of marriage where only a limited exemption is available.

Since the introduction of PETs a further extremely important exemption has been introduced by ss113A and B in relation to business property relief (with counterparts in ss124A and B for agricultural property). If a PET which proves chargeable on the death of the transferor within seven years of the gift (or indeed any other chargeable transfer made within seven years of death) would otherwise be reduced by business property relief, the resulting chargeable transfer is not to obtain such relief unless:

1. the original property (or an acceptable substitute: s113B) was owned by the transferee throughout the period ending with the death of the transferor (or of the transferee, if earlier) and is not held under a binding contract for sale; and
2. if the transferee had made a transfer of value of the property immediately before the relevant death, the property would have been relevant business property (ignoring the requirement of two years' minimum ownership).

Thus if X transfers to Y a factory which X Ltd, a company in which X has the controlling shareholding, uses for the purposes of its business, no business property relief can be available on X's death within seven years, since the factory cannot obtain such relief in Y's ownership.

Agricultural property

Sections 115–124 give relief where the whole or part of the value transferred by a chargeable transfer is attributable to the agricultural value of agricultural property. The relief is available both in the case of lifetime and death transfers and on transfers into and out of settlements.

'Agricultural value' is the value that land would have if it were subject to a perpetual covenant not to use it otherwise than for agricultural purposes. Thus if agricultural land is transferred with development value it only obtains agricultural relief to the extent of its agricultural value.

'Agricultural land' is defined by s115(2) as agricultural land or pasture in the United Kingdom, the Channel Islands and the Isle of Man, and as including:

1. woodlands; and
2. buildings used in connection with the intensive rearing of livestock or fish, if the occupation of each is ancillary to that of the agricultural land or pasture; and
3. such cottages, farm buildings and farmhouses as are of a character appropriate to the property.

In *Starke & Another (Brown's Executors)* v *IRC* [1995] 1 WLR 1439; [1995] STC 689; property on a medium-sized farm, consisting of a large farmhouse and outbuildings, was declared not to be agricultural property within the meaning of s115(2).

Section 116
The nature of the relief, as with business property relief, takes the form of a percentage reduction in the value transferred by the transfer of value. The appropriate percentage depends on the interest of the transferor. Section 116 provides, first, that the appropriate percentage is 100 per cent if the transferor:

1. had the right to vacant possession of the property immediately before the transfer, or the right to obtain it within the next 12 months; or
2. had been beneficially entitled to his interest since before 10 March 1981 and satisfied certain conditions: subs(3).

Agricultural tenancies commencing on or after 1 September 1995 also qualify for 100 per cent relief. Following FA 1996 a new provision in s116(5A) extended the relief to tenancies acquired by the succession provisions of the Agricultural Tenancies Act, and s116(5B) conserves the relief for the owner where the tenant has died but a 'new' tenancy under certain successions has not been put in place.

Section 116 provides, secondly, that the appropriate percentage is 50 per cent in any other case.

Section 117
In order to qualify for relief under s116, however, a minimum period of ownership or occupation must be satisfied: s117. Either:

1. The transferor must have *occupied* the property for the purposes of agriculture throughout the *two* years immediately preceding the transfer; or
2. The transferor must have *owned* the property throughout the last *seven* years, and the property must throughout the period have been occupied by him or some other for the purposes of agriculture.

It is not necessary to satisfy this condition by holding the same land for the whole of the requisite period. The provisions of s118 also confer relief (subject to certain restrictions) in cases where the landowner replaces one farm (or part of a farm) by another. In this case, the respective periods of ownership are aggregated, although if aggregation is necessary in order for relief to be claimed, the maximum relief available is that which would have been available had the original land been that disposed of by the chargeable transfer.

Example
X buys Whiteacre Farm for £1,000,000 in 1988. In 1995 he sells it for £1,500,000 and puts the proceeds of sale towards the purchase price of £2,500,000 of Blackacre

Farm. In 1996, when it is worth £3,000,000 and Whiteacre Farm is worth £2,000,000, he gives Blackacre Farm to his son. The maximum agricultural relief which will be available on the transfer if X dies within seven years is 100 per cent of £2,000,000, not 100 per cent of £3,000,000.

Another's period of ownership. In certain circumstances one can claim someone else's period of ownership or occupation as part of one's own:

1. When a person acquires farmland on the death of his spouse he shall be deemed to have occupied it for the purposes of agriculture and/or to have owned it for a period for which his spouse so owned or occupied it.
2. If a donee of agricultural land transfers that land on to a third party, then, even though the donee has not satisfied the rules in s117, agricultural relief will be granted if:
   - the original transfer qualified for agricultural relief; and
   - the original donee occupied the property for the purposes of agriculture at the date of the transfer; and
   - either the earlier transfer or the later one occurred on death.

Example
Farmer George gave his 3,000-acre farm, which he had occupied for the purposes of agriculture for many years, to his son Peter on 21 December 1995. Peter immediately commenced farming it. Ten months later Peter was killed by an irate bull. Agricultural property relief will be available, despite Peter's short period of occupancy.

Section 122
Agricultural property relief is also available in respect of shares in certain farming companies. Section 122 provides that where a transfer of value is of shares in a farming company, agricultural property relief is available to the extent that the value of the shares is attributable to the agricultural value of agricultural property forming part of the assets of the company, provided that the shares gave the transferor control of the company immediately prior to the transfer. Thus if a company's assets comprise £1,000,000 of farmland and £300,000 of other assets, agricultural property relief will be given (in priority to business property relief) at the appropriate rate – in other words, depending on whether the company has, or can obtain within twelve months, vacant possession of the land. The shares will probably obtain business property relief on the remainder, though in cases where the company is an investment company investing in agricultural property, the only relief available will be 50 per cent relief under s116(2). In cases where s122 applies, the company's occupation of the land for the relevant period is considered.

The restrictions on agricultural relief are of a similar nature to those applicable to business property relief:

Exemptions and reliefs available both during the transferor's lifetime and on death 309

1. There is a minimum period of occupation: see 'Section 117', above.
2. Relief is not available if at the time of transfer the property is under a binding contract for sale: s124.
3. If the transfer falls within seven years of the transferor's death, relief is given (ss124A and B) only if:
   - the original property (or an acceptable substitute) is owned by the transferor at the death of the transferor (or the transferee's death, if earlier) and is not under a binding contract for sale; and
   - the property in question is occupied by someone for the purposes of agriculture at the time of death; and
   - the property in question being shares in an agricultural company, the company continues to own the relevant agricultural property at the time of death and someone continues to occupy it.

Relief for works of art, historic buildings, etc

It will be recalled that transfers of value of works of art etc are exempt in certain circumstances when transferred to non-profit-making organisations under s26. Sections 30 and 31 extend a similar sort of relief to cases where the property is transferred to any other person, provided that certain undertakings are given by the recipient and that the Treasury is willing to 'designate' the property. Transfers of value exempted under the provisions of s30 are known as 'conditionally exempt transfers'.

Section 31(1) allows the Treasury to designate the following:

1. any pictures, prints, books, manuscripts, works of art, scientific collections or any other things not yielding income which appear to the Treasury to be of national, scientific, historical or artistic interest;
2. any land which in the opinion of the Treasury is of outstanding scenic, historical or scientific interest;
3. any building for the preservation of which special steps should in the opinion of the Treasury be taken by reason of its outstanding historical or architectural interest, together with adjoining land.

In the case of property falling within (1) the requisite undertaking is that, until the person beneficially entitled dies, or the property is disposed of, the property will be kept permanently in the United Kingdom, and reasonable steps will be taken for its preservation and reasonable access granted to the public.

For property falling within (2) it is that, for the same period, reasonable steps will be taken for the maintenance of the land and the preservation of its character, and for securing reasonable access for the public. If the property falls within (3) it is that, in addition, reasonable steps will be taken for the maintenance, repair and preservation of the building.

The exemption is available in respect of transfers on death. It is also available if the transferor or his spouse has beneficially owned the property for the last six years, or the transferor acquired it as a result of a conditionally exempt transfer on death. Where a transfer is conditionally exempt, no charge to IHT arises until a 'chargeable event' occurs. 'Chargeable events' are defined by s32 as:

1. the non-observance of an undertaking.
2. the death of the person beneficially entitled to the property;
3. the disposal of the property, by sale, gift or otherwise.

The computation of the tax on a chargeable event is complex, being made dependent by s33 on both the value of the property at the time of the relevant event and the cumulative total of the 'relevant person'. Who the relevant person is depends on the number of conditionally exempt transfers there have been in the last 30 years (a similar though by no means identical relief was conferred in estate duty). If there has been only one, he will be the transferor; if there have been several, the Inland Revenue may select from among the transferors who that person shall be, and will do so with an eye to maximising the tax payable.

With the introduction of PETs, conditionally exempt transfers are relegated to application on the transfer proving chargeable (s30(3B)) when conditional exemption of the earlier event depends on the property continuing to belong to the transferee.

22.5 Reliefs available only on death

Relief for woodlands

As has already been said, agricultural property relief may be available in respect of woodlands whose occupation is ancillary to occupation of other land for agricultural purposes. If no such relief is available under ss115–124, relief may still be available under ss125–130. Such relief is only available on death.

Section 125 provides that where any part of a person's estate immediately before his death is attributable to the value of land in the United Kingdom on which trees or underwood are growing, then an election can be made to leave the value of the trees and underwood out of account in determining the value transferred on death. The relief is not available, however, unless the deceased was beneficially entitled to the property throughout the five years immediately preceding his death, or had been given the woodlands.

On a subsequent disposal of the trees, whether by sale or otherwise, s126 levies tax on the person who is entitled to the proceeds of sale (or would be, if there were any) and IHT is charged at the top rate applicable on the deceased's death based on the consideration or value of the property disposed of. No tax is charged if the disposal is in favour of the spouse of the transferee. As the value of the trees is likely to have increased since the death, the result is that while s125 postpones a charge to IHT, when that charge eventually occurs it may well exceed that which would originally have been payable. If business property relief would have been available in respect of the woodlands on the earlier death, the amount on which tax is charged is reduced by 100 per cent.

If that subsequent disposal is itself a chargeable transfer, two charges to tax are levied, but credit is given by s129 on the chargeable transfer by reducing the value transferred by the tax chargeable under s126.

Quick succession relief

Quick succession relief is afforded by s141. That section provides relief in respect of successive chargeable transfers in two situations:

1. where the second transfer is on death; and
2. where the second transfer of value, though made during the transferor's lifetime, falls to be valued by reference to settled property in which he has an interest in possession, and the value transferred by the first chargeable transfer was determined by reference to the same property.

It is, however, profitable to discuss both cases here.

Where the value of a person's estate has been increased by a chargeable transfer made not more than five years before one of the two transfers mentioned above, the tax payable on the second occasion is reduced by a proportion of the original tax which may be deducted from the second charge and varies according to the time elapsed between the two transfers. The deductible percentage is:

100 per cent if less than one year has elapsed;
80 per cent if less than two years have elapsed;
60 per cent if less than three years have elapsed;
40 per cent if less than four years have elapsed;
20 per cent if less than five years have elapsed.

In the case of lifetime chargeable transfers calculated by reference to the value of settled property, the earlier transfer must have been either the making of the settlement or an occasion falling after the creation of the settlement.

Death on active service

Section 154 provides that where a person died as a result of a wound received on active service, or where his death was hastened as a result of a wound so received, no IHT is payable under s4(1).

23

IHT and Settled Property

23.1 Introduction

23.2 'Settlement'

23.3 'Interest in possession'

23.4 Consequence of the existence of an interest in possession

23.5 The charging provisions

23.6 'Excluded property'

23.7 Liability for tax and the beneficiary's cumulative total

23.8 The discretionary trust regime

23.9 The principal charge to tax

23.10 The charge at other times

23.11 Charitable purpose trusts

23.12 Accumulation and maintenance trusts: s71

23.13 Property becoming held for charitable purposes or by exempt bodies

23.1 Introduction

All references in this chapter, unless expressly stated otherwise, are to the Inheritance Tax Act 1984.

Chargeable transfers are defined by s2(1) as being only transfers of value made by individuals. Without more, therefore, it would be possible to avoid inheritance tax (IHT) by putting one's property into trust. Accordingly, special regimes exist to bring into charge dispositions in respect of settled property. Two entirely different methods of taxation exist, depending on whether or not there exists a person or persons beneficially entitled to an interest in possession in the settled property. Where such a person exists, he is treated as if he owned the property in which his interest subsists. Where there is no such person, tax is, in effect, imposed as if the property belonged to a notional individual who gave away such of the property as was distributed to beneficiaries by the trustees and who, in any event, gave away one third of his property every ten years.

The 'interest in possession' rules are to be found in ss49–54, and the rules relating to settled property in which no interest in possession subsists – the discretionary trust regime – in ss58–85.

23.2 'Settlement'

'Settlement' is defined by s43 as:

> 'any disposition or dispositions of property, however effected, whereby the property is for the time being –
> (a) held in trust for persons in succession or ... for any person subject to a contingency;
> (b) held by trustees on trust to accumulate ... or with power to make payments out ... at the discretion of the trustees or some other person ... ;
> (c) charged or burdened (otherwise than for full consideration) with the payment of any annuity or other periodical payment payable for a life or any other limited or terminable period;
> (d) a lease for life or lives granted ... otherwise than for full consideration'.

The following forms of trust are *not* settlements for the purposes of IHT:

1. joint tenancies;
2. tenancies in common, whether in equal or unequal shares;
3. bare trusts.

23.3 'Interest in possession'

The sole determining factor as to whether a settlement falls within one or other of the IHT settled property regimes is whether a person has an interest in possession in the settled property. The phrase is not defined by statute but has been the subject of an extremely important case in the House of Lords – *Pearson v IRC* [1980] 2 WLR 872.

The question for the House was whether three beneficiaries who were entitled to all the income arising under a settlement, subject to a power in the trustees to accumulate income during a specified period, had interests in possession. Both parties and all members of the House were agreed that a person only had an interest in possession if he had a present right to the present enjoyment of something. Just what that something was, was the core of the dispute. The trustees argued that it merely meant a right which was not in reversion, and the Revenue that it was a right to the enjoyment of the whole or part of the net income of the settled property. The majority of the House accepted the Revenue's suggestion.

Even so, there remained the question of *precisely when* a person could be said to have the present right to the present enjoyment of the net income of the trust fund. Clearly, in the simple case of 'To A for life and then to B' A has an interest in possession; no one could deprive him of his right to the net income. But what of more complicated cases? For example:

> 'To A for life, subject to the trustees' power to accumulate income, exercisable in their absolute discretion, for the next 21 years, then to B'

or

> 'To A absolutely subject to the trustees' power to accumulate income during the next 21 years'.

In each of these A is entitled to the net income of the trust fund, if the trustees decide not to accumulate income, or fail within a reasonable period to decide to do so. However, the House held that in this sort of case A did not have an interest in possession, since it could not be said of trust income, as soon as it had arisen, that it was A's; that would be so only if the trustees decided not to accumulate.

On the other hand, a *revocable* appointment, 'To A for life and then to B', did give A an interest in possession, since, although the trustees could revoke the right itself and thus deprive him of future income, he could not have taken away from him income which had already arisen, even though it had not yet been paid over to him. The distinction has been likened to a tap: if all that pours out goes to A, then he has an interest in possession, even though there exists a person who can deprive him of future income by turning the tap off; if, on the other hand, someone can divert part of that which has flowed out of the tap, then no interest in possession (IIP) exists. Whether a person has an interest in possession depends on the existence of a power in someone else to deprive him of trust income which has already arisen. It does not depend on the exercise of that power (pace Lord Keith in *Pearson*).

A distinction of much importance drawn by the House in that case was between 'administrative powers' and 'dispositive powers'. The test is not whether the beneficiary is entitled to *all* the income arising, but only whether he is entitled to the *net* income as it arises. The concept of 'net income' is designed to allow for the administrative expenses of the trust. Certain types of expense incurred by trustees, such as their own entitlement to remuneration (if any) and to maintain – though not to improve – trust property, are, in accordance with general trust principles, payable out of the trust income. Any beneficiary will always be entitled only to the residue after such expenses have been paid. If, therefore, to have an interest in possession is to have a right to income, it must be to have a right to the income after the deduction of such expenses. But a line has to be drawn between the trustees' right to have recourse to income for administrative purposes and to have recourse in a manner which diverts it away from one beneficiary in favour of another, and the distinction between such powers is that between administrative and dispositive powers. The difficulty is that no one knows where the line is to be drawn. What, for example, of a power specifically conferred on trustees to have recourse to income for the payment of what would usually be capital expenses? Does not such a power benefit the remaindermen at the expense of the life tenant, so that it should be classified as dispositive? The House appears to have thought that such a power was administrative only.

The distinction between such powers arose for decision in the Court of Session in *Miller* v *IRC* [1987] STC 108. There, the trust provided that before striking the free income or produce of the year, the trustees were to have power to appropriate such portion of the revenue as they might think proper for meeting depreciation of the capital assets of the trust. The wife obtained a vested interest in the whole free annual income or produce of the trust (subject, of course, to the power conferred on the trustees). On her death, the Revenue sought to levy IHT as if she had had an interest in possession in the fund. The trustees claimed that the power of appropriation precluded her interest being one 'in possession' within the meaning of that term, as defined in *Pearson*. The Court of Session found for the Revenue, holding that the power was administrative, not dispositive, in nature. The nature of the trust was such that any construction of a power had to lean against it being exercisable so as to divert income for the benefit of others. Thus the power could only be exercised so as to *preserve* the value of the trust fund, to keep it up to the value it had had when it vested in the trustees, and could not be exercised so as to set aside income to preserve it for the future benefit of others. That was to say, it could not be exercised to *increase* the capital value of the fund.

None of this was really conclusive; one could equally argue that the fund had already depreciated before the income in question arrived in the hands of the trustees, and so any exercise of the power increased the current value of the capital of the fund and thus benefited the future beneficiaries at the expense of the life tenant.

One illustration of a person becoming entitled to an interest in possession which is met frequently in practice (and for which special provision has had to be made by the discretionary trust regime) is that of the accumulation and maintenance settlement 'To such of my children A, B and C as attain the age of 30, if more than one, in equal shares', where A, B and C are all minors at the time of the creation of the settlement. In this situation, s31 of the Trustee Act 1925 will generally apply. If it does so (and this depends on the intention of the setlement):

1. Until a child reaches the age of 18, the section requires that his share of income be accumulated, insofar as it is not used for his maintenance, education or benefit: s31(1)(i). Accordingly, at this stage, each child will *not* have an interest in possession.
2. On attaining the age of 18, the child becomes entitled to receive a share of the trust income proportionate to his contingent share: s31(1)(ii). On reaching this age, therefore, each child becomes entitled to an interest in possession.
3. As each child satisfies the specified contingency – in the example above, attains the age of 30 – he ceases to be entitled to an interest in possession in settled property and becomes entitled to an absolute interest in a share of the property.

23.4 Consequence of the existence of an interest in possession

Section 49(1) provides that a person beneficially entitled to an interest in possession in settled property is to be treated as beneficially entitled to the property in which the interest subsists. The consequences of this have already been discussed. Even though the value of the interest itself may be small, because made under a revocable appointment, or because of the life expectancy of the beneficiary, the beneficiary is treated as entitled to, and his estate is increased by the full value of, the settled property.

Moore & Osborne v *IRC* [1984] STC 236 is of some interest. It decided that even in the case of there being a single member only of a class of discretionary beneficiaries (which class was capable of increase only until the death of the living beneficiary) that beneficiary did not have an interest in possession immediately before his death, even though the discretion was only to select the members of the class among whom to distribute the trust income exhaustively.

Section 50 makes provision for specific cases:

1. When the beneficiary is only entitled to part of the income, he is treated as entitled only to a proportionate part of the settled property.
2. Where the beneficiary is only entitled to a certain specified amount of income from the trust property, he is treated as entitled to such part of the property as produces that amount of income. Anti-avoidance rules exist to ensure that, for example, an aged beneficiary cannot be given income only out of high-income-producing assets of limited capital value.
3. If a beneficiary is entitled not to income but to the use and enjoyment of settled property, his interest is calculated by apportioning the annual value of the property he uses or enjoys among the aggregate of annual values of all the settled property. Since the whole of the settled property is treated as the life tenant's, there is no need to charge tax on the interest of those entitled in reversion: see Chapter 21, section 21.10, 'Excluded Property'.

23.5 The charging provisions

On the death of a person entitled to an interest in possession in settled property, the tax charged under s4(1) is increased by deeming his estate immediately before that time to include the settled property: see Chapter 21, section 21.7, 'Death'.

Where, however, a person's interest in possession terminates during his lifetime, IHT is charged as if he had at that moment made a transfer of value, of which the value transferred was equal to the value of the settled property in which his interest had ceased to subsist: s52(1). But s96 of the Finance (No 2) Act 1987 extends the application of s3A to include notional transfers under s52(1). Accordingly, provided that on the termination of the interest in possession another such interest immediately arises, or the property becomes held on accumulation and maintenance trusts or on disabled trusts, or for a person absolutely, the termination will be a potentially exempt transfer (PET), not liable to tax unless the life tenant dies within seven years of the event. Anti-avoidance provisions are introduced by ss54A and B to preclude gifts into discretionary trusts, for instance through the creation of a revocable interest in possession trust, the revocation of the interest and its reappointment onto the intended trusts. For example, X, who has a cumulative total of £1,000,000, wishes to create a discretionary trust in favour of his family. He settles property on revocable trusts for B (a pauper) for life, remainder to C, and subsequently revokes B's interest, reappointing the trust fund on the desired discretionary trusts. Leaving aside the possibility that the Revenue might be able to rely on *Furniss* v *Dawson*, s54A enables it to charge tax by reference either to the cumulative total of the life tenant B (which stands at zero) or to that of the settlor, provided that the termination occurs within seven years of the creation of the settlement.

Example
If X transfers property to trustees to hold upon trust to pay the income thereof to A for her life, or until she remarries, whichever is the earlier, and subject thereto upon trust as to capital and income for B absolutely, and A dies, or A remarries, then the IHT consequences will in the former case be a s4(1) charge, and in the latter case be a PET under s3A, with a potential transfer under s52(1) if A dies within seven years of remarriage.

If an interest in possession is assigned by a beneficiary to another, s51(1) provides that the disposal is not a transfer of value but shall be treated as the coming to an end of his interest. Accordingly, s52(1) is brought into operation and tax is computed in the same way.

In each case (ss51(1) and 52(1)) the disposal is only a *deemed* transfer of value. The following exemptions (contained in ss19–22) do not extend to deemed disposals:

1. the annual exemption (s19);
2. small gifts (s20);
3. normal expenditure out of income (s21);
4. gifts in consideration of marriage (s22).

However, as stated in Chapter 22, section 22.2, s57(1) extends the annual exemption and the gifts in consideration of marriage exemption to deemed disposals occasioned by the termination of a life interest in possession under s51(1). The termination is treated as a disposition made by the person beneficially entitled to the interest in possession, and that section permits him to notify the trustees that the whole or the specified part of his ss19 and 22 exemptions may be used by them to reduce the tax payable on the chargeable transfer.

There are certain exceptions and reliefs from the primary charge under s52(1):

1. If the beneficiary becomes entitled, on the termination of his interest, either to another interest in possession of the property, or to the property itself, tax is not chargeable under s52(1): s53(2). The logic of the exemption is that, in accordance with s49(1), the beneficiary has always been treated as entitled to the property. Since, as a result of the transaction, he is either still deemed to be entitled to it, or actually becomes entitled to it, it would be absurd for either event to cause a charge to tax.
2. If the charge under s52(1) arises as a result of a s51(1) disposal, the value transferred is reduced by the value of any consideration in money or money's worth received for the disposal. Thus if A sells his life interest (worth £50,000) in settled property worth £80,000 to B for £50,000, A is treated as having made a transfer of value of £30,000.
3. If the property reverts to
   - the settlor,
   - the settlor's wife, or,
   - within two years of the settlor's death, the settlor's widow,
   and
   - neither the settlor nor his wife or widow acquired the reversionary interest for a consideration in money or money's worth; and
   - in the second and third cases the wife or widow is domiciled in the United Kingdom,
   in no case is tax chargeable on the reverter.
4. Where the value of the settled property in which the interest subsists is reduced in consequence of a 'depreciatory transaction', a charge to tax arises under s52(3). A 'depreciatory transaction' is one entered into between the trustees and any person who is, or who is connected with, a beneficiary under the settlement, as a result of which the value of the settled property is less than it would be but for the transaction: for example, where the trustees sell trust assets to a beneficiary at an undervalue.

    An exception from the charge is made if the trustees can show that they would have been able to rely on s10(1) had they been an individual (for s10, see Chapter 21, section 21.3). For an example of the application of s52(3), see *MacPherson v IRC* [1988] STC 362.

23.6 'Excluded property'

Section 53(1) provides that tax shall not be charged under s52 (see section 23.5) if the settled property is 'excluded property'. 'Excluded property' is given a special meaning for the purpose of settled property by s48(3):

'Where property comprised in a settlement is situated outside the United Kingdom –
(a) the property (but not a reversionary interest in the property) is excluded property unless the settlor was domiciled in the UK when the settlement was made; and

(b) section 6(1) applies to the reversionary interest' – thus making it excluded property if it belongs to an individual domiciled outside the UK – 'but does not otherwise apply in relation to the property.'

Accordingly, where settled property is situated outside the United Kingdom, the question whether the property itself is excluded property depends only on the domicile of the settlor at the time the settlement was made, but a reversionary interest in the property is excluded property only if it belongs to an individual domiciled outside the United Kingdom. The rules thus are:

1. Where the settled property is situated in the United Kingdom:
   - An interest in possession is *not* excluded property; but
   - A reversionary interest in the property *is* excluded property (provided that it does not fall within any of the exceptions to s48(1)).
2. Where settled property is situated outside the United Kingdom:
   - If the settlor was domiciled in the United Kingdom when the settlement was made, the settled property is *not* excluded property, but if he was domiciled outside the United Kingdom when he made the settlement, the settled property *is* excluded property.
   - A reversionary interest in the settled property is excluded property if either the settlor was domiciled in the United Kingdom when he created the settlement (provided that none of the exceptions to s48(1) applies), or the settlor was domiciled outside the United Kingdom when he created the settlement *and* the interest belongs to a person not domiciled in the United Kingdom.

Save in the case of the second part of (2) above, 'domiciled in the United Kingdom' bears its narrow private international law meaning and *not* its wider IHT meaning. (The rules are the same, but become additionally complicated, if the reversion itself is settled, or if, as seems to be possible, the reversion is situate abroad while the settled property is situate in the United Kingdom or vice versa.)

23.7 Liability for tax and the beneficiary's cumulative total

Because the settled property is treated as forming part of the estate of the life tenant, the charge to IHT on any occasion when tax is charged by reference to the value of the settled property, be it under s4(1) or s52(1), is determined by adding to the beneficiary's cumulative total the value deemed to be transferred on the particular event. Thus the rate of tax chargeable will be computed by taking into account all chargeable transfers made by the beneficiary within the past seven years.

Section 201(1)(a) makes the trustees the persons primarily liable for the tax. There is no grossing-up. Nevertheless, the value deemed to be so transferred will form part of the beneficiary's cumulative total, and will thus increase the rate of tax payable by him on any subsequent chargeable transfers, even those of his own free (ie not settled) property.

23.8 The discretionary trust regime

The system of taxing settlements in which there is no interest in possession (discretionary settlements) is contained in ss58–85. Inheritance tax is levied on the assumption (by no means universally true) that a charge to tax will arise once every generation, on the death of the life tenant or the absolute owner. This charge can, of course, be avoided by an outright gift of assets more than seven years before the death of the owner (or life tenant), but in the absence of such a transfer IHT will be payable. Discretionary trusts, on the other hand, would offer an opportunity to avoid tax without losing the potential enjoyment of the property. It is thus necessary to impose tax by reference to events other than actual transfers, in order to provide for the regular collection of tax. While the effect of this was fiscally neutral for capital transfer tax (CTT), in the revised context of IHT discretionary trusts are less tax-efficient than other forms of settlement, from which property can be removed without charge.

In order to ensure regularity of charge, a periodic charge, known as the 'ten-yearly charge' is imposed every ten years (on every 'ten-year anniversary') at 30 per cent of the rate which would usually be applicable on a single transfer of the settled property. Since the current rate of tax for lifetime transfers is 20 per cent, these provisions would give rise to a charge to tax of 30 per cent of that, ie at 6 per cent. If property leaves the settlement between ten-year anniversaries, a percentage charge will be imposed by reference to the time which has elapsed since the last periodic charge. This system was intended to put a discretionary trust in a position no less favourable than that of trusts in which there is an interest in possession. As has been explained, the introduction of the PET precludes such neutrality. Discretionary trusts are not within s3A – no event of charge in relation to such settlements is ever potentially exempt.

The separate regime for discretionary trusts has its own terminology:

'Qualifying interest in possession'

A qualifying interest in possession is defined by s59 as either:

1. an interest in possession to which an individual is beneficially entitled; or
2. an interest in possession which a company whose business is the acquisition of interests in settled property has bought and to which it remains entitled.

'Relevant property'

Section 58 defines 'relevant property' as settled property in which no qualifying interest in possession subsists. It then lists exceptional situations where, though no qualifying interest in possession subsists in the settled property, the property is not to be treated as relevant property. The most important of these are:

1. property held for charitable purposes only (even if only for a limited period);
2. property held on accumulation and maintenance trusts (s71);
3. excluded property.

These exceptional cases will be dealt with at greater length below.

'Ten-year anniversary'

This is the tenth anniversary of the date on which the settlement commenced and each subsequent tenth anniversary. There is however, an important proviso to this – no ten-year anniversary could fall before 1 April 1983.

Thus, considering two settlements, one of which commenced on 31 March 1973 and the other on 2 April 1973, the first ten-year anniversary of the former did not occur until 31 March 1993, whereas that of the latter fell on 2 April 1983.

'Related settlements'

Section 62 provides that two settlements are related if they were made by the same settlor, and they commenced on the same day. A settlement held for all time for charitable purposes only cannot, however, be related to any other settlement.

23.9 The principal charge to tax

Section 64 provides that a charge to IHT is imposed where, immediately before a ten-year anniversary, any part of the property comprised in a settlement is relevant property. That charge is at a rate fixed by ss66 and 67 and is imposed on the value of the property or part which is relevant property at that time. Section 66 deals with the simple case where no property has been added to the settlement since it commenced, and s67 with that where it has. Several steps have to be taken under s66 to determine that rate, the first being to add together:

1. the value of the relevant property in the settlement, and
2. the value of any property in the settlement which has never been relevant property, and
3. the value of property in any related settlement.

One then assumes the existence of a notional transferor who makes a chargeable transfer of that amount, and who has in the previous seven years made chargeable transfers equal in value to the aggregate of:

1. the chargeable transfers made by the settlor in the seven years before the settlement commenced, and
2. the amounts on which charges to IHT have been imposed under s65 (see below) in the previous ten years.

The tax payable on such a chargeable transfer is determined by applying tax in accordance with ss66(3) and 7(2) at a rate which is currently one-half of 40 per cent, expressed as a fraction of the value deemed to be transferred. The percentage rate so determined is the 'effective rate'. The rate of tax chargeable under s64 is then three-tenths of that effective rate: s66(1). It is of the essence of ss64 and 66 that tax is *not* charged on the deemed transfer of value computed under s66(4) – which is introduced purely in order to calculate *the effective rate* – but only on the amount of 'relevant property' in the settlement.

Section 66(2) adds one further complication to this: if the whole or any part of the relevant property on which tax is chargeable under s64 was either not relevant property, or not comprised in the settlement, for the whole ten-year period prior to the ten-year anniversary, the rate at which tax is charged on the whole or part, as the case may be, is reduced by one-fortieth for every complete quarter in which it was not relevant property comprised in the settlement.

Example
On 1 July 1987, S settles £300,000 on new discretionary trusts. On 1 January 1995, he adds £50,000 to the settlement. The trustees distribute all the income of the settlement, but none of the capital. S had previously made no chargeable transfers. There is no settlement related to the discretionary trust.

The first ten-year anniversary is 1 July 1997. On that day, the amount of relevant property in the settlement is £350,000.

The effective rate of tax is calculated in the following way:

1. Calculate the value of the deemed chargeable transfer: Here there is neither any non-relevant property nor any related settlement, so the value of the deemed chargeable transfer is equal to the value of the relevant property: £350,000.
2. Calculate the transferor's previous chargeable transfers plus any value transferred under s65 in the previous ten years: There is none of either.
3. Calculate the tax on such a chargeable transfer: The value transferred equals £350,000,

so	£215,000	@	0%	=	£	0
	135,000	@	20%	=	27,000	
	350,000				27,000 tax	

and, $\dfrac{27,000}{350,000} \times 100 = 7.71\%$

and the effective rate of tax is, therefore, 7.71 per cent.

Because some of the property was added later the computation of the s64 charge must be taken in stages:

1. £300,000 × $\tfrac{3}{10}$ × 7.71% = £6,939
2. Since the £50,000 was not introduced until 1 January 1995, 30 complete quarters of the ten-year period elapsed before it became relevant property comprised in the settlement. The tax on this part of the relevant property is, therefore, computed by reducing the effective rate of tax by $\tfrac{30}{40}$, ie to 1.9275 per cent:

50,000 × $\tfrac{3}{10}$ × 1.9275% = £289,

making a total tax bill of £7,228.

Section 67 adds further complications where property has been added to a settlement after it has commenced: in determining the effective rate of tax, one can take the values transferred by the settlor in the seven years prior to the commencement of the settlement *or* prior to the date of the addition to the settlement, whichever is the higher, at stage (2) of the computation.

23.10 The charge at other times

Section 65 imposes a charge to IHT on discretionary trusts on the occurrence of certain events in the middle of a ten-year period. No tax is payable, however, if the event in question occurs in the first quarter of a ten-year period. The events are:

1. when settled property, or part of it, ceases to be relevant property, for whatever reason: s65(1)(a);
2. when the trustees of the settlement make a disposition as a result of which the value of relevant property comprised in the settlement is less than it would be but for the disposition: s65(1)(b). In this latter case, however, no IHT is chargeable if the trustees can show that the disposition would fall within s10(1) if the trustees were an individual: that is to say, if they unintentionally made a bad bargain (see Chapter 21, section 21.3).

Certain events which would otherwise fall within s65(1)(a) or (b) are excepted from tax by later provisions of the section. These events and dispositions are:

1. 'income payments'
   - payments of costs or expenses fairly attributable to relevant property; and
   - payments which are (or will be) income of any person for any of the purposes of the Income Tax Acts.

2. when property ceases to be situated in the United Kingdom and becomes excluded property under s48(3)(a) (see section 23.6).
3. when the trustees of a settlement created by a person not domiciled in the United Kingdom invest in exempt gilts within s6(2) (see Chapter 21, section 21.9).

The tax is charged on the amount by which the value of relevant property comprised in the settlement is less than it would be but for the events, listed above, whether that event falls under s65(1)(a) or (b).

If the trustees pay the IHT out of relevant property still comprised in the settlement after the events, they are obliged to gross up in order to calculate the value transferred, and the rate of tax payable on the amount so calculated is computed in accordance with rules laid down in ss68 and 69.

Section 68 applies *before* the first ten-year anniversary and s69 after it. Taking s68 first: like s66, it computes the rate of tax by determining the 'effective rate' of tax which would be payable by a notional transferor on making a notional transfer of value of all the property which has been comprised in the settlement when he is deemed, in the previous seven years, to have made chargeable transfers of an amount equal to those made by the settlor in the seven years prior to the creation of the settlement.

The consequence of this should be that, as long as no more property is added to the settlement, the effective rate will remain constant. The *actual* rate imposed on a particular event will, however, vary, fluctuating by reference to the time which has elapsed since the commencement of the settlement: the longer the period which has elapsed, the higher the actual rate of tax.

In rather more detail, to calculate the rate of tax payable on a chargeable event occurring prior to the first ten-year anniversary:

1. One computes the notional transfer of value; that is taken as the aggregate of the value of *all* the property comprised in the settlement immediately after it commenced, and the value of all the property comprised in a related settlement immediately after it commenced, and the value of any property added to the settlement immediately after it was added.
2. One then computes the amount of tax which would be payable at the rates set out in Schedule 1 (reduced by 50 per cent in accordance with s7(2)) on a chargeable transfer of an amount determined as in (1) above by a transferor who had, in the seven years previous to the transfer, made chargeable transfers of an amount equal to those made by the settlor in the seven years prior to the commencement of the settlement.
3. The tax so found is expressed as a fraction of the notional chargeable transfer: the result is the *effective rate of tax*.

The rate of tax then payable on the event falling within s65 is the 'appropriate fraction' of the effective rate (s66). The 'appropriate fraction' is:

$$\frac{3}{10} \times \frac{\text{number of complete quarters since commencement}}{40}$$

Thus, if the settlement commenced on 1 April 1994, and the event occurs on 16 July 1997, thirteen complete quarters will have elapsed since the commencement of the settlement and the rate of tax on the event will be:

$\frac{3}{10} \times \frac{13}{40} \times$ effective rate of tax

If the whole or part of the amount on which tax is payable is attributable to property which has become relevant property since the commencement of the settlement, the appropriate fraction in relation to that amount ignores all quarters in which the property was not relevant property. Thus, taking the above example, if part of the property which ceased to be relevant property on 16 July 1997 had not become relevant property until 1 April 1995 the appropriate fraction *in respect of that amount* would be:

$\frac{3}{10} \times \frac{9}{40}$

Under s69, the rate of tax charged on an event occurring *after* a ten-year anniversary is, as a general rule, the *appropriate fraction* of the rate charged on the last such anniversary under s64. In this case, the appropriate fraction is the number of complete quarters which have elapsed since that anniversary divided by 40.

If there has been an addition to the property in the settlement or some of the property in the settlement has become relevant property, the s66 calculation is recomputed, treating that property as relevant property in the settlement at that time.

Once again, as in s68, if some amount on which tax is charged is attributable to property which was not relevant property at the last ten-year anniversary, the 'appropriate fraction' in relation to that amount is calculated by ignoring the quarters in which it was not relevant property. Thus, if a settlement commenced on 1 January 1986, and a chargeable event occurred on 1 August 1997, by which property which became relevant property on 1 January 1997 ceases to be relevant property, the appropriate fraction in respect of this part is $\frac{2}{40}$.

23.11 Charitable purpose trusts

Property which is held for charitable purposes, even if only for a limited period, is not 'relevant property' within s58. Accordingly, during the period in which it is so held, no charge to IHT arises. Section 70, however, penalises limited period charitable trusts by imposing a charge in two cases:

1. on exit-charge: when settled property ceases to be held on charitable trusts otherwise than by way of application for charitable purposes;
2. where the trustees make a disposition, otherwise than by way of application for

charitable purposes, as a result of which the value of the property is less than it would be but for the disposition – a depreciatory transaction.

Tax is not, however, charged under (2) if the trustees would be able to rely on s10(1) were they an individual, nor is tax charged if the disposition is of an income nature – a payment of costs or expenses, or one which is income of any person for any of the purposes of the Income Tax Acts.

The amount on which tax is charged is the diminution of the value of the property held on charitable trusts: grossing-up is required, however, if the tax is paid out of the remaining settled property. The rate of tax depends on the length of time that the property has been held on charitable trusts:

0.25% for each of the first 40
0.20% for each of the next 40
0.15% for each of the next 40 } quarters.
0.10% for each of the next 40
0.05% for each of the next 40

23.12 Accumulation and maintenance trusts: s71

Where property is held on accumulation and maintenance trusts, a special regime applies which imposes far fewer charges than those under ss64 and 65. Property is held on such trusts if:

1. 'One or more persons will, on or before attaining a specified age not exceeding 25, become beneficially entitled to the settled property or to an interest in possession in it'.

'Will' in these circumstances is not a word of mere futurity; it means that the beneficiary cannot be disentitled from acquiring his interest under the terms of the settlement: see *Inglewood* v *IRC* [1983] STC 133:

> 'It seems to us that the ordinary meaning of those words is that the condition will not be satisfied unless it can be said that, if the person or persons attain an age not exceeding 25 they will be bound to become entitled ... There is nothing in the language of [section 71(1)(a)] to suggest that possible future events may be disregarded ... The word "will" in [section 71] does import a degree of certainty which is not satisfied if the trust can be revoked and the fund reappointed to some other person at an age exceeding 25.'

Thus if the appointment is revocable it cannot be said that the beneficiary *will* obtain his interest. On the other hand, the fact that the beneficiary could deprive himself, or be deprived, of his interest by assignments, bankruptcy, or death is irrelevant, since in such cases he will not be deprived by the terms of the settlement. The Court of Appeal was also troubled by the existence in almost every settlement of a power of advancement which may be exercised to benefit the potential beneficiary directly or indirectly. Indeed, the power conferred by s32 ICTA 1925 is so wide that it enables trustees to advance property onto new trusts which benefit the beneficiary at an age in excess of 25: *Pilkington* v *IRC* [1964] AC 612. How could such a power be squared with the requirement of 'will'?

> 'But a power of advancement has for so long been such a normal provision in a settlement for a person contingently on attaining a specified age, and since its sole purpose is to enable the trust property to be applied for that person's benefit before he attains the specified age, it would be artificial to regard the trust as not satisfying the provisions of the [section] ... it is quite unreal, in relation to [section 71] to equate it to a power of revocation. A power of advancement is not given for the purposes of revoking the primary trust and resettling the trust property. Its purpose is auxiliary. It is given as an aid to enable the trust property to be used for the fullest benefit of the beneficiary and, as such, is a normal adjunct of any trust for a person contingently on attaining a specified age ... it is a prerequisite to the transaction that the trustees should be satisfied that it is "for the benefit" of the beneficiary who is advanced. To that extent it is similar to an administrative power.'

The statute says 'a specified age'. The Revenue accepts, however, that an age is sufficiently specified if it can be identified with certainty. In most cases the specified age will be that imposed by s31(1)(ii) ICTA 1925 – the age of 18 years.

2.   'no interest in possession subsists in it and the income from it is to be accumulated so far as not applied for the maintenance, education or benefit of a beneficiary'.

Section 71 is really directed towards assisting cases where infant beneficiaries would be entitled to interests in possession, were it not for the provisions of s31 ICTA 1925 which states that where an infant has an interest which is not reversionary on any other interest the trustees shall, even if the infant would otherwise have a vested interest, accumulate the income insofar as they do not use it for the maintenance, education or benefit of the beneficiary. Accordingly, any trust to which s31(1)(i) applies will satisfy s71(1)(b).

3.   'Either – not more than 25 years have elapsed since the commencement of the settlement or, if it was later, since the time (or the latest time) when conditions (a) and (b) became satisfied with respect to the property, or all the persons who are or have been beneficiaries are or were:
i) grandchildren of a common grandparent, or
ii) children or widows or widowers of such grandchildren who were themselves beneficiaries but died before the time when, had they survived, they would have become entitled as mentioned in (a).'

The classic example of a trust falling within s71 is a contingent trust for children or grandchildren, for example:

> 'to such of my children as attain the age of 30, if more than one, in equal shares'.

Section 71(3) provides that, as a general rule, a charge to tax is made under the section:

—   when settled property ceases to fall within the scope of the section; and

- where the trustees make a disposition as a result of which the value of the settled property is less than it would be but for the disposition.

As usual, (2) does not apply if the trustees would have been able to rely on s10(1) had they been an individual.

The charge to tax is computed in the same way as that under s70. Section 71(4) provides that no charge to tax is made:

- on a beneficiary becoming entitled to, or to an interest in possession in, settled property on or before attaining the specified age; or
- on the death of a beneficiary before attaining the specified age.

Thus, no charge is made either where the trustees make an advancement of capital to or for the benefit of an infant beneficiary, or when the beneficiary obtains an interest in possession, for example on attaining 18 under s31(1)(ii).

23.13 Property becoming held for charitable purposes or by exempt bodies

Section 76 provides that, contrary to what has already been said, if property on ceasing to be relevant property or property to which s70 or s71 applies becomes:

1. property held for charitable purposes only *without limit of time*; or
2. the property of a qualifying political party; or
3. the property of a body mentioned in relation to s25, gifts for national purposes (see Chapter 22, section 22.4); or
4. the property of a non-profit making organisation, in a case where the Treasury has given a direction under s26 (see Chapter 22, section 22.4)

tax shall not, in such circumstances, be exigible under those earlier sections.

24

Administration, Assessments and Back Duty

24.1 Administration

24.2 Returns and assessments

24.3 Self-assessment

24.4 Appeals

24.5 Judicial review

24.6 Back duty

24.7 Interest

24.8 *Pepper* v *Hart* – statutory interpretation

24.1 Administration

The Commissioners of Inland Revenue, who collectively constitute the Board of Inland Revenue, are responsible for the administration and management of Income Tax, Corporation Tax and Capital Gains Tax. The statutory authority for administering the various taxes is conferred by the Taxes Management Act 1970, and references in this chapter to sections will be to that Act, unless otherwise specified. The actual day-to-day administration is carried on by collectors, who are responsible for the collection of tax, and inspectors, who are responsible for scrutinising returns and assessing tax. The inspectors and collectors are full-time civil servants appointed by the Board. The Board similarly has the care and management of Inheritance Tax. The control of that tax is separately effected by a division of the Inland Revenue known as the Capital Taxes Office (CTO) in accordance with powers conferred on it by Part VIII of the Inheritance Tax Act 1984. The administration of Inheritance Tax is not dealt with in this chapter.

24.2 Returns and assessments

Individuals and trustees

There is a positive obligation imposed on a person who is chargeable to income tax or capital gains tax and who has not delivered a return of his profits or gains or his total income to give notice to the Inland Revenue that he is so chargeable: s7 TMA 1970. This notification need only be an outline indication that he is chargeable to income tax (or capital gains tax). It is then up to the Revenue to take the matter further by sending him a document known as a 'tax return'. Whether or not the Revenue has received such a notice, an inspector may require any person by notice to make a return of his income and gains, normally by 31 January following the year of assessment (s8(1A)), specifying each source and the amount received from each source: s8. The return must includes a declaration by that person stating that to the best of his knowledge the details in the return are correct and complete. Employers are under a duty to disclose names of employees and details of any payments to them when required to do so: s15. Similar provisions exist to oblige trustees to make returns: s8A.

Section 9 provides for the return to include a self-assessment of the tax due, unless the taxpayer takes the option under s9(2) to have the Inland Revenue make the assessment under s8(3), in which case the return must be filed by 30 September following the year of assessment.

Section 9A gives the Inland Revenue power to make enquiries into the matters contained in the return within 12 months of the 31 January filing date or within the end of the calendar quarter in which the first anniversary of the actual filing date occurs. For this purpose the quarter dates are 31 January, 30 April, 31 July and 31 October.

Partnerships

The new provisions for partnership returns under self-assessment are to be found in ss12AA, 12AB and 12AC. These require the filing of the partnership return and accounts and provide for a statement of partnership income (s12AC), so that the Revenue have a means of establishing proof of the amounts which each of the individual partners will include in their respective personal returns and self-assessments, filed in accordance with the provisions for individuals, as outlined above. Provisions for amending the partnership statement where a loss of tax is discovered are contained in s30B.

Companies

In the same way, companies may be required to deliver to an inspector a return of all their profits, computed in accordance with the Tax Acts, giving particulars of disposals which give rise to a chargeable gain, an allowable loss, etc: ss10–11. Provisions similar to those in sections 9 and 9A exist in ss11AA and 11AB, to require a company to make a self-assessment and give the Inland Revenue similar powers to make enquiries. However, these company self-assessment provisions have not yet been brought into force and it is expected, according to a press release on 25 September 1996, that self assessment for companies will begin in respect of accounting periods which end during 1999.

Additional enquiry and enforcement powers

Extensive powers are conferred on inspectors of taxes by ss19, 19A and by 20 to require by notice in writing that a person deliver to them any documents that are in his possession which may contain information relevant to his tax liability or the amount of that tax liability. Such a notice may also be directed to a spouse or son or daughter of the taxpayer and, where the taxpayer carries on a business, to any other person concerned in the business.

There are further extraordinarily wide powers given to the Board by ss20A and C to obtain information which might otherwise not come to light. Under s20A, a tax accountant who has been convicted of an offence relating to tax, or who has suffered a penalty under s99 for assisting in the making of a tax return known to be incorrect, may be required to deliver all documents, other than those specifically excepted by s20B, relating to the tax liability of *any* client of his, even though there may be no evidence that any of the other clients had been making false tax returns. Under s20C, if a warrant has been obtained, the Board has power to enter premises to search and to seize and remove any documents which they have reason to believe may be evidence in a suspected tax fraud. See *R v O'Kane and Clarke, ex parte Northern Bank Ltd* [1996] STC 1249, in which it was held that notices served under s20(3) TMA 1970 were oppressive, unfair and irrational, in view of the requirements placed on the claimant bank by the notices.

Once all information has been received by the inspector and he is satisfied that it is complete and correct, he will make an assessment based on the details of the return unless the taxpayer is adopting the self-assessment method outlined above and further discussed in section 24.3. If, however, he is not satisfied that all details are present on the return, he will raise an estimated assessment. And if, subsequent to an assessment being made, an inspector 'discovers' that profits or gains exist which ought to have been assessed, or that the tax assessed was insufficient, or that a relief was given which should not have been allowed, he may make a further assessment in respect of the amount which ought to have been charged in his opinion: s29(1). The provisions for amending self-assessments are contained in new ss28A to 28F and procedures for making assessments which are not self-assessments are now to be found in s30A. The word 'discovers' has a wide meaning. It encompasses not only cases where new facts are actually discovered by the inspector but also those where he finds that he or a predecessor drew wrong inferences from facts which were known to him, or even that a mistake in law had been made by him or his predecessor whereby income which should have been assessed for tax was not assessed. There are two restrictions on this power of fresh assessment. First, time limits are imposed on the making of assessments. Under s34, an assessment may not in the ordinary cases be made more than six years after the end of the chargeable period to which it relates. Secondly, if an appeal has been made against an assessment raised by an inspector, and that appeal is settled by agreement, the subject-matter of the appeal is not capable of subsequent assessment if the inspector finds, for example, that he interpreted the legal position in a manner which was too favourable to the taxpayer (s54) see *Scorer v Olin Energy* [1984] STC 141 and *Cenlon Finance v Ellwood* [1961] Ch 634, but see also *Gray v Matheson* [1993] STC 178.

The case of *R v IRC, ex parte Matrix Securities Ltd* [1994] 1 WLR 334 in the House of Lords raised the question of the extent to which the Inland Revenue could be bound by the actions of its inspectors. It raised the issue of the extent to which full disclosure had taken place and whether the clearance given was within the normal ambit of the office in question. Due to the general reliance placed in practice upon clearances given either under statute or informally, the case was of great importance. It resulted in the issue of a Code of Practice (No 10) by the Inland Revenue explaining its position in regard to the provision of information, advice and clearances.

If a taxpayer finds that he has paid more tax under assessment than he should have because he made a mistake or error in the return by him, he may, not later than six years after the end of the year of assessment, apply to the Board for relief: s33. The Board may give such relief by way of repayment as it thinks is just and reasonable. An appeal lies to the Special Commissioners in relation to the Board's decisions. However, no application can be made if:

1. no return or an insufficient return was made by the taxpayer, with the result that an estimated assessment was raised, or
2. the assessment was in line with the general practice at the time, even though it may subsequently be decided that that practice was defective.

24.3 Self-assessment

As discussed in section 24.2 above the making of tax returns will now generally involve a self-assessment of the tax due.

Self-assessment is an option being offered to all taxpayers who complete an income tax return. For the many taxpayers who do not receive income other than from their employment and therefore are already taxed under PAYE, self-assessment will not normally apply, but any tax due under Schedule E which has not been collected in full under PAYE will be subject to the possibility of self-assessment procedure. This would include, for example, tax due on benefits in kind not dealt with in the taxpayer's coding. Any individual who receives income from other sources will be invited not only to submit a tax return but also, when doing so, to calculate the tax due on his total income and make payment of the required amounts on the appropriate due dates. Self-assessment is not compulsory, but if it is not taken up there is a requirement to submit the tax return by 30 September (s9(2)), to enable the Inland Revenue to calculate the tax due and arrange for the issue of an assessment. Under the previous provisions of TMA 1970, the onus was solely on the Inland Revenue to issue an assessment which created a legal debt. Under self-assessment the creation of that debt will be effected by the taxpayer on submitting a completed self-assessment. Self-assessment returns therefore combine the two elements of tax return and tax assessment.

The introduction of self-assessment has provided the impetus for the revision of many of the complex laws which have applied in the past to income from businesses, trades and professions, investment income and other income taxed under Schedule D. A new standard 'current year basis' will apply so that taxpayers will more easily be able to handle the additional process of getting the tax bill correct under their self-assessment. In short, the aim is to ensure that a particular year's tax is based on the income of that same year. In the past the complexities of the 'previous year basis', with detailed rules and options for the opening and closing years, would have made such a system generally unworkable.

While the switch to self-assessment has enabled these fundamental changes to the 'basis' rules to be made, it would be over-simplifying matters to say that the introduction of the two actually coincide. The change to being taxed on a current year basis has led to complex transitional rules to guard against the avoidance of tax through manipulation of the new rules, and therefore the switch to current year basis is being phased in over as short or long a period as is seen necessary according to the type of income involved.

Changes have been made to the rules for determining the income to be returned by beneficiaries of estates of deceased persons, which have been outlined in Chapter 13, section 13.7.

For partnerships, as noted in Chapter 10, self-assessment is particularly important since it ends the joint and several liability of individual partners for the whole of the partnership tax. Instead each partner will assume total responsibility for tax on his own share of profits only. For that reason the timetable for the phasing in of self-assessment and current year basis is somewhat different from that for other Schedule D taxpayers, and it also has to take into account changes in partnerships between 1994 and 1998.

The Inland Revenue has published two booklets, *SAT1* and *SAT2*, which contain respectively the detailed technical rules for the current year basis of assessment and the legal framework for self-assessment. The statutory provisions for self-assessment, most of which are designed to alter the existing TMA 1970 provisions, were introduced by the Finance Acts 1994 (ss178–199 and Schedule 19) and 1995 (ss103–116 and Schedule 21).

Dates for filing tax returns

The first of the new tax returns were issued in April 1997 to include income of the year ended 5 April 1997, or of the accounting period ended in that year, so that tax for 1996/97 can be calculated.

The tax return for those requiring the Inland Revenue to compute and assess the tax will be required by 30 September 1997, and those opting for self-assessment will have to file by 31 January 1998, and by 31 January of the year following the year of assessment thereafter.

Tax payment dates

Coinciding with the filing date for the self-assessment tax return is the date for the payment of tax related to that return of total income and capital gains. An initial payment on account for income tax only is due on 31 January during the year of assessment, followed by a second such payment, being the second instalment of tax on all categories of income (s59A), on 31 July and a balancing payment on any residual income on the following 31 January when the return is being filed, together with all capital gains tax due for the year. Payments on account should reflect one-half of all income tax due, and therefore late or insufficient payments will attract interest as at present.

By way of example therefore, a self-employed person with an accounting year ending 30 June and with capital gains for 1997/98 would make returns and payments of tax as follows:

31 January 1998 – First payment of account of Schedule D profits 1997/98
31 July 1998   – Second payment on account of Schedule D profits 1997/98
31 January 1999 – Submits return of profits for accounting year ended 30 June 1997
                (on which tax assessed for 1997/98)
             – pays any balance of Schedule D tax due for 1997/98
             – pays all capital gains tax due for 1997/98
             – pays first payment of account of Schedule D profits 1998/99

Tax on any investment income would be paid as to 50 per cent on 31 January during the year of assessment followed by a second 50 per cent payment on 31 July, with any balancing amount found to be due, on 31 January following, ie when the next return is filed.

Companies – Extension of the 1993 Pay & File system to include self-assessment

See Chapter 16, section 16.6 and section 24.2 above for details.

24.4 Appeals

An appeal lies against an assessment if notice is given within 30 days after the date of the notice of assessment. Tax appeals are heard by either General Commissioners of Inland Revenue or Special Commissioners of Inland Revenue. Powers which enable the Treasury to change the name of the bodies of general and special commissioners were added by s75 FA (No 2) 1992. This followed a review, but so far no action has been taken to implement any change of name. Other administrative changes were made by and appear in Schedule 16 of that Act.

The General Commissioners of Inland Revenue are a lay panel of usually part-time Commissioners who do not have any special qualifications in law, accountancy or tax matters. They receive no remuneration and may be considered to be the tax equivalent of lay magistrates.

The Special Commissioners are full-time civil servants who have expert knowledge of tax law, acquired either as Revenue officials or in private practice. Appeals which involve difficult questions of law are usually brought before them rather than before General Commissioners, as are any appeals which may be unusually prolonged. An appeal against an assessment made by the Board itself must be made to the Special Commissioners, whereas an appeal against an assessment made by an inspector may be made to the General Commissioners. There is, however, a procedure whereby an appeal made originally to the General Commissioners may be transferred to the Special Commissioners: either the parties may jointly apply for the transfer of proceedings to the Special Commissioners, or the General and Special Commissioners may between them agree to a transfer if they are of the opinion that an appeal brought before the General Commissioners is of such a complexity or likely length that it is more suitable for hearing by the Special Commissioners: s44(3A). Furthermore, where a taxpayer has a right of appeal to the General Commissioners he may in many cases elect to appeal to the Special Commissioners instead. That election to be heard by the Special Commissioners may be disregarded at the direction of the General Commissioners: s31(5A–E). Appeals against claims for reliefs disallowed are usually heard by the General Commissioners unless an election is made.

An appeal to the Commissioners lies on questions of both fact and law. However, an appeal from the Commissioners to the High Court lies only in respect of a point of law: s56. It is the case, though, that the Commissioners' findings of fact may be upset on appeal if those findings were such that no reasonable body of Commissioners properly instructed could have come to the conclusion at issue: *Edwards* v *Bairstow and Harrison* [1956] AC 14. The powers of the High Court on an appeal are to that extent somewhat limited, and it has shown a marked reluctance to interfere with the findings of the Commissioners. Lord Denning in *JP Harrison (Watford) Ltd* v *Griffiths* (1962) 40 TC 281 stated that it was not sufficient that the judge himself would have come to a different conclusion.

Either a taxpayer or the inspector (who usually represents the Crown) may appeal from the Commissioners to the High Court on a point of law, and an appeal to the High Court may only be brought if the appellant has expressed dissatisfaction immediately after the decision of the Commissioners hearing the appeal. FA 1984 enables appeals from the Special Commissioners to proceed directly to the Court of Appeal if a direction to that effect is obtained from the High Court.

Once dissatisfaction has been expressed, the appeal proper commences by notice being given in writing to the Clerk to the Commissioners, within 30 days from the hearing of the appeal, requiring the Commissioners to state a case for the opinion of the High Court. From the High Court there is a further right of appeal to the Court of Appeal, and from there, with that court's leave, to the House of Lords.

If an appeal is made to the High Court, that court may make an order for costs against either party. Each party to the appeal before the Commissioners normally has to bear its own costs, but following a press release on 10 March 1992 legislation was included in Schedule 16 FA (No 2) 1992 permitting the Special Commissioners to award costs in any case which has been pursued unreasonably. Legal aid is not available before tribunals such as the General and Special Commissioners. A taxpayer may appear in person at an appeal to the Commissioners or be represented by his solicitor, or by counsel or an accountant. The Crown will normally be represented by the inspector at the hearings before the Commissioners and by counsel at the High Court.

Once an assessment has been made it can only be varied by the General or Special Commissioners or a higher court making a formal determination on that particular point, or by agreement between the taxpayer and inspector under s54 TMA 1970. By s54, if a taxpayer and an inspector agree to confirm or vary or discharge an assessment it has the same effect as a determination by the Commissioners or the court. Once agreement has been made under s54 it precludes any further assessments in relation to the matter in dispute: see the *Cenlon, Scorer* and *Matheson* cases referred to in section 24.2.

Where the amount of the assessment is the point in dispute the onus of proof is on the taxpayer. It is for him to bring evidence showing where the assessment is defective. However, in the case of fraud or wilful default the onus of proof lies on the Crown.

ICTA 1988 provides dates on which taxes computed under the various Schedules become due and payable. In the event of an appeal against an assessment, the date of payment used to be deferred until the appeal had been determined. This provision was often used as a device by the taxpayer for the sake of the interest earned during the period of deferment. It has, therefore, been provided by s55 that the appellant must either agree the tax to be postponed with the inspector or apply to the Commissioners to determine that amount. If the appellant fails to make application to postpone the payment, the tax is payable as if no appeal had been made. The application to postpone payment is heard and determined in the same way as an appeal, and if the application is successful the Commissioners will postpone payment of the tax on which the appellant contends he has been overcharged until the appeal has been heard. The remainder of the tax which is not postponed becomes due and payable in accordance with the usual rules. On determination of the appeal itself, any tax payable becomes due and payable as if charged by the original assessment notice, and any tax overpaid must be repaid. Under self-assessment, 'statements of account' are issued to taxpayers for the initial payment on 31 January during the year of assessment, with provisions to enable the amount contained in the statement to be varied, based on the further information provided by the taxpayer at that time.

Section 86 provides that tax due under an assessment shall carry interest at the prescribed rate from 'the reckonable date'. The reckonable date is either the date mentioned in a table contained in s86(4), or that on which tax would have been due and payable had there been no appeal, whichever is the later.

24.5 Judicial review

Alternatively, in a limited number of circumstances, the decision of the Commissioners or the Revenue can be challenged by means of judicial review. As Lord Wilberforce stated in *IRC v National Federation of Self Employed and Small Businesses Ltd* [1981] STC 260, the Revenue is an 'administrative body with statutory duties' and consequently is not immune to judicial review.

In *R v IRC, ex parte Preston* [1985] STC 282 the taxpayer and the Revenue made an 'agreement' by which the taxpayer agreed to withdraw his claim to relief for interest and capital gains tax losses, and in return the Revenue said that it would not pursue any further enquiries into his affairs. Later, however, when new information came to light, the Revenue initiated another investigation into the taxpayer's affairs under s460 ICTA 1988. The taxpayer applied for an order prohibiting the Revenue from making any further enquiries on the grounds that its conduct constituted an improper exercise/abuse of its statutory powers of collection and management. The House of Lords found against the taxpayer on the grounds that the Revenue's action did not constitute an abuse of power. Nevertheless the House went on to hold that in principle there was no reason why a taxpayer could not obtain judicial review of a decision of the Revenue or Commissioners if the decision was unfair to the taxpayer because the conduct of the decision-maker was equivalent to a breach of contract or breach of representation. The House also accepted that, in certain circumstances, delay could convert otherwise lawful action by the Revenue into an abuse of power.

For decisions where the court has considered whether to grant judicial review of the Revenue's decisions see *R v HM Inspector of Taxes, ex parte Kissane* [1986] STC 152, *R v Commissioner, ex parte Stipplechoice Ltd* [1988] STC 556, and *R v IRC, ex parte MFK* [1989] STC 873. In *ex parte MFK* the taxpayer sought judicial review of the Revenue's decision to depart from the earlier assurances that it had given to the taxpayer concerning the taxation of index-linked bonds. The House of Lords reaffirmed the principle that the taxpayer is entitled to judicial review of the

Revenue's decision if the Revenue, as a public authority, conducted itself so as to create a legitimate expectation for the taxpayer that a course of action would be followed, and then proceeded to deviate from that course. However, on the facts the House found that the Revenue in its statements had not promised to follow the course indicated, and consequently its departure from the course did not constitute an abuse of power.

In considering ways of challenging a decision by the Revenue or Commissioners one must therefore consider both the appeal procedure and the possibility of an application by way of judicial review in order to determine which is the most suitable way to proceed.

24.6 Back duty

Where a taxpayer is found not to have disclosed his true income, or to have claimed any reliefs or allowances to which he is not entitled, or in any other way to have evaded tax, the Revenue may:

1. commence criminal proceedings;
2. make assessments in respect of the lost tax with interest;
3. claim penalties.

Criminal proceedings

Criminal proceedings cases are on the whole relatively rare. The cases that do go to court generally fall within s5 of the Perjury Act 1911, in that the defendant knowingly and falsely made a statement in a material matter in one of the relevant documents. Alternatively, the charges may come under common law offences of making false statements or accounts or of 'cheating the Revenue'.

Assessments for past years

Under s34 TMA 1970, as revised for self-assessment, an assessment to income tax or capital gains tax can generally be made by the Revenue not later than five years after the 31 January which follows the year of assessment. An assessment to corporation tax may be made not later than six years after the end of the chargeable period to which the assessment relates. In the case of fraud or wilful default a time limit of 20 years applies: s36 (unless an assessment is made against personal representatives, when an assessment may be raised for any year of assessment ending not earlier than six years before the death of the taxpayer, at any time before the end of the third year of assessment next following that of the death). Such a late assessment itself may only be made with the leave of the General or Special Commissioners. The Revenue may also make assessments for the years before the usual six-year period where the taxpayer is guilty of 'neglect', but once more the leave of the General or Special Commissioners must be obtained first.

The situation in cases of neglect is as follows:

1. Where an assessment has already been made for 'a normal year' – ie one of the six previous years – to recover tax lost because of fraud or wilful default or neglect, then an assessment can be made for any one of the six years preceding it – 'the earlier years'. But an assessment may only be made for the earlier years where the loss of tax is attributable to the taxpayer's neglect. Such an assessment must be made within one year after the end of the year in which the tax for 'the normal year' was finally determined – that is to say, in which the date after which no appeal was possible or outstanding arose. No assessment can be made for an earlier year unless tax is shown to have been lost through fraud, wilful default or neglect in one of the normal years (ie, in one of the past six years).
2. If a back duty assessment has been made by the Revenue as a result of fraud, wilful default or neglect in 'an earlier year', the Revenue may go back still further to any of the six years prior to the year of the existing back duty assessment and make an assessment in respect of any of those years. In this case, though, an assessment may only be made by leave of the Special or General Commissioners if it is proved that there are reasonable grounds for believing that such neglect has occurred.

Penalties

Penalties may be charged for various failures – for example, failure to make returns – or for submitting an incorrect return. Under s93, there is an automatically penalty of £100 for failure to deliver a tax return date by the relevant 31 January, followed by further penalties if the failure continues for a further six months. The penalties to which the taxpayer may be liable depend on the nature of the offence and are prescribed by the Act by reference to maximum amounts chargeable. Thus, in the case where a trader has negligently or fraudulently submitted an incorrect account to an inspector the maximum penalty in respect of each year would, under s95(2), be the amount of tax lost to the Revenue.

Penalties must normally be recovered within six years from the date of the offence. In the case of fraud or wilful default, though, they may be recovered within three years of the date of final determination of the tax.

24.7 Interest

An assessment to income tax under Schedules A, D or E, or assessment to capital gains tax or to mainstream corporation tax, will bear interest from the 'reckonable date'. The Revenue also has a power to charge interest on tax not assessed at the due date by reason of fraud or wilful default or neglect of the taxpayer. The interest runs from the date on which the tax should have been paid. Under the self-assessment provisions, if the payments required under ss59A and 59B Taxes Management Act 1970 are not made on time, s59C imposes a surcharge of 5 per cent of tax not paid within 28 days of the due date and a further 5 per cent where tax remains outstanding six months after the due date. As at 6 February 1997, the rate of interest charged on unpaid tax was set at 8.5 per cent. It is varied by statutory instrument from time to time as bank interest rates change.

24.8 *Pepper* v *Hart* – statutory interpretation

The decision of the House of Lords in *Pepper* v *Hart* [1992] 3 WLR 1032; [1992] STC 898 (before Lords Mackay of Clashfern, Keith of Kinkel, Bridge of Harwich, Griffiths, Ackner, Oliver of Aylmerton and Browne-Wilkinson) lent a prominence well beyond its original scope to a tax case. Having had to determine whether the cash equivalent of the benefits enjoyed by schoolmasters at Malvern College in respect of their sons' education was to be determined on a marginal cost basis or an average proportional cost, the Lords could not determine the appeal without overcoming constitutional questions in the matter of statutory interpretation.

Before the outcome of the tax issue at stake could be pronounced in *Pepper*, the Law Lords set up a second hearing with an enlarged membership (see [1992] 3 WLR at 1045) to investigate the issue of whether it was permissible to refer to *Hansard* (official parliamentary reports) when interpreting ambiguous and obscure statutes, so as to bring to bear the outcome which Parliament had intended when enacting that piece of legislation. Lord Mackay of Clashfern, although agreeing to allow the appeals, dissented on the issue of allowing the use of *Hansard* for the purpose of statutory interpretation.

Having determined that such references to parliamentary reports were in certain circumstances permissible, the House of Lords' decision immediately became more celebrated for this non-tax aspect of the judgment and the wide application of the principles regarding statutory interpretation. *Pepper* v *Hart* has been cited in a number of cases since the judgment, for the most part in cases not involving tax statutes.

Circumstances in which reference to parliamentary reports is permissible

The circumstances in which it would be permissible to utilise parliamentary reports as a guide to interpreting statutes were clearly limited by the case and were spelt out in the judgment of Lord Browne-Wilkinson ([1992] 3 WLR 1033):

> 'My Lords, the underlying subject matter of these tax appeals is the correct basis for valuing benefits received by the taxpayers who are schoolmasters. However in the

circumstances which I will relate, the appeals have also raised two questions of much wider importance.

The first is whether in construing ambiguous or obscure statutory provisions your Lordships should relax the historic rule that the courts must not look at the parliamentary history of legislation or Hansard for the purpose of construing such legislation.

The second is whether, if reference to such materials would otherwise be appropriate, it would contravene article 9 of the Bill of Rights 1688 or Parliamentary privilege to do so.

... in 1975 the Government proposed a new tax on vouchers ... On 1 July 1975 in the Standing Committee on the Finance Bill ... the Financial Secretary was asked about the impact of the clause on railwaymen. He was then asked to explain why they would not be taxable and replied:

> "... clearly the railways will run in precisely the same way whether the railwaymen use this facility or not, so there is no extra charge [cost] to the Railways Board itself, therefore there would be no taxable benefits."

... the very question which is the subject matter of the present appeal was also raised ... The Financial Secretary responded to this question as follows:

> "He mentioned the children of teachers. The removal of clause 54(4) will affect the position of a child of one of the teachers at the child's school, because now the benefit will be assessed on the cost to the employer, which would be very small indeed in this case."

... in my judgment the user of clear ministerial statements by the court as a guide to the construction of ambiguous legislation, would not contravene article 9 ...

... I therefore reach the conclusion ... that the exclusionary rule should be relaxed so as to permit reference to parliamentary materials where
(a) legislation is ambiguous or obscure, or leads to an absurdity;
(b) the material relied upon consists of one or more statements by a minister or other promoter of the Bill together if necessary with such other parliamentary material as is necessary to understand such statements and their effect;
(c) the statements relied upon are clear.

... Parliamentary privilege

It follows from what I have said that in my view the outcome of this appeal depends upon whether or not the court can look at parliamentary material. If it can the appeal should be allowed. If it cannot, the appeal should be dismissed.

... I trust when the House of Commons comes to consider the decision in this case, it will be appreciated that there is no desire to impeach its privilege in any way. Your Lordships are motivated by a desire to carry out the intentions of Parliament in enacting legislation and have no intention or desire to question the processes by which such legislation was enacted or of criticising anything said by anyone in Parliament in the course of enacting it. The purpose is to give effect to the intentions of Parliament.'

The most important limitation on the use of ministerial statements is the 'ambiguous or obscure' aspect referred to in the second paragraph of Lord Browne-Wilkinson's judgment. It is not therefore an all embracing directive for interpreting complex legislation. But given that complexity leads to ambiguity and obscurity of intention, the scope for its application is sufficiently wide.

25

Value Added Tax

25.1 Introduction

25.2 Taxable supplies

25.3 Importation

25.4 Exempt supplies

25.5 Zero-rated supplies

25.6 The computation of the charge

25.7 Special cases

25.1 Introduction

Value added tax was introduced by the Finance Act 1972 in anticipation of obligations which were to be imposed on the United Kingdom on its admission to the European Economic Community. The tax is very much the creature of the EEC and its current form is derived from the Sixth Council Directive of 17 May 1977 reference EEC/77/388. The day to day management of the tax is under the jurisdiction of the Commissioners of Customs and Excise ('the Commissioners').

Inherent in the doctrine of the supremacy of Community law is the primacy of Community legislation which holds that provided the terms of the legislation are clear, unconditional and precise, it is capable of having direct effect in member states – to the extent that national statutory provisions which conflict with it must be ignored. Not every provision of the Directive is intended to have such direct effect – for example, where the Directive confers some form of discretion on the member state in connection with the implementation of an Article. In some cases, the European Court has found that the United Kingdom legislation does not accord with the provisions of the Directive; on other occasions, the VAT Tribunal has implemented the Sixth Directive in preference to the terms of the Value Added Tax Act 1994. Permissible 'derogations' from the standard provisions of the Sixth Directive on VAT permit the United Kingdom to continue with its zero rating categories, although some, if not all, of these derogations have an implied time limit within which the derogations are expected to be ended in favour of the common system of harmonisation which the Directive seeks to impose. It is against this background that the 1994 Act must be read. The decisions of VAT Tribunals (to whom appeals are made against numerous decisions and assessments of the Commissioners) are reported in the official VAT Tribunal Reports ('VATTR').

VAT was consolidated by VATA 1994, and references in this chapter to statutory provisions are references to that Act unless otherwise stated. Much of the operation of the VAT system is provided for in regulations, the principal ones being the VAT (General) Regulations 1995 (SI 1995/2518) which consolidated the previous general regulations 1985 with all subsequent regulations and which deal particularly with registration, tax invoices, time of supply, input tax recovery for partially exempt businesses, input tax on specified capital items, importation and exportation and customs warehouses, and accounting for and payment of VAT. It should be noted that other VAT Orders, as opposed to regulations, are still in force and have not been affected by the consolidation of the regulations mentioned above.

The scope of the tax is explained by s1:

'a) Value added tax shall be charged ... on the supply of goods or services in the United Kingdom (including anything treated as such a supply).
(b) on the acquisition in the United Kingdom from other member States of any goods, and
(c) on the importation of goods from places outside the member States.'

The wording of the above is that which applied from 1 January 1993, from which date VAT ceased to be charged on the import/export of goods between taxable persons in the EC. Under these provisions VAT is accounted for by the importer of the goods, in other words on the acquisition of goods as opposed to the normal procedure of accounting for VAT on sales. However, that same amount of VAT so accounted for is treated as input tax which can be recovered by set-off, subject to the normal input tax restrictions, if any, imposed by ss24 and 26.

It should also be noted that (b) and (c) relate to goods only and not to services, which are separately dealt with under what are termed the 'reverse charge' provisions of s8 for supplies of professional services and other services listed in Schedule 9. Other international services are zero rated under Schedule 8 Group 7.

Tax is charged at one of two rates on taxable supplies: the standard rate of 17.5 per cent and the zero rate (of 0 per cent). Certain other supplies are exempted from VAT altogether. Some transactions are regarded not simply as exempt but as 'outside the scope' of VAT – eg, non-business transactions. It is one of the oddities of the legislation that since it is the ultimate consumer alone who bears the tax, and the business supplier may recover tax on supplies made to him for the purposes of a trade in which he makes taxable – but not exempt – supplies, it is more advantageous to make supplies which are standard or zero rated than exempt supplies.

Theoretically, VAT is levied at each stage of the production of an item on the 'value added' by the trader; in practice a trader making only taxable supplies is liable in each quarter to pay to the Commissioners the difference between the VAT charged on supplies made to him for the purposes of his business (his input tax) and the tax he charges on his own supplies (his output tax). Since the input tax paid by the trader may have been on items not used in making supplies during the period, the value added principle, at least in the short term, is not strictly true.

25.2 Taxable supplies

Section 4 provides:

> '(1) Tax shall be charged on any supply of goods or services made in the United Kingdom where it is a taxable supply made by a taxable person in the course or furtherance of any business carried by him.'

VAT is thus not charged on supplies which under the terms of the VAT legislation are considered to be made outside the United Kingdom. However, special rules are contained in s6 to determine whether a particular supply should be treated as made within or outside the United Kingdom.

'Business' is not fully defined by the Act but has been given an extremely wide meaning by the courts. Section 94 provides that 'business' includes any trade, profession or vocation, and that the admission of persons to premises for a consideration and the provision by a club or other organisation (for a subscription or other consideration) are both to be deemed to be the carrying on of a business. In *Customs and Excise Commissioners* v *Morrison's Academy Boarding House Association* [1978] STC 1 the Court of Session held that the word 'business' did not import any requirement of commercial purpose or, indeed, any intention to make a profit; but one had to show a course of activities carried on over an appreciable tract of time and with such frequency as to amount to a recognisable and identifiable activity of the particular person on whom the liability was to fall and, further, that those activities were predominantly concerned with the making of taxable supplies to consumers for a consideration. The wording in the corresponding section of the EC Sixth Directive does not refer to business expressly, but is much wider in referring to any 'economic activity'. In *Wellcome Trust Ltd* v *Customs and Excise Commissioners* [1996] STC 945, on the meaning of 'business' for the purpose of VAT, the European Court of Justice ruled that, in the instant case, the buying and selling of shares by the trustees of the charitable trust were not to be regarded as an economic activity for the purposes of the Sixth Directive. HM Customs and Excise later made an announcement that the *Wellcome Trust* decision does not affect organisations other than charitable trusts.

VAT is levied only on 'taxable persons'. Section 4(2) defines such a person as:

> 'a person who makes or intends to make taxable supplies ... while he is required to be registered under this Act.'

It is a peculiarity of the VATA that it defines liability by reference to a registration requirement. Nothing similar appears in the Sixth Directive and, to the extent that that requirement precludes a genuine intending trader from recovering VAT on inputs made to him prior to his first supplies, it is invalid: *Merseyside Cablevision* v *Customs and Excise Commissioners* [1987] VATTR 134. VAT law in the United Kingdom now permits intending traders to register and therefore to reclaim VAT suffered on their expenditure.

Nevertheless, the United Kingdom persists in requiring registration before a person is either entitled to charge VAT on outputs or to reclaim VAT paid on inputs. These requirements are contained in Schedule 1 to the Act.

In outline a person who makes taxable supplies is obliged to register as a taxable person if:

1. at the end of any month the value of his taxable supplies in the period of one year ending at that time has exceeded £48,000 unless the Commissioners are satisfied that for the period of one year beginning at that time the value of his taxable supplies will not exceed £48,000, or
2. there are reasonable grounds for believing that in a period of 30 days commencing at any time the value of his taxable supplies will exceed £48,000.

In addition if a business is transferred as a going concern to a non-registered transferee that transferee is required to register if:

1. the value of taxable supplies in the year ending at the date of transfer has exceeded £48,000 unless the Commissioners are satisfied that for the period of one year beginning at that time the value of his taxable supplies will not exceed £48,000, or
2. there are reasonable grounds for believing that in the 30 days beginning from the date of transfer, the value of his taxable supplies exceed £48,000.

Once registered, the trader is obliged to make returns at the end of every 'prescribed accounting period' of his inputs and outputs for the period, and to pay any VAT shown to be due.

A taxable supply is described by s4(2) as:

> 'a supply of goods or services made in the United Kingdom other than an exempt supply.'

Accordingly, a trader who only makes exempt supplies is not entitled to register as a taxable person since he makes no taxable supplies.

In turn, 'supply' is defined by s5(2) as:

> 'all forms of supply, but not anything done otherwise than for a consideration;'

and 'supply of services' as:

> 'anything which is not a supply of goods but is done for a consideration (including, if so done, the granting, assignment or surrender of any right) ... '

Thus whenever a taxable person is paid for doing something in the course or furtherance of his business, provided it is done in the United Kingdom and is not an exempt supply, it will be liable to VAT. So, in *Neville Russell* v *Customs and Excise Commissioners* [1987] VATTR 194 the Tribunal held that the acceptance by a lessee of a reverse premium, for example, a sum paid by a landlord to encourage a potential tenant to enter into a lease, was liable to VAT as a 'supply of services' since it was something done for a consideration.

In the case of *BJ Rice & Associates* v *Customs and Excise Commissioners* [1996] STI 273, the Commissioners of Customs and Excise sought to charge VAT on supplies of the business made before the requirement to register arose but which were paid after the requirement for VAT registration occurred. The Court of Appeal held that supplies made when a person was not a 'taxable person' were not liable to VAT. The important aspect of the above reasoning is that a 'taxable person' under basic VAT law – s3 – is one for whom the requirement to register has arisen – not when actual registration has been made.

Schedule 4 contains rules (mainly derived from the Sixth Directive) determining cases to be treated as supplies of goods or services. Many of these rules are inconsistent with the usual position in English law:

1. The transfer of the *whole* property in goods is a supply of goods; however, the transfer of an undivided share of the property, or the possession of goods, is a supply of services.
2. If the possession of goods is transferred under an agreement for the sale of goods; or under an agreement which contemplates expressly that the property also in the goods will pass at some time in the future (eg on a sale or return basis or under a hire purchase agreement), that is the supply of goods.
3. If a person produces goods by applying a treatment or process to another person's goods, then he makes a supply of goods. The classic example of this is said to be the tailor who makes a suit from the customer's own cloth. There must be some doubt, though, whether this amounts to a treatment or process. In any event, the laundry which subsequently cleaned the suit would certainly be supplying services not goods, since it would produce nothing new (albeit that what it did to the goods *would* amount to subjecting them to a process).
4. The supply of any form of heat or power is a supply of goods.
5. The granting assignment or surrender of a major interest in land is a supply of goods. A major interest is defined by s96(1) as the fee simple in the land or a tenancy for a term certain exceeding 21 years. The supply of a shorter tenancy would be a supply of services.

The importance of the distinction between supplies of goods and of services lies in part in the determination of where the supply is made. As has been said, if the supply is, under the terms of the VAT legislation, considered to take place outside the United Kingdom, it is not subject to VAT. Section 7 provides separate rules for each type of supply:

The place of the supply of goods

1. If the goods are in the United Kingdom and the supply does not involve their removal from it, they are treated as supplied in the United Kingdom (and thus as a taxable supply).
2. If the goods are out of the United Kingdom and the supply does not involve bringing them to the United Kingdom, they are treated as *not* supplied in the United Kingdom.
3. If the supply involves the removal of the goods from the United Kingdom, they are treated as supplied in the United Kingdom. In this case, although the supply is taxable, it may well be zero-rated under s16.
4. If the supply involves the removal of the goods to the United Kingdom from abroad, the supply is treated as made outside the United Kingdom.

The place of the supply of services

The place of the supply of services depends on where the supplier 'belongs':

1. if he belongs in the United Kingdom, the supply is made in the United Kingdom – but may be zero-rated by Schedule 8 Group 7, as the supply of international services, if involving an overseas consumer; and
2. if he belongs abroad, the supply is made abroad.

Most importantly, however, Schedule 5 lists a number of services which are treated as made in the country where they are received – including various financial, legal and professional services and dealings in copyright, patents and trade marks, etc. This constitutes the 'reverse charge' scheme referred to in section 25.3.

Section 9 provides further rules to determine where a supplier belongs. Primarily, the test is whether he has a business (or some other fixed) establishment in the country, and no such establishment elsewhere. If, though, he has no such establishment, one looks to his place of residence.

Finally, if he has more than one business or other fixed establishment, one looks to the country where the establishment which is most directly connected with the supply is situated. A branch and an agency through which the trader carries on business are two forms of 'business establishment' for this purpose.

In a 1996 VAT Tribunal decision on 'place of supply' in the case of *The Chinese Channel Limited (Hong Kong) Limited* v *Customs and Excise Commissioners* [1996] Decision No 14003, it was held that the Hong Kong company did not have a business establishment in the UK as a result of the appointment of a UK marketing company for its broadcasting activities. Further legislation as to the place of supply of telecommunications and internet services both from within and to the European Community Member States is expected during the course of 1997.

Detailed regulations in the VAT (Supply of Services) Order 1992 (SI 1992/3121) cover the place of supply of certain services relating to land, transport and the services of intermediaries.

In other areas of VAT law it is sometimes important to ascertain whether what is supplied is a supply of services or a supply of goods. At times the Act directs certain items to be a supply of services so that their VAT treatment falls within the relevant general provisions for services or for goods.

Mixed supplies

As can be seen from some of the VAT cases to come before the courts, it is often not clear what the supply being made is or what the consideration received represents. The question arises as to whether the consideration passing is related to a composite supply of several matters or a single supply to which others are merely ancillary. For example, in *Virgin Atlantic Airways Ltd* v *Customs and Excise Commissioners* [1995] STC 341 the question at issue was whether free transport to the airport for its passengers was part of the zero-rated supply of passenger transport under Schedule 8 Group 8 or a separate and therefore standard-rated supply. It was held that the passenger contracted for a single supply of transport from home to the destination, and that the two elements of car and aircraft were therefore indivisible. Accordingly the zero rating under Schedule 8 applied in its entirety. See also the decision reached in *British Airways plc* v *Customs and Excise Commissioners* [1990] STC 643, where in-flight meals were held to be an integral part of the supply of air transport and therefore similarly zero rated. In the case of *Customs and Excise Commissioners* v *Leightons Ltd* and *Customs and Excise Commissioners* v *Eye-Tech Opticians* [1995] STC 458, it was held that in the supply of spectacles the dispensing activities were distinguishable from the physical supply of the spectacles and that only the latter constituted a standard-rated supply, the former being exempt. The consideration was therefore to be properly apportioned.

In such situations, the decisions will lead either to the charging of VAT on the otherwise non-chargeable supply (or supply made for no consideration) or to the inability to recover input VAT in full if certain supplies are found to be exempt ones.

The latter position arose in another case involving *British Airways* v *Customs and Excise Commissioners* [1996] STC 1127. British Airways supplied meal vouchers to passengers whose flights were delayed, meals being taken in a restaurant. The passengers paid the restaurant any excess of the cost of the meals over the face value of the vouchers. BA paid the restaurant the value of the vouchers redeemed and attempted to recover the VAT paid on the meals. It was held that BA were not the recipients of the supply of meals and could not therefore deduct the VAT incurred. The meals were held to have been supplied to the passengers by the restaurant and not to BA.

25.3 Importation

Supply of goods in the EC after 1 January 1993

Whereas importation of goods was subject to a VAT charge at the time of importation, from 1 January 1993 the first stage of the harmonisation of VAT systems (not rates) went into operation and overnight the entire system was altered. Goods were no longer held and then taxed but were allowed to cross freely across the borders of the EC member states.

For supplies between VAT registered businesses in any of these countries VAT is no longer charged on the despatch of goods nor at the time of importation. Instead the recipient business customer accounts for VAT on the acquisition of the goods. These are effectively now zero-rated supplies.

For supplies to non-VAT registered customers VAT is charged and is paid by the supplier on despatch. This is another new feature of the changes.

It should be remembered that supplies to and from countries outside the EC are not affected by the changes which came into force to create what is termed the Single Market.

Importation from non-EC member states after 1 January 1993

VAT is charged on the importation of goods into the United Kingdom 'as if it were a duty of customs': s1(4). It is also payable on the supply of services to a United Kingdom resident by an overseas supplier under Schedule 5 in what is known as the 'reverse charge', since the United Kingdom recipient rather than the supplier is required to account for VAT to the United Kingdom authorities for such services received from outside the EC (before 1 January 1993 it included the EC) as are listed in Schedule 5. In practice this means declaring VAT as a liability and recovering the same amount as a credit for payment of it. Being treated as a duty of customs, the tax on the supply of goods is payable at the time of importation, rather than at the end of some prescribed accounting period. Unlike VAT on supplies in the United Kingdom, it is levied without regard to whether the importer is registered, so that everyone who imports goods is liable for import VAT. Section 21 provides the amount on which the tax is payable:

1. If the goods were imported at a price in money, tax is payable both on the price *and* the taxes and other duties (apart from VAT) levied outside the United Kingdom or on importation *plus* all costs by way of commission, packing, transportation and insurance up to the port of entry.
2. If the importation is not taking place at a price, the value of the goods is taken as their open market value plus all taxes and shipping costs, as in (1).

Thus whilst VAT is not levied on the supplier of the goods where the goods are supplied abroad, nevertheless, it is collected from the importer in its alternative form as a customs duty.

25.4 Exempt supplies

Section 31 states that:

'A supply of goods is an exempt supply if it is of a description for the time being specified in Schedule 9 to this Act.'

Since a taxable supply is any supply of goods or services made in the United Kingdom other than an *exempt supply*, an exempt supply is not liable to VAT; correlatively, though, it is not permissible to recover the input tax on any taxable supply made to the trader for the purposes of his exempt supplies – thus, as an example, a bank may not recover the VAT element of its telephone bill.

It is not proposed to list exhaustively all forms of exempt supply described by Schedule 9. Some of the most important are as follows:

Group 1: Land

The grant of any interest in or right over land or of any licence to occupy land *other than*:

1. the grant of the freehold ('fee simple') of non-residential buildings or buildings not occupied for charitable purposes and civil engineering works;
2. the provision of accommodation in a hotel, boarding house, or similar establishment;
3. the provision of holiday accommodation in a house, flat, caravan etc.

Land and the 'option to tax'

Schedule 10 paras 2–4 contain further provisions relating to land and its exempt status. These provisions allow the person by whom the exempt grant of an interest in the land is made to treat supply as a standard-rated taxable supply, subject to certain conditions and the making of an election to that effect. This 'election to waive exemption' allows for the charging of VAT and similarly enables the person concerned to recover part or all of the VAT incurred on his acquisition, development etc. Section 26(2) allows only for recovery in regard to input tax on taxable supplies. The recipient of the grant of interest in the land, either tenant or purchaser, would also be able to recover the VAT charged on his rent or on the sale, in accordance with his own VAT status – in other words according to the extent to which his business makes non-exempt supplies.

Section 37 of Finance Act 1997 made a fundamental change to the 'option to tax' regime. Until then, property owners generally had an unrestricted right to opt to charge VAT on properties which they let out or sell. This enabled the property owner to recover any VAT paid on construction, acquisition or refurbishment of the property. The tenant or purchaser will have to pay VAT on his rental or purchase price and will be able to recover that VAT only if he himself uses the property for activities which are 'taxable' in VAT terms. He will suffer a restriction on his ability to recover the VAT if he is exempt or partly exempt (for example, most banks and insurance companies).

Various schemes had been devised in the past to mitigate the effects of VAT on a partly exempt business wanting to buy or occupy property. Mostly these schemes operated merely to defer VAT, rather than avoid it altogether, but even this cash-flow saving proved unpalatable to Customs and Excise. There had been piecemeal anti-avoidance legislation in the past, but it had often been possible to circumvent this.

The 1997 Finance Act measures, which inserted new paras 3AA, 3A into Schedule 10 of VATA 1994, aim to end these avoidance schemes once and for all. The rules provide that the option to tax does not apply to any future letting or sale where the tenant or purchaser does not use the property at least 80 per cent for VAT-'taxable' business purposes and took effect from 26 November 1996.

Developer's self-supply charge
Further provisions in Schedule 10 relating to charging VAT on a self-supply basis for development for own use are being phased out, following the Finance Act 1995, which arose, inter alia, from the anomalies encountered in cases such as that involving Robert Gordon's College. *Customs and Excise Commissioners* v *Robert Gordon's College* [1995] STC 1093 resulted in the college (whose normal activities of education were VAT exempt) being subject to a developer's self-supply charge based on the value of the site and the works after developing and leasing its playing fields to a wholly owned company (Countesswells), while continuing to occupy them along with others after the development. The position was reversed by the House of Lords ([1995] STC 1093). The Lords ruled that the sixth directive operated to impose a self-supply charge on such a development only where the goods or services were created by the taxpayer and not when acquired from a third party. Since the college's use arose from the grant of a licence by the Countesswells company the self-supply condition was not fulfilled. In addition, the Lords ruled that the college could recover VAT incurred in developing the site on the basis of the decision of the European Court of Justice in *BLP Group* v *Customs and Excise Commissioners* [1995] STC 424, the VAT being attributable to a taxable supply of the grant of a lease by the college to Countesswells.

The Finance Act 1994 made provision for the abolition of the developer's self-supply charge in respect of work undertaken after 1 March 1995. The final payment in respect of work in progress at that date was made on 1 March 1997.

Lubbock Fine v *Customs and Excise Commissioners* [1994] STC 101 dealt with VAT liability on the payment by a landlord to a tenant to surrender a lease – the European Court of Justice held that the surrender was exempt.

The VAT (Land) Order 1995 (SI 1995/282) redefines the 'grant' of an interest to include a reverse surrender as well an assignment and (ordinary) surrender.

Group 2: The provision of insurance

Group 5: Finance

Item 1: the issue, transfer or receipt of, or dealing with, money
Item 2: the making of any advance or the provision of credit
Item 7: the operation of any current, deposit or savings account

An interesting point arose in the case of *Primback Ltd* v *Customs and Excise Commissioners* [1996] STC 757 in determining the VAT liability of what had become widely advertised as 'interest-free credit' retail sales. The transactions involved the customer entering into a finance agreement with a finance house to pay £x by instalments, corresponding to the retail sale price of the goods. The credit was arranged by the retailer, who therefore was making a supply of both the goods and of the 'arranging of credit'. The supply by the finance house was that of the credit itself. The finance house in turn paid a lesser total sum to the retailer. The issue which therefore arose was the treatment for VAT purposes of the credit charge, which was not disclosed to the customer.

Primback accounted for VAT under one of the special Retail Schemes, which accounts for VAT as a percentage of total sales. No VAT invoice was issued to the customer. In the Court of Appeal it was held that the making of arrangements for the supply of credit remained exempt within what is now VATA 1994 Schedule 9 group 5, irrespective of whether it was disclosed to the customer or not. The statutory status of the special Retail Scheme A used by the company also implied that VAT was to be accounted for on actual sales and not on sums not actually received – particularly where these sums were represented by an exempt supply of the actual credit itself.

The case is expected to be decided ultimately in a further appeal by Customs and Excise to the House of Lords.

Group 6: Education

Item 1: the provision of education or research by a school or university
Item 2: the provision, otherwise than for profit, of:

1. education or research of a kind provided by a school or university; or
2. training or retraining for any trade, profession or employment.

25.5 Zero-rated supplies

Section 30 provides that if a supply of goods or services made by a taxable person is zero-rated, then –

1. no VAT is charged on the supply; but
2. it is in all other respects treated as a taxable supply.

Most important amongst the consequences of (2) is that, as a taxable supply, any input tax paid by the trader on supplies to him in connection with the zero-rated output is recoverable from the Commissioners. Where a person makes only zero-rated supplies, he will be a 'repayment trader' – one who will not be paying tax, but reclaiming it. For obvious reasons, the Commissioners permit repayment traders to be exempted from registration if they so wish; see Schedule 1, para 14. This saves the Exchequer the obligation to make tax payments to the trader, and the trader the inconvenience of the administrative duties of the taxable person.

There are five basic categories of zero-rated supplies (see s30):

1. supplies of goods or services which are of a description specified in Schedule 8; and
2. supplies of goods to taxable persons within the member states;
3. a supply of goods in the United Kingdom to a person who has exported, or will export, them himself from the United Kingdom and who satisfies administrative conditions imposed by the Commissioners;
4. supplies of goods which are exported from the United Kingdom to a place outside the United Kingdom;
5. goods supplied for use as stores or for retail sale on voyages or flights outside the United Kingdom.

Clearly, in categories (2) and (3), zero-rating is given only for supplies of goods and not for services – but the nature of the goods is irrelevant. All that is significant is whether the goods in question are properly exported by the supplier or the recipient.

Again, there is little point in an exhaustive list of the zero-rated goods or services to be found in Schedule 8. The most significant are these:

Group 1: Food

Item 1: food of a kind used for human consumption (other than confectionery)
Item 2: animal feeding stuffs (but not pet foods)

One important exception is that a supply in the course of catering (including a supply of hot food for consumption off the premises) is standard-rated.

Group 3: Books

Item 1: books
Item 2: newspapers, journals and periodicals
Item 4: Music

Group 5: Construction of buildings

Item 1: the granting by a person constructing it of a major interest in, or in any part of, the building or its site if the building is designed as a dwelling or number of dwellings or is intended for use solely for a relevant residential purpose or a relevant charitable purpose.

A relevant residential purpose means use as:

1. an institution providing residential accommodation for children;
2. an institution providing residential accommodation with personal care for people needing personal care by reason of old age, disablement, past or present dependence on alcohol or drugs or past or present mental disorder;
3. a hospice;
4. residential accommodation for students or school pupils;
5. residential accommodation for members of the armed forces;
6. a monastery, convent etc;
7. an institution which is the sole or main residence of at least 90 per cent of its residents.

Hospitals, prisons and hotels are excluded from this definition.
A relevant charitable purpose is use by a charity other than in the course of a business.
Item 2: the supply in the course of construction of any building for residential or charitable use or any civil engineering work for a relevant permanent park for residential caravans.
Item 3: the supply by a person supplying services within item 2, of and in connection with those services: materials or builder's hardware etc or other articles of a kind ordinarily installed by builders as fixtures.

The scope of Group 5 was very considerably reduced in order to give effect to the decision of the ECJ in *EC Commission* v *UK* [1988] STC 456 where it was held that Directive number 77/388/EEC art 28(2) did not allow zero rating of supplies other than to final consumers in respect of the construction of industrial and commercial buildings

Group 7: International services

The supply of various kinds of services to persons belonging to other commuinity member states or to businessmen based in non-EC countries. Not all services qualify for such zero-rating: principally they will be of a consultant nature (such as lawyers or engineers) or relate to the transfer of intellectual property or financial services and therefore fall within Schedule 5 as 'supplied where received' and subject to the reverse charge.

Group 8: Transport

Items 1 and 2: the supply of large ships and aircraft
Item 4: transport of passengers in vehicles designed to carry more than 12 passengers or on scheduled flights

Group 16: Clothing

Item 1: articles designed as footwear or clothing for young children and not suitable for other persons
Item 2: protective boots and helmets otherwise than for the use of employees of the person providing the protective gear
Item 3: protective helmets for motorcyclists

25.6 The computation of the charge

Value of the supply

Section 19 provides that the value of a supply is determined in the following ways:

1. If the supply is for a consideration in money, its value is such amount as, *with the addition of the tax chargeable*, is equal to the consideration.
   In other words, when a contract for a taxable supply fails to mention VAT, the tax is already to be treated as included in the price.
2. If the supply is not for a consideration in money, or for a consideration not consisting wholly of money, the value is taken as its open market value on which, of course, VAT is then levied at 17.5 per cent. In *Empire Stores Ltd* v *Customs and Excise Commissioners* [1994] STC 623 the European Court of Justice held that free goods given by mail order firms for customer introductions were taxable supplies, and therefore tax was to be levied on their value.
3. In another case, *Fine Art Developments plc* v *Customs and Excise Commissioners (No 2)* [1996] STC 246, the House of Lords ruled on the value to be imposed under what is now VATA 1994 Schedule 6 para 2 on supplies made to agents (not registered for VAT) by one of the company's subsidiaries, Express Gifts. Some of the goods supplied were for retail sale and others were to be retained by the agents. It was held that the goods be valued for VAT purposes at open market value on a sale by retail and not at the price received by the suppliers from the agents. It was held that the presence of the word 'part' (of the business) in para 2 was to charge VAT on this type of supply. Failure to do so would result in a loss of VAT by directing retail sales via multiple non-taxable agents.

Credit for input tax against output tax: ss24 and 26

At the heart of the VAT system are the principles that the tax should be borne by the ultimate consumer alone, and that the intermediate supplier should only be liable for the value he has added to the asset supplied at his stage of the on-supply. This is achieved by allowing a taxable person credit for the VAT charged on standard-rated supplies made to him against the output tax which he is liable to pay to the Commissioners.

Section 25(1) requires that a taxable person account for and pay VAT by reference to 'prescribed accounting periods'. Usually, these are three-monthly periods, and will begin at the start of such a calendar month as may be agreed with the Commissioners. Supposedly, s1(2) makes the tax due and payable at the time of supply: in fact this is overridden by a combination of s25(1) and the VAT (General) Regulations 1985, regs 58 and 60, which allow the VAT return which is to be made by the trader to be furnished, together with the tax due, within one month after the end of the prescribed accounting period to which it relates. Since the tax due is an amalgam of all VAT charged on taxable supplies for that period, less VAT suffered, it may be that the trader has had the benefit of the VAT which he charged on a supply for up to four months. There are a number of special schemes for retail businesses which can be used by agreement with Customs and Excise to calculate VAT liability.

Sections 24(1), 25(2) and 26(2) determine the amount of input tax to be deducted by defining 'input tax' by reference to the types of supplies and acquisitions and by limiting the deduction of input tax if appropriate, to that which can be attributed directly to the supplies listed at s26(2), including tax on supplies outside the United Kingdom which would be taxable if taking place inside the United Kingdom.

The amount of credit to be given is dependent on rules contained in s26: only if all the trader's supplies are taxable supplies (ie standard or zero-rated) is the whole of the input tax deductible. If all of his supplies are exempt, none of his input tax may be deducted. Furthermore, if some but not all of his supplies are taxable the deduction is controlled by rules for 'partial exemption', in the VAT (General) (Amendment) (No 2) Regulations 1987. The partially exempt trader may, unless he comes within certain de minimis limits, only deduct input tax on supplies or importations wholly to be used in making taxable supplies. If a supply is partly used in making taxable, and partly in making exempt, supplies the input tax on it must be apportioned according to actual usage.

Schedule 4 provides a number of exceptions, designed to preclude the loss of tax after input tax has been claimed on the receipt of a taxable supply by a trader:

- where goods forming part of the assets of a business are transferred or disposed of by the trader so that they no longer form part of those assets *whether or not for a consideration*. For example, X buys a desk for the office, and after a few months decides to take it home: that would be a deemed supply under Schedule 4 para 5.
- where a person ceases to be a taxable person, any goods then forming part of the assets of the business are deemed to be supplied by him in the course or

furtherance of his business immediately before he ceased to be a taxable person: Schedule 4, para 8.

Restrictions on input tax recovery

Section 24(3) states that if goods or services are supplied to a company or goods are imported by a company which are then used by the company:

1. in the provision of accommodation, and
2. that accommodation is domestic accommodation which is used by a director of the company or any person connected with the director,

then such goods or services shall not be treated as used or to be used by the company for the purpose of any business carried on by it.

Consequently any VAT which is paid or becomes payable on such goods and services does not constitute input tax within s24(1). Recovery of input tax is also denied where the expenditure relates to business entertainment, as laid down in the Value Added Tax (Input Tax) Order 1992 (SI 1992/3222), which also contains provisions denying input tax recovery in relation to VAT paid on motor car purchases even if used wholly for business purposes (see reg 7(1)) as well as tax on secondhand goods, works of art etc (reg 4), where tax is accounted for under a special scheme. However, from 1 August 1995 businesses purchasing cars wholly for business use may deduct the input tax on those which they elect to treat as 'qualifying cars'. Correspondingly there will be VAT on the full sale price when disposed of. See *Royscot Leasing Ltd and Royscot Industrial Leasing Ltd* v *Customs and Excise Commissioners*; *Allied Domecq plc* v *Customs and Excise Commissioners*; *T C Harrison Group Ltd* v *Customs and Excise Commissioners* [1996] STC 898 concerning cars purchased for part business and personal use and for leasing. The three cases, which were pre-the August 1995 changes, were considered together and in each case input tax recovery was denied. See Chapter 27, section 27.7, for further details.

By s25(3),(5), if the trader's input tax for a period exceeds his output tax, the excess is to be repaid to him unless he has failed to make a return for an earlier period – when it may be withheld until he has complied with his obligations.

Bad debt relief

Relief from payment of VAT on supplies for which the trader never received payment was substantially changed by s39 Finance Act 1997. Prior to these changes the system of relief operated so that such a person can claim a full refund in respect of the amount of VAT paid on the outstanding debt providing:

1. the consideration payable for the goods and services does not exceed open market value, and
2. he has written off the consideration payable as a bad debt in his business accounts, and

358 *Value Added Tax*

3. one year has elapsed since the date of the supply.

Under the amended rules brought in by s39 and Schedule 17 Finance Act 1997, new ss36(4A) and 36(5)(ea) are added to VATA 1994. The changes made to the old rules were as follows:

1. In regard to supplies made with effect from the passing of FA 1997 title to any property supplied to the recipient need not have been passed.
2. The recipient may no longer claim input tax credit when the supplier makes a claim for bad debt relief.
3. No claims under the old rules may be made in respect of supplies made after the passing of the 1997 Finance Act.

25.7 Special cases

Groups of companies: s43

Two or more bodies corporate are eligible to be treated as a group if:

1. one of them controls the other or others; or
2. one person controls them all; or
3. two or more persons carrying on business in partnership control them all.

In any of these cases all or some of the companies may make an election that the business of the group be treated for VAT purposes as carried on by the 'representative member', in which case:

1. any supply of goods or services by one member of the group to another may be disregarded; and
2. any other supply by or to a member of the group is treated as a supply by or to the representative member.

The effect is to enable the group to be treated as having a single identity – that of the representative member – and to be obliged to submit one tax return only. Perhaps even more importantly, it ensures that taxable supplies by one member to a partially exempt member do not suffer irrecoverable input tax in the hands of the latter – inter-group supplies being ignored for VAT purposes. The Finance Act 1996 introduced a new Schedule 9A into VATA 1994 to counter the misuse of the inter-group supply rules. Customs now have power to direct that certain supplies will be subject to VAT or to bring an associated company into a VAT group in exceptional circumstances. These powers became necessary following the *Thorn* case. In this case input VAT on the supply of cars was claimed through a scheme involving one of the companies leaving the group at an appropriate point in the chain of supply and payment, and utilising the non charging of VAT between group members.

All members of the group are jointly and severally liable for VAT payable by the representative member.

Sections 40 and 41 Finance Act 1997 amend the rules on the treatment of VAT groups which have effect from 26 November 1996. The new rules, contained in ss43(1AA) and 43(2A), are aimed at ensuring that the deemed treatment of a VAT group as a single taxable person does not enable VAT group members to take advantage of the VAT group's representative member's special status as, eg a charity, permitted insurer or eligible supplier of education, to alter the character of the supplies made by them.

Also with effect from 26 November 1996, the rules for making retrospective applications to Customs and Excise for treatment as part of a VAT group are relaxed to allow a limited period of retrospection where a company is applying to be treated as leaving one group and joining another.

Section 44(4) provides that certain capital items shall not be treated as self-supplied to the representative member of the group within s44(5) if they are assets within VAT (General) Regulation (SI 1995/2518) reg 113. Examples of such assets are computers and computer equipment valued at more than £50,000 and interests in land and buildings having a value greater than £250,000.

Partnerships: s45

A partnership is assessable in the name of the firm, and changes in the constituent membership of it are ignored for VAT purposes. The firm is thus, in part, treated as a separate entity from its members but just as an individual is entitled only to one registration for VAT, however many businesses he carries on by himself, two partnerships comprising the same members are only entitled to a single registration: *Commissioners* v *Glassborrow* [1975] QB 465. If, however, A carries on business both as a sole trader and in partnership with B, each business would require a separate registration. Every member of a partnership is jointly and severally liable for all VAT debts of the partnership incurred before the date on which he notifies the Commissioners that he has ceased to be a partner.

Agents: s47

If goods or services are supplied through an agent, the legal position (subject to the rules of undisclosed agency) is that the supply is made by the principal to the third party; or vice versa. The Commissioners would normally adopt this approach and hold the principal alone liable for the VAT on the supply. Section 47(3) gives the Commissioners power, though, to treat the supply as being one made to the agent by the principal and by the agent to the third party – or vice versa, if they think fit. This power would be exercised in a case of undisclosed agency. It would be open to the Commissioners also to apply it where there were unable to recover tax due from the principal.

26

Anti-avoidance

26.1 Introduction

26.2 *The Duke of Westminster's Case* and beyond

26.3 *Ramsay* and the 'new approach'

26.4 Pre-ordination

26.5 The tax avoidance motive

26.6 Summary

26.1 Introduction

Until relatively recently the only control of tax avoidance schemes was by specific statutory provision. Attempts at avoidance were identified by the courts and Parliament subsequently plugged the gap in a rather piecemeal fashion. Most of these anti-avoidance provisions are contained in Part XVII ICTA 1988. Other examples are the treatment of certain premiums as Schedule D rather than Schedule A income (see supra 4.8). There were, however, no common law principles of general application to control tax avoidance. This may be seen as a corollary of the principle that tax statutes should be given their strict literal interpretation. If a transaction falls within the scope of a statutory provision that provision should be given effect without regard to the purpose of the transaction.

> 'In a taxing Act one has to look merely at what is clearly said. There is no room for intendment. There is no equity about a tax. There is no presumption as to a tax.' (Per Rowlatt J, in *Cape Brandy Syndicate* v *IRC* [1920] 1 KB at p71.)

This chapter will seek to explain the history of the so-called 'new approach' and describe its likely present extent.

26.2 *The Duke of Westminster's Case* and beyond

> 'Every man is entitled if he can to order his affairs so that the tax attaching under the appropriate Acts is less than it otherwise would be.' (Per Lord Tomlin [1935] 19 TC 490 at p520.)

The starting point in any discussion of tax avoidance is *The Duke of Westminster's Case*. At first sight the above statement by Lord Tomlin in this case would seem to give taxpayers carte blanche to arrange their transactions in such a way as to avoid or lessen their liability to tax. The new approach, however, significantly qualifies this entitlement. More emphasis should be placed on the words '... if he can'.

In *The Duke of Westminster's Case* the Duke entered into a number of covenants with his domestic staff whereby he agreed to covenant an amount to them which would have the economic effect of paying them their salaries, or at least part of their salaries. The significance was that covenanted sums could be set-off against the Duke's surtax liability, whereas salaries could not.

The staff were required to sign a letter which stated that whilst they could, in addition to the covenanted sums, still claim the full amount of their salaries, it was to be understood that staff would not. The Revenue sought to tax the Duke on the economic effect of these transactions; their substance over form. It was argued by the Revenue that the covenanted sums were in reality payments of salaries and therefore should fall to be treated as such. It is this approach that a majority of the House of Lords rejected. The covenants could not simply be disregarded for these purposes as they were bona fide legal transactions and not mere shams.

> 'The subject is not taxable by inference or analogy, but only by the plain words of a statute applicable to the facts and circumstances of his case.' (Per Lord Russell at p524.)

The House of Lords affirmed, however, that in construing the true legal effect of a transaction, regard may be had to all the surrounding circumstances.

In the years after *The Duke of Westminster's Case* the approach which the courts adopted to determine the tax effect of composite transactions (ie those with an ultimate objective yet with intermediate steps inserted) encouraged planning and avoidance. The tax effect of each step in a composite transaction was determined individually without regard to the overall purpose of the whole. This accorded well with the principle stated above that tax statutes are to be interpreted strictly. This approach led to the emergence of so-called 'off the shelf' schemes. These schemes were designed to manufacture a tax benefit by means of tax avoidance steps inserted into an otherwise genuine commercial transaction. These steps were inserted solely for that reason, having no other commercial purpose. In this sense the inserted steps were artificial. The benefit could, for example, take the form of an allowable loss or even a deferral of liability.

It was against a background of increasing loss of tax to the Revenue and increasingly artificial schemes that led to the decision in the related appeals to the House of Lords of *WT Ramsay* v *IRC* and *Eilbeck* v *Rawling* 54 TC 101. The *Ramsay* decision marks the clear beginning of the new approach in the attitude of the courts to tax avoidance schemes.

In the earlier case of *Floor* v *Davis* [1978] STC 436 the judgment of Eveleigh LJ in the Court of Appeal shows the first signs of a change in judicial approach. In that case the taxpayer wished to sell his shares in a company called IDM to another called KDI. If done directly this would have realised a very large capital gain on the disposal. The scheme actually used involved an intricate share exchange transaction which the taxpayer hoped would attract a tax benefit under the gain deferment provisions in ss77 et seq CGTA 1979 – now ss126 et seq TCGA 1992. The gain produced was hived off to a foreign resident company effectively free of tax (although details of ownership of that company were not available). The case was decided on appeal to the House of Lords on another point. The judgment of Eveleigh LJ however is important as it was expressly approved of by the House of Lords in *Ramsay*. Eveleigh LJ decided that for the purposes of capital gains tax the true legal effect of the transactions was a 'disposal' directly from the taxpayer to KDI thus producing the chargeable gain, notwithstanding the interposed transactions.

26.3 *Ramsay* and the 'new approach'

In the related appeals of *WT Ramsay Ltd* v *IRC* and *Eilbeck* v *Rawling* [1981] STC 174, both cases involved a scheme which was intended to create an artificial loss which could then be offset against previous capital gains realised on separate transactions. The *Ramsay* scheme involved the following steps:

1. R bought all the shares of a specially created company (Caithmead Ltd 'C').
2. R agreed to make two equal long-term loans to C on the following terms:
   – the loan could be repaid before the maturity date if C wished, and had to be repaid if C went into liquidation. If they were repaid at such an earlier date, they were repayable at the higher of face value and market value (calculated on the assumption that the loans would remain outstanding until maturity);
   – R had the right, exercisable once only, to reduce the rate of interest on Loan 1 and increase the rate on Loan 2 to a corresponding extent.

A variation of the interest rates would not affect the total amount of interest payable, but the market value of R's rights under Loan 2 would increase and of C's rights under that loan would decrease; the opposite effect would apply to Loan 1.

It was hoped that neither loan would be a 'debt on a security', thus enabling R to sell its rights under Loan 2 at a tax free profit. On C's liquidation, the loans were repayable; the loan whose market value had increased would be repayable at that increased value but the other loan would be repayable at par. C's repayment obligations were therefore increased (and the value of its shares correspondingly decreased) by an amount equal to the change in market value of the loan caused by the alteration in interest rates. Thus on a disposal of R's shares in C a loss was realised approximately equal to the gain realised on the disposal of its rights under Loan 2.

(The scheme failed on the alternative ground that Loan 2 was a debt on a security so that a chargeable gain was realised on its sale which offset the loss on the shares, leaving no net loss for other purposes.)

Lord Wilberforce stated some principles to explain the position of the law:

'1. A subject is only to be taxed on clear words, not on "intendment" or on the "equity" of an Act. Any taxing Act of Parliament is to be construed in accordance with this principle. What are "clear words" is to be ascertained on normal principles; these do not confine the courts to literal interpretation. There may, indeed should, be considered the context and scheme of the relevant Act as a whole, and its purpose may, indeed should, be regarded: see *IRC v Wesleyan and General Assurance Society* [1946] 2 All ER 749 at 751 per Lord Greene MR and *Mangin v IRC* [1971] 1 All ER 179 at 182 per Lord Donovan. The relevant Act in these cases is the Finance Act 1965, the purpose of which is to impose a tax on gains, less allowable losses, rising from disposals.
2. A subject is entitled to arrange his affairs so as to reduce his liability to tax. The fact that the motive for a transaction may be to avoid tax does not invalidate it unless a particular enactment so provides. It must be considered according to its legal effect.
3. It is for the fact-finding commissioners to find whether a document or a transaction is genuine or a sham. In this context, to say that a document or transaction is a "sham" means that while professing to be one thing, it is in fact something different. To say that a document or transaction is genuine means that, in law, it is what is professes to be, and it does not mean anything more than that. I shall return to this point.
Each of these three principles would be fully respected by the decision we are invited to make. Something more must be said as to the next principle.
4. Given that a document of transaction is genuine, the court cannot go behind it to some supposed underlying substance. This is the well-known principle of *IRC v Duke of Westminster* [1936] AC 1. This is a cardinal principle but it must not be overstated or over-extended. While obliging the court to accept documents or transactions, found to be genuine, as such, it does not compel the court to look at a document or a transaction in blinkers, isolated from any context to which it properly belongs. If it can be seen that a document or transaction was intended to have effect as part of a nexus or series of transactions, or as an ingredient of a wider transaction intended as a whole, there is nothing in the doctrine to prevent it being so regarded; to do so is not to prefer form to substance, or substance to form. It is the task of the court to ascertain the legal nature of any transaction to which it is sought to attach a tax or a tax consequence and if that emerges from a series or combination of transactions, intended to operate as such, it is that series or combination which may be regarded. For this there is authority in the law relating to income tax and capital gains tax: see *Chinn v Collins* and *IRC v Plummer*.' (But see *Moodie v IRC* [1993] STC 188.)

The essence of the approach is contained in the last paragraph. The court's task, according to Lord Wilberforce, is to determine the true legal effect of a transaction in order that it may attach the proper tax consequences to that transaction. If the true legal effect emerges only from scrutiny of all the surrounding circumstances then that task is within the court's function. This approach has been criticised in that it appears to prefer judge-made law over the expressed intentions of Parliament. The courts, it is argued, are denying the literal interpretation and corresponding application of statutes to transactions which, as a matter of fact, have been found to exist.

The answer to this argument is succinctly stated by Lord Oliver in another case, *Craven v White* [1988] STC 477 at p497:

'... judges are not legislators and if the result of a judicial decision is to contradict the express statutory consequences which have been declared by Parliament to attach to a particular transaction which has been found as a fact to have taken place, that can be justified only because as a matter of construction of the statute, the court has ascertained that that which has taken place is not, within the meaning of the statute, the transaction to which those consequences attach.'

Returning to *Ramsay*, in addition to enunciating the preferred approach, Lord Wilberforce expressly stated that the courts should not confine themselves to the previous method of assessing the tax consequences of each step individually in a composite transaction:

'To force the courts to adopt in relation to closely integrated situations a step by step, dissecting approach which the parties themselves may have negated, would be a denial rather than an affirmation of the true judicial process. In each case the facts must be established, and a legal analysis made: legislation cannot be required or even be desirable to enable the courts to arrive at a conclusion which corresponds with the parties' own intentions.'

The *Ramsay* case was closely followed by the case of *Furniss* v *Dawson* [1984] STC 153 which gave the House of Lords further opportunity to define the criteria for application of the 'new approach'.

In *Dawson* the taxpayer wished to sell the shares in the 'operating company' to another company called Wood Bastow. If done directly this would have produced a large capital gain immediately. The taxpayer wished to defer this liability. To this end a company called Greenjacket Investments Ltd was incorporated in the Isle of Man. The following two transactions were executed:

1. The taxpayer entered into a share for share exchange of the operating company's shares in return for shares issued in Greenjacket. (This, it was hoped, would attract the tax benefit, viz a deferment of liability under what is now ss135–138 TCGA 1992. Under those provisions the exchange is not treated as a disposal, the new shareholding and old shareholding are treated as the same asset.)
2. The shares in the operating company were then sold by Greenjacket for cash to Wood Bastow.

Lord Brightman in his speech at p159 explained the facts, in the appeal. He then dismissed two limitations which, it had been argued, constrained the approach.

It was contended, firstly, that the new approach only applied to so-called 'self-cancelling' schemes like *Ramsay* and not to those as in the instant appeal which had enduring legal consequences. This idea was rejected by Lord Brightman.

Lord Brightman also dismissed the contention that for the approach to apply the steps in a composite transaction must be contractually bound together.

'In a tax-saving scheme, no distinction is to be drawn for fiscal purposes, because none exists in reality, between (1) a series of steps which are followed through by virtue of an arrangement which falls short of a binding contract, and (2) a like series of steps which are followed through because the parties are contractually bound to take each step seriatim.

Thus in this case, although there was no contract directly between the taxpayer and Wood Bastow, that did not prevent the application of the approach provided that the steps to sell the shares ultimately to Wood Bastow were "pre-ordained".'

What then are the criteria for the application of the new approach? According to Lord Brightman they are as follows:

'But first there must be a pre-ordained series of transactions; or, if one likes, one single composite transaction. This composite transaction may or may not include the achievement of a legitimate commercial (ie business) end ... Secondly, there must be steps inserted which have no commercial (business) purpose apart from the avoidance of a liability to tax – not "no business effect".'

If these two criteria are fulfilled, Lord Brightman then goes on to describe the effects of the application of the approach.

'If those two ingredients exist, the inserted steps are to be disregarded for fiscal purposes. The court must then look at the end result. Precisely how the end result will be taxed will depend on the terms of the taxing statutes thought to be applied.'

The so-called 'new approach' is thus essentially a principle of statutory interpretation and the effects of its application reflect this. The interposed steps conferring the benefit are ignored and the ultimate objective of the taxpayer is taxed accordingly. The reason why the steps are ignored is that in the overall scheme of things the interposed steps have no real independent life of their own, ie they are artificial. A share exchange scheme in this situation whilst remaining a bona fide transaction for other purposes is not a 'share exchange' within the meaning of the Capital Gains Tax Act 1979, and therefore does not attract the benefit of the relief. The real issue is determining the criteria to be fulfilled for the courts to be justified in determining that the interposed steps are artificial, bearing in mind that artificial does not just mean prejudicial to the Revenue.

It should be noted that, according to Lord Brightman, the above criteria are findings of *fact* for the Commissioners. If they are found to exist then the only grounds on which that decision may be overturned by a court are those elucidated in *Edwards v Bairstow*.

The result in the *Dawson* case was that there was a disposal by the taxpayers of the shares in the operating company to Wood Bastow for a consideration equal to the amount paid by Wood Bastow to Greenjacket.

26.4 Pre-ordination

The extent of the new approach was discussed further in the conjoined appeals in *Craven v White* [1988] STC 476. This case gave their Lordships opportunity to determine whether transactions were 'pre-ordained' according to Lord Brightman or as Lord Wilberforce in *Ramsay* termed them a 'single composite transaction'.

In the case of *Craven* v *White* the taxpayer had effected an exchange of shares in his family company 'Queensferry' with an Isle of Man shelf company 'Millor" with a view to the ultimate sale to a third party of the Queensferry shares. Again the object of the exchange was to obtain a deferral of capital gains tax. The significant difference in this case was that at the time of the exchange, negotiations to find a final purchaser were still taking place. The identity of the final purchaser and to some extent whether the sale itself would take place was at that time uncertain.

One of the issues which their Lordships had to address was whether the final transaction, that is the sale to the ultimate purchaser which in fact took place, was 'pre-ordained'.

The majority represented by Lord Keith took a narrow view of the meaning of 'pre-ordained'. At p481 Lord Keith stated:

'In my opinion both the transactions in the series can properly be regarded as pre-ordained if, but only if, at the time when the first of them is entered into the taxpayer is in a position for all practical purposes to secure that the second also is entered into.'

It must also be noted that the question of whether the final transaction is pre-ordained should, according to Lord Keith, be determined at the time of the *share exchange*, that is at the time of the interposed tax avoidance step.

Similarly according to Lord Oliver 'pre-ordained' means:

'that there was at that time (ie when the intermediate transaction was entered into) no practical likelihood that the pre-planned events would not take place in the order ordained, so that the intermediate transaction was not even contemplated practically as having an independent life.'

A broader approach, however, was adopted in the minority judgment of Lord Templeman, who expressed concern that this narrow interpretation placed limitations on the judgment of Lord Brightman in *Dawson*.

'I have read the drafts of the speeches to be delivered in these present appeals. Three of those speeches accept the extreme argument of the taxpayer that *Dawson* is limited to its own facts or is limited to a transaction which has reached an advanced stage of negotiation (whatever that expression means) before the preceding tax avoidance transaction is carried out. These limitations would distort the effect of *Dawson*, are not based on principle, are not to be derived from the speeches in *Dawson*, and if followed would only revive a surprised tax avoidance industry and cost the general body of taxpayers hundreds of millions of pounds by enabling artificial tax avoidance schemes to alter the incidence of taxation. In *Dawson* Lord Brightman was not alone in delivering a magisterial rebuke to those judges who sought to place limitations on *Ramsay* because they disliked the principle that an artificial tax avoidance schemes does not alter the incidence of tax. In my opinion, a knife-edged majority has no power to limit this principle which has been responsible for four decisions of this House approved by a large number of our predecessors. Adapting the words of Lord Diplock in *Burmah*, it remains disingenuous to suggest, and dangerous on the part of those who advise taxpayers to assume, that *Ramsay* and *Dawson* did not mark a significant change in the approach adopted by this House in its judicial role to artificial tax avoidance schemes (whether or not they include the achievement of a legitimate commercial end) which include steps that have no commercial purpose apart from the avoidance of a liability to tax which in the absence of those particular steps would have been payable.'

The necessary requirements for the new approach to apply are, according to Lord Templeman:

'First, the taxpayer must decide to carry out, if he can, a scheme to avoid an assessment of tax on an intended taxable transaction by combining it with a prior tax avoidance transaction. Secondly, the tax avoidance transaction must have no business purpose apart from the avoidance of tax on the intended taxable transaction. Thirdly, after the tax avoidance transaction has taken place, the taxpayer must retain power to carry out his part of the intended taxable transaction. Fourthly, the intended taxable transaction must in fact take place.'

It is submitted, however, that the narrow approach of the majority reflects the ratio of the decision in *Craven* v *White* and is to be preferred.

It is important lastly to note some of the factors which their Lordships considered important to be taken into account to determine whether a transaction is pre-ordained.

Lord Keith:

'It may be many months before a possible purchaser is found, and many more before a bargain is concluded.'

Lord Templeman:

'Of course, if there are two transactions separated in time, the commissioners may conclude that the two transactions did not form part of an artificial tax avoidance scheme planned at the time of the first transaction and completed by the second transaction.'

Thus the length of time between the two transactions is important although not conclusive either way. A planned, prolonged period between transactions would not of itself prevent the application of the approach. It must be a genuine interruption.

Other factors identified by Lord Keith at p481 are:

1. Whether the intention actually to carry out the ultimate transaction is present at the time of the intermediate transaction, or whether it is merely carried out to put the taxpayer in a better position if he ultimately chooses to carry out the deal.
2. The state of negotiations for the ultimate transaction.

Lord Oliver concentrated on the nature of the intermediate step:

'There is a real and not merely a metaphysical distinction between something that is done as a preparatory step towards a possible but uncertain contemplated future action and something which is done as an integral and interdependent part of a transaction already agreed and, effectively, predestined to take place.'

Lord Jauncey identified the following factors as relevant to consider:

1. The extent to which at the time of the tax step negotiations or arrangements have proceeded towards the carrying through, as a continuous process, of the remaining transactions.
2. The nature of such negotiations or arrangements.
3. The likelihood at the time of the tax step, of such remaining negotiations being carried through.
4. The extent to which after the tax step negotiations or arrangements have proceeded to completion, without genuine interruptions.

26.5 The tax avoidance motive

As we have seen the new approach, according to Lord Brightman, requires that there must be steps inserted:

'which have no commercial (business) purpose apart from the avoidance of liability to tax'.

This is reflected in the judgment of Lord Keith in *Craven* v *White*:

'It is also relevant to take into account, if it be the case, that one or more of the steps was introduced with no business purpose other than the avoidance of tax.'

The rationale behind this requirement is explained by Lord Oliver in *Craven* v *White* at p501:

'The absence of any commercial motive underlines the artificiality of the interrelated transactions and entitles the court to disregard them because they are not intended to produce anything other than an artificial result.'

It should be noted that the essence of this requirement is the absence of any commercial or business reasons for the inserted steps 'apart from the avoidance of a liability to tax'. It is not intended to affect steps for which there are genuine commercial reasons. The striking point is artificiality. The approach also does not force a taxpayer always to choose the least efficient method of transacting.

'The principle does not involve, in my opinion, that it is part of the judicial function to treat as nugatory any step whatever which a taxpayer may take with a view to the avoidance or mitigation of tax. It remains true in general that the taxpayer, where he is in a position to carry through a transaction in two alternative ways, one of which will result in a liability to tax and the other of which will not, is at liberty to choose the latter and to do so effectively in the absence of any specific tax avoidance provision.' (Lord Keith in *Craven* v *White* at p480.)

Thus the taxpayer may prevent the application of the new approach if he can show genuine commercial reasons for the inserted steps other than an attempt to gain a tax benefit. It should be stressed, however, that this is a question of fact to be determined primarily by the Commissioners.

The importance of genuine commercial reasons for the inserted steps is demonstrated by the case of *Shepherd* v *Lyntress Ltd* [1989] STC 517.

Lyntress, the taxpayer company, was wholly owned by Grendon and a member of the Grendon group. Lyntress owned the shares in MH which were showing a substantial loss. Because of the previous transactions, if Lyntress ceased to be a 75 per cent member of the Grendon group or sold the MH shares outside the group, the loss on those shares would crystallise. In 1979 Grendon decided to utilise the loss by selling Lyntress to a company with chargeable gains, against which Lyntress's losses on the MH shares could be set. At the same time Grendon wished to keep MH within the group: there were hopes of turning around its fortunes. News International became interested in purchasing Lyntress for the losses. A three-part scheme was devised to avoid the pre-emption provisions of MH's articles, and to avoid the provisions of s62(3) CGTA 1979. The scheme was:

1. On 26 November 1979 News acquired 35 per cent of Lyntress. This broke the group relationship with Grendon and crystallised the losses in Lyntress.
2. On 27 November 1979 Lyntress sold its shares in MH to another Grendon subsidiary.
3. On 28 November 1979 News acquired the remaining 65 per cent of Lyntress.

The inspector raised an assessment against Lyntress on the basis that the three transactions of 26, 27 and 28 November were a single composite transaction with the pre-planned end of the sale of Lyntress to News. The sale of 35 per cent had no commercial purpose, only a fiscal purpose, and fell to be ignored, leaving 100 per cent of the Lyntress shares to be regarded as sold on 28 November (ie at stage (3) with the consequence that the sale of the MH shares on 27 November crystallised the losses in Lyntress while Lyntress was still a member of the Grendon group, and hence on account of s62(3) they were not available for set-off by News.

Lyntress appealed to the Commissioners who reduced the assessment. The Crown appealed to the High Court.

Vinelott J held that the sale of the first tranche of shares did have a commercial purpose; viz the avoidance of the pre-emption provisions of MH's articles and also to avoid s62(3).

The latter part of the decision is extremely important in that it confirms the ability of a taxpayer to take advantage of a specific fiscal privilege, namely the ability to channel losses into a subsidiary in order to sell the subsidiary pregnant with such losses. Thus, taking advantage of a fiscal privilege is not necessarily tax avoidance. Vinelott J (in *Shepherd* v *Lyntress*):

> 'It is clear from the decision of the House of Lords in *Craven* v *White* and related appeals that a transaction cannot be disregarded or treated as fiscally ineffective merely because it was entered into with a view to avoiding tax or taking advantage of some fiscal exemption and for no other purpose.'

Although, as stated above, the existence of genuine commercial reasons is a question of fact, it seems clear that the courts are reluctant to apply the new approach with its consequent drastic effects if the taxpayer has some other genuine motive for carrying out the intermediate steps or if he is merely taking advantage of some benefit for which Parliament has provided. The real question is how genuine the other motives for the transaction are. See the decision in *IRC* v *Willoughby* [1995] STC 143 on a case involving the application of s739 where the commercial aspects were fully explored and great stress was laid on being within an alternative statutory framework provided for by Parliament. One of the side effects of this case has been the amendment to s739 brought in by s81 Finance Act 1997 as s739(1A), so that it can be applied to income arising on or after 26 November 1996, irrespective of whether the taxpayer was ordinarily resident in the United Kingdom at the time when the 'transfer of assets' took place.

For further discussion see the judgment of Lord Templeman in *Ensign Tankers (Leasing)* v *Stokes* [1992] STC 226 at p229 which set the rule of looking at the true construction of the whole transaction.

26.6 Summary

In summary it is submitted that the new approach may be applied where according to the ratio in *Craven* v *White* the following are present:

1. There must be a pre-ordained series of transactions or a single composite transaction; and
2. Steps have been inserted into the transaction which have no other commercial purpose than the avoidance of a tax liability. Taking advantage of a fiscal advantage provided for is not sufficient.

These are facts to be determined primarily by the Commissioners.

In order for the approach not to apply the taxpayer may demonstrate a genuine uncertainty or interruption in the continuation of transactions or a genuine commercial reason for the intermediate steps.

If the above criteria, however, are satisfied the approach treats as a fiscal nullity the inserted steps. The intended ultimate transaction is then taxed accordingly. The new approach may specifically apply a charging provision or prevent the application of a tax benefit, eg a deferral. Furthermore it does not apply only to capital gains tax.

In *Customs and Excise Commissioners* v *Faith Construction Ltd* [1988] STC 35 the approach was applied to a scheme which attempted to avoid a VAT tax liability.

In *Fitzwilliam (Countess) and Others* v *IRC* [1993] STC 502; [1993] 1 WLR 1189 the Court of Appeal was clearly of the opinion that the *Ramsay* principle could be applied to IHT schemes. On the facts, however, it was held that there was not a composite transaction to which the new approach could be applied. In June 1993 the House of Lords confirmed in favour of the taxpayer.

It should be noted, however, that dicta are not to be read as one should read a statute. The application of the new approach depends very much on the facts of the particular case at hand. Rather than apply a factual checklist students should have an understanding of the principles which lie behind the often conflicting dicta.

Lord Wilberforce's summary of the state of the law in *Ramsay* remains as pertinent now as it was then.

Although the new approach may have been limited to some extent in its narrow definition by the majority in *Craven* v *White*, it may yet prove to have Medusa-like qualities given the difference in judicial opinion with regard to its scope (see the judgment of Lord Templeman in *Craven* v *White*).

Moreover, whilst the new approach remains merely a principle of judicial statutory construction, with its consequent uncertainty, the planning of transactions will continue no doubt with ever-increasing sophistication. This is perhaps one activity the 'new approach' was designed to restrain.

The case of *Piggott* v *Staines Investments* [1995] STC 114 involved a scheme to recover corporation tax paid by an acquired company by introducing it into a group whose parent company (BAT Group) had surplus ACT. A dividend was paid to Staines by another group company without ACT under a group election, followed by a dividend payment out of Staines to its parent company which could then pay a dividend to its shareholders. BAT did not have to account for ACT since the dividend it had received had borne tax (see Chapter 17). Despite the time delay of ten months in the respective 'steps' it was held that they were still within the *Furniss* v *Dawson* doctrine and had to be ignored as being for no purpose other than the avoidance of tax. This has taken the 'certainty' aspect of the steps further than before, to a stage of being caught unless the opposite was very unlikely to occur.

Whittles v *Uniholdings Ltd* [1996] STC 914 was a case of an attempt to reverse the normal application of *Furniss* v *Dawson* previously relied upon only by the Revenue as an attack argument. Here it was argued successfully in defence by the claimant company in the High Court (but overturned in the Court of Appeal) that the two elements of a foreign exchange transaction were not to be treated separately for capital gains purposes by the Inland Revenue, on the grounds that they constituted a single 'composite transaction' and should be taxed according to their overall effects. The Court of Appeal held that the *Ramsay* principle could not be relied upon to combine a gain on a foreign currency futures contract with the expense, claimed as a loss, of repaying associated dollar loans, resulting in a 'single composite transaction'. The loan 'deficit' or expense did not arise from the disposal of a chargeable asset and could not therefore be set off against the gain resulting from the futures contract.

In *IRC* v *Universities Superannuation Scheme Ltd* [1997] STC 1, concerning a 'transaction in securities', a company purchased its own shares from the appellant giving rise to a distribution. The appellant was entitled to exemption from tax as an exempt pension fund. The issues were whether the appellant received an 'abnormal amount by way of dividend', whether the transaction was carried out for bona fide commercial reasons or in the ordinary course of making or managing investments, and whether the appellant obtained a 'tax advantage' – ss703, 704 and 709 ICTA 1988. It was held that a person who was exempt from tax might be said to obtain a 'relief' from tax within the meaning of the definition of 'tax advantage' in s709(1). The definition of 'tax advantage' was amended by s73 FA 1997 to include the receipt of tax credits. See Chapter 27, section 27.8, for further details.

27

Recent Cases

27.1 Schedule D Cases I and II

27.2 Capital allowances

27.3 Schedule E

27.4 Settlements – anti avoidance

27.5 Corporation tax

27.6 Close companies

27.7 Value added tax

27.8 Anti-avoidance

27.1 Schedule D Cases I and II

Deeny and Others v *Gooda Walker Ltd (In Voluntary Liquidation) and Others (Inland Revenue Commissioners as Third Party) and Related Appeals* [1996] STC 299 House of Lords (Lords Goff, Browne-Wilkinson, Mustill, Nicholls and Hoffmann)

Damages – underwriting agent's negligence – whether damages taxable in the hands of the Lloyd's Names as receipts of trade – s171 Finance Act 1993

Facts
The plaintiffs (Deeny and others) were awarded damages against the managing and members agents of various Lloyd's underwriting syndicates (Gooda Walker Ltd and others) as a result of the agents' failure to exercise due care in the exercise of their functions on the members' ('Names') behalf. The quantity of the award to the members was to be such that they would be in the same position as if they had been insured against such losses. The issues in the instant case were whether in determining the amount of the damages, regard had to be taken of the tax element, for which the agents sought a reduction in the amounts awarded against them. The agents contended that the Names had and would continue to save tax on the sums awarded and that accordingly the amounts awarded against them should be reduced by an amount equivalent to the tax so saved.

Held
The House of Lords dismissed the agents' appeal, holding that the business of an underwriting Name at Lloyd's consisted of a single business and that the agency agreements were contracts made in the course of that business. The damages received by the Names were, therefore, a trading receipt of the business, to be taxed according to ss171 and 184 Finance Act (FA) 1993 . As no tax saving had or would accrue to the names, no deduction should be made from the amount of damages awarded against the agents.

Commentary
This case did not directly concern the Inland Revenue, since it did not involve the collection of tax comprised in assessments made by them on a taxpayer, but they consented to be joined as a third party, in view of the importance of the tax matters at issue between the Names and their agents, in determining whether reduction should be made in the amount of damages which the agents were ordered to pay as a result of their negligence. The agents contended that the damages did not arise to the Names from the carrying on of their (the Names') businesses but that the source of the cause of action was the rights and obligations between the names and the agents. They sought to prove that the Names had therefore saved tax on the awards because of the source (as contended by them) of the award.

Lord Hoffmann, approving the dicta of Diplock LJ in *London and Thames Haven Oil Wharves Ltd* v *Attwooll* (1966) 43 TC 491 at 495, confirmed that the receipt of a sum by a trader as compensation for the failure to receive what would have been a revenue receipt of his trade was sufficient to demonstrate that the compensation was itself a receipt of the business. The source of the award was therefore the business conducted by the Names. See s184(1) FA 1993 for the definition of 'underwriting business'.

Wharf Properties Limited v *CIR* [1997] STC 351 Privy Council (Lords Browne-Wilkinson, Lloyd of Berwick, Nicholls of Birkenhead, Steyn and Hoffmann)

Hong Kong – Revenue Profits tax – whether interest on loans 'expenditure of a capital nature' – whether deductible in ascertaining taxpayer's chargeable profits – Inland Revenue Ordinance (Laws of Hong Kong, 1995 rev, c112), ss16(1)(a) and 17(1)(c)

Facts
Wharf Properties Ltd ('Wharf') was a Hong Kong property development company. In 1987 it decided to acquire and redevelop the old tramway depot at Causeway Bay. By a contract dated 3 August 1987 it agreed to buy the depot for HK$3,039 million. Part of the price was paid at the time of the contract and the rest on two dates in 1988. Wharf obtained the purchase money by borrowing from various banks

and financial institutions. The loans were for short periods, ranging from a week to a month, but were always renewed. The issue was whether Wharf was entitled (under the relevant Hong Kong statute) to deduct the interest payments on these loans for the purpose of calculating its taxable profits.

Held

The appeal was dismissed on the grounds: (i) that although the interest payments were prima facie deductible as having been laid out for the purpose of earning profits in future years, no deduction could be permitted under the relevant statute for payments of a capital nature; and (ii) that the nature of the payment as a capital or revenue one depended on the purpose for which it was incurred and, since the interest was incurred for the purpose of creating a capital asset, the interest had been paid for a capital purpose.

Lord Hoffmann:

> 'Prima facie ... the interest was deductible under s16(1)(a). It was incurred for the purpose of earning taxable profits in future years ... But s17 contains a list of various kinds of expenditure in respect of which "no deduction shall be allowed". Their Lordships think that in the absence of express contrary language, expenditure which comes within s16 will not be deductible if it falls within one of the prohibited categories in s17. ...
>
> The relevant head of prohibition in s17 is subs(1)(c): there shall be no deduction of "any expenditure of a capital nature". The question therefore is whether the interest payments were expenditure of a capital nature. ...
>
> It is true that on the hands of the recipient, interest ... will have the character of income. From the point of view of the payer, however, a payment of interest may be capital or revenue expense, depending on the purpose for which it was paid. ... The wages of an electrician employed in the construction of a building by an owner who intends to retain the building as a capital investment are part of its capital cost. The wages of the same electrician employed by a construction company, or by the building owner in maintaining the building when it is completed and let, are a revenue expense. ...
>
> ... the purpose of the loan during the period for which the interest payment was made is critical to whether it counts as a capital or revenue expense. In the present case, during the whole of the two years in question, the loan was clearly being applied for the purpose of acquiring and creating a capital asset rather than holding it as an income-producing investment. It follows that the interest was being expended for a capital purpose.'

Commentary

In this case some of the dicta are important in establishing the dividing line between capital and revenue expenditure and as such are equally applicable in a UK context. Lord Hoffmann said that recurring and periodic payments were not necessarily revenue expenditure. It may be that the UK Inland Revenue will seek to rely on this decision to enquire more closely into, for example, the deductibility of salaries or other recurrent payments where they can point to some underlying capital purpose related to the payments being made.

27.2 Capital allowances

Bradley v *London Electricity plc* [1996] STC 1054 Chancery Division (Blackburne J)

Capital allowances – machinery or plant – whether electricity substation 'plant' – s44 FA 1971 (now s24 CAA 1990)

Facts
London Electricity constructed a substation comprising a substantial underground structure which housed transformers and other machinery and equipment. The company claimed that the whole of the substation constituted 'plant' for the purposes of a claim to capital allowances under what is now s24 Capital Allowances Act (CAA) 1990. They succeeded in their claim before the Special Commissioner and the Crown appealed.

Held
Reversing the finding of the Special Commissioner, that the structure of the substation did not perform any plant-like functions and that the expenditure relating to its construction did not qualify for capital allowances under the provisions relating to machinery and plant.

Blackburne J said that, in his judgment, the Special Commissioner had failed to ask himself what plant-like function the structure performed in London Electricity's trading activity, and that if he had, the true and only reasonable conclusion he could have come to was that the structure functioned as the premises in which London Electricity's trading activity was carried on, rather than the apparatus with which it was carried on. No plant-like function had been identified for the structure as a whole. The fact that features of the structure were carefully designed to accommodate the equipment within did not, in his view, convert what was otherwise the premises in which the activity was conducted into the plant or apparatus with which that activity was conducted. He concluded:

> 'In my judgment the structure of the substation is no more plant than the purpose-built kennels in *Carr* v *Sayer*, the specially designed planteria in *Gray* v *Seymours Garden Centre*, or the car wash halls in *Attwood* v *Anduff Car Wash Ltd*. The appeal therefore succeeds.'

Commentary
In reversing the conclusion of the Special Commissioner, the High Court has continued to develop the findings of the cases mentioned above, that it is not sufficient to look at whether a structure performs a business function, in determining whether capital allowances are due under the machinery or plant provisions. Blackburne J relied upon the judgment of Hoffmann J in *Wimpey International Ltd* v *Warland (Inspector of Taxes)* [1988] STC 149 at 170–171 in

which he 'mapped' out what he described as 'the boundaries of the concept of plant'. The description came from *Yarmouth* v *France* (1887) 19 QBD 647 at 658:

> '... in its ordinary sense, it includes whatever apparatus is used by a businessman for carrying on his business, not his stock-in-trade which he buys or makes for sale; but all goods and chattels, fixed or moveable, live or dead, which he keeps for permanent employment in his business.'

Thus, the following were excluded:

1. Anything not used for carrying on the business.
2. Stock-in-trade – although used for the purposes of the business, it lacks permanence.
3. Things which are not 'apparatus ... goods and chattels, fixed or moveable, live or dead' or not employed in the business – this excludes the premises where the business is conducted.

In arriving at his decision the Special Commissioner failed to distinguish the structure from what it housed and erroneously concluded that the two could not be looked at separately. Although the structure performed a business function, it was not used in the actual generation of electricity, but housed the equipment and machinery utilised by the business in the generation of electricity.

27.3 Schedule E

Templeton v *Jacobs* [1996] STC 991 Chancery Division (Jonathan Parker J)

Schedule E – benefit to director or higher paid employee – employer providing for office in employee's home before commencement of employment – construction completed after employment taken up – whether provided when employed by the employer – s154 ICTA 1988 – meaning of 'provided'

Facts

On 14 January 1991 an offer of employment was made to the taxpayer by the company to commence on 1 May of that year. As part of that offer, the taxpayer would work from home. The company agreed to provide at its expense an office by means of a loft conversion at the taxpayer's home. The company signed the order for the loft conversion on 30 January and made part payment on the same date. From 1 April 1991 the company paid rent to the taxpayer in respect of the part of the taxpayer's house which it occupied. The loft was available for office work from the beginning of September 1991. The taxpayer was assessed to income tax under Sch E for the year 1991–92 on the whole cost of the conversion as the provision of a benefit in kind under s154(2) Income and Corporation Taxes Act (ICTA) 1988. The taxpayer appealed contending that the loft conversion was not assessable as a benefit in kind under s154 as it had been provided during the tax year 1990–91, which was before the commencement of his employment with the company. In addition the employee claimed that even if it were a benefit for that year, it fell within the job-related accommodation exemption of s155(2)(b).

The Crown contended that, since the conversion was not completed until September 1991, it was not 'provided' to the taxpayer until the income tax year 1991–92, and was therefore assessable under s154 for that year. The Special Commissioner held that the benefit of the loft conversion had been provided before 6 April 1991 because the company had done everything which it had to do in order to fulfil its commitment to the taxpayer before that date and that the benefit was therefore outwith the terms of s154. The Crown appealed.

Held

The Court held that in order for a benefit to be regarded as 'provided' for the purposes of s154(1), the benefit had to be available to the taxpayer, and until such time as the benefit was capable of being enjoyed by the taxpayer, there was no relevant benefit for s154 purposes. As to the exemption claimed under s155(2)(b), what was provided for the employee was not 'accommodation' as required by the language of that section. The provision of a loft conversion was therefore a taxable benefit and assessable for the year 1991–92.

Commentary

The case centred on whether the contractual arrangements for the provision of the loft conversion for the prospective employee's use as an office were sufficient to determine the date on which the benefit was provided to him and therefore to settle the income tax year in which it was to be considered for assessment. If the contractual arrangements were sufficient to trigger a charge to tax, in this case there was no employment carried on in that year and therefore there would be no liability under s154.

The Judge ruled that the arrangements for the provision of the work were not the touchstones for determining when the benefit was provided and that the Special Commissioner had therefore erred in the interpretation of the statute's requirements. He also held that there was no merit in the taxpayer's additional argument for exemption under s155(2)(b), noting that occasional use by the taxpayer's family removed any contention that it was exclusively used for the purposes of the employment.

27.4 Settlements – anti-avoidance

Young v *Pearce; Young* v *Scrutton* [1996] STC 743 Chancery Division (Sir John Vinelott)

Meaning of settlement – gifts between spouses – taxpayers directors and sole shareholders of trading company – issue of preference shares to wives of taxpayers –

shares carrying no rights to participate on a winding up of company – substantial dividends paid on preference shares – whether an arrangement constituting a 'settlement' – whether preference dividends to be treated as income of taxpayers – outright gift between spouses to the other – whether property given was wholly or substantially a right to income – ss672, 674A(1) and 685(4A) ICTA 1988

Facts

The taxpayers were the sole shareholders and directors of a profitable trading company. They determined that part of the profits should be paid to their wives. In November 1990 the share capital of the company was reorganised into ordinary and preference shares. The preference shares carried the right to a dividend of 30 per cent of the net profit of the company for the relevant financial year but the shares carried no rights to participate in the surplus assets of the company on a winding up, other than the price paid for the shares, and carried no voting rights in regard to general meetings. The Revenue raised assessments on the taxpayers in under ss672(1)(a) and 674A(1)(b) ICTA 1988 on the basis that the dividends paid to the wives were income of their respective husbands. The Revenue's contentions were that the actions of the taxpayers amounted to an arrangement sufficient to create a 'settlement' as defined in s681(4)(c) ICTA 1988 and that the income of the settlement was to be treated as the income of the taxpayers as settlors either: (1) pursuant to s672 because the settlement was revocable since the taxpayers as owners of all the voting shares in the company had power to revoke the settlement by winding up the company; or (2) pursuant to s674A(1) which deemed income payable under a settlement to be treated as that of the settlor unless, inter alia, the settlor had divested himself absolutely of the income under the settlement (s674A(1)(d)) or the income of the settlement was treated as that of the settlor under another provision (s674A(1)(f)).

The Special Commissioner allowed the taxpayers' appeal, holding that the dividends paid to the wives were taxable on each of them separately since the taxpayers' actions had not amounted to an arrangement sufficient to create a settlement, and further that the power of the taxpayers to wind up the company at any time did not constitute power to revoke the alleged settlement within s672 ICTA 1988.

The Crown appealed, contending, inter alia: (1) that the creation of a new class of preference shares, the application by the wife of each of the taxpayers for 25 of the new preference shares to be issued at par and the allotment of the shares together constituted an arrangement or disposition and therefore a 'settlement' within s681(4) ICTA 1988; and (2) that none of the exceptions excluding the application of s674A(1) were relevant since the taxpayers were deemed not to have divested themselves absolutely of the preference shares within s674A(1)(d) because the transaction was an outright gift by one spouse to the other of property which property was 'wholly or substantially a right to income' within s685(4A)(d) ICTA 1988.

Held

1. The creation of the new class of preference shares, the application by the wife of each of the taxpayers for 25 of the new preference shares to be issued at par and the allotment of the shares together constituted an arrangement or disposition within the meaning of the definition of settlement in s681(4) ICTA 1988. The judge followed the decision in *Copeman* v *Coleman, for Coleman Minors* (1939) 22 TC 594.
2. The preference shares entitled the holders to a preferential dividend if the taxpayers determined to distribute the whole or part of the profits arising in any given year. Apart from that right to income, the only rights conferred on the preference shareholders were the right to repayment of the nominal sum paid on the allotment of the shares and the right to attend and be heard, but not to vote, at general meetings. The fact that the allotment of shares was an outright gift of property from one spouse to the other comprising 'wholly or substantially of a right to income' within s685(4A) meant that s674A(1) was not excluded, and therefore the taxpayers as settlors were deemed not to have divested themselves absolutely of the preference shares. The income of the settlement and, therefore, the preference dividends were to be treated under s674A(1) as income of the taxpayers. The Crown's appeals would therefore be allowed.

Commentary

The settlement provisions under which this case arose were updated and restated by FA 1995 and are now to be found in ss660A to 660G ICTA 1988. Since the essence of the provisions were not altered in their effect by the 1995 Act, this judgment will still apply to settlements determined under the law as currently stated. Under s660A income arising from property under a settlement remains that of the settlor unless the settlor has no interest in the property. In the situation such as arose in this case, the continuing reservation to the husbands of all rights other than income represented by the preference shares and the retention of control as to whether the dividends would be paid or not, would be sufficient to confirm that an interest in the property continued to exist for the settlors.

27.5 Corporation tax

Imperial Chemicals Industries plc v *Colmer (Inspector of Taxes)* [1996] STC 352 House of Lords (Lords Keith, Browne-Wilkinson, Mustill, Nolan and Nicholls)

Corporation tax – Consortium relief – s258 ICTA 1970 – holding company – whether business of holding company consisted wholly or mainly in the holding of shares or securities of trading companies which were its 90 per cent subsidiaries – whether group relief available only where holding company's 90 per cent subsidiary trading companies are bodies corporate resident in UK – s258(2), (5), (7) and (8) ICTA 1970

Facts
The appeal concerned the interpretation of s258 ICTA 1970 (now ss413(3)(b) and 413(5) ICTA 1988) and related to claims for consortium relief for the years 1985 to 1987. ICI Ltd (ICI) and the Wellcome Foundation Ltd (W), which were UK incorporated companies, formed a consortium in which ICI had a 49 per cent interest and W had a 51 per cent interest. The consortium owned all the share capital in CAHH, a holding company which was also a UK incorporated company. CAHH owned 100 per cent of the shares in all but one of its 23 subsidiary trading companies, four of which were UK resident, six were resident in other EU Member States and 13 were resident outside the EU.

One of the four UK resident subsidiaries (Coopers Animal Health Ltd) ('CAH') sought to surrender to ICI trading losses for the three accounting periods ending on 31 August 1985, 30 August 1986 and 29 August 1987 thereby enabling ICI to claim group relief by reference to its 49 per cent share in the consortium under the consortium relief provisions of s258(2)(a) and (8) ICTA 1970 (now s402(3) and (4) ICTA 1988). The Inland Revenue rejected ICI's claims, on the basis that CAHH was not a 'holding company' within the definition of holding company found in s258(5)(b) (now s413(3)(b) ICTA 1988) because its business did not consist wholly or mainly in the holding of shares or securities of trading companies resident in the UK. The condition that the companies, whose shares are held, must be UK resident, is to be found in s413(5) ICTA 1988. The Court of Appeal had held that the residence condition did not extend to the subsidiary companies. The Crown appealed.

Held
The House of Lords held that the proper and intended interpretation of the words in the subsection (now s413(5)), 'references in this Chapter to a company apply only to bodies corporate resident in the United Kingdom' was that it included not only the claimant and surrendering companies but the holding company and the companies whose shares comprised 'wholly or mainly' the shares held by the holding company.

Commentary
Despite reaching the conclusion that the statute as written, both historically and currently, imposed a general requirement of UK residence, the House of Lords have referred the matter to the European Court of Justice before the appeal can finally be determined. It is a question of whether this construction conflicts with the obligations of the United Kingdom under Community law and the applicability of arts 52 and 58 of the EC Treaty (which are against restrictions upon the freedom of

establishment of nationals, including companies, of one Member State in the territory of another) needs to be considered by the ECJ.

27.6 Close companies

Steele (Inspector of Taxes) v EVC International NV (formerly European Vinyls Corp (Holdings) BV) [1996] STC 785 Court of Appeal (Neill, Morritt and Hutchison LJJ)

Double taxation relief – dividends paid by UK company to Dutch joint venture company – joint venture company owned as to 50 per cent by two companies – whether Dutch company entitled to tax credits in respect of dividends paid – whether Dutch company controlled by two or more connected persons – s839(7) ICTA 1988 – Double Taxation Relief (Taxes on Income) (Netherlands) Order 1980

Facts

EVC was a private company established in the Netherlands in 1986 as a joint venture between two groups of companies, ICI and EniChem. The terms of the joint venture were contained in a shareholders' agreement between ICI and EniChem. Under the provisions of the agreement ICI and EniChem each transferred to subsidiaries of EVC all their interests in the PVC market in return for a 50 per cent shareholding in EVC. The venture was to continue for a minimum period of five years but with the expressed intention that it should continue without any time limit. EVC had a management board and a supervisory board appointed by ICI and EniChem. The management board was required to report to the supervisory board and was subject to the supervisory board's approval for certain decisions. At general meetings no resolution could be passed by either the ICI shareholders or the EniChem shareholders independently without the support of at least one shareholder from the other group. The arrangements for electing members of the boards and the voting powers ensured that EVC was as deadlocked at board level as it was at general meeting level.

EVC appealed against the Crown's decision that it was not entitled to tax credits in respect of dividends which EVC received in 1988 from one of its UK subsidiaries in accordance with s231(3) ICTA 1988 and article 10(a) of the Double Taxation Relief (Taxes on Income) (Netherlands) Order 1980 (SI 1980/1961). The Order (the double taxation agreement between the UK and the Netherlands) imposes a condition that relief (in the form of the tax credits) is not due unless it could be shown that the claimant company is not controlled by two or more connected persons together, who or any of whom would not have been entitled to a tax credit if he had been the beneficial owner of the dividends' within the meaning of art 10(3)(d)(i). It was common ground that EniChem would not have been entitled to a tax credit if it had been the beneficial owner of the dividends, due to the absence of a corresponding treaty provision with its country of residence.

The Inland Revenue contended that ICI and EniChem were persons acting together to secure or exercise control of EVC and should therefore be treated as 'connected persons' as defined in s839(7)(b) ICTA 1988.

Held
1. Control of the affairs of a company meant control at the level of general meetings of shareholders as control at that level carried with it the power to make the ultimate decisions as to the business of a company and in that sense to control its affairs. The terms of the shareholders' agreement imposed control over EVC at the level of general meetings of EVC. The shareholders were acting together and thereby exercising control of EVC at the time that the dividends were declared in observing and performing the agreement and voting at general meetings of EVC in the manner required by the shareholders' agreement and they were therefore connected persons within the meaning of s839(7).
2. The use of the word 'could' in conjunction with 'any purpose' in 'persons shall be treated as associated or connected if under [UK law] they could be so treated for any purpose' in art 10(3)(d)(ii) excluded any requirement that there should be some substantive issue between the Revenue and EVC other than the availability of the tax credit for the purpose of which the connection arose or was relevant. It did not mean that they had to be treated as connected for all purposes.

Commentary
The Court of Appeal upheld the decision reached in the High Court, holding that the connection under article 10(3)(d) clearly included the connection under s839(7) as art 10(3)(d) provided, inter alia, that persons were deemed to be connected if under UK law they could be so treated for any purpose and that therefore, as a condition of entitlement to the tax credits claimed, EVC was required to show that its shareholders were not 'acting together to secure or exercise control' of EVC within the meaning of s839(7) at the time when the dividends were paid.

The High Court had found that the shareholders' agreement constituted the necessary 'acting together' and that by acting according to its terms, ICI and EniChem were in 1988 acting together to secure (in the sense of safeguarding and protecting) their control of EVC. EVC appealed contending, inter alia, that its shareholders did not exercise control over the company as the meaning of that word in s416(2) ICTA 1988, included 'control over the company's affairs' which, EVC unsuccessfully contended, implied control at board level and not just at general meetings of the company.

The conclusion that parties to a joint venture agreement are connected within s839(7) would have the effect of denying an ACT refund to the joint venture company on dividends from a UK subsidiary if *any* shareholder (however small) of the joint venture company was itself resident in a country which did not have a treaty with the UK containing an ACT refund provision.

Prior to this decision, the courts had firmly held that 'control' for s416 purposes, which was the test applicable for s839, was shareholder (general meeting) and not board level control, this conclusion being reinforced by the fact that s416 appeared in the 'close company' provisions which were concerned primarily with ownership rather than management of the company. *Irving* v *Tesco Stores* (1987) TC 1 had been distinguished on the basis that it was dealing with s840 control in the context of group relief 'arrangements' under s410.

The Revenue had accepted that one effect of the decision was that, in a purely domestic context, consortium relief would never be available between shareholders of a UK joint venture company, at least if there was a shareholders' agreement in force. In the Finance Act 1997 s68 amended s410 ICTA 1988.

The strict wording of the domestic and the treaty provisions relating to control of the joint venture company do not precisely correspond: under the domestic provisions, 'control' was a necessary ingredient of 'connection', whereas under the treaty connection was a necessary ingredient of (but not necessarily sufficient for) control. However, it is unlikely that another court would seek to have regard to this distinction.

27.7 Value added tax

Royscot Leasing Ltd and Royscot Industrial Leasing Ltd v *Customs and Excise Commissioners; Allied Domecq plc* v *Customs and Excise Commissioners; T C Harrison Group Ltd* v *Customs and Excise Commissioners* [1996] STC 898 Queen's Bench Division (Turner J)

Value Added Tax – Input tax – Exclusion of credit for input tax – Motor cars – cars purchased (1) for leasing (2) for employees for business use (3) by motor dealer as demonstrators and for leasing whether exclusion of input tax credit ultra vires – whether compatible with EC law – whether validity of UK legislation should be referred to ECJ – EC Council Directives 67/228, art 11(4) and 77/388, art 17(6) – s14(10)(a) Value Added Tax Act 1983 – art 7(1) Value Added Tax (Input Tax) Order 1992

Facts

These three appeals were considered together, since they concerned in essence the same matter of law.

The Royscot companies carried on a car leasing business. The cars were used for business only. Although deduction of input tax incurred in respect of the supply of a motor car to a taxable person was excluded by art 7(1)(a) Value Added Tax (Input Tax) Order 1992 (SI 1992/3222) the appellant companies claimed input tax on the purchase of cars for leasing in their VAT returns for periods ended September 1993 and December 1993. Appealing against assessments issued by the Commissioners, the appellants contended that art 7(1) was ultra vires the enabling provision, s14(10)(a) Value Added Tax Act (VATA) 1983. The VAT Tribunal dismissed the appeal, on the grounds that art 11(4)(c) EC Council Directive 67/228 (the Second Directive) allowed Member States to exclude 'certain goods and services in particular those capable of being exclusively or partially used for the private needs of the taxable person or of his staff', and did not exclude the right of Member States to limit deduction of input tax by reference to the description of the goods supplied.

On that basis art 7 was not therefore ultra vires s14(10)(a) interpreted in accordance with Community law. The Tribunal further held that the transitional measure in art 17(6)(d) EC Council Directive 77/388 (the Sixth Directive), whereby Member States could retain all the exclusions provided for under their national laws until new rules to determine the expenditure eligible for deduction came into force, did not expire at the end of the four-year transitional period there provided for in the absence of new rules.

The tribunal concluded that the issues raised on the appeal could be decided by it 'with complete confidence' making it inappropriate to refer the case to the Court of Justice of the European Communities for a preliminary ruling. The appellants appealed, contending, inter alia, (1) that s3(6) FA 1972 and s14(10) VATA 1983 (now s25(7) VATA 1994) under which art 7(1) and its statutory predecessors had been made, were ultra vires respectively art 11(4) of the Second Directive and art 17(6) of the Sixth Directive, since power was given to the commissioners to make provision in 'any circumstances whatsoever', which went beyond the limited power to exclude the right of deduction conferred by arts 11(4) and 17(6), and (2) that the exclusion of the right to deduct input tax was inconsistent with one of the principles underlying the VAT system contained in the Second and Sixth Directives, which was the prevention of double taxation.

In the second appeal Allied Domecq plc was the parent of a group of companies carrying on retailing, brewing, food and wine and spirits businesses. It purchased cars for the use of employees which included an element of private use. The issues in that appeal were similar to those in the appeals of Royscot Leasing Ltd. Allied Domecq appealed against the VAT Tribunal's decision not to refer to the European Court of Justice, contending further that art 7(1) was incompatible with art 17(5) of the Sixth Directive, which permitted apportionment in cases of use which was partly business and partly private, and that a partial exclusion of the right to deduct could have been adopted to deal with fraud or the difficulty of determining the proper proportions of business and private use.

In the third appeal T C Harrison Group Ltd was a motor dealer which purchased cars for leasing and for use as demonstrators. There was a possibility of private use of some of the cars by senior staff, but that was minimal in extent. Cars purchased for use as demonstrators could also be used by prospective customers for private purposes while in their possession. The issues were similar to those in the other appeals.

Held

That the VAT Tribunal had decided correctly in not referring the question of validity of the law to the European Court of Justice and that deduction of input tax on cars purchased in the circumstances of the three appeals was correctly ruled out. All the cases were actes claires, so the Tribunal was able to decide the appeals with sufficient confidence. The tribunal correctly directed itself as to the applicable law, in accordance with the judgment of Sir Thomas Bingham MR in *R v International Stock Exchange of the United Kingdom and the Republic of Ireland, ex parte Else (1982) Ltd* [1993] QB 534 at 545 when he said:

> 'In relation to [such] questions, I understand the correct approach in principle of a national court (other than a final court of appeal) to be quite clear: if the facts have been found and the Community law issue is critical to the court's final decision, the appropriate course is ordinarily to refer the issue to the Court of Justice unless the national court can with complete confidence resolve the issue itself. In considering whether it can with complete confidence resolve the issue itself the national court must be fully mindful of the differences between national and Community legislation, of the pitfalls which face a national court venturing into what may be an unfamiliar field, of the need for uniform interpretation throughout the Community and of the great advantages enjoyed by the Court of Justice in construing Community instruments. If the national court has any real doubt, it should ordinarily refer, I hope I am fairly expressing [the] essential point.'

Commentary

Apart from dealing with the substantive question, the decision is a useful insight into the relationship between UK VAT law and the European Community VAT law under the Sixth Directive, and also clarifies the circumstances in which it is appropriate to refer matters to the European Court of Justice for a ruling. Since 1 August 1995 a new scheme permitting partial or full deduction of input tax on cars bought for business use and for leasing, has been in force in the UK.

27.8 Anti-avoidance

Inland Revenue Commissioners v *Universities Superannuation Scheme Ltd* [1997] STC 1 Chancery Division (Sir John Vinelott)

Transaction in securities – distribution – purchase by company of its own shares from appellant giving rise to distribution – appellant entitled to exemption from tax – whether appellant received abnormal amount by way of dividend – whether transaction carried out for bona fide commercial reasons or in the ordinary course of making or managing investments – whether appellant obtained 'tax advantage' – ss703, 704 and 709 ICTA 1988

Facts

USS was the trustee of an approved pension scheme and was thereby entitled to exemption from income tax. In 1984, it was agreed, (1) that USS would advance finance to the developer of a business park (TSH); (2) that USS would have the right to acquire part of the development; (3) that USS would make a further advance to TSH to be secured by a debenture repayable ten years after the first draw down; and (4) that USS would have the right to acquire 1,000 A ordinary shares in TSH which carried with them a put option entitling the holder to require TSH's parent to buy the A shares for 7.5 per cent of a net asset valuation of TSH's interest in the business park development. In consideration of the put option, the rate of interest on the first loan to TSH was fixed at 10 per cent (ie 3 per cent below the market rate). Following a takeover of TSH's parent company in 1987, USS declined to join in the proposed reconstruction and decided to realise its investment through the exercise of the put option. The figure at which TSH's parent was required to purchase the A shares was valued at £3,517,000 but it was agreed that TSH would purchase the A shares itself instead for £2,662,750. After deducting the amount of £100,000 representing the repayment of capital on the A shares, that payment gave rise to a distribution of £2,562,750 by TSH which when aggregated with the associated tax credit of £854,250 resulted in USS receiving £3,517,000 in total. USS claimed and received payment of the tax credit from the Revenue.

Subsequently, the Inland Revenue notified USS that it considered that s703(3)(a) ICTA 1988 applied on the grounds that USS had obtained a 'tax advantage' through the receipt of an abnormal amount by way of dividend which had been taken into account for an exemption from tax.

Held

A person who was exempt from tax might be said to obtain a 'relief' from tax within the meaning of the definition of 'tax advantage' in s709(1).

Where the Revenue alleged that a tax advantage had been obtained by way of a relief or increased relief from or repayment or increased repayment of income tax, it did not matter whether this accrued to a taxable or to a tax-exempt person. Such a contrast was only required when the advantage sought to be established had been achieved by the avoidance or reduction of an assessment to tax or the avoidance of a possible assessment thereto. That conclusion was reached by reference to the origin of the tax avoidance provisions in the Finance Act 1960, and was reinforced by the fact that a contrary interpretation would have meant that the substitution of advance corporation tax and tax credit for the deduction of Sch F tax at the standard rate would have had the unexpected consequence of removing charities and other exempt bodies from the scope of the anti-avoidance provisions. Moreover, it was well established that a narrow construction of the tax avoidance provisions was to be avoided. 'Relief' was a word of wide import. It was natural to refer to the exemption from tax of the income of a charity or of an approved pension scheme which was, in the one case, applied for charitable purposes or, in the other case, was income from investments held for the purposes of the pension scheme, as a relief from the tax that would have been payable if those conditions had not been met. Accordingly, a person who was exempt from tax might be said to obtain a 'relief' from tax within the meaning of the definition of 'tax advantage' in s709(1). *Sheppard and Another (Trustees of the Woodlands Trust)* v *IRC (No 2)* [1993] STC 240 not followed; dicta of Lord Wilberforce in *IRC* v *Parker* (1964) 43 TC 396 at 441 explained.

The Special Commissioner had erred in his assumption that it was common ground that the distribution amounted to £2,562,750. He had been wrong to treat that sum as the amount of the distribution for the purposes of s709(4). The scope of Sch F tax was set out in s20(1)(d), which brings into charge all dividends and other distributions of a company resident in the United Kingdom and in para 2 it was provided that, 'for the purposes of this Schedule and all other purposes of the Tax Acts', any such distribution in respect of which a person was entitled to a tax credit should be treated as representing income equal to the aggregate of the amount or value of that distribution and the amount of that credit. The 'purposes of the Tax Acts' included the provisions aimed at cancelling tax advantages arising out of transactions in securities. When determining whether an amount received by way of dividend should be treated as abnormal pursuant to s709(4), 'dividends' had to be read as references to the aggregate of the distribution and any associated tax credit. Accordingly, the Crown's appeal succeeded.

Commentary

Section 709(1) ICTA 1988 contains a reasonably detailed definition of the meaning of 'tax advantage' when applied specifically to the anti-avoidance legislation in ss703–708, the chapter of the Act dealing with withdrawing tax advantages obtained in any of the ' prescribed circumstances' set out in s704. Included in the definition is the term 'relief from tax'. The High Court ruling provides some further clarification of how wide the term is to be applied, including an exemption from tax. The definition of 'tax advantage' in s709 ICTA 1988 was altered by s73 FA 1997 to include the receipt of tax credits.

Old Bailey Press

The Old Bailey Press integrated student library is planned and written to help you at every stage of your studies. Each of our range of Textbooks, Casebooks, Revision WorkBooks and Statutes are all designed to work together and are regularly revised and updated.

We are also able to offer you Suggested Solutions which provide you with past examination questions and solutions for most of the subject areas listed below.

You can buy Old Bailey Press books from your University Bookshop or your local Bookshop, or in case of difficulty, order direct using this form.

Here is the selection of modules covered by our series:

Administrative Law; Commercial Law; Company Law; Conflict of Laws (no Suggested Solutions Pack); Constitutional Law: The Machinery of Government; Obligations: Contract Law; Conveyancing (no Revision Workbook); Criminology (no Casebook or Revision WorkBook); Criminal Law; English Legal System; Equity and Trusts; Law of The European Union; Evidence; Family Law; Jurisprudence: The Philosophy of Law (Sourcebook in place of a Casebook); Land: The Law of Real Property; Law of International Trade; Legal Skills and System; Public International Law; Revenue Law (no Casebook); Succession: The Law of Wills and Estates; Obligations: The Law of Tort.

Mail order prices:

Textbook £10

Casebook £10

Revision WorkBook £7

Statutes £8

Suggested Solutions Pack (1991–1995) £7

Single Paper 1996 £3

Single Paper 1997 £3.

To complete your order, please fill in the form below:

Module	Books required	Quantity	Price	Cost
		Postage		
		TOTAL		

For UK, add 10% postage and packing (£10 maximum).
For Europe, add 15% postage and packing (£20 maximum).
For the rest of the world, add 40% for airmail.

ORDERING

By telephone to Mail Order at 0171 385 3377, with your credit card to hand

By fax to 0171 381 3377 (giving your credit card details).

By post to:

Old Bailey Press, 200 Greyhound Road, London W14 9RY.

When ordering by post, please enclose full payment by cheque or banker's draft, or complete the credit card details below.

We aim to despatch your books within 3 working days of receiving your order.

Name

Address

Postcode   Telephone

Total value of order, including postage: £

I enclose a cheque/banker's draft for the above sum, or

charge my   ☐ Access/Mastercard   ☐ Visa   ☐ American Express
Card number

☐☐☐☐ ☐☐☐☐ ☐☐☐☐ ☐☐☐☐

Expiry date   ☐☐☐☐

Signature: ……………………………………….Date: ………………………………………